mexico under spain

1521 - 1556

PEGGY K. LISS

mexico under spain

1521 – 1556

Society and the
Origins of Nationality

THE UNIVERSITY OF CHICAGO PRESS
Chicago and London

PEGGY K. LISS has taught history at Hiram College, Case Western Reserve University, the University of Pennsylvania, and Swarthmore College. She has edited (with Sheldon B. Liss) *Man, State, and Society in Latin American History.*

The University of Chicago Press, Chicago 60637
The University of Chicago Press, Ltd., London
© 1975 by The University of Chicago
All rights reserved. Published 1975
Printed in the United States of America

Library of Congress Cataloging in Publication Data

Liss, Peggy K.
  Mexico under Spain, 1521-1556.

  Bibliography: p.
  Includes index.
    1. Mexico—History—Conquest, 1519-1540.   2. Mexico—
History—Spanish colony, 1540-1810.   3. Spain—Colonies
—America—Administration.   I. Title.
F1230.L76   972'.02   74-33507
ISBN   0-226-48495-5

The Mexican is not an essence
but a history

—Octavio Paz

Contents

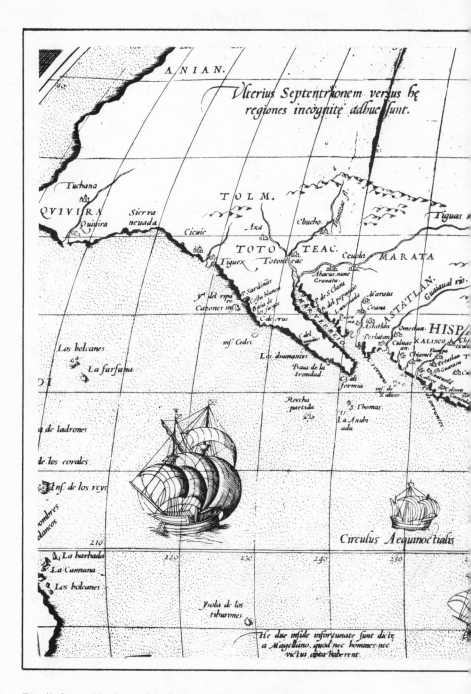

Detail from Abraham Ortelius' map of America in
Theatrum Orbis Terrarum (1575 edition). Courtesy of
The University of Chicago Libraries, Special Collections.

Preface

What follows is an essay on the beginnings of Mexican society and an inquiry into the origins of some of the sentiments and symbols early associated with being Mexican. It is also an account of the initial impact of the Spaniards on Mexico, a discussion of the attitudes and institutions they brought to bear in establishing control over Mexico, and of the relations between Spaniards and Indians. My study stresses the interplay of events and attitudes, reporting what happened, how it was perceived by participants, and how this interaction of event and perception in turn affected subsequent Mexican history.

This book is, in part, somewhat of a massive brush-clearing, the result of my attempt to answer certain questions and to resolve some of the problems I found obscuring the broader terrain of the history of Mexico under Charles V. Yet primarily it is a response to an enigma and a paradox. For me, the enigma was medieval Spain; the paradox how a sense of Mexican-ness could evolve among Spaniards in Mexico. My search for edification on both points led to the social and political theory and practices of late fifteenth- and early sixteenth-century Spain, to the political commonplaces prominent in that period of national consolidation and expansion, and to thinking about precisely what being Spanish meant to Spaniards at that time. I wanted to know what the words "empire" and "nation" connoted, first to Spaniards and then to the new society forming in the land Fernando Cortés called the Kingdom of New Spain. I wanted to find out how, and in what sense or senses, Spanish loyalty could be extended overseas to Mexico and there maintained among the various segments of society. I also sought to understand more fully the processes enabling Spain to control millions of Indians. Finally, I found it necessary to make sense of the interaction between imperial policies and interests, internal Mexican arrangements, and the indications of Mexican particularism discernible even in this earliest period of Mexico under Spain.

My findings are presented here as a hypothesis, a tentative reconstruction of a period crucial to modern Mexican history. This study is offered as an ordering device, giving shape to the rather amorphous mass of previous specialized research, and as an inventory of riches and inadequacies. The notes are designed to cite sources and to explain something of the history of scholarly approaches to the points under consideration. I hope this book will indicate new directions awaiting exploration, as well as exposing old ones which like the roads built by many a caudillo led only through miles of nowhere to his own hacienda.

I have had moments of what, in this dawn of a post-Freudian era, I shall once more call soul-searching, of asking whether or not any attempt at national history is worthwhile. Is it too broad an endeavor, or too artificial a construct? I think not. Nations now give promise of being with us for some time. In addition, Mexico is a very real and important entity to her peoples and many others. To Mexicans many aspects of their past have become a source of communal pride, of national cohesion, and of an individual sense of esteem and well-being. Within this context, in concentrating on the roots of the sentiment of Mexican nationality, this essay responds to current interests. It is not meant to support an interpretation of history particular to any one interest group. We know that nineteenth-century conservatives tended to extol the Spanish heritage, and that there has been a twentieth-century reaction, born of the Mexican Revolution of 1910, to focus positively on Indian and creole traditions, usually at the expense of the Spanish. There has even been a more pro-Spanish reaction to that reaction. I trust my portrait of the immediate postconquest period will place Indian, Spanish, and nascent creole traditions within a comprehensive historical context lessening simplistic distortion of the Mexican past. I hope it will help to perpetuate those distinctions born of time and conducive to individual and social well-being and to the retention by Mexicans of a unique national character.

Members of nations, including those of Mexico, often tend to see themselves and their countries at least partially as expressions of historical existence, as indeed they are. The way they perceive their own situation involves how they view their nation's past. As one historian has explained, "What do we mean by the history of a country? We mean the way that country has acquired self-consciousness, and the play of interests, political, social, cultural, within the perimeter established by language, by geography, and by relations, acquisitive or concessive, with its neighbors."[1] To begin to understand Mexico today, then, we must look into its history, material and ideational.

A crucial earlier period, in terms of its continuing importance to Mexican society and institutions and to the Mexican self-image, was that of Mexico under Charles V. And to understand that period more fully, we must in turn know something of perceptions of history at that time. We must investigate, then, not only the material conditions of society, including social, economic, and political arrangements, and the dynamics of all of them, but also the vantage point of peoples in time and place, including their grasp of their past. Thus, how historical perception influenced the Spanish conquest and immediate postconquest Mexico is a theme of this book. Through better comprehending that era we can go on to appraise more clearly subsequent Mexican history, and to understand better the many present attitudes toward the colonial past.

After writing this book, I have discovered that much of my approach to my subject matter accords with the theoretical formulations concerning individual relations to society, its history, and to the universe, made within the framework of the sociology of knowledge.[2] Since my approach to Mexico under Spain varies from that of many other historians, some explanation of it, of certain key terms and concepts I employ, may be of value to the reader. Like some sociologists and cultural anthropologists, I discuss culture as the totality of man's products, among them being society, including national society. The origins of modern Mexican society can be said to lie in the impact upon each other of two cultures, the Spanish and the Indian, in the domination imposed by the former culture on the latter, in the resulting new syncretic, plural, regional society, and in institutions that evolved within that situation.

As a sociologist states, "to be in culture means to share a particular world of objectives with others."[3] Society is an aspect of culture, "a product of human activity that has attained the state of objective reality," and also a coercive power over individuals. In a society shared attitudes and beliefs concerning individuals and groups, the state, other organizations, the universe, and relations among them all provide its members with their perception of social reality. These same assumptions infuse habits of behavior, which can in turn form institutions. And institutions then function as structures for social maintenance. Some ways institutions themselves may change or become redirected will also be indicated in this book. Ultimately, as an anthropologist has said, institutions are "but cultural patterns for group relationships."[4] This is not to say institutions necessarily remain in a pristine state, retain vitality, or respond well to changing situations. Specific evidence for these general statements will be forthcoming in the body of this work.

Shared attitudes and beliefs are also thought of as the elements making up common sense within a society, or within one group; they need not be construed as such within another. The comment attributed to the Duke of Wellington, that Spain was the only country in the world where twice two did not make four, can be viewed as a comment by a redoubt of one society's common sense upon that of another's. Notions involved in attitudes, beliefs, norms, values, common sense—all are part of a society's general stock of knowledge, although all of them are usually not part of an individual's knowledge. Certain clusters of notions and symbols thought to define reality by an interest group may be called an ideology. Ideology has been well described as "the tendency at a given time to make facts amenable to ideas, and ideas to facts, in order to create a world image convincing enough to support the collective and individual sense of identity."[5] Formulating ideologies has often been an unconscious tendency and has underlaid religious and scientific, political, and social thought. Ideology used in this sense is synonymous with legitimation. That is, at bottom, ideologies present and are components of, particular views of the universe, and of the reality of society and self within it. Obversely, "when a particular definition of reality comes to be attached to a concrete power interest, it may be called an ideology."[6]

Some ways in which ideologies became current will be touched upon in this book. An ideology can be superimposed by one powerful group upon a society as an overlay supporting dominance. As such, in other members of society it can become sincere belief, or only acquiesced to, or rejected. In addition, portions of it may be accepted or rejected selectively. It can be an official set of social and political ideals, or a challenging one, offering an alternative. Ideologies, that is, can be discerned and discussed, but with care, and with attention to their precise components.

In contemplating writing this book, I was struck by accumulating evidence that under Spain ideological elements appeared in Mexico which became concepts and symbols associated with Mexican nationality. Some of them, as we shall see, initially supported Spanish domination, yet came to be viewed as elements of Mexican nationalism. I felt that investigating their roots in Spain and advent in America would shed light on an entire historical epoch crucial to Mexican culture, on the process of forming a new society, and on the interaction between history and society. Making sense of early Mexico, I soon saw, involved studying nation-making in Spain. For clearly, as Leopoldo Zea has stated, "the order of the colony ... depended on a previous mental order"[7]—yet not, it must be stressed, on a mental order alone, divorced from material elements.

Here two caveats are necessary. First, the study of ideas in history need not, and should not, be relegated to the category of intellectual history.[8] Ideas are spawned within social reality and have consequences. They are an important and integral part of history. This leads to my second point. As Peter Berger, a sociologist, says, "the course of history has little to do with the intrinsic logic of ideas that served as causal factors in it."[9] That is, while ways of thinking do influence future history, neat concepts do not propel it along. Deprecators of the history of ideas, however, often claim that its proponents believe so, and they sometimes (I think mistakenly) do. Disembodied ideas do not of themselves make history, but men espousing them and institutions embodying them have done so. Ideas can and do direct and limit, and are in turn limited and directed by, what is and what happens. They cannot be ignored as historical components, particularly in the case of nation-forming. I must add two further observations. First, affecting history are not simply concepts themselves but their dynamism, that is, the spirit animating them and given off by their proponents. Second, historical context is extremely important when discussing ideas. For one thing, men and women whose thought appeared radical to the nineteenth century may appear rather conservative today, since people now holding seemingly similar ideas may be of that disposition. Yesterday's proponents of a particular idea may have been in different circumstances, faced different problems, and been of different temperament. It should be noted that the spirit propelling notions involved in change, or maintenance, within a historical ambience, makes a good deal of difference and should be taken into account in assessing ideas.[10] Thus "isms" can harbor, and be employed by, people of differing tempers and interests, in differing times and places, for different ends, none perhaps more so than nationalism.

In this study I stress mental conditions in the consolidation of Spanish control and in the acquisition of Mexican self-consciousness, and I emphasize the dynamics of those processes, because previously historians in the United States in writing of colonial Mexico have tended to underrate these factors. The writing of history, I think, must in part be—today as in the sixteenth century—either implicitly or explicitly a comment on previous historical exposition. It also, consciously or unconsciously, in one way or another, responds to assumptions, values, and concerns of the historian's society. Where my own assumptions, preferences, and proclivities intrude themselves, I can only plead human fallibility and a belief in the tentative nature of all historical writing. Once again, this book is intended to be a progress report, not a definitive statement, to promote further investigation and to open debate, rather than to shut them off. My conscious concern is directed to breaking habits of looking at history from an approach unconsciously oriented by national or cultural background. It is also meant as an affirmative response to a perceived need for ideological self-examination among historians in the United States and to a sense of worldwide questioning of the worth of history. These preoccupations combine with great admiration for the Mexican attempt to enrich the present and the future through shedding light on the past. I seek the origins and content of a web of relationships evolved, among groups in Spain and Mexico, into cultural forms or mechanisms now associated with Mexican character.[11] This is not to say that an integrated society has even yet coalesced in Mexico. Conflict among groups is still a fact of life. Yet to the extent Mexico is a national society, as indeed it is, elements mentally associated by Mexicans today as components of national identity, and of national tradition, can be isolated and their historical evolution investigated, though very carefully, with recognition of the existence of distorting proclivities in the thinking of us all, and with "that watchful critical anxiety for a closer approximation to the truth which is perhaps the chief virtue to which historians ... are entitled to aspire."[12]

Mexico under Charles V was officially known as the Kingdom of New Spain. The two designations are sometimes used interchangeably, although "Mexico" then generally referred to the city and its environs, the central valley. New Spain was bounded on the south by Guatemala, on the north by Zacatecas, the province of the Guachichiles. The territory beyond was not fixed until the Adams-Onís treaty of 1821. New Spain included the area of the Pacific coast from Navidad, Jalisco, to Soconusco, Chiapas, on the Gulf coast from Soto la Marina, (now Tamaulipas) to Coatzacoalcos (now Puerto México) in Veracruz. Each time I have used the term "Mexico" I have tried to indicate the extent of territory meant.

There is hopeless inconsistency in my choice of forms of proper names. Thus I have yielded to current scholarly practice of referring to Fernando, rather than Hernán or Hernando, Cortés. Yet I have retained the Anglicized forms Ferdinand and Isabella, and Charles, feeling that consistency would then require España, Nueva España, and so on. History, despite historians, is never neat.

My deep gratitude to those teachers who have helped me either to formulate the questions or to value historical analysis, to Walter Ferree, Michael Jameson, and Arthur P. Whitaker, and to the many others whose work has pointed the way. My thanks to Charles Gibson and to Arthur Whitaker for their helpful comments on the content and style of this manuscript, respectively, and to my family for their patience and encouragement. To Peter and Maggie. To Shel, my husband, a special appreciation—both for the understanding and advice of a fellow historian and for making possible near-ideal living and working conditions.

P.K.L.

August 1974

1

Spain under Ferdinand and Isabella: Background to Empire

The men who conquered Mexico expressed strong feelings of attachment to the Iberian regions of their birth. Their leader, Fernando Cortés, explained to Motecuhzoma II, the Aztec ruler, that hostilities between his own followers and those of a rival captain, Panfilo de Narváez, stemmed from a traditional enmity between Narváez's Biscayans and his own men who were born, for the most part, in Castile.[1] He then placed himself within that tradition by equating the Biscayans to the Otomís, thought by the Aztecs to be among the most savage and barbarous of peoples. Yet the conquistadors went beyond such regional allegiances to take pride in being Spanish. Bernal Díaz del Castillo, in his recollection of the conquest, boasted, "Of such magnificent stuff are we Spanish soldiers made!"[2] Cortés also demonstrated a sense of belonging to a larger, national entity, writing of "our nation" and of "these kingdoms of Spain where I am native."[3]

Spain in 1519, the year Cortés reached Mexico, was a congeries of semiautonomous kingdoms, only recently united under a single monarch. How, then, explain these expressions of national identity and Spanish patriotism? They must be understood if we are to make sense of Mexican history. For the body of beliefs supporting the feeling of attachment early Spaniards in Mexico articulated for Spain also affected their perception of the new land they had conquered and had great bearing on the organization of the society they established there. Moreover, this corpus of assumptions originally associated with Spanish patriotism lent form and content to a new body of regional ideas and activities that later would, with justification, be looked upon as origins of Mexican nationalism.

1

We shall see that the sense of loyalty to a Spanish national community expressed by Cortés and his fellows fit within a broader context of shared beliefs concerning themselves and the world. That is, they held in common a number of underlying assumptions concerning social and political organization, and defining relationships among Spaniards, to the king, to other peoples, to all human society, and ultimately to the universe. Their cast of mind encompassed a complex of beliefs not necessarily consistent, yet particularly Spanish. Conversely, men and women in Spain and America with the same general outlook accepted as fellow Spaniards those people recognized to be of similar ethnic background who shared their ideas-become-assumptions. Accordingly, in order to make sense of the formative period of modern Mexican society, we must first examine some of the mental, as well as material, conditions making up the Spanish background of the generation of the conquest.

Spaniards in 1519 can be said to have existed within concentric circles of communal attachment. They generally assumed the family, in the sense of extended family, to be the central and basic social unit, then the local and regional communities, next the nation, and finally universal Christendom. By 1519, however, Spanish history had made possible and Spanish rulers were making certain that all political power coalesced in the monarchy. They were claiming absolute authority, identifying that authority with the nation, imposing it on smaller social units of family and locality, and presenting it as most authentically representing universal Christendom. In a period when throughout western Europe dynastic monarchs were forging nation-states, insisting that the nation, under them, must define limits of effective community, in Spain Ferdinand and Isabella had established the foundations of a national community, unifying it, and maintaining unity, through allegiance to the crown and the faith, and through a common history.

This is not to say that the Spanish monarchy was in fact all powerful, only that it was making an increasingly successful effort, with minor setbacks, to become so politically. Spanish kings had traditionally governed with the support of certain magnates or lords, and corporations or groups, and through popular belief in their legitimacy. That is, consensus had long existed on the right of the monarch to represent the highest political authority as overlord, *señor natural y universal,*[4] although the nature and limits of actual royal power tended to shift in accord with conditions and the character of the incumbent. In fact when Isabella, as aspirant to the throne of Castile, in 1469 married Ferdinand, heir to Aragon, Spain was not a political entity. Not only was it dominated by the two powerful kingdoms of Castile and Aragon but the former was rent by civil war. There, within each region, noble families contested for power and engaged in struggles and intrigues over control of city governments. And when, in 1474, the young Isabella was accepted as monarch by the *cortes* or parliament of that kingdom, it was largely due to the weaknesses of Enrique IV, to aristocratic military backing, and to the support of a number of semiautonomous towns and some of the powerful and militant clergy. In 1479, on Ferdinand's accession in Aragon, Christian Spain was at last unified, but only through the royal personages. Effective unity required additional measures.

To change tenuous seignorial authority into government and control, Ferdinand and Isabella employed warfare, diplomacy, patronage, law, religion, history, and psychology. They succeeded in curbing dissident nobles, clergy, and strong towns tending to autonomy, and in imposing over urban councils royal officers, the *corregidores*. They established royal ascendancy over Spanish society and overcame much regional particularism adverse to their authority. They regained royal property fallen into private hands, standardized coinage, imposed royal law, and, allaying the political aspects of seignorialism they found developing in Castile—such as military and political de facto regional control by powerful nobles—they welded the disparate kingdoms into a pluralistic and patrimonial national state.[5]

Their majesties understood that Spanish unity involved a supportive state of mind. They saw, as did their admiring contemporary Niccolò Machiavelli, the worth to the monarchy of favorable public opinion.[6] Together they worked consciously to unify the diverse and often conflicting interests and factions of the period, by awakening in all their subjects a sense of a broadly national Spanish identity. To this end they made a political policy of forming a national mystique of what had been the military ideals and attitudes of Castile. Castile was larger and more populous than Aragon; in 1530 it was estimated to have had perhaps four and a half million inhabitants, while all the other provinces of Spain combined had only two and a half millions.[7] Castile was the traditional as well as geographical heartland of the peninsula, and it had been the leader of the greatest Christian victory over Spanish adherents to Islam. Ferdinand and Isabella now graphically reinvigorated Christian militancy under the banners of Castile.

The Christian reconquest (*reconquista*) had in fact been largely achieved by the mid-thirteenth century. The kingdom of Granada alone had remained a Moorish stronghold, but tributary to Castile. Nevertheless, Ferdinand and Isabella rallied men and resources and personally laid siege to Granada, so that, in successfully channeling Spanish energies into a concerted cause, and in reawakening the old crusading zeal, they at once provided Spaniards with a sense of participating in Christian and national mission and of heightened royal prestige. To support this holy war, the monarchs caused to be sold indulgences called bulls of crusade and collected immense amounts of money, men, and matériel from the Castilian towns, whose militias, *hermandades,* formed the bulk of troops, as archers, against Granada.[8] Sons and nephews of such Spaniards were among the men who conquered and governed Mexico.

Christian Spaniards, then and subsequently, hailed the conquest in 1492 of that last Islamic outpost as a popular victory and as the climax of the reconquest. Its fall also signaled a direction of royal energies to greater internal consolidation and to Spanish expansion overseas. Internally, Isabella and Ferdinand introduced reform in the name of renovation. They knew the Spanish tendency to believe political and social institutions were arranged for all eternity, as was the universe, by unchanging natural laws. They appealed to this predominant conservatism by carefully inaugurating change in the guise of putting the constitutional system of medieval Spain into working order. They played on the theme of historical sanction for a Spain composed of one people unified under the law and the faith. They repudiated as historical aberration the previous century of weak kingship and civil wars in Castile. They sought to sap the customs and traditions infused with political individuality and supporting regional distinctions. And in part they were successful in doing so through directing their subjects to see in the taking of Granada a Spain united under a Castile that had triumphantly completed seven centuries of leading a continuous and broadly Spanish Christian offensive. The victory did dim the popular memory of the intervening strife-torn years and evoked instead an increasingly popular myth of a Spain ever united in Christian endeavor under warrior kings.

As intended, this policy aggrandized the reputation of its architects, Isabella and Ferdinand, now to be known as Their Catholic Majesties, and of monarchy as an institution. It also linked in the popular mind morality, Christianity, and Spanish civilization. Thereafter, what Spaniards— including those who took Mexico—thought Spain to be depended to a great extent upon what they believed Spain to have been. And their articulated view of the past if differing in specifics tended to concur in broad outline with the official one, indicating among other things that manipulating the present has involved revising the past. We shall see that early Spaniards in Mexico generally adhered to an interpretation of their European past as one of an ongoing Christian crusade for king and faith, and that this sense of history colored conquest and settlement there.

Although in the campaign against Granada their highnesses emphasized the traditional royal role of military leader, they knew that for civil purposes royal authority extended only to men and communities submitting to the crown's jurisdiction. Accordingly they sped consolidation of their government through recourse to that other great traditional royal attribute—supreme temporal judge. The Council of Justice they made the center of their governing system. They relied on their own regional courts, the *audiencias* and *chancillerías,* to interpret and enforce their edicts, and used the tribunal of the Inquisition to circumvent regional jurisdictions.[9] Claiming to follow older laws and customs, they enacted new ordinances and issued executive decrees. They also promulgated civil law, notably the 1505 Laws of Toro, designed to buttress royal authority and maintain social stability.

In legislating for most of Spain, the precedent they fell back upon was Castilian. To cut across local customs and cherished *fueros,* rights or privileges—depending on the point of view—and to diminish regional autonomy, they had available to them, and used as precedent, earlier sporadic attempts by kings of León and its offspring, Castile, and their chanceries to assert civil supremacy over all Christian Spain through the law.[10] Most organized and applicable to their own interests and needs was the work of Alfonso X, the Learned, who in 1252 inherited with the crown of Castile much of the former Moorish domain of al-Andalus, for his father, Fernando III (consequently San Fernando), had completed the true reconquista. Moreover, at his accession Alfonso X, his authority acknowledged in seignorial fashion from the Cantabrian Sea through Andalusia, was monarch over the majority of Spaniards in a period when throughout western Europe secular rulers were pressing claims to pre-eminence over local nobility, asserting temporal independence from the power of the papacy, and countering the pretensions to universal dominion of the Holy Roman Emperor. Alfonso not only strove to assert strong kingship in Spain but sought the imperial office, unsuccessfully.

His general policy had been to change the emphasis on the king as military leader to that of civil monarch. His chosen instrument was law. In Castile he staffed the royal chancery with *letrados,* men trained in Roman and canon law, many of them at the new University of Salamanca. He oversaw completion of a legal code, *Las Siete Partidas,* corporate in philosophy, national in scope, and infused with what were at the time grandiose notions of kingship.[11] In addition, political theory supporting royal power and authority, and patriotic pronouncements eulogizing Spain and its monarch emanated from his court. Events proved his attempt to strengthen royal authority overly ambitious. Regional and local power vested in both powerful men and entrenched custom triumphed, deposing Alfonso. The theory he employed and the ways he did it nonetheless were part of Spanish history, and as such provided fine precedent for Isabella and Ferdinand. In brief, political and social theories and attendant policies that in the thirteenth century bordered on wishful thinking and were confined to the king and his chancery, by the end of the reign of Isabella and Ferdinand had become thought of as traditional concepts. By 1519 there was indication of widespread Castilian

5

acceptance of the world view implicit in Alfonsine law and theory—and a good deal for Alfonso's view of civil society, Spain, and its monarch. Therefore, since these states of mind are important to Mexican and all Spanish American history, we shall take a closer look at some of the theoretical and symbolic elements making up this essentially imperial and Christian outlook, their social roots, their relation to royal policy, their more general acceptance in Spain, and their exportation to America.

Fernando Cortés, it will be recalled, expressed a patriotic attachment to Spain as his *nación,* the land of his birth. He and other conquistadors also asserted loyalty to the king, the faith, and Spanish civilization. The notions of social and political community found in their patriotic avowals are markedly similar to the patriotic content implicit in documents emanating, once again, from court circles under Alfonso X. In particular, one Vincentius Hispanus wrote strongly and explicitly of patriotism in similar terms and advertised his concept of *patria* in his surname. He insisted the Spanish homeland worth dying for and—as Cortés, Bernal Díaz del Castillo, and other conquerors of Mexico would also claim—he declared Spaniards "had acquired an empire by their valor."[12]

He located national identity in Spanish history, discerning the roots of a broad Spanish communality in an undefined but shared "body of prescripts and traditions." Other late medieval theorists, the authors of the Partidas, and the Laws of Toro also assumed a Spanish-ness based on a common heritage, and by 1519 many Spaniards did, too. Patriotic statements, broadly Spanish law, and political theory, all confined to royal aspiration until given wider currency during the reign of Ferdinand and Isabella, were in turn compounded of elements derived from still earlier European traditions with connection to Spain. All were adapted from theory sanctified, it was claimed, by time, and particularly from notions associated with imperial Roman law and rule in Spain, and the continuous presence and institutions of Christianity. That is, royal law, political theory, and avowals of Spanish patriotism—sometimes explicitly, sometimes not—incorporated, indeed relied on as authoritative precedent, ideological elements which had accompanied previous attempts at both Spanish unity and domination and supranational *imperium.* Both Rome and the church had advanced social and political ideas within a cohesive world view, and these ideas and their proponents Spaniards could and did claim, when it seemed useful to do so, as integral to Spanish history.

Specifically, from Rome, through use in canon law and royal cause, came the association of patria with religion and civilization. It appeared as early as the seventh century in the *Etymologiae* and *De laude Spaniae* of the powerful Isidore, archbishop of Seville.[13] Rome lent the idea that the homeland was less a definite or limited territory than a cultural entity embracing an entire way of life. Early Rome presented the effective social community as the *república,* while the later empire and the legal compilations of the Emperor Justinian sanctioned and exalted royal power and authority over the body politic. Christianity, particularly as explained by Augustine, offered the concept of an ultimate, eternal, heavenly homeland, and in Spain Christian authorities, usually allied with kings, had long claimed that country as its outstanding earthly manifestation and *the* temporal reflection of the ideal community. Notable here, again, is Isidore of Seville.

Roman and Christian habits of thought in turn owed much to Greek philosophy, two aspects of which continued to be particularly important in Christianity and in Spanish thought. One, the concept derived from Plato of the abstract Ideal being more real than its transient temporal reflection. The other, the political theory of Aristotle, insisting on the static, organic nature of human community, on people being by nature political animals, on the importance of custom, and, akin to Plato, on the numerous individual communities as emanations of and sharers in the universal concept of human community. Augustine was influenced by Platonic philosophy, medieval political theorists by him and by Aristotle.

Most medieval theorists were members of the clergy. Christianity gave Spain its most stable and durable institutional structures. Religion invested with coherence the Spanish outlook on the universe and gave sacred sanction to the king, as God's vicar. Canon law incorporated much imperial Roman law. With its attendant imperial theory, churchmen-jurists supported Christian monarchy, so that church-state relations in Spain came to resemble a closely woven web. A reinforcing element, introduced by the Visigoths, was that of the monarch as first lord or *señor.* [14] By the 1200s, the concept of seignorial kingship extended among Spaniards to a patriotic loyalty to the king as *señor natural.* In Castile Alfonso X could not turn this seignorial notion of kingship, the idea of lord among lords, into one of national monarchy. Isabella and Ferdinand could and to a great extent did.

A similar view of the universe and, within it, all human community and its microcosm, Spanish society, infused the writings of Isidore, Alfonsine thought and the Partidas, late medieval social and political theory in general, and, as we shall see, the attitudes of many Spaniards involved in Mexico. It was consonant with the view of human society presented in imperial Roman law, when overlaid by Christian doctrine. Within the ecumenical, medieval Christian construct, Spain was thought of as a single society, a subdivision of mankind, set in a divinely ordered universe and based upon the primary Christian (Augustinian) assumption that temporal life was fleeting, serving only to prepare human beings for eternal salvation. Natural law, construed to be a reflection of divine intent, ordered the physical universe and the relations of its inhabitants. [15]

7

Political activity was believed to have as its purpose maintaining the social community—conceived of as an organic, corporate entity or mystical body—in peace, harmony, and equilibrium. While all human beings were members of *the* social community, universal Christendom, Spanish theorists and compilers of codes, in a period of emerging nation-states, assumed Spain to be the effective community, the nation. And it, in turn, was thought of as being subdivided into small replicas of the whole, into regional and local communities, corporations, orders, households, and families.

All society was assumed to be naturally hierarchical, unchanging in structure, its basis the family unit. The ruler, reflecting the ordering function of *the* Lord, was represented as endowed with office in order to regulate society and its subdivisions. He was to maintain the social community in peace and harmony, defending it as military leader and governing it as judge and lawgiver. He personified the divine principle of justice, the other face of order. He was obligated to direct society toward ethical ends and to uphold principles of divinely ordained natural law.[16]

As this universal system was thought to originate in divine authority, so the principle of authority was mirrored in every facet of it. It is necessary to understand relations between law and government within this context. Law rested upon the authority of tradition and had to be interpreted by men who were considered authorities in their own right, the monarch and his counselors. Thus, the Partidas cited the authority of the Old and New Testaments, of the church fathers, and of Roman jurists, as well as that of consonant Spanish custom—thought of as sanctified by time and in conformity with natural law. And although natural law theoretically could be perceived by individual reason, only the rational ability of recognized authorities counted in interpreting it. To legislate correctly, the ruler was expected to investigate tenets of civil and canon law with the help of jurists, to translate moral and religious principles into rules, and to respect customary usage.

Isabella and Ferdinand ostentatiously followed this traditionally prescribed legal procedure in consulting jurists, often churchmen, to ascertain proper principle, and in so doing to give to their statutes and edicts religious, legal, and customary sanction. In particular, they increased the prestige and application of the Partidas, which were invested with welcome assumptions supportive of Spanish cohesion and patrimonial monarchy. Although under Alfonso X the strength of regional and local custom, of corporate and private fueros, and of individuals, had prevented that code from becoming the law of the land, in the intervening period it had come to be consulted as supplementary law and, beginning in the fourteenth century, used in university law courses. Under Isabella and Ferdinand, advisers and administrators trained in law were familiar with it. Jurists glossed it. And it was cited as precept for royal ordinances and as the main basis of their own code of 1505, the Laws of Toro.[17] Both codes and all royal law, explicitly citing imperial Roman precedent and Christian principles, conformed to, disseminated, and reinforced notions advancing Spanish unification under the crown. Law favored by their majesties described the natural social community as the national one, and the king as its natural head and lord of the land, with the authority of emperor in his realm.[18] In sum, law, consonant with religion, political theory, and nationality, was an ideal and prime royal instrument.

Ferdinand and Isabella in their policies and practices, in their use of selected Spanish tradition, and in their royal persons personifying justice, fostered dissemination of a normative view of social and political reality, indeed an ideology. It proceeded from Christian universalistic principles and their Spanish adaptations, had an unmistakably imperial cast, was elaborated in political theory and law, and gained widespread support for the newly expanded, Spanish monarchy during the early, formative years of those Spaniards who would conquer and govern in Mexico. Three further ramifications of its content, particularly of assumptions relating to social organization, the king as natural ruler, and the importance of law for royal authority, deserve mention, since they have a good deal of bearing on Mexican, and all Spanish American, history. First of all, it is evident that, contrary to a current tendency, it is fallacious to explain sixteenth-century Spanish legal and political philosophy as derived chiefly from the great theologian of the thirteenth century, Thomas Aquinas, for many Spanish principles concerning the social community and its government came of parallel, indigenous Spanish development. Aquinas' monumental *Summa Theologica,* which among other achievements revived systematic political thinking as a respectable pursuit, was roughly contemporaneous with the Partidas. At the same time the Italian Dominican theologian (influenced by Aristotle) was finding the earthly city more worthy of interest than had Augustine, whose censure of it in the fourth century had long outlawed systematic political theorizing as a Christian activity, Spanish jurists were borrowing from Roman and canon law (similarly Aristotelian) notions of politics and society as suitable working principles for monarchical purposes. Thomistic theory subsequently reinforced, but it did not occasion, Spanish views concerning temporal community, nor did it introduce in Spain their Aristotelian, Roman, and Christian bases.

Second, previous Spanish theory and practice help to explain royal tendencies to consult jurist-theologians publicly, and to ascertain and strengthen monarchical authority through claiming and exercising jurisdiction based on religious sanction. They also shed light on why Spanish royal edicts have appeared to be so much an expression of Christian ideals, and why law and legal forms figure so prominently in Spanish history. They make more understandable what has been referred to often as the legal cast of the Spanish mentality and help to relate it to what some scholars have described as the Spanish mania for seeking or imposing order. They also indicate how written law and monarchy were mutually supportive and ultimately how justice was employed as a royal instrument. Related is the Spanish tendency to appeal to authority and tradition to establish and buttress legitimacy, and to shun innovation as an explanatory device.

Finally, although the Spanish model of society, as it came to be accepted more widely, endowed human community with divine approbation, and invested royal government with both secular and religious purpose, there was not general agreement in our period on the immediate source of royal dominion, or systematic consideration of the nature of sovereignty. The Partidas exposed the problem: "Kings," it explained, "are vicars of God, appointed over people to maintain them in justice and in truth in temporal matters."[19] Its compilers, concerned primarily with strengthening royal claims to jurisdiction, simply listed all current notions of the sources of sovereignty, stating that a king could inherit office or gain it through "all the people of the kingdom," by marriage, or through the pope.[20] The Partidas admitted a popular source of royal authority, but only as one possibility. Much stronger is the concept of subjection of all inhabitants to the king, the idea that "the king possesses in his dominions *merum imperium,* the clear and absolute right to judge and command the people of his country."[21] They are his vassals and owe him service. Vassalage is a natural relationship, "a great and important debt which those who are vassals owe to their lords, and which their lords owe them."[22] Here in the Partidas is found theory, invoked as traditional by the crown in governing Spain and Mexico, which implies a mutual obligation, pact, or contract between king and vassal, but the debt of the vassal is the one emphasized. Moreover, the code asserts direct royal control over all individuals, implying all are royal subjects, and thereby obviating a relationship wherein an ennobled royal vassal in turn may independently govern his own vassals. The concept here is seignorial, the king as overlord above other señores, a lord of lords. He holds civil and military authority, the right to judge and command. All men of his realm owe him military service and all its people are subject to royal justice.

Further definition of the locus of political authority, and of relations between king and people, became important to the crown during Spanish expansion into America, as we shall see, when questions requiring more precise answers arose concerning American dominion.

Problems associated with expansion overseas also exposed gaps in the logic of the official view of Spanish society, and highlighted discrepancies between official and popular political notions. A new environment, and the contest for spoils and power among conquistadors, jolted memory, recalling an unofficial oligarchic, regional, and autonomous past, and its traditions and institutions. A history, competing with the official vision of all Spaniards united for centuries in ongoing reconquest under Christian rulers, provided Spaniards in the New World with useful tradition and frontier institutions. This non-official view of the past, purposefully obscured by the official version disseminated by court, schools, and church, was closer to previous social reality, and particularly to that of the period of weakened royal power between the reigns of Alfonso X and Isabella and Ferdinand, and of the unsettled years following Isabella's death in 1504. Their majesties had dimmed the memory, but had not eradicated completely the old tendency, of challenge to strong kingship. The important point here is that Spaniards on both sides of the Atlantic were heirs to two historical traditions, joined at the apex by religion and crown but conflicting in many lesser particulars, among them notions of political organization. A deeper look at certain aspects of Castile in the fourteenth and fifteenth centuries is in order.

In the late Middle Ages, civil strife, visible in the deposition of Alfonso X, and culminating in the mid-fifteenth century, had exposed as fantasy the Alfonsine vision of a single harmonious Spanish community. It had emboldened smaller political units so that they and notions lending them legitimacy posed a historical problem as well as a real threat to the power of the young rulers at the start of their joint reign. In areas under Castile, in a society organized for war, ecclesiastics, religious orders, and nobles had gained at royal expense property, wealth, and a habit of exercising political power. Nobles and towns in seignorial relation to the crown had tried to change that arrangement to a more autonomous one, especially to exercise formally absolute jurisdiction in their precincts and to establish the king politically only as first among equals. Local power and sentiments burgeoned; regional differences and customs accentuated.[23]

A spokesman for the dominant oligarchic point of view was the cortes, originally composed of lay and ecclesiastical magnates, but by the fifteenth century in Castile also of representatives of the towns. In the period of civil war responsible for Isabella's ascending the throne, this body in its representations to the crown developed certain aspects of late medieval political theory supporting oligarchic authority, customary in Aragon but relatively little voiced in Castile, variants of the concept of the organic nature of society and of the idea of a pact existing between king and community.[24] Thus, although in 1445 the cortes of Olmedo declared, in terms reminiscent of the Partidas, that the king was God's anointed and his vicar, head and heart and soul of his people, who were his members, this elevated notion of near-sacred kingship gave way to one stressing its communally delegated nature, when in the turmoil of 1474 the cortes of Madrigal, in agreeing to recognize the shaky claim of Isabella to the crown of Castile, informed her that government was the result of a contract between ruler and community and that the community had endowed her with office.[25] Society, it implied, conferred headship; true sovereignty resided in the corporate social community—that is, in local leaders.

Two years later the cortes made explicit this point in stating that authority did derive from the social community (adding, however, that the ruler was obligated to God, who had to be paid in the administration of justice). It thereby provided example and precedent to later proponents of the notion that sovereignty ultimately resided with the "populace," that is, in the community or body politic. It must be remembered, however, that in this Christian, Spanish, and organic concept of community the *ricos hombres*—the oligarchy of the most propertied and noble—were the constituents proper of the "populace" and that this was no democratic idea of popular sovereignty.

Subsequently, conditions traditionally signaling weak monarchy recurred in Spain, giving rise there and in Spanish America to further assertions of organic popular sovereignty. Similar theory, supported by medieval precedent, accompanied the 1520–21 risings of the *comuneros*, shortly after the accession of Charles V, and later characterized Spanish American struggles of 1808. In the course of Spanish history, support for monarchy or oligarchy was often connected to how one viewed whether or not the community had ceded sovereignty permanently in investing the ruler with authority. Within traditional Spanish political theory, then, lurked the potentially subversive idea of popular sovereignty. Yet Spanish theoreticians could, and would, also take this idea up in defense of strong monarchy. Notable among theorists who did was the Jesuit Francisco Suárez (1548-1617). We must remember that until 1789 the ideas of monarchy and popular sovereignty were not necessarily incompatible or mutually exclusive.

For our purposes, two points are important here: that precedent was established by the oligarchic use of political theory made in the power struggles with monarchy, and that Fernando Cortés and many of his fellows were born at a time when Isabella and Ferdinand had just begun to redirect older institutions, and to counter political assumptions, reflecting weak central government. Although the political power of local lords was waning, they continued to hold half the land. Their wealth and social prestige remained tremendous. The earliest Spaniards in Mexico had been raised in an atmosphere likely to impress upon them the military and individualistic values of experience, opportunism, and personal resourcefulness. Their parents had known years of resurgent oligarchic power in Castile. Nor did the crown forget those years, or the mentality accompanying them. Spanish monarchs remained understandably leery of the power, in Spain and America, of town councils and regional señores—aversions that were to prove important for Mexico.

Among Spaniards a strong sense of belonging to the restricted and concrete reality of the village, town, and region in which one was born paralleled and reinforced the continuing strength of local custom in the face of royal law. A case in point is the explanation given by Cortés for the animosity based on regional origin between his men and those of Narváez. Yet by 1519 certain shared allegiances bridged such differences. Common to Spaniards was a rather mystical notion of the greater homeland, Spain, and of supreme temporal authority vested in a remote but powerful king. Here Cortés' tendency to think on two levels of patriotism—often referred to now as *patria chica* and *patria grande*—provides evidence of the Spanish tendency to hierarchies of thought, and to the conclusion that after Isabella regional allegiance, while strong, was becoming subsumed to a broader, Spanish sense of nationality.

Ultimately, the continuing success of Isabella's and Ferdinand's imposition of political unity was intimately tied to the relations of royal legitimacy and Spanish identity with religion. To enhance monarchy, those rulers successfully used not only law and political theory but also the church, identifying their nation with the universal Christian community—as its most perfect manifestation. They sought not merely to associate but to equate Spanishness with Roman Catholicism. Religion, implicitly the ultimate unifying factor in all medieval political thought through the true reconquest, but treated cavalierly by Juan II and Enrique IV, was raised by Isabella and Ferdinand to a *raison d'être* of their monarchy. They made the defense and propagation of Christianity the supreme end of their state, confident of the reinforcing tendencies of being associated with the church. Here we must remember that the church then connoted the body of the faithful, and not just the institutions of the clergy. In 1492 the Spanish monarchs ordered Jews, and in 1502 Moslems, to be converted or banished from Castile. The resulting expulsion of non-Christians and the increase of statutes rigorously limiting activities of converts and of all those subjects who could not prove *limpieza de sangre,* "purity of blood," made Spain appear a Christian citadel, while remaining a plural society. Non-noble Spaniards proving four grandfathers baptized were imbued with an aristocracy of sorts as Old Christians, and throughout the realm pride intensified in a broadly national identity.[26]

Royal policy heightened the association of honor, a Castilian military value, with Christian religion, and of being Spanish with race, and it exacerbated hatred of foreigners, especially of those of other faiths, who were also usually people who differed from Spanish Christians in appearance or culture. Bogus notions of *race* and *blood* tended to become intertwined with the concept of *nation,* although in fact many aristocrats known to be of Jewish descent and many other Christianized Jews—*conversos*—and Moslems—*moriscos*—and their descendants retained positions through the legal fiction of being of limpieza de sangre, and thus they incidentally also served as living examples of the idealistic, as opposed to the literal, nature of Spanish law. Moreover, their presence indicates another instance where a notion of continuous unity—in this case ethnic and religious—coexisted with real and long-standing diversity.

To maintain orthodoxy, religious and political, their majesties introduced the Inquisition in Castile and revitalized it in Aragon; perhaps two thousand converso heretics were burned at the stake in the 1480s. They also used the tribunal as a national court capable of circumventing regional and local customs and fueros. In addition, confiscations by the Inquisition, the huge resources of the military orders, semireligious organizations dedicated to crusade, and the sale of bulls of crusade greatly helped to increase royal income and to finance centralizing policies. Of greatest benefit in this respect were the spoils of crusade reaped from conquered Granada.

The notion of precise boundaries between sacred and profane belongs to a later age. Royal policies united many institutions and individuals exercising religious and lay authority in Spain in a sense of carrying out national mission under the direction of the crown. For practical purposes the Spanish clergy became an energetic arm of the state. Ferdinand requested and received a papal delegation of *patronato real,* which included rights of general patronage and ecclesiastical appointment, and to oversee tithes collected from royal subjects in Spain and in the Indies.[27] He secured through a mixture of diplomacy, coercion, and election the masterships of the three major military orders and so supervision of their huge revenues, of their vast landed estates, of the people who existed by working them, and of the powerful members of those orders as well.

The intimate working accord between crown and clergy in the process of bringing about a more closed and Christian society, and the advantages both derived from that partnership, is illustrated in the activities of Francisco Jiménez de Cisneros, the Franciscan friar who ended his career as regent of Spain, and whose work is also important to the history of Spain in America. Cisneros, appointed archbishop of Toledo, primate of Spain, in 1495 sped reform in the Spanish clergy. Well before Luther made a stand for a cleansing of the church, Cisneros strove to impose greater orthodoxy and a more primitive Christian austerity on the older religious orders, that is, on the regular clergy, those who lived under a monastic rule, and especially upon his own Franciscans.[28] They in turn worked to intensify popular faith. An official effort was made initially to assimilate the remaining Moors of Granada into Christianity through persuasion. Then in 1499 Cisneros introduced a program of forced conversion and, the following year, he is said to have made a public spectacle of burning over a million Islamic books.[29] In 1505 in the tradition of the fighting bishops of the reconquest, he led an expedition against the Moslems of Oran. From 1507 on he was also Inquisitor General. He was twice regent of Spain, after the death of Isabella and in the last year of his life, when he ruled in the interregnum between the death of Ferdinand in 1516 and the arrival in Spain in the last days of 1517 of Isabella's and Ferdinand's grandson, Charles I of Spain. In both periods Cisneros discouraged aristocratic and regional divisiveness, through his person projecting strength in union of monarchy, church, and nation.

At first glance, it may appear surprising that in 1508 Cisneros founded the University of Alcalá, where the best of Spanish humanism flourished. It is often pointed out that under his direction at Alcalá began (in 1510) the compilation of the great Complutensian Polyglot Bible, published in 1522 and considered the crowning achievement of the Renaissance in Spain. On reflection, however, the school and the scholarship pursued there can readily be understood as falling within a broader, and royal, program of Christian reform tied to national consolidation. That is, Alcalá was established primarily to educate future clerics and royal servants, young men zealous to find advancement in service to church and state. In its emphasis on education for the church, it joined the older University of Salamanca, where the specialty was law, in educating Spaniards primarily for combined state and church purposes.

The humanities—the teaching of Latin and Greek grammar, poetry, and rhetoric, using as models for emulation selections from works of classical authors—and attendant training in techniques of textual criticism were introduced in Spanish universities under Isabella and Ferdinand, and with royal impetus, to prepare Spaniards and particularly Castilians for Christian life and civil service. For some students, humanistic studies were a prelude to the higher disciplines of law, Christian philosophy, and theology, taught by scholastic method. Within this context the teaching of the humanities and the compilation (by converso scholars) of the multilingual Bible, as well as Cisneros' offer to Erasmus of a chair at Alcalá, appear more as testaments to a revitalized Roman Catholicism associated closely with consolidating government than—as some scholars have tended to depict them—as evidence of an atmosphere of free rational enquiry.[30]

Spanish humanism, which was to be important to the history of Mexico, under Isabella and Ferdinand abetted the royal policy of national unification in several specific ways and with the help, from 1490 on, of the first generation of master printers. Humanistic scholars worked to give Castilian language and culture a national aspect. Antonio de Nebrija, schooled in the humanities in Italy, returned to his native Spain, published a Castilian grammar in the key year of 1492, and, dedicating it to Isabella, informed the queen that it was his intention "to engrandize the affairs of our nation," and that the study of history had shown him the value of language as "a companion to empire."[31] Isabella was undoubtedly not unaware of that coalescence, for in a period when humanistic study renewed interest in classical history, she read in their original Latin Romans steeped in patriotic spirit—Cicero, Seneca, and Livy—and set a fashion at court for such reading. She also employed Peter Martyr d'Anghiera, the Italian humanist, as tutor to the children of the court. Martyr, in turn, wrote an account of Columbus' discovery of a new world for Spain, and later of Spanish conquest in America.[32] And Nebrija supervised the publication of the first edition of the latter work, Martyr's *Decades,* at Alcalá in 1516. The book was a popular success, heightening the prestige and renown of Martyr, Nebrija, Columbus, and their majesties, and ultimately contributing to pride in being Spanish. We might note in passing that Nebrija, for his textual criticisms of the Vulgate Bible during work on the polyglot edition, was called before the Inquisition —and was released upon the intervention of Cisneros.[33] The humanist's brush with the Holy Office is further indication that thought was free in this period only in relation to subsequent restraint and only insofar as it pleased those in positions of authority. It should also be kept in mind that the authorities maintained a militant attitude toward all learning and looked upon schooling as a cure for temporal ills—including lack of gainful employment, an excessive provincialism, and an attendant, unenthusiastic national loyalty. Well-born Spaniards, although they did not generally esteem higher education or Renaissance culture, became more disposed to study the classics since it appeared the thing to do at court.[34] The study of the humanities, then, was a basis of professional education. In those exposed to it, including some Spaniards in Mexico, and probably Fernando Cortés, were reinforced the classical concepts of *república* and *patria* as synonymous with nation.

Graduates of university courses in humanities actively facilitated Spanish unification under the crown. Isabella and Ferdinand moved toward central administration and a rudimentary state organization through the system of councils, including those of justice, state, finance, the hermandad (until 1495), the Inquisition, and the military orders. All required staffing. As more Castilians participated in central government, the possibility of such prestigious and potentially lucrative employ attracted increasing numbers of ambitious *hijosdalgo,* lesser nobility, to the study of those professions recognized as stepping-stones to royal preferment, the clergy and the law.

Government position was thought of as a sinecure, where an intelligent man could find ways to wealth and standing. Yet training and royal surveillance, while Isabella lived, as well as her example, set standards of moderation and pride in government service and supported feeling for tradition and responsibility in crown service. Men of middle strata now filled the royal councils, replacing conversos and also those greater nobles who, retaining social and economic power, were losing political control to the central government. In this sense, as the chronicler Hernán del Pulgar noted, a growing number of ambitious individuals saw no incompatibility between freedom and a greater degree of subservience to royal authority. Many wished, Pulgar reported, "to escape from lordship to royal liberty."[35] To these Spaniards and to others in America, including Fernando Cortés, regional ties meant restriction while adherence to the crown and loyalty to the expanded patria, or nation, enabled relative freedom of action. In Cortés' Extremadura, to 1515 emigration was due largely to the seignorial tendency, especially on the part of the largest landholders, the military orders, to charge large fines, compel work on castles, and put pressure on communities through seignorial jurisdiction.[36]

In sum, in numerous ways the Spain of Isabella and Ferdinand provided fine support, and impetus, for overseas expansion, which in turn helped to sustain and spread the acceptance of much of the official political ideology and to increase royal authority. They established an official ideology claiming as its basis traditional Spanish theory. It was reinforced and given additional validity by tenets and men associated with Christian humanism, and it helped to unify Spain in monarchy, faith, and culture. Concomitantly, however, an unofficial ideology was also broadly disseminated, an ideology rooted in the military mentality of a traditional social sector, the urban oligarchs and nobility. At issue between the two outlooks was the relative power of monarch and oligarchs, and the value of constituted authority as opposed to the worth of individual experience. Initially, expansion allowed harmony through ongoing military endeavor. Military activities and ideals permitted Spain to put on the façade of a monolithic society. Ferdinand launched campaigns in Africa, waged in a spirit of holy war, and in Italy. In America Spaniards subdued the indigenous peoples of the Caribbean against great odds and with an astounding confidence in themselves and in the justice of their endeavor, bolstered by faith in divine guidance and in being spiritual heirs to the civilization-bearing heroes of ancient Greece and Rome.

Not surprisingly, their highnesses sought to establish greater royal authority over the inhabitants of the Indies than they exercised effectively over those of Spain. Following the first voyage of Columbus, Ferdinand and Isabella immediately secured papal sanction to hold the new territories and to evangelize their peoples, Isabella specifically claiming the Indians as vassals directly subject to the crown of Castile. (However, in 1495 royal jurists adjudged that Indians taken in "just war" could be sold.) Papal bulls also sanctified New World dominion by the Spanish crown and established the patronato real over the Indies, in effect granting to the crown absolute religious authority in Spanish America.[37]

Ferdinand set up a House of Trade (*Casa de Contratación*) in Seville to enable monopolistic royal control of people and merchandise crossing the Atlantic. He also, after Isabella's death, allowed Indians to be parceled out (*repartimiento*) among *encomenderos,* as the Spanish recipients of such grants came to be known, and in a sort of indirect tribute arrangement then sought to tax encomenderos for the Indians they held. And he authorized Spanish expeditions to read to Indians they encountered the *requerimiento,* a document insisting the natives immediately accept the faith and royal dominion based on papal concession.[38]

It should be noted that when, between Isabella's death in 1504 and the 1520s, the monarchy and Spanish unity perceptibly weakened, the Spanish situation had ramifications for America. Ferdinand, although king in Aragon, became regent in Castile in 1509, only after his Habsburg son-in-law, Philip I, died and his mentally disturbed daughter, Philip's wife, Juana, was thought unfit to rule. With no royal title to Castile or its dependencies, and with an interest in the Indies granted him by Isabella, his policy in America was to enrich himself and his cohorts. When Dominican friars in 1510 publicly condemned as inhuman the Spanish treatment of the natives and excoriated galloping depopulation in the Caribbean, jurists, some of them theologians, at royal behest drew up the Laws of Burgos. These laws, containing an official, moral injunction to Spaniards to give better care to the natives and to see to their spiritual welfare, also viewed Indians as natural slaves.[39] Although upon Ferdinand's death the energetic nonagenarian, Cisneros, as regent of Spain dispatched fellow churchmen, Hieronymite friars, to oversee the Indies, and issued ameliorative ordinances, Spaniards continued to treat Indians much as they had before. And when in 1519 Diego de Velásquez, governor of Cuba, planned an expedition to the west, it was probably with a mind to gold and slaves. As its leader—a momentous decision he would later regret—Velásquez named an encomendero and town councilman, Fernando Cortés.

2

The Conquistadors

From the original settlement on Española, Spaniards had spread to neighboring islands and to the Caribbean mainland. In 1519 some 654 of these *isleños,* most of them born in the Castile of Isabella and Ferdinand and its Andalusian domain, with years of experience in the Indies and now lured by reports of populous lands rich in gold, sailed westward from Cuba under Fernando Cortés. These conquistadors shared a sense of national identity, undoubtedly heightened by their being Spanish in a part of the world where everyone else was not. In the conquest of Aztec Mexico they strove to embody the Castilian ideal of a life spent in aggressive military endeavor, permeated with religious ardor, dedicated to crusade. In their first battle on Mexican soil they invoked the patron saint of the reconquest, advancing against their Indian adversaries to the shout of "Santiago y a ellos!" ("St. James and at them!").[1]

Had Cortés, Bernal Díaz, or any of the others been asked what Spain meant to him, the answer would probably have included the concepts of national patriotism nurtured by Isabella and Ferdinand. Spain, those who wrote indicate, evoked a deep feeling of loyalty to the crown, to the faith, and to *the* civilization as the proper way of life. In engaging in military crusade against the heathen they believed themselves not only to be busied in a most laudable and very Spanish project but also to be discharging the highest form of service to country. They bore the symbols of the crown and the faith—the royal coat of arms and the holy cross—emblazoned on their battle standards.[2] Bernal Díaz explained, "My ancestors having always been servants of the crown, and my father and one of my brothers being in the service of the Catholic monarchs, Don

Ferdinand and Doña Isabella, of very glorious memory, I wished in some sort to emulate them."[3] He, Cortés, and many of the others had come to the Indies from Isabelline Castile; Cortés had arrived in 1504. They fought and some died not to defend national boundaries but to expand them. Certain of their God-given prowess and of the righteousness of their cause, the conquistadors took Mexico in the name of Spain.

These Spaniards saw no disparity between doing one's religious and patriotic duty and serving oneself. "We came here," Bernal Díaz added, "to serve God and also to get rich." The Dominican friar Bartolomé de Las Casas was more acerbic: "All volunteered for greed and expected much gold."[4] Cortés, his secretary later wrote, initially had believed that he had only to arrive at Santo Domingo to be weighed down with it.[5] They risked their lives and whatever fortune they possessed in a gamble on getting more. At the same time, they also sailed in search of esteem, in the eternal human pursuit of higher social status and repute. Esteem they assumed would come, as it usually does, with achieving goals and positions their own society held to be most honorable and worthy of attainment, and in Spanish society, as they knew it, among the most revered of all were the military virtues of honor and glory and their material manifestations, wealth and nobility. Great and relentless service at arms in the name of the king and the Lord had led to riches and titles in this world and they would lead to the salvation of one's soul in the next. Patriotism and self-interest dictated that it was noble, it was virtuous, and it would undoubtedly prove eminently worthwhile, to engrandize the homeland through expanding the domain of the crown. In military endeavor, then, private and royal interests coalesced.

Fernando Cortés exemplified the conquistador mentality. He was born in 1485, during the ten-year-long siege of Granada, in Extremadura, the Castilian frontier on Portugal and Andalusia. His father, Martín, had earlier fought as cavalry officer in the forces of a dissident lord who opposed Isabella's having appointed Ferdinand master of the military order of Alcántara.[6] The elder Cortés, poor but claiming the status of hidalgo, was later reconciled to the widening power of royal government to the extent that he sent his son to study (royal) law in Salamanca. There the man who would lead Spaniards conquering Mexico spent several years studying Latin, through the humanistic method—reading selections from the classics—but he probably never pursued higher studies at the university.[7] Cortés was a notary in Española and in Cuba, where he also sat on a town council—signifying a degree of property and prestige and some familiarity with government.

Certain of Cortés' actions and attitudes shed light on those of the conquerors in general. Some were important to Mexico under Spain, and some to Mexico thereafter. In his letter of 3 February 1544 to the king, he conveyed his thoughts on a worthwhile life, his own, assuming that what had been of value, morally and materially, to Cortés had equally profited Spain. He wrote:

> I have toiled without cease for 40 years, eating poorly, through times good and bad carrying arms on my shoulders, placing myself in danger, spending my fortune and my life, all in the service of God. I brought sheep into His fold in unknown lands, far away from our hemisphere and not inscribed in our chronicles. I spread the name and increased the patrimony of my king, winning for him and bringing under his yoke and royal scepter many large kingdoms and lordships of many barbarous peoples and nations, while gaining for myself appropriate esteem and wealth.[8]

Note that in exchange for honor in this world and in anticipation of eternal glory, Cortés claimed to have found in Mexico the sort of political entities both men understood and wrote of adding them to the domain of his monarch.

From his arrival there he commented in dispatches to the crown on the well-ordered governments he was encountering in many indigenous communities. Indian social and political organization facilitated his increasing the royal patrimony by gathering up the more settled *peoples* and *nations* in a pattern of seignorial subjugation to the Spanish crown. In his letter of 1544 when writing of "Indian nations," he used the word *nation* in the generally accepted sense of his time, as meaning an extended social community, one united politically, culturally, and ethnically, although not necessarily geographically, and much like the *tribe* in the Old Testament. Initially, he reported finding Indians living in cities and villages governed by lords (señores) who "have offered their service to your majesty and given it through their subjects and vassals."[9] Such offers, of course, most frequently followed Spanish application of varying amounts of coercion. Cortés was aware that, earlier, Indians had reacted with disbelief to the *requerimiento* and other Spanish requests, when preceded or accompanied by no resort to force, that the natives acknowledge the foreign monarch as overlord. Bernal Díaz, citing the example of the natives of Tabasco who answered, when members of the earlier expedition under Juan de Grijalva had so importuned them, that they already had a chief, observes that "we had only just arrived and knew nothing about them, and yet we wanted to give them a señor."[10]

Cortés presented much the same argument to the same Indians, first formally stating Spanish intent by reading, as had Grijalva, the *requerimiento,* but then going on to convince them through exposure to Spanish might in battle. Afterward the native "señores" proved more disposed to join the Spanish political system. Cortés requested and received an oath of fealty from these Indian leaders "to the greatest princes in the world," followed by a plea to their new friends to leave the land as soon as possible.[11] This procedure was repeated frequently during the march to Tenochtitlán—the Aztec metropolis and now Mexico City—and again later during Cortés' expedition to Honduras. It is very probable that the political aspects of the *requerimiento,* when stated through an interpreter, were comprehended by peoples already paying tribute to the Aztecs.[12]

The conquistadors gained at least the temporary loyalty and at times the effective support of entire peoples through recognizing that the exercise of political authority in the more sedentary Indian communities bore similarities to Spanish arrangements. Perceived structural parallels enabled at least nominal imposition of Spanish overlordship upon indigenous governments. They facilitated control, in the name of the crown, by relatively few Spaniards of millions of Indians during and after the conquest. They also permitted an apparent continuity of political authority within many communities. Most important, the Spaniards in Mexico understood that groups of natives could be controlled through manipulating their leaders.

On occasion, however, Cortés and other Spaniards overstated similarities, sometimes through error, at other times to suit their purposes. In a report meant to impress the king, Cortés described Motecuhzoma as the greatest of all Indian lords, ruling in royal fashion as an overlord, having as vassals many lesser señores, and comparable in power to the greatest rulers on earth. "No prince of the world was ever more feared by all his subjects, both near and far."[13] In reality, Motecuhzoma's Tenochtitlán has perhaps best been described as a state in the process of formation. It dominated the neighboring cities of Texcoco and Tlacopan and governed the surrounding area through Aztec nobles and justices. In the rest of the region it dominated—the southern part of present-day Mexico—most, but not all, communities paid tribute but remained self-governing. Within them Indians lived in traditional tribal societies, their chiefs chosen from first families by a nonhereditary warrior aristocracy. The great majority were peasants farming communal lands and belonging to a *calpulli,* perceived as an extended clan based on common ancestors.[14] Their leaders were their link to Aztec domination.

The conquistadors noted differences among Indian groups. The non-sedentary Chichemecas Cortés described as "barbarous people of less rationality than those of all other provinces," while the Tlaxcalans, living in houses, holding markets, governed by recognizable señores, were "a people of all reason and harmony."[15] Man, Cortés assumed in accord with current Spanish notions, was a social being naturally inclined to family and communal life. Living habits qualified certain Indian groups as a whole as rational and civilized and excluded others. The Spanish conquerors initially tended to correlate the degree of native mental capacity with the degree of political organization. That is, they judged intelligence to be a communal endowment reflected in social order. Thus, when Spaniards discovered Indian communities living in "all manner of good order and polity" they extrapolated, from what they observed to be the state of civilization of a community, the degree of rationality possessed by its members. Order of one sort to them implied order of another. Reasonable beings, Cortés assumed, lived in communities most like those of Europe. If conforming to the Spanish norm, that is, they were adjudged to lead civilized lives. Moreover, it must be borne in mind that when Cortés reported his subjugation of men living in organized societies as "civilized" in the literal sense of the word, in no way did it diminish the importance of his own achievement. Self-interest would continue to play a large part in determining whether certain Spanish individuals and groups would accept or reject the idea of the rationality of the Indian.

Although comfortable with Indian political arrangements, Cortés grew livid when first confronted with indigenous religious beliefs and practices. He raged against the rites of their gods, those lies and deceptions invented by the devil to bring eternal damnation. He was certain that he had to intervene to save native souls from hell. Initially, he jeopardized Spanish subjugation of Indian towns by insisting that all negotiation be prefaced by idol smashing, or at least removal, and by replacing the local deities with the Christian cross. Paradoxically it was a friar, the Mercedarian Andrés de Olmedo, who most often restrained him from iconoclasm, counseling prudence, reminding him that the Indians would far sooner swear obedience to an absent overlord than accept the sudden demise of their present gods.[16]

To Cortés, in the tradition of the reconquest, the religious obligation was a primary one, understood in military and crusading terms. He informed the natives that the Spanish rulers, those greatest of lords, in turn obeyed an even mightier Prince.[17] Cortés' God was the supreme Lord, the *Señor Universal.* His own relationship with God he conceived of as a felicitous one based on mutual understanding and a sense of reciprocity, in short a kind of compact. He expressed a belief in divine direction of his own affairs: ". . . since Almighty God, our Lord, has vouchsafed to advance and favor me in the discovery and conquest of New Spain and all the provinces subject thereunto," in return he, Cortés, felt obliged in his last will and testament to follow the custom of Spanish nobility, ordering that religious foundations, a hospital, a convent, and a school be built and dedicated to the greater glory of God[18]—and at the same time, of course, to the renown, the temporal glory, of Fernando Cortés.

Concerned with saving his own soul, Cortés assumed this to be contingent upon doing his utmost to salvage the souls of the Indians. He had friars with him throughout the conquest, and afterward urged the king to send more of these regular clergy as missionaries. He decreed in 1524 that encomenderos, Spaniards holding Indians, maintain clerics to instruct their natives.[19] In his last will, he directed his heirs to look to the religious instruction of the Indians in the towns he held as Marqués del Valle de Oaxaca. Clearly, although to us his behavior appears often at odds with such a sentiment, he believed temporal activity a preparation for eternal life. Yet thought and deeds can be reconciled if we remember that, to Cortés, in this world adherence to Spanish military values paved the road to heavenly bliss, and that his statements and actions were generally acceptable within the prevailing system of belief.

Cortés also understood that on earth religion reinforced political authority. To him, the Spanish king was vicar to God, and the conqueror strove to establish the same sort of mutually advantageous arrangement he assumed he had with the heavenly Lord with His earthly representative and counterpart, his own señor natural, Charles, the Habsburg grandson of Isabella and Ferdinand, the new king of Spain and also, even more recently, the Holy Roman Emperor. Accordingly, shortly after landing in Mexico, Cortés threw off the authority delegated to him by his heretofore immediate superior, Diego de Velásquez, governor of Cuba, and, as had many Spaniards before him, took steps to escape into the royal liberty. He and his men gained relative freedom of action by foreswearing their ties to a delegated royal (Fernandine) official and claiming a more direct obligation to the more distant crown and its new wearer. Especially with the new young king not firmly established as the royal power in Spain— their letter was addressed to both Charles and his mother, Juana—they felt the crown would circumscribe their activities far less than would Velásquez, who had sent them only to explore and trade, to get gold and slaves and report on the land, but not to settle there themselves. What can be construed as their declaration of independence from more effective restriction (or so they thought) was made shortly after their arrival on the mainland.

Cortés, in the fashion of a military leader of the Castilian reconquest, arranged the founding of the town of Villa Rica de la Vera Cruz and appointed from his lieutenants its council (*cabildo*). A letter from that council then went to the crown. In it these public spirited royal vassals, as they characterized themselves, declared Velásquez unjust and tyrannical in his dealings with them and, by not allowing settlement, acting contrary to royal interests: "Since it appeared to us not conforming to the service of Your Majesties to do in this land as Diego Velásquez had ordered the Captain, Cortés, it seemed better to all of us that a town be founded and peopled here in the name of your royal highnesses."[20]

During the Spanish reconquest, particularly in the eleventh and thirteenth centuries, towns had been established in newly won areas under Castile as seats of defense and of government for urban inhabitants and for the surrounding countryside. Soldiers wishing to settle then became the nucleus of a new civil community. At times they chose their lord; always, however, they recognized the king as overlord, as did the council members of Vera Cruz. Further, they gave evidence to a more general tendency to equate maintenance of public order and justice with royal authority. "Justice should be done," their letter explained, "so that you will have lordship (*señorío*) in this land as is customary in your kingdoms and dominions." Recognizing the royal right of appointment, the cabildo petitioned the crown to designate Fernando Cortés governor and chief justice, that is, to delegate to him local authority for the civil royal functions. "And once this country is populated by Spaniards, thereby adding to the kingdoms and dependencies, and the income, of Your Majesties, you might see fit to bestow your favors upon us (*hacer mercedes*)." As additional earnest of service to the crown and as indication of the value of the new land, they were sending, they said, "all the gold, silver and valuables obtained in this country."[21]

Cortés and the council probably followed earlier Caribbean practices derived from Spanish precedent, rather than Spanish usage directly. In Spain autonomous communities such as Vera Cruz were anachronistic, but they resurfaced, as did other frontier institutions, in the Indies. Moreover, on Española royal officials had founded some Spanish towns dependent directly on the crown, circumventing the authority of the governor, Diego Colón, while others had revolted against him and placed themselves directly under the monarch. In Cuba Velásquez himself ignored Colón, his more immediate superior, to treat directly with officials in Spain. In sum, Cortés and his men were following an American variant of a familiar, time-hallowed Spanish pattern.

Implicit in the explanation of founding Vera Cruz was the device of a compact between lord and vassals. The conquistadors stated they had served the crown well and would continue to do so. In return, the monarch was to govern justly, to reward their loyalty and service through grants of position, wealth, and titles, and to delegate authority locally. Another assumption underlay this one: these Spaniards assumed a town, in accord with medieval political notions, to be at once a microcosm of human community, a natural corporation, an embodiment of civilization, and a seat of sovereignty. Their notion of association was in the same tradition as the one explicitly stated by the cortes of Castile in reminding Isabella that sovereignty was bestowed by God upon the social community and that the community in turn had vested it in the ruler in contractual form, so that he or she must govern justly to retain authority. The Vera Cruz cabildo revealed similar political assumptions regarding constituted community in declaring the terms of its relationships to superior authority. It assumed a reciprocal agreement with its overlord, the crown. To Velásquez it ascribed both tyranny and disservice to his overlord. As lord and governor he had violated a compact with his people, and as a vassal and royal official had breached his contract with his king. In accord with this line of thought, the cabildo could find the old agreements invalid and, in constituting a new community, establish the basis for operating within a proper, natural, contractual relationship with the monarch. Thus, essentially military notions of relations between lord and vassals combined with essentially civil concepts concerning relations of king and community (or subjects) in the foundation of Spanish government in Mexico.

Cortés and the other conquistadors probably did not notice inconsistencies and inherent tensions in the mélange of time-honored theory they cited to support their acts. That is, their interest was not (as was that of the cortes in addressing Isabella) in asserting where sovereignty ultimately resided, nor was it in testing their right to depose a tyrant-prince. They sought to posit the political supremacy of their self-constituted social community not above that of the monarch but only above that of the governor of Cuba. But they did put forth the community's right to make, and to declare valid or invalid, contracts with higher authorities. Their endeavor was in some respects similar to the efforts of the comuneros in Spain then seeking freedom from overbearing superiors and a return to the rights enjoyed by medieval towns. Yet the founding of Vera Cruz was an exercise in popular government only if popular is taken in its medieval corporate sense, as an organic concept signifying not the sum total of individual citizens but the essence of community, and one in which the more powerful and wealthier members were thought of as representing the commonwealth, itself in turn a microcosm of all polity. Paradoxically, in employing Spanish political theory and precedent to gain direct royal patronage, the cabildo of Vera Cruz incidentally set a Mexican precedent concerning the notion of popular sovereignty, one that Mexicans in 1808 would cite against Spain itself, asserting that the community had delegated sovereignty to its ruler in a contractual manner and going on to claim that sovereignty resided ultimately, and remained, in the social community.[22]

Subsequently, Cortés became governor and captain-general of all Spanish Mexico. As highest civil and military authority, he strove to ensure permanent Spanish settlement and, at the same time, to control, protect, and preserve the Indians. To achieve these goals he introduced *repartimiento-encomienda,* another variant on institutions earlier utilized by Castilians in Extremadura and Andalusia, and by Spaniards among the Moors, the Canary Islanders, and as repartimiento, among the Caribbean natives. Individual Spaniards and the military orders in newly acquired territories had been granted in similar fashion groups of newly conquered peoples—at times charged with their protection and with overseeing their introduction to, or continuance in, the faith. In return, these recipients were to have certain amounts of service (usually labor), tribute (usually in kind or money), and jurisdiction. This system had a variety of forms and designations; at bottom all were seignorial arrangements.[23]

In Mexico Cortés "deposited" Indian señores and their followers with Spaniards who were to reside in the land. His grants reflected the favor-dispensing function of military leaders (and thus of the supreme military leader), previous practice in the West Indies, and were provisional upon royal approval, reading "for the present, I entrust in you ..." the services of Indians and señores of such a such a town (*pueblo*) or towns.[24] Citing the unhappy precedent of the annihilation of the Caribbean peoples, in his ordinances he promised encomenderos they "could keep their Indians if they multiplied," and to request of the king holdings in perpetuity.[25]

More will be said of encomienda as an institution in later chapters. Here we note that its introduction altered both the theory and practice of Mexican political arrangements. Where during the conquest Cortés had written of Indian lords as becoming directly subject to the overlordship of the king, by his ordinances and activities afterward he established a chain of authority whereby encomenderos held effective power over vast numbers of Indians through native chiefs, while he and his lieutenants governed the encomenderos and in turn acknowledged the superior, but distant, authority of the monarch. In effect, he assigned a de facto lordship to Spanish encomenderos, removed the Indians from direct royal authority, and assumed a mediating stance between the king and his Mexican subjects. He also reserved for himself the tribute and services of choice Indian towns in various heavily populated areas. This mixed civil and military system briefly made him lord of the land.

Dissident factions among the Spanish and steady imposition of royal authority soon eroded his power. By 1530, although held in awe, particularly by the Indians, as the embodiment of Spanish might, Cortés found his political authority in New Spain, the kingdom he had conquered and named, confined to the rather nebulous duties and prerogatives of captain-general. In 1529 Charles granted him the title of Marqués del Valle de Oaxaca, a true señorío with the right to hold 23,000 vassals and "all rents, taxes, rights, tributes, and contributions belonging to His Majesty, exactly as these lands were held by their lords before the country was conquered."[26] That is, Cortés was granted a huge and important domain, one previously recognizing Motecuhzoma as overlord. The Spanish king, however, retained overlordship, the right to coin money and to call to arms, and reserved to Cortés' vassals the right to appeal to the crown.[27] And while the grant appears magnanimous, it fell far short of Cortés' real holdings at the time. Subsequent *mercedes* (royal grants—

literally, favors) to Spaniards in Mexico frequently had the same result; royal bequests to conquistadors often tended in fact to be restrictions. Thus, as customary among Spanish nobles, Cortés surrendered ultimate political authority but enjoyed—in his case, increased—social prestige and economic well-being.

With limited but unique regional authority, his wealth unsurpassed except by the monarch's, Cortés remained a loyal Spanish subject.[28] He had come to the Indies a commoner, if of hidalgo stock.[29] He died, in 1549, lord of a goodly part of the land he had named the Kingdom of New Spain. His fortunes had risen during a decade of expanding conception of the extent and nature of royal power and authority. Presenting to the king a cannon cast of Mexican gold, silver, and copper, embellished with a phoenix, Cortés summed up his assessment of both his own and the royal position in its inscription: "This bird was born without equal. As a servant I have no second. And you have no peer in this world."[30]

The Spanish conquest and initial settlement had taken place just after Charles I of Spain secured election as Charles V, Holy Roman Emperor, thus joining in his person the Spanish tradition of kingship, itself invested with pretensions to empire, with the imperial title. This conjunction of the two titles in his acknowledged overlord allowed Cortés, a year later, to view himself as the instrument of "the great emperor" in effecting a splendid increase of the royal domain. He wrote to Charles in 1520, referring to his Mexican conquests as "these kingdoms of Your Majesty" whereof he, Charles, could be considered emperor "with no less a title and merit than that of Germany, which by grace of God you possess."[31] Cortés did not write in terms of New Spain as being within a Spanish empire, or in terms of a single world empire but, rather, with the view that he was adding to the royal patrimony a distinct region of great magnitude. He wrote of carving out another empire for his lord.

Cortés personified the old Castilian military mentality, magnifying its heroic qualities in his dispatches and deeds and embroidering Spanish endeavor with notions of classical and chivalric heroism. To many contemporaries and subsequent admirers, he typified, in a manner larger than life, Spanish individualism. In conquest he thought and dared in grandiose style. He displayed the Spanish ability to order dominion initially in militant fashion and within a theoretical framework of neat social and political bundles, but he also displayed qualities that made maintenance a problem for Spain throughout its history. Barely a decade before the Mexican conquest, Francisco Guicciardini, Florentine ambassador to Ferdinand's court, observed of Spaniards "that perhaps they make better soldiers than generals.... They may be more apt for combat than for governing or command."[32] Events proved him wrong about command. Spanish armies soon became acknowledged by Europeans, often to their discomfiture, as the best on the Continent. But in Europe and in Mexico, tensions were inevitable between the static, corporate, hierarchical, and authoritarian crown-supported concepts of civil and social arrangements and dynamic, individualistic, even anarchic military qualities. Dissimulation became an instrument of reconciliation. The setting up of the Vera Cruz cabildo, for example, in theory the product of a civil and corporate society, was in reality that of Cortés' own assertion of militant individualism. Wise in the value and uses of guile and the worth of experience, he could conquer and—with experience too in some aspects of law and public order and in controlling Indians—he could establish social and political institutions of part civil, part military nature, perceived as traditional and designed for use, by a military aristocracy. He did not, however, succeed in retaining control of them. For other Spanish practice, now becoming accepted and competing tradition, made social maintenance, in fact as in theory, a royal function, performed by other sorts of men.

The conquerors of Mexico could not know what sort of king Charles would be. The model they had was Ferdinand, if diluted with a bit of Cisneros. Cortés had come from Spain and prospered in the Fernandine years, when exploitation and corruption flourished in the Caribbean. Spaniards mined its native peoples and its resources. And in doing so, they discovered better ways of handling both, a knowledge which they brought, along with mercantile experience, to New Spain. In the islands, under Ferdinand the crown had acted largely to ensure its own share of wealth and to prevent civil strife among resident Spaniards, only admonishing, when brought to it by the clergy, that encomienda Indians and slaves be better treated; and the difference between those two conditions was then largely one of how the natives had been obtained.

Against this background, Cortés appears to have been fairly enlightened. He may well have been aware that the best way to subdue huge numbers of Indians and gain the product of their labor was, as Vasco Núñez de Balboa had shown earlier in Darién, by conquering in the sense of winning over their chiefs. He also probably understood the efficacy of Christianizing for control, although insisting on conversion out of a strong sense of the need to legitimate conquest through crusade and implanting the true faith. His was a religious fervor reminiscent of Isabella's. He saw church and state as joint responsibilities of the Spanish crown and its representatives—indeed, of any true leader.

Now that the Spanish monarch was also Holy Roman Emperor and as such traditional temporal champion of the faith, in theory if not so often in fact, Cortés and other Spaniards in Mexico could usefully append to the Fernandine mentality concerning America a revitalized and militant religious purpose combining the spirit of Cisnerian reform with the crusading zeal rekindled largely by Isabella. This they did, and continued to do, while Charles and his counselors and officials pursued a divergent policy grounded in principles of civil government. It, too, was in large part a legacy of their Catholic majesties. Spain offered to America sufficient precedent and ideological elements to bring into being and continue to bolster both the views from above and those from below.

Cortés was a Spaniard acutely aware of the political and ideological possibilities of imperial organization. His belief in his own right to lordship over a sizable portion of the lands and peoples of Mexico, through conquest and under the aegis of the most powerful and very remote overlord who wore the crown of Castile (and now that of Holy Roman Emperor), was a traditional Spanish one, mirrored and perpetuated not only in the outlook of many of his companions but also in that of other early Spanish arrivals. Many of their attitudes and beliefs came to be held as articles of faith by subsequent generations of Mexican claimants to Spanish ancestry. Meanwhile, in Spain itself Habsburg rule, anchored in differing interpretations of many of the same beliefs, became synonymous with Spanish imperialism.

3

Charles I and Mexican Policy

When Charles I of Spain, the Habsburg grandson of Ferdinand and Isabella, secured election in 1519 as Charles V, Holy Roman Emperor, he joined in his person the Spanish tradition of kingship, itself invested with pretension to empire, with the imperial title. Alfonso X, with the aid of jurists and long before the consolidation of the kingdoms into a national complex, had embellished the Castilian crown with attributes of imperial sovereignty. Earlier kings, too, had borrowed concepts supporting their imperial aspirations directly from canon law and, usually through it, from imperial Rome. During the reconquest, for example, Alfonso III (866–910) of León, the parent kingdom of Castile, had expressed a rudimentary sense of imperial mission in claiming to be heir to Gothic and Roman rule in the peninsula, not only taking the title "King of the Spains," but on occasion also seeing to it that his sons and his subjects hailed him as *magnus Imperator* or *Imperator nostro*.[1] Spanish tradition and the imperial title consequently allowed Spaniards, among them Fernando Cortés, to think of Spain and empire as coterminous.

We have seen that in 1520 Cortés wrote of adding another empire to Charles' domain. In that year, too, in October, Cortés addressed him as "Most high and powerful and very Catholic Prince, most invincible Emperor and Lord," employing a set of separate titles. By September of 1526, however, he had adopted the then customary, more compact, and grandiloquent form of address: "Holy Catholic Caesarean Majesty."[2] It was a salutation combining Christian and Roman elements in one all-embracing title, at the least implying that supernatural sanction existed for a single, Roman-like, Christian, and essentially Spanish empire. The ways Cortés chose to address Charles not only exemplified the evolution of acceptable form but, more important, kept pace with and indicated expansion of current assumptions concerning royal authority.

As Spaniards conquered Mexico, Charles' supporters in Spain advanced the imperial concept. The bishop of Badajoz, Ruiz de la Mota, presiding over the cortes at Santiago-Coruña in 1520, explicitly stated what the salutation of 1526 was only at most to imply: "By will of Divine Providence," that churchman declared, "Your Majesty rules the universe!"[3] In the same period the Fleming and royal minister, Mercurio Gattinara, dreamed in medieval and Dante-esque fashion of uniting Christendom into a true universal domain for the emperor. It was also Gattinara who had stipulated that Charles be addressed officially as Christian Caesar.[4] Although religious schism between Roman Catholics and Protestants soon doomed the vision of an ecumenical empire, more and more Spaniards tended to view their monarch as Christian champion, vicar of God, and shepherd to the faithful.[5] The role of the crown as defender of the faith, stressed by Isabella and Ferdinand, was combined with the traditional Christian imperial title by Charles V. His son, Philip, even without that title, was to Spaniards later *the* Christian prince and temporal head of all true Christendom.

Charles himself, as one historian has astutely remarked, "defined his position and his aims in chivalric, religious, and dynastic terms, rather than in terms of political domination, [and] he set no limits to them."[6] Bringing Burgundian, knightly values to Spanish rule, where they coalesced with the spirit of Christian crusade, Charles referred to himself as God's standard bearer.[7] He ruled as a traditional dynast, governing as overlord, that is, as if wearing the separate crowns of many principalities and kingdoms in Spain, the Lowlands, Austria, Italy, and America. Within his Spanish domain, moreover, he claimed direct lordship over all peoples as subjects and vassals. ("Subject" and "vassal" were employed rather indiscriminately at the time.) In a letter he wrote to his son, Philip, upon leaving the prince as regent of "the kingdoms and lordships" of Spain in 1543, his dynastic cast of mind is unmistakable, as are his ideas of the obligations of monarchy. Philip must trust in God, do his duty as ordained by Him, guard his own honor and, should his father die, look to, as his own, the Spanish kingdoms, lordships, and vassals.[8]

Charles came to Spain in 1517. Born and raised in Flanders, this elder son of Philip I and Juana (known to history as *la Loca,* the Mad) was viewed with suspicion, then open hostility, by numerous Spaniards of all social strata who disliked a foreign-born and foreign-reared king and his non-Spanish, rapacious officials and courtiers.[9] In the comunero uprisings of 1520–21, dislike flared into open revolt against the royal officials. Castilian towns and nobles fought to bring back the more halcyon days, experienced before Isabella and Ferdinand, and after Isabella's death, of greater autonomy. Royal triumph over the dissidents, Charles' subsequent attachment to Spain and preference to Spaniards in government and the clergy there, and his stance as defender of religious orthodoxy won him increasing Spanish respect and loyalty. Spanish pride grew in the monarch's vast domain and imperial title. Growing recognition of the seriousness of Christian schism and Charles' stance as Christian warrior-king defending Europe against infidel and heretic fed Spanish attachment. And in the 1520s, the now traditional Spanish belief that all communities belonged to one great society embracing all mankind abetted the ideological fusion of dynastic and imperial rules, as did Charles' tendency to see Spain increasingly as the hub of his empire.

Mexico came under Spain in the first years of Charles' reign. Even as Cortés took the land it was formally incorporated into the dynastic system as an American kingdom dependent upon the crown of Castile.[10] Thus, the monarch wrote to Cortés concerning his American subjects and, in 1523, informed the conqueror that the Kingdom of New Spain could not be alienated from the crown.[11] In that year the king also formally established within the governing system of Spain, as part of the machinery expediting the workings of an informal imperial complex, a Council of the Indies. That title was given to a de facto administrative group evolved within the Council of Castile. Charles employed it, as he did the other royal councils, to aid him in carrying out the ruler's traditional functions —waging war and doing justice (including legislating, adjudicating, and administering).

From the outset, revenues were clearly his primary interest, as they had been Ferdinand's. The first royal officials sent to Mexico, immediately after the conquest, were dispatched to supervise the *real hacienda* or royal treasury.[12] They replaced the *veedor,* the overseer chosen, as was customary, by the conquistadors to guard for the crown a fifth of whatever was gained of value.[13] The earliest royal decrees for Mexico, those issued from 1519 to 1524, were directed to securing the crown's share of booty, to imposing tribute payments, import duties, and the traditional tax, the tenth or tithe, as patron of the church.[14] The injunction to Cortés to grant no encomiendas may be viewed within the context of these decrees, as an attempt to safeguard sources of royal income and to circumscribe his authority. By these means, the court sought to bring practice into line with the royal belief that the Indies in general, and New Spain or Mexico in particular, were part of the señorío of the crown of Castile, and that the Indians were free, direct, taxable royal subjects.[15] Charles, that is, sought direct seignorial control in Mexico over all Spaniards and Indians as royal vassals or subjects.

Isabella and Ferdinand had established ample precedent for their grandson's American policies. First to claim the Indians as free subjects or vassals was Isabella. Ferdinand, however, had delegated effective authority over Indians and the direct fruits of their labor to individual Spaniards. Cisneros had then returned to the Isabelline policy, instructing that Indians should pay tribute as royal subjects. Their majesties had based their title to the Indies upon the papal concession, justifying dominion on the grounds of bringing Christianity to the Indians. Charles, then, was endowed with these spiritual and material precedents for dominion as their heir. The royal request for patronato real in the Indies and the papal compliance, it will be remembered, represented the sort of traditional arrangement wherein the highest temporal and religious authorities supported one another's prerogatives. Thus church and state in Spanish America were enabled freely to reinforce one another.[16] Yet their Catholic majesties were among the last of European monarchs who did feel free to pay great formal and theoretical deference to the See of Saint Peter without attendant loss of sovereignty or independence of action. Subsequently Charles and Philip vigorously employed the patronato real and close association with the clergy for royal purposes but did not want their American title to rest solely on the papal donation, or their American subjects to be controlled and taxed by any but royal authority.

Charles insisted that all natives were his own subjects, owing him service and tribute as their monarch and overlord.[17] Implicit in the claim was a prohibition against conquistadors setting up a seignorial domain of their own in Mexico. He initially outlawed encomienda. He also ordered Spaniards to enslave no Indians unjustly, that is, unless taken in war or held previously by other natives.[18] These royal orders combined political and financial interest with limited humanitarian concern. Political, economic, and humanitarian considerations will be seen to continue to be invoked, and frequently to coalesce, in the unfolding of royal policy for New Spain.

From the outset, Spanish clerics in their traditional role as jurists and royal advisers both supported and influenced royal policy in Mexico. Cisneros had set precedent. Jurists at court provided theory to justify the incorporation of New Spain into the crown of Castile, and in America churchmen worked to implement it. Spanish crown and Spanish church were to afford one another continuous reciprocal reinforcement. Throughout his reign Charles strove to expand and defend the faith. It must be emphasized that he did so as he understood it, in accord with dynastic interest, and often at odds with the Farnese and Medici popes, or at best in uneasy alliance with them against infidels and heretics. In this spirit he advised Philip to respect the papacy but to keep a sharp eye on the encumbent.[19] Nor was he averse to suggestions of how to lessen royal dependence upon Rome, and some of the best advice to that end came from the clergy.

Throughout Europe, by the 1520s religion, nationalism, and royal power were linked and fought over. Even where Catholicism held, royal national and protonational interests increasingly challenged papal power. It is well to remember that even sixteenth-century European rulers loyal to Roman Catholicism frequently vied with the papacy for control of regional and national religious institutions, and that they tended to bolster their claims to the exercise of sovereignty free of papal interference by recourse to traditional Christian political theory. Europeans in general continued to invoke heaven's sanction for all political authority and to assume political and ethical theory inseparable (except on occasion and then usually in the immediate papal neighborhood—where, for example, Niccolò Machiavelli represented one kind of reaction to the omnipresent reality of papal involvement in power politics).

Charles, like his Spanish grandparents, believed in the indissoluble union of government, ethics, and religion, and, like them, he understood it as a traditional obligation "to discharge the royal conscience" through concern for the moral well-being of his subjects.[20] He extended this sense of responsibility to his Indian subjects, repeatedly throughout his reign consulting ecclesiastics, requesting their aid in defining justification for the Spanish presence in America and norms for relations with the Indians. In so doing, or course, he was following correct legal procedure, as Spanish political theory and law outlined it. In brief, it appeared to the king essential to find proper precedent and authority to reconcile with the will of God Spanish expansion, royal sovereignty, and the augment of the royal fisc.

It appeared so to his counselors as well. Spanish churchmen, schooled in canon and civil law, and called upon to elaborate political theory supporting Spanish royal sovereignty in the Indies, endeavored to justify the crown's title there, to circumvent sole reliance on the papal donation, and to limit the power of private Spaniards in America—and they succeeded. The 1512 Laws of Burgos had asserted royal authority based on religious mission, and had relied only partially on the papal grant. Under Charles, convocations of theologians discussing American problems instead of seeking to minimize abuse of repartimiento-encomienda, as Ferdinand's counselors had, directly attacked the institution itself. In 1519, the year the Indies were incorporated into the crown and Cortés landed in Mexico, a junta of ecclesiastics at Barcelona declared the institution of encomienda, in that it diminished the number of tribute-paying vassals, opposed to the royal interest as well as to Indian welfare.[21] The ecclesiastics further proclaimed encomienda contrary to the intent of God, an obstacle to preaching that gospel meant to save indigenous souls. In 1520 Charles declared the Indians free royal subjects, and in 1523 a royal order to Cortés prohibited entrusting Indians to Spaniards in repartimiento or encomienda. That edict also forbade slaving, and stated that the Indians, whom God created free, must pay tribute to the crown and undergo peaceful conversion.[22] Under Charles, then, the tide turned against encomienda (although subsequently, acquiescing to Mexican conditions, the king and his Council of the Indies allowed provisional grants of Indians and some Indian slavery). Thus the court condemned as exploitative and opposed to royal interests an institution, repartimiento-encomienda, that Spaniards, including the crown, had originally justified as a means to ensure the religious instruction of Indians. This about-face represented two conclusions drawn by the king and his advisers, both important to Mexico: that the interests of Spain and of individual Spaniards in America were not necessarily identical, and that royal championing of native welfare and conversion was also a means to effective political control of Indians, of encomenderos, and of all Mexican inhabitants.

In formulating norms of government for Mexico and all Spanish America, throughout his reign Charles also sought advice from officials, clergy, and prestigious Spanish subjects in America, experimented through orders and instructions, and sent *visitadores* to investigate and mediate on behalf of the monarch. The general principles of crown policy for New Spain, then, were elaborated during its conquest. Supportive theory, specific institutions, and problems of social relations and of government were worked out by mid-century. Except for briefly toying, in the late 1520s, and perhaps again in the later 1540s, with the idea of granting encomiendas in perpetuity in order to ensure permanent Spanish settlement in Mexico, royal policy was consistent. Settlers were to have as little political authority as possible and no political power; yet to hold the land they must be permitted to retain social, and some economic, power. Indians, like Spaniards, were royal vassals. While encomienda endured, encomenderos might have provisional use of Indian tribute, with the understanding that it was by right a royal prerogative only delegated to them. Encomenderos were to pay certain tithes, ultimately derived from Indian tribute. Indian service was to be separated from tribute and discouraged. The monarch must exercise jurisdiction over all inhabitants of Mexico.

In the twin processes of justifying royal policy and protecting Indians from Spaniards in America two Dominican friars, Bartolomé de Las Casas and Francisco de Vitoria, were the formulators par excellence of theories grounded in religion and advancing royal authority and power, Indian welfare, and the value of missionary activity as opposed to that of military conquest. Las Casas as an encomendero in Cuba had witnessed Spanish ruthlessness and laid blame to settlers for the virtual extinction of the indigenous peoples of the Caribbean. He renounced his holdings, joined the Dominicans in 1524, and divided his life between Spain and America, energetically dedicating it to saving Indian bodies and souls. He made his first trip to court during the regency of Cisneros and favorably impressed and influenced the Indian policy of that sagacious man.[23] Gattinara, Charles' minister and a leading exponent of the emperor's universal Christian dominion, then became Las Casas' protector.[24] The junta of 1519 resulted from Las Casas' zeal, as did several later convocations. He became and remained influential among Charles' advisers and in formulating royal Indian policy. He lobbied and wrote tirelessly in a lifelong crusade to protect and Christianize Indians, to advance religious and crown interests, and to hem in lay Spaniards in America. The histories he wrote remain of prime importance for our knowledge of Spanish America. His influence on royal policy is incalculable. Until his death in 1566, past ninety years old, he harangued and cajoled, crisscrossing the Atlantic, experimenting with peaceful conversion in America, gathering evidence of Spanish cruelty, prevailing on Charles to draw up the New Laws of 1542—a mortal blow to encomienda—debating in 1550 in favor of Indian rights and rationality. Therefore it is worthwhile to have a brief look into his frame of mind and especially to touch upon some of his political notions important to Spanish policy.

Las Casas endorsed the royal title to America. He excoriated mistreatment of Indians as foul deeds of the conquistadors, berated inhumane officials, but placed no blame for abuse of natives on Charles V. It was his achievement to leave to posterity accounts damning Spaniards who took part in the conquest of the Indies while heaping praise on the king in whose name they conquered. Although he stated that the Spanish royal title to the Indies derived indirectly from God through the papal donation, he managed to throw the weight of the royal right to that title on the divine, rather than on the papal, bestowal of it. Thus he wrote, in his *Brevisima Relación . . .*, or *Very Brief Account of the Destruction of the Indies,* published in Spain in 1552, of "those great and vast kingdoms . . . that most vast and new world of the Indies, concealed until commended by God and his church to the kings of Castile in order to rule and to govern them, to convert and enrich them temporally and spiritually."[25]

Monarchs, said Las Casas, were ordained by God.[26] King, God, and the Indians would best be served, he insisted, if encomienda was abolished, for it was a true invention of the devil, designed to depopulate the world.[27] Encomenderos were Spanish tyrants impeding the spread of the faith. Moreover, the conquest had been unjust and now encomienda was invalidating Spain's title to the New World. The native rulers, as the true lords of the Indies, must be converted peacefully.[28] Only then would the royal title granted by the pope be in force, and "all the kings and lords [señores naturales], cities, communities, and peoples of the Indies be obliged to recognize the kings of Castile as universal and sovereign lords and emperors."

Like Cortés, Las Casas admired Indian rationality. He also approved of many aspects of Indian life and wrote of natives of the New World as superior in certain Christian virtues to those of the Old.[29] Also like Cortés, he took as point of departure essentially medieval notions concerning seignorial political association. Both men, for varying reasons, contributed to the establishing of an initial seignorial relationship between crown and Indians, one which would stabilize in a patrimonial arrangement. The conqueror, however, sought to place native chiefs under Spaniards as regional lords, whereas Las Casas believed the native rulers were themselves lords directly dependent upon the Spanish crown. In addition, while the churchman insisted Spanish control follow the cross, the conquistador found more convenience in reversing that process.

In comparison to Las Casas, Francisco de Vitoria, lecturing from his chair of theology at the University of Salamanca, in the 1530s voiced relatively secular, and more systematic, justifications for extending royal authority to America. As a student and teacher at the University of Paris, he had been exposed to the Christian humanism of the Lowlands. He had studied languages and the classics there, and admitted great admiration at that time for the work of Erasmus.[30] He also studied that scholastic masterpiece of the thirteenth century, the *Summa Theologica* of Thomas Aquinas. Back in Spain, Vitoria followed the general tendency at Salamanca and Alcalá to incorporate humanistic scholarship within a framework of scholastic theology. He helped to revitalize scholastic philosophy, and brought scholastic thought to bear on certain problems of current interest.[31] His specific contribution to Mexican history was to examine ethical questions in political relations, and particularly to lecture on the bases of the Spanish right to the Indies. By 1541 the conclusions he reached had proved him dedicated to expanding royal jurisdiction and had gained him acceptance as a trusted royal adviser. His theories relating to Spanish enterprise and subsequent history in Mexico are worth examining.

Assuming that Spain had just titles to America, Vitoria sought to find them. Unlike Las Casas, he based his supporting argument on precepts of natural law, which he understood to be the communication of the will of God, that is, of eternal law—he termed it "the will of the Legislator"— and thus an absolute good, perceived by reason. He stated that in accord with natural law, the pope was not ruler of the world.[32] Rather, public power came directly from God through natural law and was vested in the king.[33] Royal power was identical with the power of the state.[34] Many nations, in fact, could be governed by one prince who had the right to trade, to wage war if that right was interfered with, and to exact tribute from defeated opponents.[35] Following both Aquinas and earlier Spanish legal and political tenets and, like them, employing a mixture of medieval Christian, imperial Roman, and Aristotelian political theory, Vitoria subsumed but separated the temporal world from the eternal and assumed that man was by nature gregarious, living in a single human community subdivided into separate, smaller states or "perfect communities." The community or state, in fact, was natural and legal even among non-Christians. The relations among all such social and political organisms were regulated by the *jus gentium,* the law of nations or international law. Vitoria, here following Roman legal theory, found international law to be a body of general deductions derived from natural law through common agreement among communities. He also echoed Aristotle, medieval Spanish theory, and Aquinas in asserting that the goal of all communities or states was the common good and that, within them, society was a corporate body best regulated by a single head or ruler. Public power was derived from natural law and invested in states; the community in turn created the king, in the act transferring not only power but its own authority.[36]

Vitoria insisted that native American communities were sovereign entities. The Indians he argued, as had Las Casas and Cortés, were rational beings, as proved by their well-ordered communal life, and thus capable of self-government and receiving Catholicism.[37] They were not, through unbelief, barred from exercising true dominion, nor should they be despoiled of their property or lands.[38] The *requerimiento* was a farce, for "God did not deliver the Indians to the Spaniards as He did Canaan to the Jews."[39] Thus papal right to temporal donation was denied implicitly. The pope, however, might give Spaniards the exclusive right to preach and teach in the Indies in order to propagate Christianity; then a number of legal possibilities would allow the American aborigines to come under the power of Spain.[40]

His exposition on just titles to the Indies is couched as comment on Saint Matthew's "Go ye, therefore, teach all nations, baptizing them in the name of the Father, and of the Son, and of the Holy Spirit." Vitoria was certain that individual Spaniards had no señorío in America, and that the royal right to dominion there rested not on the work of conquistadors, except as "ambassadors," but on that of the clergy. Like Las Casas he believed that after receiving Christianity voluntarily, Indian "nations" would recognize the kings of Castile as overlords and emperors. In short, he saw Spanish-Indian relations as arrangements between nation-states, within an imperial, seignorial framework allowing ascending levels of political control and also bringing Indian nations directly under the authority of Spain's monarch.

His contribution to Spanish title, and incidentally to international law, was in using as justification for the initial Spanish presence in America the principle of the right to trade, in accord with the law of nations as set down in Justinian's *Institutes,* the imperial Roman legal compilation.

Moreover, the Spanish *entrada* into New Spain, he specified, might be justified as supporting the cause of allies and friends in Cortés' response to the Tlaxcalan request for aid in defensive war against the Aztecs.[41] The conquistadors, however, were not entitled to exercise lordship. Vitoria's loyalties can be adduced from his strong arguments supporting monarchy and his statements that according to natural law the love of country "is right of itself," and that, of course, international trade must not be hindered because "grave hurt to the royal treasury would be intolerable."[42]

In the 1530s and 1540s, abetted by such opinions, Charles V and his officials pursued a three-pronged policy. They strove to curtail the political prerogatives of Spanish settlers in Mexico and attempted to regulate in some detail their daily lives. They worked to control Indian labor and tribute, perceiving that in doing so lay the key to effective control of both Europeans and Americans. And they attempted to protect "Indian subjects" from Spanish abuse, although less from that of local officials than from private Spaniards.

Charles initially had forbidden all unlicensed Indian slavery and, by 1530, grants of encomienda were to be made by royal officials for a limited period only. Then, in 1542, he issued the New Laws, declaring encomienda, Indian slavery, and personal service abolished.[43] And at the specific request of Las Casas, the following year the *requerimiento* was replaced by a letter, to be delivered by missionaries to native chiefs, reflecting the thought of Vitoria in respectfully requesting agreements to trade, and in stating that Spain was certain they would prove mutually advantageous.[44] Subsequent pronouncements under Charles and Philip II repeated the principle that the Spanish right to America was the royal one.

When the New Laws caused unrest in Mexico and civil war in Peru, the crown reopened discussion on extending encomienda. A subsequent convocation at mid-century, and the royal decision against general and perpetual encomienda, attest to the consistency of the official viewpoint and to the ongoing importance to it of political theory and of that theory's clerical proponents. It is hardly surprising that royal counselors, among them Melchor Cano—who succeeded Vitoria in the first chair of theology at Salamanca and had his predecessor's lectures published—in 1548 opposed publication of the tract *Democrates Alter,* by the humanist scholar Juan Ginés de Sepúlveda.

Sepúlveda, who stated he had been influenced in his opinions by conversations with Cortés, wrote it specifically to support the conquistadors and the validity of the military conquest. He declared the Spanish conquest a just war, for "the Spanish nation" was naturally superior to the Indians, and he justified ongoing war and Spanish dominion as a civilizing mission to barbarians. He cited Aristotle, writing that "It is licit and just that the best and those who excel by nature, customs, and laws rule over their inferiors."[45] Employing these cultural criteria, he concluded that "with perfect right the Spaniards exercise dominion over those barbarians of the New World ... who in prudence, intelligence, and all manner of virtues and human sentiments are as inferior to the Spanish as are children to adults, women to men." The Indians he adjudged to be "slaves by nature."[46]

Sepúlveda's argument was not original. He restated opinions expressed by earlier Spanish theorists who had assumed the superiority of Spanish culture and had asserted that the Indians were by nature inferior.[47] He and the others can also be viewed, in this sense, as forerunners of the sort of thought which supported notions of the white man's burden and social Darwinism in the nineteenth century. Vitoria had thought Indians rational, but less so than Spaniards, and was unsure whether it was due to their lack of wits or to "a bad and barbarous upbringing," thus modifying the doctrine of natural servitude by raising the possibility of behavior caused not by genetic heritage but by environment.[48] The later official displeasure Sepúlveda incurred was undoubtedly due to his two principal discretionary errors, however, rather than simply to his disdainful attitude toward the Indians. These were that he had the bad sense to undercut the prevailing theory of religious mission by emphasizing only the Spanish civilizing one, and that he wrote of New World dominion by the Spanish nation when more prudent men referred to that of the monarch. In effect, he argued from a principle of political justification, anathema to theologians, that of reason of state. His outlook was essentially secular, substituting patriotism for religion rather than, as was more customary, and politic, reconciling the two. His thought ran counter to the Catholic Reformation mentality and to the established Spanish justifications for royal authority.

Sepúlveda came off badly. Cano—who is said to have declared elsewhere, "To the Pope, first tie his hands, then kiss his feet"—had taken issue with Sepúlveda's defense of Spanish domination based on military conquest, since it ran counter to Vitoria's opinion. In 1550 Cano and thirteen other savants—theologians and royal council members—met at Valladolid on crown business. As one of them, Domingo de Soto, explained, they were to ponder how best to govern and legislate in order to preach the faith in the New World, and how best to keep "those peoples subject to the majesty of the Emperor, our lord, without lesion of his royal conscience and conforming to the bull of Alexander VI [granting the Indies to Spain]."[49] Las Casas had also contested Sepúlveda's theories and both men appeared before this not impartial junta. Sepúlveda spoke for three hours, Las Casas for five days.

This rather prolix exchange, in which Sepúlveda insisted conquest through war was licit and in Spanish tradition and Las Casas, unconcerned with the history of the *reconquista,* swore it was not, has been described as a highlight of "the Spanish struggle for justice in the conquest of America."[50] However that may be, it must be remembered that justice was the supreme theoretical and practical political instrument of the Spanish monarchy. Indeed, the great medieval principle of justice was often claimed as the royal *raison d'être,* so that when Charles came to the throne one of the major general beliefs supporting royal power and authority was that monarchy had been established by God for the purpose of doing justice. Moreover, in imposing royal authority upon New Spain and justifying that process, all participants invoked the twin basic, and now traditional, principles supporting royal government: that the monarch's authority came from God and that the king must rule justly.[51] Thus it was encumbent upon the king to seek justice in all matters, and thus the perceived royal need to justify American dominion. Again, since royal authority not only rested on the principle of justice but was expanded and maintained through its use, purveyors of royal justice, magistrates (*oideres*), were the first officials, after the treasurers, assigned to New Spain. And there the crown employed law, the operative aspect of justice, and particularly made use of decrees (*cédulas*), law originating as royal will and which became, as in Spain, a favorite royal instrument. Sent to royal officials, such edicts contained arbitrary legislation composed of statements of principle, findings of right, and ethical injunctions. Most often, they contained findings relating to specific data based on Christian moral principles. As in the Spanish entry into America in general, in laws made by the crown specific decisions were usually explained and justified by Christian purpose.[52] In sum, the notion of the Spanish monarch as the source of justice and ultimate mediating agent in society explains the Spanish emphasis on, and struggle for, justice in relation to American dominion. Moreover, the king as temporal embodiment of the principle of justice was a concept introduced in Mexico by the conquistadors. Reinforced by government and clergy, it would become a prime ideological component tying Mexico to Spain.

In 1550, it should be added, no verdict in favor of either Sepúlveda or Las Casas was handed down, nor was an explicit decision necessary. Sepúlveda's argument advancing reason of state divorced from religious sanction was of no use (*ius?*) to the crown.[53] Cano, who perceived the real issue and supported strong monarchy, opposed Sepúlveda's secularity but also disapproved of Las Casas' recognizing papal authority in temporal matters. One indication of royal preference was the fact that the treatises of Las Casas appeared in print shortly thereafter, while Sepúlveda's manuscript did not.

Habsburg rulers, after 1550, endorsed the theory that Spain must occupy the Indies to instruct the natives in the faith and the way of life consonant with it, until the Indians reached full cultural maturity, as measured by Spanish norms. The crown thus claimed direction of both Christianizing and civilizing efforts, sidestepping papal authority and minimizing conquistadors' rights through conquest and ongoing control. To this extent royal policy was in accord with principles stated by Las Casas. Yet its focus fell somewhere between the positions of Sepúlveda and Las Casas. Rather, the official attitude toward Indians and, by extension, lordship in America continued to conform most closely to the theory of Francisco de Vitoria. For Indians were considered royal vassals, owing tribute to the crown, and—a possibility mentioned by Vitoria— wards similar to minors. His opinion was now the official one: ". . . they need to be ruled or governed by others as sons to parents until of age."[54] The sincere, and extremely expedient, royal policy of Christianizing and civilizing the Indians was not only cited in official documents to justify the Spanish presence in America, but also helped to maintain that presence in further justifying the imposition upon, and domination of Spanish government, faith, and culture over, native societies.

The concept that the natives were free subjects in a state of tutelage carried as a concomitant certain other notions justifying Spanish dominion and use of Indian labor. The same body of theory yielded to royal government, which had also to maintain Spanish presence and prosperity in America, concepts useful to support Spanish settlement and, at the same time, to appear to protect the Indians. For example, it was early stated in the Laws of Burgos that since the Indians' idleness constituted an injury to them, the king out of kindness must relieve them of its burden.[55] Royal instructions to Mexico's first viceroy, Antonio de Mendoza, in 1535, and a letter to the audiencia of Mexico in 1548, expounded this moral principle in support of forced labor, stating that Indians were naturally lazy, that idleness was a sin, and that the natives were not to be abused but that they must be made to work.[56] Unemployment was thereby held to be synonymous with delinquency. This official characterization of Indians as lazy by nature and of work as a virtue served as justification first for encomienda, in 1512, and then for its officially designated successor institution in Mexico, the *cuatequil,* the forced labor draft, authorized in 1549. It also permitted, as suggested by Mendoza, forced labor by "lazy Indians" on royal *estancias,* or farms.[57]

Although Indians were to work for Spaniards, the crown decreed that they must live separated from them. Natives were to remain in their own communities, often termed by the Spanish government *repúblicas,* and so apart from the undesirable influence of Spanish immigrants and in a condition most amenable to official control. Royal orders to this effect in 1523 inaugurated in New Spain a rudimentary apartheid policy.[58] Mexico was to remain two repúblicas, one Spanish, the other Indian—but events dictated otherwise.

In accord with theories advanced by Las Casas and Vitoria, the crown recognized native sovereignty to the extent that royal policy sought to retain Indian aristocrats in limited authority and power, and also—as was implicit in both expositions—to hispanize them to a malleable point. Thus, a cédula of 1526 directed that two noble Indians, despoiled of their lands, be given two villages each.[59] An advisory junta in 1529 suggested that natives be instructed in the faith and adopt Spanish customs, to some extent after the fact. Royal instructions to the audiencia of Mexico in 1530 stated, "it is necessary for Indians to begin to understand our manner of living and government."[60] Acculturation was the goal, but not complete hispanization, for the Indian governors and justices were instructed to guard the traditional social order and good customs of their people, if they were not contrary to Christianity.

Earlier, religious indoctrination, primarily of *tlatoanis,* chieftains, and especially of their sons and those of other prestigious natives, the *principales,* began under royal order. The king sponsored schools for young Indians and mestizos, and also favored missionaries' learning native languages. All education in Mexico was basically religious. Decrees urged Mendoza in 1536 and the Augustinians in 1550 to have Indians learn Castilian, and, in the cédula establishing the University of Mexico, in 1551 expected that natives, too, would there be instructed "in things of the faith and other faculties."[61] Indians were to be made aware of royal concern for their welfare, as the New Laws, for example, so explicitly stated.[62]

It was deemed important to royal control that not only Indians but all sectors of Mexican society were to be kept ideologically bound to Spanish norms and values. When a second generation of Spaniards appeared in New Spain, the king sponsored the establishment of formal institutions for them, such as societies tend to employ to reinforce cultural adhesion, including schools and a printing press. This first generation of Spanish Americans, like other peoples in Mexico, were soon thought by Charles and his counselors to exhibit a goodly share of human weakness. The crown sent out innumerable decrees prodding them to live in a reasonable state of morality and civilization, and in peace—by which was meant, in the traditional Christian, Augustinian sense, a condition of order or equilibrium within an unchanging society. Although Charles allowed subjects from his non-Spanish domains to go to America in the 1520s, in the late 1530s the Indies were officially closed to all foreigners from abroad. As we shall see, the government had a less clear-cut policy, and Spanish theory provided few guides, concerning the problem of assimilating free blacks and people of mixed parentage already present in Mexican society.

The king continued to legislate to ensure royal income, as then understood, in what are now called bullionist terms, imposing on Mexico an economy geared to the requirements of the crown. To this end, Charles sought both to regulate economic relations between Spaniards and Indians and to fit Mexico as an economic component into the larger informal, but de facto, empire. Royal economic policy was not systematically formulated nor divorced from social theory or concern with the royal fisc. It was based not on peninsular needs but on exigencies affecting the royal treasury. Charles needed gold and silver to finance the expenses of farflung empire and all economic interests primarily derived from that simple principle. Thus on 9 December 1526 it was decreed that the crown possessed full rights to the soil and subsoil in the Indies and could give individuals usufruct in order to increase the economic activity of Spaniards, especially the discovery and working of mines.[63] The crown, as was customary, was to receive a share of all metals mined. True wealth was thought to be only precious metals, gold and silver; however, other activities assessed as taxable and translatable, directly or indirectly, into revenue were also encouraged, thus one reason for royal orders to raise sugar and cattle and, ultimately, one explanation for royal interest in abetting Spanish settlement in America. Throughout this period, all duties and taxes, a share of New World booty, the granting of monopolies, and licensing the trade in African slaves increasingly swelled royal revenues.[64] In practice, it should be noted, leading members of the ruling coterie, preeminent among them the royal secretary, Francisco de los Cobos, amassed a great amount of wealth, some of it at the expense of the treasury, from their close connections with Mexican trade and finance.[65] In Indian policy, too, financial considerations often overrode humanitarian ones. At mid-century the crown allowed moderation of Indian tribute rates. But when royal revenue dropped as a consequence, a cédula of 1556 ordered moderations rectified since they adversely affected the royal patrimony.

Over the years, crown policy, influenced by financial straits, religious schism, and Charles' hardening attitude against religious deviation, became less flexible and, by mid-century, was set for Mexico in a mold largely unbroken until the latter part of the eighteenth century. Thus, by the 1550s, numerous books and activities associated with the earlier, more ecumenical proponents of Christian humanistic notions were prohibited.[66] Advocates of ideas earlier associated with religious reform and Christian humanism but now suspect as heterodox were, with luck, only in political and academic limbo. The Inquisition and anti-converso statutes were broadening in scope and effectiveness. The crown's continuing insistence on royal protection of Indians and its patronage of learning had little to do with liberalism. These activities could in fact be viewed as neo-conservative, in much the same spirit as Vitoria, who, early inclined toward Erasmus, showed himself to be a neo-scholastic and adept at incorporating new currents of thought bolstering old usages. When Charles resigned his throne to his son Philip in 1556, he gave over an absolute royal authority—if with effective limitations at work curbing absolute power—to govern the Spanish empire.

As Spain had expanded from a frequently contentious group of kingdoms into the center of a dynastic empire, it missed development, more pronounced in France and most of all in England, into an integrated nation-state. A full sense of national community did not develop, and broadly national governing institutions were not imposed, throughout the country. Instead, among Spaniards a sense of regionalism and of local customs and rights, a shared faith, the mystique of a semisacred monarch, and expansion overseas supported and fed a unity essentially symbolic, ideological, and imperial. Within this context, the Kingdom of New Spain was linked to the metropolis in conformity with the prevailing mode of political adhesion—that is, through the monarch—and in accord with royal principles.

Isabella and Ferdinand through proclivity and policy had kept Spain bound to all Europe culturally, economically, and through Christian ideal and Habsburg alliance. And internally, the same universal Christian principles they invoked to strengthen the monarchy and abet national unity later made Charles' broader European activities appear a traditional Spanish duty, associating with the raison d'être of Spain the destiny of all Christendom. Indeed, Habsburg hegemony over Christendom seemed possible to the court and Spanish supporters in the first decade of Charles' reign, which was also that of the discovery and conquest of Mexico.

Charles' broader European concerns strongly influenced Mexican policy and its administration in Spain. Before religious schism, his imperial title and tremendous domain made eminently suitable ecumenical political theory, supporting his far-flung *imperium* and *dominium,* derived from Spanish medieval thought and Roman law, and grounded in a universal Christian purview. His counselors specifically tailored imperial concepts based upon Christian universalism to extend and maintain royal authority and power over all the inhabitants of Spanish America, and particularly of Mexico.

It has been said that three elements at least are crucial to political theories: a set of assumptions regarding the nature of man, a discussion of the nature and location of sovereignty, and, consistent with these two, a set of practical principles of governing. The king and his advisers had definite ideas about the nature of man in America and specific, although unsystematized, and essentially imperial concepts of sovereignty, and they evolved policy consonant with these beliefs. The crown sent administrators to New Spain to introduce institutions and measures putting principles into practice. Charles did not, however, insist on rigid adherence by

Mexican officials to royal measures. His instructions were often couched as suggestions, encouraging experiment in means to reach desired royal goals in organizing the new society. That is, in Mexico by 1530 royal purpose was clearly understood by officials sent from Spain, as was the fact that decisions on ways and means to implement it were only expected to conform to royal policy and to broad norms of government as practiced in Spain, but in the Spain of Charles and not that of Ferdinand.

A number of circumstances allowed Mexican policy and institutions introduced under Charles' aegis a more humane and socially integrative basis than was the case earlier, or would be later, either in Mexican government or in that established in South America. The nature of Christian universal principles appealed to and employed as justifications in making decisions both in Spain and Mexico regulating the lives of Mexican residents and their relations to one another had allowed the incorporation of numerous societies under the monarch. By the end of Charles' reign, however, a certain rigidity in attitudes and institutions and in political and social organization, and a narrower royal dominance were observable.

Charles, then, had relied on ecclesiastical jurists to elaborate political theory supporting expansion and dominion in Mexico within a broadened, and now imperial, Spanish context. Compounded of traditional elements, this theory allowed Spanish patriotic attachment to the monarchy, the faith, and Spanish civilization to be transplanted into Mexico, as it had been earlier in the Caribbean. Yet as we shall see, and as we have had some indication in the attitudes of the conquistadors, resident Spaniards and the crown and clergy held divergent opinions on the nature of American man, of sovereignty, and of government. Nevertheless, a shared Spanish world view enabled the crown to implement principles of royal policy among men at least paying lip service to royal authority, and to do so through dispatching to Mexico Spaniards experienced in government and imbued with the Christian principles supporting it. There such deputies were to, and would, introduce and maintain imperial authority and disseminate a mentality supporting it, in accord with royal notions.

4

New Spain: The Imposition of Royal Authority

During the reign of Charles V, Mexico came under Spanish domination and Spaniards instituted formal and informal mechanisms to control and regulate society. As we have seen, the king and his advisers elaborated general governing principles for New Spain. We shall also see that Spanish government was introduced there, and practiced by royal administrators in Mexico, in continuing interaction both with royal policy and with society—that is, that specific aspects of royal policy were worked out, and at times modified, in Mexico itself, that Spaniards there carefully tailored royal administration, in order to fit policy to ways they wanted to direct economic and social conditions, and that as Spanish government evolved in New Spain it contributed to implanting and maintaining a supportive official ideology. In order to understand this process we must assess the men who were responsible for consolidating Spanish control, and also evaluate the Mexican impress upon the Spanish system and upon Spanish institutions and ideology as they took root in New Spain. Here, then, we shall look into the role of royal government in Mexico as it was and as it was perceived by both the governors and the governed, in theory and in practice.

Cortés, as the first European governor introduced Spanish rule as a seignorial regime within an informal imperial system. In the name of the monarch he imposed his own jurisdiction. He appointed lieutenants to head the cabildos of the city of Mexico and of the handful of new, Spanish towns, strategically located in recently conquered populous areas. The members of these town councils, the encomenderos who were also propertied *vecinos,* townsmen, in turn controlled much of the settled Indian population through its chieftains.

The principles Cortés stated in his letters and ordinances were for the most part in accord with royal goals and remained general objectives of Spanish government in Mexico.[1] He argued that Spanish permanence there depended on holding the land through domiciled Spaniards and on sufficient Indians to work it. Indian labor must support the Spanish presence. He was certain that Spanish well-being, the preservation of the Indians, and the ensuring of royal rents were interdependent. As first governor he set precedent for many Mexican institutions and attitudes seemingly in conformity with royal purposes. At the same time, however, he employed approved institutions and an important unapproved one, encomienda, to begin to establish seignorial enclaves under Spaniards dependent upon his own de facto lordship while he acknowledged the Spanish monarch as señor universal.

During the conquest Cortés, in His Majesty's name, had Motecuhzoma order all Indians to pay tribute and had it collected as an extraordinary but precedent-setting measure, and without royal fiat. He then distributed the proceeds, mostly gold and jewels, to the conquerors.[2] Equating Spanish power and prosperity with control of Indian communities rather than of land per se, after the fall of Tenochtitlán he ordered a convocation in Coyoacán of all chiefs and principales of the central Mexican area and there explained to them: "Know that now you do not have to render tribute to Motecuhzoma . . . you have only to serve the emperor." He went on: ". . . and in his name these Spaniards."[3] Afterwards, he distributed the native señores and their followers in repartimiento-encomienda, having encomenderos contract with communal leaders for Indian goods and services. He also, as we noted, reserved for himself in encomienda a goodly portion of the Mexican labor force.

Cortés, then, cited the royal right in both Spanish and indigenous political tradition to tribute and service in order to justify real control of Indians by individual Spaniards through encomienda. And while paying lip service to the notion that all residents of Mexico were now vassals and subjects of the crown, he nonetheless fell back to the older Spanish seignorial system wherein communities were ruled by regional lords—in Mexico, conquistadors—who wielded effective local power. It was the sort of political system Isabella had found in force on ascending the Castilian throne and against which she and Ferdinand had fought. Its resurgence was also an element in the comunero uprising the crown now faced in Spain.

To the king he explained that he had virtually been forced to grant encomiendas by the need to induce Spaniards to remain in Mexico, in order to repay them for services rendered and debts contracted during conquest, and by officials demanding funds for the royal treasury.[4] He endorsed encomienda as a better alternative to unrestricted slavery and depopulation such as he had witnessed in the Caribbean islands. It was the best means, he was certain, to preserve both Indian lives and Spanish prosperity, and thus also the best insurance that Spaniards would pay royal taxes.[5] The Indians of New Spain, he added, while much more rational than those of the Caribbean, were not *that* rational; they needed to be overseen by individual Spaniards. Accordingly, he established the conquerors as a military aristocracy, ordering in 1524 that they must settle in the land and maintain arms for its defense.[6] By decree and example he encouraged them to engage in mining, agriculture, and stock-raising. Spanish society as he knew it should be reproduced in Mexico. He limited Indian slavery, but it should be kept in mind that unregulated slavery could undercut the power of patronage, and of income from licensing the business of slaving.[7]

Thus, while Cortés enunciated traditional Spanish political theory, as did the crown, in his case it was to support an older Spanish system of dominance modified by Spanish experience in the Caribbean under Ferdinand. In Spain tribute was usually in agricultural goods or money. Service meant labor in fields or construction. Cortés' extraordinary collection of tribute and its distribution to Spaniards was hardly what Charles had in mind. And while, in making encomienda the pivotal institution of Spanish control, his grants were provisional and did not mention tribute or jurisdiction, they did stipulate that Indians must serve—that is, work for—individual Spaniards. Moreover, although he earlier distinguished between royal tribute and personal service to en-comenderos, at first the two exactions were meshed by encomenderos' simply extorting as much as possible in goods and services from their charges.

Royal theory was in many ways similar to his, but royal priorities differed markedly. Of prime concern to the crown were its own revenues, thought of in terms of precious metals. Indians were to ensure Spanish settlement, and thus royal income, by their labor, but to be thought of as direct royal vassals and subjects, and to be preserved in body and soul. In the royal view in this period, the Christianizing process, not private military conquest, justified Spanish dominion, abetted conquest, and reinforced royal control. Officials, not encomenderos, must administer for the crown in New Spain. With the appearance of treasury officers sent from Spain began the royal program to find means to maximize crown revenues, limit Cortés' power, and establish effective and direct royal authority over Spaniards and Indians. It is not surprising that at least three of them, Alonso de Estrada, Rodrigo de Albornoz, and Gonzalo de Salazar, had fought against the comuneros. There followed a steady erosion by juridical and administrative action of the freedom of Spaniards to compel Indian labor. For from the outset, as the letters of the first royal tax collectors reveal, officials in New Spain saw that the ability to regulate native slavery, tribute, service, and encomienda would guarantee control of both Indians and Spaniards. Thus the royal *contador* (accountant), Albornoz, insisted that of most benefit was the Indian tribute paid directly to the treasury.[8] Cortés, Albornoz complained, had hampered tribute negotiations with caciques of major towns; Albornoz requested that a governor and a prudent audiencia "without greed" be sent to New Spain. He also suggested encomienda be retained but restricted. His opinion corresponded with the thinking at court. From there he received advice to investigate further and to go slowly.

There ensued a power struggle in Mexico between royal officials and Cortés. The first treasury officials became embroiled in factional struggles among the conquistadors, dating from the Cortés-Velásquez dispute and complicated by subsequent alignments resulting from private interest. Squabbling among the four treasury officials over who was to govern, during Cortés' absence on expedition to Hibueras-Honduras from 1524 to 1526, brought Mexico to the verge of anarchy. As Cortés caustically remarked on his return, "the country is somewhat fatigued by recent disturbances."[9] By 1527 the crown had begun subdividing New Spain into provinces under independent governors, but two royal visitadores charged with investigating Cortés' conduct, replacing him as governor if necessary, and looking into the possibility of levying direct royal tribute in Mexico, had failed.[10] The interim governor, Marcos de Aguilar, and Franciscans in Mexico then suggested that the crown allow perpetual encomienda and assign and regulate tribute payment to Spaniards, but retain jurisdiction —that alienating jurisdiction was the real harm.[11] In 1528 Mexican government was placed under an audiencia, a council of magistrates who were to impose the king's justice and authority. Its president was Nuño de Guzmán, recently come to New Spain from court and governor of the newly created province of Pánuco. Four lawyers were appointed as oidores; two died soon after reaching Mexico. The survivors, Diego Delgadillo and Juan Ortíz de Matienzo, with Guzmán composed the audiencia.[12]

Published royal instructions, designed to quiet Spanish factionalism and ensure settlement, appeared to acquiesce to some of the wishes of Spaniards in Mexico. This first audiencia was publicly charged with promoting stability by arranging the granting of encomiendas in perpetuity. Reserved to the crown, however, were the Indians in many of the more important towns, cities, and ports, and in them the justices were to ascertain what the natives should give the king in "gold and other things."[13] Clearly the opinion proffered by Aguilar and the Franciscans accorded with royal sentiments; justice was to be the primary instrument of royal control in Mexico. In return for their services and to sustain them, Spaniards might hold Indians in encomienda, but their relations with those Indians were to be regulated through law by the crown. In an order of 4 December 1528, the crown explicitly allowed encomenderos tribute or service, but with restrictions explained as being in the interests of the Indians.[14] The relatively experimental and tentative nature of this first audiencia was not made public, but was indicated by a secret order from the crown to do nothing before advising it.

Guzmán and his two colleagues bungled their opportunity to institute a permanent encomienda system. They largely ignored their instructions and, though forbidden to hold Indians, used their official positions as opportunity to appropriate to themselves and to their retainers, friends, and relatives innumerable pueblos in encomienda. They also made other grants and revoked them at will, forced Indians to labor in mines and on private projects, and enslaved large numbers of them.[15] Undoubtedly established to counter the power of Cortés, the initial audiencia instead of assuming a mediating posture above local interest, thus reflecting the royal position, pursued self-interest directly among the Spanish factions in Mexico. And while it joined the contest for spoils of conquest, Cortés became Margués del Valle de Oaxaca, thereby, while his possession of a large share of the spoils was confirmed, he was also pensioned off, if on grand scale, with limited authority and a title held by largess of the crown. The royal gesture can be construed, as it was undoubtedly meant to be, as both great honor and effective restriction.

The crown also decided to appoint a viceroy and to send, as an interim governing body, a second audiencia, made up of four jurists of high integrity, experienced in royal service, and presided over by Sebastian Ramírez de Fuenleal, then bishop of Santo Domingo, an appointment he held from Cisneros.[16] It should be noted that not only was a churchman placed in charge of this body, but that in the troubled twenties clergy in Mexico had been relied on to advise the court and further its interests, that the first audiencia was ordered to consult important churchmen, and that no clear line existed between the religious and the civil (all to be discussed more fully in the next chapter).

Between 1530 and 1550 this second audiencia and Antonio de Mendoza, the first viceroy, successfully adapted Charles' priorities to the Mexican situation. Many of the institutions they introduced endured until the last third of the eighteenth century. These appointments and royal instructions to the second audiencia reflected a now-hardened resolution to curb all encomenderos, to assert governmental jurisdiction over all residents of New Spain, to establish Indians as free royal subjects, and, in practice, to vie actively with resident Spaniards for direct and effective authority over all natives, whether under the crown or in privately held towns. The oidores were to rescind grants made by the first audiencia to relatives and retainers and "all who should not have them."[17] They were to entrust no more encomiendas to individuals, to put those reclaimed directly under the crown, to appoint royal overseers to adjudicate and collect tribute in Indian towns not privately held. These officials were to be called corregidores "so that even by their name Indians would know they were not señores." The oidores were also to regulate, and to secure for the crown, a share of whatever Indians gave encomenderos. Within private encomiendas, Indians—it was again ordered—were not to be enslaved, forced to work in mines, lent, or hired out. Slaving was prohibited, and slaves held were to be reported—although a cédula of 1534 superseded this order, allowing enslavement of rebelling Indians or those taken in war.[18]

Indians, the royal orders stipulated, "must begin to understand our manner of living and government." Their political arrangements must approximate those of other royal subjects. But their worthwhile customs were to be taken into account in the process of introducing Spanish government and way of life. Specifically, the oidor Vasco de Quiroga was to examine preconquest practices of slaveholding and to respect indigenous tradition in settling conflicting claims to headship and lands, and lawsuits in general.

Royal orders to bridle Cortés further were indicative of a broader policy aimed at subordinating all Spaniards to the crown's authority. Several instructions were designed not only to restrict Cortés but to do so publicly. Although he was still, as captain-general, the ranking military officer, civil authority was to be displayed as superior. The audiencia was to take a census of Indians he held as Marqués, and to make certain he controlled no ports or *cabeceras* (leading towns). Moreover, they were to commandeer, by purchase, for their own official use his palace in the capital. Again, the crown forbade its officials to hold encomiendas. Latitude in implementing these royal instructions was intended and explicitly stated: "What now must be done is to try out and experiment for the future. Provide and decree as best you can.... When someone complains about tribute, do what is most suitable to the service of the king and always look to the welfare and pacification of the land."[19]

Members of the second audiencia functioned as dedicated royal administrators and expressed opinions echoing royal principles and approved theory. For example its president, Bishop Ramírez de Fuenleal, argued concomitantly with Vitoria that royal authority over the Indians was based only in part on papal concession. But this administrator's primary interest lay not in justifying royal dominion theoretically but in converting theory into practice by establishing in Mexico the monarch's central role in conquest and its consolidation. In a written opinion his ideas on Spanish government strongly reflected court views. The Spanish king, he explained, was to the Indians their "señor universal, who through great expense and loss of subjects has pacified and led them to Catholic union, has had them taught religion and good customs, and has defended and maintained them in justice."[20] Now, however, "the interests and rents of this land require populating it with Spaniards who will discover mines, raise cattle, and plant, and to do all this the natives must be employed as tools." Spaniards must be assured enough to eat; "Indians must know that they are royal vassals and that Spaniards are entitled only to what the crown orders they be given." Indian chiefs were to receive their customary tribute. That owed to the government, and previously received by Motecuhzoma, should go to encomenderos, but the audiencia should regulate amounts and the crown retain tributes in its own towns. Fuenleal's was, in fact, a classic statement of then current royal purposes and policy in regard to Mexico. Henceforth, Spaniards who held encomiendas were to receive tribute, but they and their Indians were to acknowledge royal jurisdiction, and the institution of encomienda was to be discouraged juridically.

These oidores, as instructed, called consultative juntas of dignitaries—including Cortés and other prestigious settlers, the bishop of Mexico, and representatives of the Franciscan and Dominican orders.[21] They also immediately reviewed their predecessors' conduct in office—that is, took their *residencia*—and sought to circumscribe the authority of Cortés. They attempted to count his Indians, known to number far more than the 23,000 allotted him, even if interpreted as 23,000 heads of families, removed towns from his jurisdiction, and encouraged settlement of the Spanish town of Antequera de Oaxaca as a royal enclave in the core of his marquisate.[22] They also sought an alternative to encomienda in sponsoring the founding of Puebla, hoping to attract Spaniards who had no Indians by offers of good land and the lure of the large, free labor force in nearby Tlaxcala. They ordered—as Cortés had earlier—encomenderos to bring over their wives and to reside in New Spain. They inspected the land, revoked the holdings of more than a hundred encomenderos, and put their Indians under the crown. They appointed corregidores, drew up lists stipulating tribute (*tasaciones*) to be assessed in both private and royal encomiendas, and began to introduce Spanish governmental organization into Indian towns.[23] They began to implement the royal policy of allowing encomenderos to collect tribute but regulating that right, thus also making jurisdiction rather than direct taxation the measure of royal authority. Goods and services, when assessed by royal officials and not requisitioned without royal license, would lose much of the appearance of seignorial dues. This regulatory principle, coupled with guaranteeing Indians due process and royal justice, served as the wedge whereby royal government legally split Mexico into two sectors, Spanish and Indian, then occupied the breach betwen them so that both recognized negotiation with the other was dependent theoretically on royal fiat.

These oidores outdid the court in attempting to protect Indian subjects in the early 1530s. Although in 1531 the opening of the first silver mines, coinciding with a smallpox epidemic, put a premium on Indian labor, the audiencia continued to oppose the extension of native slavery. In 1534 when the crown conceded that Spaniards might enslave Indians, the oidores refused to publish that concession, one of them, Vasco de Quiroga, insisting Indian slavery benefited miners, settlers, and Indian leaders at the expense of *maceguales,* commoners. Yet the oidores did not work rigorously to abolish either slavery, personal service, or forced labor in general, one of them remarking they could not, "for it [Indian labor] was the nerve sustaining the land,"[24] and it is known that Quiroga, for example, held slaves, ultimately freeing them in his will. Instead, the audiencia worked to restrict the more flagrant abuse by Spaniards of Indian servitude and to safeguard and strengthen royal authority over Indians not held by individual Spaniards. Their predecessors had become a Spanish faction. These magistrates remained more aloof from involvement in resident Spanish society (with the exception of Alonso Maldonado, who married the daughter of Francisco de Montejo, *adelantado* [military governor] in Yucatán).[25]

All the oidores were churchmen or jurists or both. They were professional administrators, imbued with an elevated sense of duty and in general conversant with the Christian humanism introduced into Spanish schools during the reign of Isabella and Ferdinand. They expressed familiarity with the humanistic revival of interest in the classic ideals of Western culture and sought to apply some of them in Mexico in behalf of the king's Indian subjects; the Spaniards there, they felt, were beyond reforming. The president-bishop wrote of Spanish corregidores and *alguaciles,* bailiffs, who only worked to rob Indians and enrich themselves.[26] The oidor Juan de Salmerón expressed distaste for the purely material inclinations of all Spanish colonists, terming them ambitious, grasping, and mean-minded.[27] He thereby, in viewing them as living corrupt and immoral lives, incidentally also provided a very early example of a peninsular Spanish feeling of superiority to Spaniards earlier domiciled in Mexico.

Most renowned for being influenced by humanistic ideals associated with European renaissance was Vasco de Quiroga, who found in a recent book, Thomas More's *Utopia,* a model of communal organization for Indians cut loose from their old societies. Quiroga organized at least two hospital-villages for Indians on classical utopian principles of simple living, hard work, and education in farming and crafts.[28] His stated object was to lessen human misery, and he went about it in accord with advanced European notions of his day. Thus, although these villages sheltered hundreds of natives and protected them from less principled Spaniards, he had them built by forced draft of native labor.

Throughout their careers Quiroga and his fellows judiciously tempered humanistic idealism where it did not conform to the interests of royal government. Often, however, it did. For example, although supporting church efforts to impose upon Indians the Spanish religion and related social customs, such as monogamous marriage and clad bodies, in many instances these officials and the clergy viewed Indian usages as compatible to classic universal ideals, and to natural law, as well as to Christian morality and strove to preserve them. Quiroga in investigating Indian customs and in hearing Indian cases chose to consult natives learned in preconquest law and lore. And in seeking precedent for setting tribute rates and in gathering information requested by the crown on the history and state of the land, the audiencia sponsored the first of a number of Spanish accounts that would later be cited as a basis for a new distinctly Mexican, Spanish-Indian cultural synthesis.[29] The oidores knew they could facilitate control of the natives by preserving and using indigenous traditions, that indigenous adherence to Spanish rule could be strengthened by urging upon Indians Spanish ways as an overlay upon their own morally consonant customs, or as an addition to them.[30] The audiencia thereby demonstrated interaction between Spanish imperial government and a broad sense of universal morality predicated on classical European ideals. Its members also revealed some insight into the advantages of acculturation to political control. In short, the second audiencia introduced principles of royal government in accord with crown policy, modified by conditions in New Spain, and within an ideological context of a broader Western Christian idealism adapted to official Spanish needs and goals.

The first viceroy, Antonio de Mendoza (1535–50), built on their foundations, but whereas the oidores appeared proficient and proper royal magistrates, Mendoza in his person and as the monarch's surrogate, presented a far more resplendent and impressive symbol of royal, indeed imperial, authority. He belonged to one of the five or six most powerful and prestigious families of Castile.[31] He came of a functioning aristocracy, active in military leadership, civil administration, and the church hierarchy, wealthy in lands and livestock, and responsible in royal service. He was a younger son of Don Iñigo López de Mendoza, Count of Tendilla and Marquis of Mondéjar, the first Christian governor of Granada. In the years of Ferdinand's regency in Castile, when nobles and towns once again tended to autonomy, Tendilla had remained loyal to the principle of centralized authority and by his example and influence kept Andalusia at peace.

The governor's household in Granada, however, attested to a certain laxity in enforcing the official policy of Spanish ethnic and cultural exclusivity. The future viceroy's mother, a cousin of Ferdinand, was herself of Jewish, Moorish, and Spanish Christian descent. Antonio de Mendoza was raised in the royal palaces in the Alhambra, and accustomed to the Arabic dress, food, and furnishings adopted by his father, who also employed converso and morisco retainers. The first viceroy of New Spain had also been educated within the broader European context provided by humanistic study. When ambassador to Rome his father had brought to Spain Peter Martyr d'Anghiera, the Italian humanist, who with Hernán Nuñez, a converso learned in Greek, Latin, and Arabic, had tutored his children. One of them, Diego Hurtado de Mendoza, became himself a noted humanist and royal ambassador; another, María Pacheco, was a leading *comunera*.

Tendilla, governing mixed peoples for the monarchy, ruled Granada benevolently, in close accord with the bishop, Hernando de Talavera. When official policy hardened to persecution of non-Christians, he did his best to serve both the crown and his morisco subjects. His son the viceroy on occasion cited as precedent for his own concern for Indians his father's patriarchal interest in the moriscos of Granada.[32] Antonio de Mendoza early sought royal patronage and attached himself to Charles' court. In 1516, on news of the death of Ferdinand, he traveled to Flanders, became chamberlain to the queen, and married a lady-in-waiting, Catalina de Vargas, who died before he took the Mexican office. As viceroy he carried on a family tradition of a self-interest intertwined with serving Castilian kings, advising and supporting them, defending their honor and their realm. His career represents both a late manifestation of an essentially medieval sense of privilege and seignorial obligation and an early one of the transatlantic expansion of European nation-states. In New Spain Mendoza maintained a court, a bodyguard of thirty to forty gentlemen, and a staff of sixty Indians, and employed many more. As viceroy he was also president of the audiencia of Mexico, vice-patron of the church, and prime dispenser of patronage. He could and did frame laws, subject to review by the Council of the Indies. He ruled as father to the Indians, governor and mediator among Spaniards, and lesser version of the king.[33]

His tenure coincided with a period of boom for Spaniards—of mine development, territorial expansion, doubling and redoubling of royal revenues, of sizable Spanish immigration but also of Indian decimation by plague and famine. He was expected to continue the work of the second audiencia, taking care to suit government to Mexican conditions. Royal instructions reminded him that Mexico "being so far off and so different from these kingdoms, we confide in your loyalty and conscience and zeal for our service."[34] Specifically, Mendoza was to put greater order into tribute assessment and collection and to bring into the tribute system Indians on the frontiers—in Guatemala, Nueva Galicia, and Pánuco—to extend present encomiendas for another life but to make few new allotments, to investigate slaving by Spaniards and by native principales and chiefs, and to oversee the welfare of the Indians. Industries were to be encouraged for the benefit of New Spain and of the royal treasury, whose accounts he was to examine.[35]

In deciding whether or not specific royal instructions suited the Mexican situation as he understood it, Mendoza pursued an adroit and temporizing policy, recognizing his function to be a mediating one and seeking to reconcile Spanish and indigenous interests under royal authority. He informed his successor, Luis de Velasco, of the obvious and basic dilemma continually facing the government, that the twin policies of increasing revenues and protecting Indians were mutually contradictory.[36] He explained, as had Cortés, that royal rents accrued from Spanish enterprise in mining, farming, stock-raising, and from the silk industry, that Indian products were of little worth and Indian labor of value only when employed by Spaniards. Indian tribute per se was not a prime source of royal income. In the interest of crown revenues, therefore, he had chosen to limit and license, rather than to forbid as directed, Indian slavery and personal service in the mines. In general he followed a policy where, instead of prohibiting where directed by royal decree, he strove only to regulate and control. He could thus extend effective authority while appearing exceedingly benevolent. To Velasco he suggested minimal intervention in society, that the secret of good government was to do little and to do it slowly. It was a maxim cited and adhered to by viceroys down through the 1760s. Mendoza's regulations nevertheless affected all aspects of Mexican life.[37] He defined and set bounds to relations between Spaniards and other peoples, and also to exploration, to the form and content of economic activity, to local government, moral practices, and to cultural, and some religious, institutions. He employed delegated royal authority, arbitrating, adjudicating, and legislating in order to bring New Spain, in practice as in theory, within the Spanish imperial system.

He reinforced certain trappings of seignorialism useful to the crown, while dispensing with others he deemed less savory. He called upon Spanish settlers to do their military duty as guardians of the land, relying on encomenderos, for example, to help put down warring seminomadic Chichemecas in northwestern Nueva Galicia in 1541–42, during the Mixtón Wars; yet he forced those Spaniards to accept the general principle that all Indians were royal subjects. He regulated both inheritance of encomiendas and tribute payment and labor within them. He allowed occasional transfers of encomiendas to new holders, granted new ones sparingly, and, as directed, forbade encomenderos to lend or hire out Indians for mining unless the natives consented. Although other royal officials thought Indians directly under the crown should pay tribute by working in mines, Mendoza opposed this sort of service in lieu of tribute. His most outstanding use of discretionary power was his delay in publishing the New Laws of 1542 until the clause most offensive to encomenderos, stating that on the death of present holders all encomiendas would revert to the crown, was revoked in 1545. Then, again directed to abolish slavery, he again temporized, instead continuing to prohibit its abuse in the mines and liberating only those Indians who brought successful suit for being illegally enslaved in the first place.

Mendoza not only interposed royal authority in relations between Spaniards and Indians but also, through widespread and judicious use of patronage, increasingly made Spaniards dependent upon royal favor, and often on his own. He turned many Indianless conquistadors, their heirs, and later immigrants into royal pensioners. He put many privately held Indians under the crown on the death of their second holders, and doled pensions from their tribute to the widows and orphans of the defunct encomenderos. Pensions of sorts, too, were his appointments to the posts of corregidor and *alcalde mayor*, bestowed on Indianless Spaniards, some of them conquistadors, empowering them to oversee political, economic, and judicial matters, including tribute collection, in Indian villages, in lieu of granting their petitions for encomiendas.[38] His most important assertion of authority was the final hemming in of Fernando Cortés. Ordered to continue the process begun by the second audiencia, Mendoza reduced Cortés' subjects and towns, restricted his use of his office of captain-general, competed successfully with him for power and esteem among Spaniards, vied with him in exploration, and, by 1540, drove the marqués to seek redress at court and residence in Spain, where he died in 1547. One result of Mendoza's triumph over the conquistador was the visita of Francisco Tello de Sandoval. On Cortés' recommendation, the visitador had been sent to subject the viceroy to residencia and, during 1544–47, took depositions concerning viceregal activities. Mendoza, and his office, won out, certainly not harmed by the appointment in 1545 to the presidency of the Council of the Indies of one of his brothers, Bernardino.[39]

In accord with his instructions, Mendoza took measures to ensure Spanish prosperity, and thus to build the economy of New Spain and, through it, royal revenues. He regulated mining, encouraged agriculture, particularly the planting of sugar, wheat, and mulberry trees for silkworms, and stock-raising. He fired Spanish interest in breeding fine horses and introduced merino sheep, and he also favored raising mules for export and to replace Indian carriers in Mexico. He abetted Spanish expansion by founding towns, began systematic land distribution for herds and wheat, imported skilled workers of textiles, encouraged cloth manufacture, opened roads, favored commerce, oversaw foundation of a mint, and standardized coinage.[40] During his term of office royal income increased sixfold.

Mendoza continued the policy of tightening royal control over the native populace through manipulating its leaders. By his power of appointment to posts in Indian towns he worked to lessen the prevalent collusion of principales and chiefs with clergy and encomenderos at the expense of native commoners and of the royal treasury. He ordered both Indians and Spaniards to pay tribute. He imposed royal supervision in examining, evaluating, and registering tribute due from Indians, and assigned corregidores and alcaldes mayores—similar officials—to collect it and to oversee native cabildos, as we have noted. These decrees applied first to encomienda pueblos directly under the crown, then by 1550 to all Indian towns. He also worked with church leaders to minimize abuse of Indians by Spaniards, strove to protect communal lands and property, but never lost sight of where the royal interest lay.[41]

His measures, like those of the second audiencia, extended Spanish control over Indians through superimposing Spanish ways on their own. Thus he sought to preserve indigenous traditions compatible with European morality and custom while introducing into native life selected aspects of Spanish culture and furthering Indian reliance on royal authority. Enjoined to govern Mexico in accord with the Laws of Toro, Mendoza also followed the precedent of the second audiencia in choosing to respect many regional customs, indeed seeking them out in making decisions and decrees. He personally heard cases brought by Indians and strove at least to appear to fill their new, Spanish-inspired town offices with recognized community leaders. In addition, he advocated eventually training a native priesthood—"when this nation [the Indians] is at our state of civility"—and was a sponsor of the Colegio de Santa Cruz de Tlatelolco, opened in 1536 for sons of Indian aristocrats and designed to educate future directors of Indian society in Spanish faith and government, norms and values—as intermediaries between the dominant and indigenous cultures.[42]

Throughout Spanish society, as well as Indian, he sought to guard morality in conformity with European ideals, working closely with the clergy in putting into effect royal orders for single men to marry, forbidding gambling and sumptuous attire, and in general issuing edicts conducive to permanent settlement and social stability. And in conjunction with Juan de Zumárraga, bishop of Mexico, Mendoza urged bringing in instruments of cultural support and dissemination: a printing press and schools. He not only encouraged the founding of the colegio at Tlatelolco for Indians but also supported—as had the president of the second audiencia—the Colegio de San Juan de Letrán to teach "Christian doctrine, good customs," trades and letters to mestizo boys, an asylum for mestizo girls—"so they may get husbands"—and the various other educational activities of the religious orders.[43] By 1539 he had requested royal sponsorship for a university of Mexico.

In sum, in striving to bring all social groups in Mexico under the control of the Spanish crown he thought it important to lead them to know and to esteem a European, and specifically Spanish, style of life. Moreover, while never advocating the possibility of an American utopia, he believed that firm and prudent government could effect a workable harmony among the diverse elements of Mexican society, and that religious and social conformity to Spanish norms would help greatly to ensure the survival of New Spain.

He treated both the Spanish and Indian segments of society in patrimonial fashion but with differences and in accord with royal principles. As the highest royal representative in the land, the viceroy took special care to instill a sense of his own superiority to individual domiciled Spaniards.[44] Non-Spanish peoples he handled as more childlike subjects. His stated opinion of Indians in large part paralleled Vitoria's. He suggested to Velasco that Indians be treated as sons, that while he distrusted their cunning, lying, and proclivity to litigate, and condemned them for drinking excessively, they were not beasts; indeed many were intelligent and must be dealt with as "any other nation."[45] They tended to be lazy by nature, however, and so must be made to work, but they must also be protected from abuse where possible. He recognized Indian aristocrats as such, and also their value to Spanish government. In addition, he went beyond official attitudes to appreciate, and on occasion appropriate, the more highly elaborated indigenous aesthetic achievements, sending (for instance) idols of green jade to his brother, the humanist and ambassador to Italy, Diego Hurtado de Mendoza, and he encouraged ongoing Franciscan investigations into the old indigenous cultures.

Initially, too, the first viceroy assumed a benevolent attitude toward Mexicans of mixed parentage. We know that schools for mestizo children received his patronage. He also confirmed as legitimate heirs mestizos recognized by Spanish fathers, permitting in at least one case an encomienda to go to the husband of a mestiza daughter of the former encomendero. He suggested Velasco arrange marriages for Indian daughters of "honored persons," including to corregidores. By the late 1540s, however, as mestizo vagrants became commonplace and were reported to harass and rob travelers and Indian villagers, he perceived mestizos in general as footloose, outside of society, and a threat to law and order. And where at first he had urged importing African slaves to replace Indians working in mines, by mid-century he characterized their more mobile mixed offspring as mulatos and dangerous social parasites.[46]

Mendoza came increasingly to identify his own fortune with that of New Spain. Early he fitted out, at his own expense, expeditions of exploration, including Francisco Vázquez de Coronado's. As his brother Diego Hurtado observed, the viceroy had caught conquistador fever.[47] With the failure of Coronado to find new peoples and wealth comparable to the Mexican, like other Spaniards Mendoza turned to extracting his fortune from known resources. Despite royal orders to the contrary, he acquired encomiendas, wheat estancias, horses and sheep, and interests in textile workshops and in other commercial ventures.[48] To their mutual advantage, he continued the arrangement begun by treasury officials of steering a large share of trading privileges in the New World to Francisco de los Cobos, the royal secretary. Under Mendoza these included monopolies in flax, wine, black slaves, and on sales of bulls of crusade, or indulgences, to Christianized Indians.[49]

In the 1540s while royal policy increasingly was directed to freeing Indians from private Spanish control, the viceroy of New Spain more and more diverged in sentiment. He allowed wholesale slavery in the Mixtón campaign, delayed putting into effect the New Laws, argued the need of Spaniards to convert Indian goods and services to treasury income—and thus for continuing control of Indians by individual Spaniards—granted estancias to stockmen without royal authority and on the basis of prior use, and urged a general repartimiento among Spaniards of all Indians toward the end of the decade. His own interest came more and more to conform to that of other Spanish inhabitants. He and his family had acquired ties to the land. He had brought two illegitimate half-sisters to New Spain. One of them, Leonor Beltrán, married a latterday conquistador, Martín de Ircio. The other, María de Mendoza, soon possessed substantial mines.[50] It can be argued that these connections increased his primary interest in general Spanish prosperity, his concern for Indian welfare and preservation, and his inaugurating government strong enough to vouchsafe Spanish occupation but not to hamper private economic endeavor, particularly his own. His outlook on Mexico came to resemble that of a propertied lord loyal to his overlord. Relieved of his post in 1550, although worn out and ailing, he accepted as his duty viceregal office in Peru, acquiescing, too, in the royal refusal to make his son his successor in New Spain.

The first viceroy undoubtedly enjoyed—in both senses—wielding delegated, but widely discretionary, authority and power. An English contemporary, Francis Bacon, recalled Mendoza's only complaint of the Peruvian post was that it was too close to Spain.[51] In the same spirit and in terms reminiscent of his late relative, Ferdinand of Aragon, Mendoza told Velasco to listen to everyone, then do what he had planned in the first place.[52] He explained that distance and slowness of communication prevented tight control of Mexico by the Council of the Indies, yet while the viceroy could rule much as he wished, he would be wise to delay executing unwelcome laws and to respect local custom. In sum, Mendoza's ordinances and correspondence reveal that by 1550 he had synthesized older Fernandine practice with new imperial policy, and his own private with Spanish-dominated public interest, that he governed New Spain not simply as viceroy of a revenue-producing dependency of the crown but as resident lord of a great region within the Spanish empire, having many of its own distinct needs, customs, and traditions, some of them evolving during his tenure as viceroy.

Luis de Velasco, the new viceroy, was also a Castilian noble, but of somewhat less illustrious birth than Mendoza.[53] He had had military and administrative experience as inspector general of the Spanish armies and as viceroy of Navarre. Sent to refine, invigorate, and maintain governmental institutions and arrangements now introduced in New Spain, his instructions from the crown were relatively brief.[54] He was to rule the Indians paternally, visit the land, use oidores as traveling justices, collect more information concerning tribute, lowering rates he found too high, and to levy more precise assessments so that Indians clearly understood them. He was also to try to define more exactly the responsibilities of officals and of the clergy. He was to found a university.

Other royal orders of the period were concerned with ensuring closer royal supervision of labor and tribute. They stipulated that the viceroy free remaining Indian slaves but see to it that the natives worked regularly, paid taxes, and were instructed in religion. In particular, copious tribute regulations flowed from court during 1550–56, among them orders to abolish personal service, to curb caciques cheating maceguales, to allow no contracts for tribute rates between encomenderos and caciques "for they destroy maceguales," and to ensure that officials other than corregidores collect tribute. In other words, he was to put teeth into the remaining New Laws. He was also to enforce strictly the cédula of 1549 decreeing all Indians must hire out for pay, rather than be enslaved or perform services in lieu of tribute.[55]

Velasco found in New Spain an organized central government, but also a society growing more complex, with Spanish immigrants increasing and a generation of Spanish Americans maturing, the Indian population decreasing, down perhaps from the 1530s by as much as two-thirds in the central area, with great loss due to famine, typhus, and smallpox during 1545–48, and the social situation complicated by a growing number of what the government viewed as troublesome inhabitants of mixed descent.[56] In the first years of his term he faced ascending tensions between crown policy and Mexican conditions, between Spaniards and other inhabitants, and within both Spanish and Indian society. The earlier, seemingly unlimited advantage offered by the new land had shrunk to a more restricted range of possibilities for Spain and for Spaniards and their offspring in Mexico. Competition now frequently existed where there had been cooperation. Rewards appeared to have become more defined and their supply shortened. As the reign of Charles V drew to an end, in Mexico as in Spain, men and women looked less to a promising future and harder at the present reality. A general loyalty to authority had been established; Velasco was now confronted with the practical business of managing competing assertions of self-interest.

The new viceroy in general continued Mendoza's policies. He initially responded quickly to immediate problems. In the aftermath of the plague he urged hospitals for Indians and funded one himself. He established a Santa Hermandad, a variety of civil militia utilized by Isabella and Ferdinand, to patrol roads, do summary justice, and protect the settled populace from the increasing depredations of vagrants. Finding a silver rush to the north underway, he caused the towns of San Miguel and San Felipe to be inhabited by Spaniards as waystations and garrisons. Initially, too, he strove to enforce the royal edicts against slavery and supported the visita of encomiendas made by the oidor Diego Ramírez in 1552-53, leading to new and more forceful tribute regulations and, briefly, to reduced assessments. Under Velasco, it has been said, tribute legislation became effective for the first time.[57] There is evidence, however, that within two years of his arrival, he imposed much of the legislation curbing Spanish use of Indian labor reluctantly. In a letter of 1552 to the crown, for example, he requested, as had Mendoza and other Spaniards in Mexico, a perpetual repartimiento be made of native villages.[58] In 1553 he wrote opposing further freeing of Indian slaves and reform legislation in general. By 1554 he complained of economic crisis, writing that royal rents had dropped because of lack of Indian slaves and personal service, and because of lowered tributes, that as a consequence silver production lagged and with it the commerce and prosperity of the land. Indians, he concluded, must be forced to work. At a time when three-quarters of the encomiendas in central Mexico had reverted to the crown, he approved of encomienda as an Indian-conserving institution and an object of royal patronage.[59]

He founded the University of Mexico, primarily for "sons of Spaniards," continued viceregal support of the Indian colegio at Tlatelolco, yet his reports to Spain indicate that his opinion of all inhabitants of Mexico was generally low. He wrote of Spaniards as arrogant and disobedient, refusing to work and dependent on Indian labor, many simply vagabonds living off Indian villages. Some of the old conquistadors who once held Indians, he added, had frittered them away. He expressed less solicitude than had Mendoza for public esteem, gave less of an appearance of relying on public opinion, vented a more aristocratic hauteur, and appears to have lived a richer and more ostentatious life. Velasco maintained great pomp and ceremony in his court, indulged in hunts, was devoted to fine horsemanship and falconry, and kept an open house and table.[60] The second viceroy provided the example of a Renaissance *caballero* to the wealthy of New Spain. His conduct helped to associate with aristocracy the pleasures of horse racing, drinking, gambling, masquerades, and bull-fights, and to turn a working military aristocracy into a more decorative and ceremonial one. Yet he wrote of the majority of Spaniards in Mexico as of common sort, with only a few domiciled caballeros competent for magisterial posts, and those few with ability seeking too much salary. His disdain for lowborn recent immigrants—he wanted immigration stopped —was surpassed by that for other, newer components of society. He found cause for alarm in Negro conspiracies of the 1540s and in the numbers of vagrant blacks, mulatos, and mestizos who, he said, stirred up and preyed upon Indians, increased rapidly, and were evilly inclined. He also wanted Negro importation ended.[61]

Although previous governors had encouraged Spanish colonization— members of the second audiencia had hoped settlers in Puebla would soon "love the land"—Velasco was now wary of the obvious and growing exclusive attachment of Spaniards to their Mexican lands. Where, previously, ensuring permanent settlement had been cause for royal headache, now Velasco thought settlers too devoted to their new residence, warning the crown that "Spaniards would risk their lives for their estancias."[62] He inadvertently sped regional divergence from Spain, however, when, for example, he authorized the oidor Vasco de Puga to make a compilation of royal cédulas specifically directed to Mexico, thereby enlarging on the work the second audiencia and Mendoza had begun of giving order to a body of regional precedent distinct from the law of Spain. He also continued Mendoza's practices of encouraging Franciscan inquiries into indigenous history and custom, and relied on native tradition when opportune, consulting, for example, the old Indian pictographs as guides to effecting flood relief for the city of Mexico.[63]

Putting less emphasis than did Mendoza on actively promoting harmony with other directing agencies of Mexican society, Velasco was soon at odds with encomenderos, their representatives—the *regidores* (members), of the *ayuntamiento* (council), of the city of Mexico—stockmen, some of the regular clergy, the archbishop, the audiencia of Mexico, and the new one in Nueva Galicia as well.[64] By the middle of the decade, moreover, his own vested interest came into conflict with others. From his arrival in New Spain he had complained of inadequate salary. Apparently, however, he soon found extraofficial means to sustain himself and his family. His brother Francisco had accompanied him to Mexico and became one of its principal wealthy vecinos, marrying the widow of Juan Jaramillo, whose first wife had been Marina, Cortés' native translator, confidante, and the mother of his bastard son, Martín.[65] In 1556 Velasco's son Luis, later to be viceroy also, married María de Ircio y Mendoza, the Mexican-born daughter of Mendoza's sister Leonor and Martín de Ircio, and his daughter Ana de Castillo wed the mine-rich conqueror of Nueva Vizcaya, Diego de Ibarra. The second viceroy and his family, too, despite royal orders to the contrary, became actively involved in the economy and society of Mexico.[66]

Here Velasco, it appears, followed the lead of Mendoza and members of the audiencia, although he scored oidores for the same sort of "corruption."[67] By the 1540s Mendoza had denounced the oidor Lorenzo de Tejada for trading Indians bad land for twice as much good and also for buying property which he improved and built upon for very profitable resale.[68] In 1554 oidores in Nueva Galicia, too, were known to be active in slaving, in mining in Zacatecas, and in related commerce.[69] The royal orders at mid-century forbidding oidores and the viceroy to hold landed property in New Spain now serve more as comments than they ever did as effective constraints on this state of affairs.[70] While Habsburgs ruled Spain, governors in Mexico tended to juggle implementing royal policies with improving their own material condition and that of their dependents.

At mid-century, royal government centered and was most effective in the city of Mexico and its environs. In practice it had less control at local levels outside of the capital region. Encomenderos continued to sit in the cabildos of smaller Spanish enclaves and to negotiate in great freedom with communal caciques for the goods and services of their Indians. Local officials appointed by the government to advance royal control in native communities often became petty tyrants perhaps worse than encomenderos because without vested interest in their charges. The second audiencia had first placed corregidores empowered with jurisdiction and collecting tribute over the governments of Indian towns not privately held, but soon accused them of collusion with chiefs and Spaniards and of rapacious practices. Mendoza had put them over all Indian towns, although in frontier areas and in new mining towns he preferred to introduce for the same purposes alcaldes mayores.[71] Competition for the corregimientos was great by the 1540s, salaries small and paid in kind from tribute collected, and extortion inevitable. In a political system where lower offices were customarily granted as payment for services rendered, thought of as livings, and at mid-century beginning to be sold, the sort of professionalism associated with pride in performance was seldom apparent.[72] Local office was looked upon by incumbents as a private holding, a sinecure, and not as a delegation of royal authority.

Central government also had least effective control in the most outlying provinces. In 1545 the audiencia of Guatemala was instituted and, in 1548, one named for Nueva Galicia to curb abuse occurring under the governorship of Coronado. Yet the now familiar formula of introducing royal justices to regulate Spanish-Indian relations in the royal interest did not have the desired effect in these provinces, just as it did not at first in central Mexico.[73] In the 1550s, the Mexican periphery resembled the loose political situation in the central valley of a generation earlier, before 1530.

In sum, the first officials' interest in eliciting royal revenues and to a greater extent in their own fortunes nearly proved disastrous to organizing Mexican society as an ongoing concern under Spain. Cortés, however, as conqueror and first royal governor, had introduced political and religious institutions, and effective leadership, though of mixed Fernandist and imperial structure, providing an adequate framework for Spanish domination. The second audiencia, composed of professional administrators exclusively and attuned to Charles' policies, then skillfully introduced official principles and a supporting ideology. Antonio de Mendoza, the first viceroy, wise in ruling peoples of mixed ethnic background and in conciliating royal, religious, and private interests, functioned less as a faithful royal servant than as a scaled-down mirror image of his overlord. Emulating the royal stance within a more limited area, and in accord with prevailing political theory, he implemented royal policies. By decrees, decisions, and setting the tone for Spanish society in Mexico, Mendoza and to a lesser extent other officials continued to impose royal authority over political, social, and economic aspects of all Mexican society, and to reinforce the imperial ideal of allegiance to the crown and Christianity, and of esteem for the material and ideal components of Spanish civilization. In particular, the second audiencia and the viceroy imposed royal justice, established the concept of Indians and Spaniards as royal subjects owing their monarch tribute, and made of encomienda a dinosaur institution, destined for extinction. They also escalated royal revenues.

Mendoza and the oidores had purposely sought to gain a consensus supporting royal authority over all peoples, including what they referred to as Indian "nations."[74] They saw to it that Spaniards, often wielding real power as encomenderos and increasingly as landed proprietors, showed respect for crown authority, although they did not always obey it. The theory of Indians as royal subjects was generally understood as they meant it should be, including by the more settled natives themselves, and substantiated by royal ability to do justice, to regulate labor and tribute, and to defend frontiers. Royal officials in Mexico, although regarding conquistadors and first settlers as the dominant aristocracy, succeeded in limiting them politically through adroit use of royal justice, patronage, taxation, and the imposition of a supportive seignorial and imperial ideology.

Yet those affected by the lure of landed wealth and by the attendant attachment to New Spain (noted by Velasco) included officials, which meant that among the first generation of Spanish Americans born in

Mexico and raised to be its aristocracy were children of royal officials and their families as well as of private Spaniards. It also meant that Mendoza, Velasco, and other lesser appointees at first exerted a good deal of vigor in carrying out royal orders and implementing royal policy, then settled into the dual role of attempting to combine offical duties with de facto señorío.

Velasco was viceroy at the formal accession in 1557 of Philip II. That monarch received as part of his dynastic inheritance the Kingdom of New Spain, where an essentially imperial government machinery had been introduced as well as the theory to sustain it. King's men had consolidated and institutionalized conquest in behalf of the Spanish crown, carefully, if by trial and error, and permanently. Governmental supervision of the elaborate festivities celebrating the advent to the throne and the swearing of allegiance to Philip, and participation by all sectors of Mexican society in the celebration, attested to imposition, over the social and economic reality of dominant Spaniards and subservient Indians and newer peoples, of the concept of the supremacy of royal authority and the institutions of royal government.[75] The imperial and patriarchal system allowed super-imposition of Spanish domination over older Spanish and indigenous, and newer syncretic, attitudes and structures. Thus the Kingdom of New Spain, to a great extent through the labors of royal government there, had been politically attached to Spain. Mexico was incorporated to the crown of Castile as a distinct region, one inhabited by numerous "nations," one with strong material and ideological ties to the economy, the crown, the faith, and the civilization of the Spanish empire. And sharing responsibility for the success of this process of imperial consolidation was the clergy.

5

The Friars, Christianity, and the Crown

Friars, many of them barefoot and clad in patched homespun, were of tremendous help to Charles V, one of the most powerful of European rulers, in imposing Spanish domination over New Spain. Just as the Spanish monarch relied on churchmen in key government posts, and on theologians to justify the Spanish presence in America, initially he also counted on members of the clergy to help ensure Spanish permanence in Mexico, to implement theories bolstering royal power there, and particularly to bring Indians and to keep Spaniards within the imperial system. In turn, the friars who came to Mexico believed that the church had the dual mission of bringing Indians to the faith and under the crown, that it was a religious duty "to open the door to the apostolic conquest and to augment the royal domain."[1]

Two priests came to Mexico with Cortés and several more with other expeditions. In 1521 Pope Adrian VI, who had been Charles' counselor, permitted Franciscans (Friars Minor) extraordinary powers as parish priests in the Indies, in effect enabling those friars, and later other religious orders, to perform as secular clergy there.[2] In accord with this papal directive, and empowered by the patronato of the Indies, the king appointed men who valued and taught humility, and whose appearance was unquestionably humble, to attend to Indian welfare, and to attract and subject the natives to God and the Spanish monarchy. In 1523 three Franciscans from Flanders began to introduce institutions to make permanent the spiritual conquest of Mexico. Nine months later Charles sent a group of Spanish Friars Minor to organize formally a Franciscan province in Mexico. Other regular clergy—more Franciscans, Dominicans from 1526, and Augustinians from 1533—continued to arrive, to fan out among the more settled indigenous peoples, to preach and teach, build churches and monasteries, uproot the old gods, and baptize hundreds of thousands of Indians. Among them were a few nuns and a small group of women (*beatas*) unordained but affiliated with the Franciscan order. By mid-century the regular clergy had succeeded in establishing themselves as the most visible and directly accessible intermediaries between the natives and government and God.[3]

Cortés, who took for granted the efficacy of spiritual conquest and had specifically requested regular clergy for Mexico, assembled the highest Spanish and Indian dignitaries to welcome the first group of Spanish Franciscans, then indicated the threadbare friars' prestige by kneeling and kissing their hands.[4] The Franciscans, in turn, upheld his authority, during the turbulent 1520s, seeing in its continuance the best possibility of preserving and Christianizing Indians and of calming Spaniards. Their support of his interests and those of the Indians and their insistence on their own delegated authority in civil and criminal jurisdiction over the natives caused sufficient hostility by 1526 among resident Spaniards to bring the Order to the brink of abandoning the Mexican enterprise.[5] Tenacity won out. Moreover, Charles buoyed their spirits in obtaining license from the pope for 150 more Friars Minor for New Spain, and in naming as Protector of the Indians—a title earlier held by Las Casas—and as first bishop of Mexico one of their Order, Juan de Zumárraga. The king also dispatched the first contingent of Dominicans who, although allying themselves to a faction opposing Cortés, also engaged in energetic missionary work and guarded the royal prerogative.[6] One of the most notorious of them, in Mexico as in Spain, then and now, was Bartolomé de Las Casas. He first came to New Spain in 1531 with Ramírez de Fuenleal—in 1516 appointed by Cisneros bishop of San Domingo, and now president of the audiencia of Mexico.[7] Las Casas, who became bishop of Chiapas in 1543, continued to shuttle between Mexico and Spain, influencing the crown in developing the principles and articulating the ideology underlying American policy.[8]

It was one of the first Flemish Franciscans, Pedro de Gante, however, who set the pattern for the theory and method of missionary work generally followed in Mexico. Many of his views on Indians, Spaniards, and royal authority became accepted norms and his ways of teaching precedent for practice among the early missionary clergy. His career inspired many others.[9] He brought to New Spain an outlook and ideals having much in common with advocates of Christian renaissance and reform in his native northern Europe. Throughout his correspondence and activities Gante displayed a Christocentric faith and a renovating spirit, not unlike that of his fellow countryman, Desiderius Erasmus, and also a strong commitment to live as had members of the primitive church. He demonstrated that, to him, to Christianize meant to educate Indians in religious principles and Western cultural practices consonant with ideals associated with Christian humanism, and that such education was necessary to equip men and women for daily life. He put into practice in Mexico a program to instill in Indians a Christianity based upon a combination of essentially classical European, and early Christian, cultural ideals, certain that a life well spent, as defined within the context of these ideals, was a prerequisite to salvation. Gante refused ordination, office, and honors and remained a Franciscan lay brother until, past ninety, he died in 1572.[10] He was active to the last, instructing Indians in the European religion and morality he viewed as of universal content and application, and retaining his belief in the value and efficacy of education. In effect, Gante carried out the injunction of Vitoria's text, "Teach all nations...."

Gante learned Nahuatl during his initial stay in Texcoco and, though a stutterer, was an excellent linguist, preaching and writing catechisms in that tongue. In the city of Mexico his work began with over two hundred sons of native leaders, or at least with boys assumed to be. They had been brought from twenty-four leagues around to the Franciscan house, on order of Cortés, to learn "the law of God and Christian doctrine."[11] Since Pedro de Gante's work and attitudes, and those of other early churchmen, made a strong and continuing impact on life in New Spain in this crucial, formative period, their activities and outlooks are worth a closer look.

In the school attached to his church of San José de Belen de los Naturales, Gante taught these Indian boys to write and to read Latin, and to sing and play instruments as Europeans did, transmitting Christian language, faith and culture to them—at first so they could help friars by acting as interpreters and teachers to their peoples. He also set up workshops and trade schools to train indigenous commoners in European arts and crafts. Indian girls were taught domestic arts and to value monogamous marriage. His students, as planned, became intermediaries between Spaniards and natives. Some fulfilled that role as judges, alcaldes, and regidores in Indian communities, or as their wives. Some trained as artisans competed successfully with Spanish craftsmen in producing European-style products.[12] With others he was less successful.

Gante insisted that Indians were rational beings innately and spiritually equal to Europeans. He found them, he wrote, "apt in all things, especially in receiving the faith. Habit rather than their nature makes them servile, for they were accustomed to be taught through fear, not love."[13] The Flemish Franciscan was convinced, in accord with the dominant social assumptions of western Europe, that all human beings were equal before God, but also that all humanity was subdivided into social communities having innate, static, hierarchical structure. Thus he taught Indians to live and to work energetically within what he assumed to be the social station of their birth. At the same time, he introduced them to a religion and to a concept of culture incorporating the values and practices of a broadly conceived and idealized European civilization capable of encompassing compatible Indian customs. He denounced to the king mistreatment of Indians by Spaniards, whose essentially secular claims to hold Mexico by right of conquest he contested. The Indians had been discovered, he wrote, only to ensure their salvation; the Spaniards had been sent by God solely to open Mexico to Christianity, and they now impeded the very end heaven meant them to serve. The Fleming expressed no loyalty to Spain itself, only to its monarch who was also the Holy Roman Emperor. His allegiance was Christian and universal. He believed, as Augustine had stated, that "this heavenly city . . . while it sojourns on earth, calls citizens out of all nations."[14] Although his primary allegiance was to the eternal patria, he came to feel, and wrote, that Mexico was to him the most important of all temporal kingdoms. By 1529, instead of indulging in the European fashion of classical allusion, Gante indicated his new affinity in peppering his correspondence with Nahuatl phrases.[15]

Gante spoke of Spain and New Spain as equal kingdoms, ruled separately by the emperor, his principal ally in Christian mission. He addressed Charles with a more than customary flourish, as "Holy Catholic Caesarean Majesty, Emperor and King, Our Lord" and also referred to him as "the vicar of Christ."[16] And although Philip II was not Holy Roman Emperor, in his reign Gante—as did contemporary Spaniards—continued to associate imperial Christian authority with the ruler of greater Spain. In 1558, writing to congratulate Philip on his accession, the Franciscan recalled his own labors in support of the dynasty, reminding the new monarch that, as ruler of "the state and with it these kingdoms of New Spain," he, Philip, had inherited from Charles a moral obligation "to augment and to conserve Christianity."[17] His letters, too, provided Mexican precedent to a number of the early clergy who in writing to the king continually reported on government, denounced abuses, and suggested remedies. As a body, the mendicants thought of themselves as royal chaplains, in keeping with contemporary Christian political theory obliged to evaluate and, when necessary, complain of government policy or practice to the king, so that he might seek reform and thereby rid the royal conscience of responsibility for bad government.

Spanish Franciscans who followed Gante to Mexico, the Twelve, meant to recall the first apostles, were led by Martín de Valencia, who, although sickly and in his fifties, was rigorously ascetic and devoted to poverty, simplicity, Christ, and to saving Indian souls—as were the others. Best remembered and representative of the group was Toribio de Benavente, who on arrival, goes the story, heard Indians remark on his bare feet and patched robe, calling him *motolinía*. Learning that the word meant "poor one" he immediately adopted it as his name. Motolinía's writings and other Franciscan correspondence and chronicles affirm that these mendicants came from Spain with reforming attitudes similar to Gante's, that in Mexico they sought to do the same sort of work, that they too combined religious fervor with universalistic ideals generally associated with the Christian renaissance but that, unlike him, the men who expanded upon Gante's activities at times employed harsher methods —Valencia, for example, meted out capital punishment—and always exhibited great Spanish patriotism.[18]

The Twelve had been educated in Spain during a period of perceived crises in church and state when, as in northern Europe, educational renovation along humanist lines often went hand in hand with advocacy of religious reform. In both regions of Europe, meticulous scholarship was associated with humanistic methods of textual criticism applied to studies of Christ, Paul, the Bible in general, and the church fathers. Selections from classic authors in Greek and Latin were employed as adjuncts to Christian learning, as part of secondary education preceding studies of law, scholastic philosophy, and theology. Two reformist movements had converged, the mystical and the pietistic, and Christian humanism served to reinforce both. The mystical, traditionally, stressed the value to society of individuals imbued with direct divine inspiration and guidance. Their example was thought to be most important to others, since they were vessels of divine purpose. Mystics of this nature usually were activist and held utopian and apocalyptic hopes. The other, pietistic movement, was more closely associated with new, humanistic scholarship and thought. It emphasized the power of human reason, the social worth of an intellectual aristocracy, and the efficacy of education.[19]

In Spain we have seen that much impetus to reform, in both the schooling and life of the clergy, had come from a Franciscan, Cisneros, who as archbishop of Toledo, primate of Spain, had established the humanistically oriented University of Alcalá primarily to improve the education and caliber of the clergy, and had endorsed compilation there of the Complutensian Bible. He had also pressed all friars to live in poverty, austerity, and greater humility, in greater conformity to Christian ideals. Further, he had evinced a militant dedication, indeed crusading zeal, in warfare, conversion of Moslems, renovation of education, clerical reform, and Spanish patriotism, in centralizing political control under the crown, and in Indian affairs. Friars, and several friar-bishops, in Mexico followed his lead—Sebastian Ramírez de Fuenleal, president of the second audiencia, among them.

A militant spirit of reform had cropped out, more intense in Spain than in Flanders. Manifested not only by Isabella and her bishop, Cisneros, it had also appeared within a general impulse to monastic reform among certain radical Franciscans who imposed variant, austere rules in several provinces.[20] Martín de Valencia had governed one of them, that of San Gabriel in Extremadura, subscribing to the most rigorous observance. He had drawn the Twelve from among his charges there and in Mexico continued to insist on poverty and extreme severity of discipline.[21] Like Gante, his Spanish brethren exhibited a reforming zest unhampered by doubt, by fear of falling into heterodoxy, by narrow strictures on missionary methods, or by an organized hierarchy. But in addition to Gante's Erasmus-like faith in education and example, they introduced a fervent mysticism, akin to that of the fiery, book-burning Italian monk, Savonarola and other apocalyptic visionaries, but evolved in Spain and conducive to intense proselytizing and to reinforcing militant reforming proclivities.[22] The Twelve, eager to propagate a world-embracing Truth, were proponents of ecumenical Christianity, of spiritual human brotherhood, of the real presence of the Devil and the need to prepare for the Day of Judgment, all concepts well suited to their gargantuan task. Like Cisneros, who had managed Spain for Charles, the first Franciscans served both God and his temporal vicar. Perhaps above all, they were sustained by a sublime faith in the Indian need for their ministry, material and spiritual, and thus by an enviable belief in their own usefulness.

Motolinía's own missionary achievement—he claimed to have baptized 300,000 Indians—remains a monument to positive thought. Throughout central Mexico and Guatemala he preached, taught, baptized, and established religious enclaves—including churches, schools, and hospitals—introducing the faith and with it imperial authority. Indeed, it was he who in 1525 vied with secular officials over the right to dispense royal justice. He was the prototype of the missionary who consolidated the Spanish conquest, enabling a relatively few Europeans to control millions of natives. His writings show him to have been practical, blunt, patient, and industrious, and in everything he did to feel in direct contact with God. As did Pedro de Gante, Motolinía credited heaven with achieving the conquest. The Lord had directed Spaniards to Mexico, caused Cortés "to open the door to us in order to preach the Holy Gospel."[23] Then God had intervened, working miracles, to aid friars and Indians, and now He watched over churchmen and those royal officials who desired that "He might be known and adored."

Motolinía combined a tremendous zest for apostolic achievement with a pungent and at times caustic wit. Thus, scoring the Dominican Las Casas for stirring up trouble between Spaniards and Indians—as a man who "made rams of sheep," and "put the cart before the oxen" by tale-bearing rather than directly ministering to Indians—he acridly reported as a case in point that the Dominican had forced an unconscionable number of native bearers to carry his huge collection of documents denouncing the employ by Spaniards of Indian carriers.[24] Unlike Las Casas he also believed, as did the great majority of clergy in Mexico, that missionary success depended on Spanish prosperity, that it was achievable only through allowing Spaniards to control Indian labor, that, although Mexico was more Christian and less corrupt than Spain, there too weaknesses in human nature derived from social ills, and that there these weaknesses afflicted both major components of the populace, Spaniards and Indians, for all Indians were not good nor all Spaniards wicked.

Spaniards, he lamented, oppressed Indians by too heavy demands for tribute and personal service and inflicted on them labor in the mines and the building of the city of Mexico. By 1555, however, he declared that encomenderos treated their Indians well—in what was probably an implicit comparison to the earlier encomienda and to other Spaniards. And he gave Spanish greed a purpose in explaining it as chief among the plagues visited upon the natives for their past sins of idolatry and human sacrifice.[25]

By nature, stripped of pagan belief and practices, he found the Indians remarkably virtuous, rational, and worthy,

> not proud and ostentatious like the people of other nations. . . . Why should not God give His grace and bounty to these Indians, whom he created according to His image, and why should he not bestow His blessing upon them as well as upon us [Spaniards]? . . . Their souls did not cost Jesus Christ less than the souls of the Spanish nor of the Romans.[26]

In particular, he praised the natives for quickly learning to read and write Spanish and Latin and to paint, sing, and play flutes, delighting in their ability through so doing to come to Christianity and to acculturate to Spanish ways. For to Motolinía and his friar-compatriots Spanish culture embodied the highest development and ideals of Christian civilization. Their missionary activity included instilling in Indians esteem for Spanish cultural traditions as part of a broad Christian heritage and a concomitant of respect for king and God.

Motolinía enthusiastically sponsored religious *autos*, adapted from European morality plays. The friars used them to graphically instruct Indians in European history, warfare, politics, morality, and religion. Enacted on feast days, they also mirrored the current political climate. A very early one presented Indians with a Spanish version of the conquest. Its theme was the baptism of the kings of Tlaxcala and it included a most respectable Cortés, as governor for Charles V, giving reasons for Spanish dominion.[27] Motolinía, in celebration of the peace between Spain and

France in 1538, directed Tlaxcalans in another extravaganza of mixed religious and political nature—as was the occasion. In it the armies of Spain and New Spain besieged Jerusalem for Charles V. Mendoza led them. Cortés was depicted now as a sultan, Pedro de Alvarado as captain-general of the infidels. Europeans and Mexicans, repulsed, prayed. Saint Hippolyte—on whose day, 13 August, Tenochtitlán fell—and Santiago appeared on horseback to lead them to victory. In triumphal procession they then marched past three more autos. In one Indians enacted the temptation of Christ, indicating enticements to be avoided. Thus the devil was shown recounting the attributes and wealth of New Spain and of goods imported from Castile, and the joys of Spanish wine. (Elsewhere, too, Motolinía lamented native tendencies to emulate Spanish vices.)[28] Indian villages continued to enact specific plays annually, often freezing in time the passing political scene, endorsing Christianity and in its name Spanish political domination.

In missionary activity in general a cultural synthesis was Motolinía's goal, and that of most friars, in the sense of imposing Spanish upon Indian civilization. They did not seek integration of Indians into a single Mexican community. Although initially some Franciscans supported mixed marriages between Indians and Spaniards as a preferable alternative to informal cohabitation and children born out of wedlock, the Order generally sought to maintain a separate Indian society, with a Spanish veneer and in subordination to the European community. The friars thus implemented royal principles, Motolinía coming to advise the king, for example, not to allow Indians to ride horses or in any way set themselves up as equals to Spaniards.[29]

Like Pedro de Gante, Motolinía came to be both respected and esteemed by Indians and consulted by Europeans directing the church and the government in New Spain.[30] In the 1530s he first wrote an account of indigenous history as a report to the government.[31] In current Spanish fashion he referred to Indian groups as "nations," in particular recounting the glories and fatal defects of the Aztecs. He told of the grandeur of Motecuhzoma II, of how the Aztec-Mexica had enriched the land with industry, agriculture, styles of clothing, and buildings of stone and adobe, favorably comparing what he adjudged to be Aztec civilizing activities with the more recent ventures of the Spaniards. Yet Tenochtitlán fell, punished by God for its pagan "sins and abominations."[32] Heaven's instrument was the Spanish and especially the "remarkable resourcefulness and strategy displayed by Fernando Cortés." Thinking within the traditional universal Christian context enabled Motolinía easily to admire both the indigenous peoples and the Spanish conquest. And in time his view of Mexican history as a joint European and Indian legacy itself became part of the Mexican heritage, important to later generations in their search for national roots and identity.[33]

The friar's political ideas were those common to the period in Spain. Governing was a regulating and peace-keeping activity, meant to ensure communal harmony and to be carried on under religious principles. It was the royal duty, he wrote, to maintain Mexico "in justice and continual peace";[34] so far his majesty had on balance done well. Motolinía, who with his fellow Franciscans had opposed the abuses committed by the earlier officials, thanked him for aiding the Indians by sending the second audiencia, "very deserving of everlasting memory," and the mendicant praised God for Antonio de Mendoza, who, governing wisely, had placed the land "on a sound basis of Christianity and civilization."[35] He argued, however, that Mexico, properly called Anáhuac, would profit through greater autonomy, for "large and remote, separated from the mother country, it cannot be well governed from such a distance."[36] He viewed Anáhuac as a political entity in its own right, with its own history and traditions equal to any. Its capital, Mexico, was "another Jerusalem, the mother of provinces and kingdoms ... in all of Europe I doubt there is any town so excellent, opulent, and thickly populated."[37] New Spain, he suggested, deserved rule by a prince of the royal household. That is, he proposed a more direct, but at the same time more autonomous, form of rule for the kingdom under a member of the imperial dynasty. He perceived crown and clergy joined in bringing the faith to the Indians and lay Spaniards necessary in limited numbers as the military arm of that endeavor.[38]

Motolinía played a pivotal role between Spaniards and Indians in Mexico in a seminal period, taking part in and recording for posterity the hispanizing process. Among the first to promote acculturation, he equated Spanish civilization with a universal Christian ideal and, as such, also transmitted select aspects of it to the natives. Universal terms made easier the introduction of Spanish ways and at the same time, although fostering Spanish cultural superiority, did not press for exclusivity. One previously mentioned result of his cast of mind and activities was that they enabled him to combine both the Spanish and indigenous heritages into a new, regional historical synthesis, and as such to present it to contemporaries and preserve it for posterity. Related was his large contribution to the working out of an ideology ground in Christian, universal principles, acceptable to both Spaniards and Indians, supporting adherence of both groups of peoples to the imperial Spanish system. His contributions in these respects were notable, but not unique.

Perhaps even more illustrative of the sort of mutual reinforcement between church and crown during the consolidation of conquest is the career in New Spain of yet another Franciscan, Juan de Zumárraga, Protector of the Indians, Inquisitor, bishop and archbishop of Mexico. In Spain Zumárraga had been in charge of over eleven hundred friars in a strict observant province, on royal commission had investigated a report of witches in Pamplona, and had subsequently been chosen by Charles to institute church organization in Mexico. Arriving with the first oidores in 1528, the austere and often outspoken Basque prelate continued to live simply and sought to pursue all of his offices in a direct and militant manner.[39] He immediately faced the overlapping civil and religious tasks of insulating his native charges from enslavement and abuse by Spaniards and from the blandishments of idolators among their own people. He battled the first audiencia for jurisdiction over the Indians incensed, he said, at seeing Nuño de Guzmán and his fellows brutally mistreat them.

He charged the oidores, correctly, with commandeering Indians to work for them—forcing natives to carry corn, beans, and chickens, also requisitioned illegally, to feed mining gangs—with selling or gambling away slaving licenses, and with themselves enslaving, branding, and sending to the mines numbers of Indians. He also gave refuge to harassed Indian principales from the encomiendas of the absent Cortés, to whom he wrote deploring "this Babylon." When the oidores violated sanctuary to seize the native leaders, then had a Franciscan, denouncing the judges' conduct as sacrilegious, pulled from the pulpit in mid-sermon, Zumárraga marched through the city of Mexico with cross aloft and draped in black, surrounded by his fellow friars, and placed the capital under interdict. Although the oidores intercepted several of his letters denouncing them to the crown, he managed to smuggle one out. It was instrumental in bringing about their dismissal.[40]

The bishop found the second audiencia and Mendoza much more satisfactory. And although named an executor in Cortes' will, he came to favor Mendoza over the conqueror. The second audiencia used the tasaciones he drew up, stipulating tribute to be paid by certain Indian communities, as precedent for their own assessments.[41] Zumárraga also worked closely with the oidores, and later Mendoza, to establish cultural institutions. He and the viceroy jointly sponsored the Franciscan Colegio de Santa Cruz de Tlatelolco, the school for noble Indian boys modeled on Gante's of San José. They secured the importation of a printing press, and they urged a university be founded. The bishop also opened the Hospital del Amor de Dios (Hospital of God's Love), popularly known as the Hospital de las Bubas, to treat venereal disease. He encouraged Indian *cofradías*, sodalities, in native churches, founded other schools for Indian boys and convent schools for Indian girls, and wanted one of each established in every cabecera. He urged girls be taught selected Indian and Spanish domestic arts and, most important, the Christian practice of monogamous marriage in houses "where they can live and may escape the accursed lechery of the caciques."[42] That is, all such schools, actual and projected, were to make use of indigenous elements but to emphasize Spanish religion and cultural components.

Working with Pedro de Gante, Motolinía, and other religious, and in correspondence with Francisco de Vitoria, the bishop strove to protect the Indians up to the point where royal authority and Spanish settlement were not endangered. He praised Indian abilities and virtues, and the dedication to indigenous welfare of Las Casas, who reciprocated in kind. He thought encomienda necessary, however, and he held one himself—and both black and Indian slaves as well.[43] Zumárraga also opposed enforcement of the New Laws, as did the majority of the clergy, supporting Mendoza's decision not to implement them. He condemned abuse of Indians, but not the Spanish right to insist that the natives work. The land needed Spaniards, he informed the king in unquestionably organic terms, "as the flesh of the human body needs bones, to sustain it."[44] Spaniards could give Indians examples of Christian goodness, be to them as fathers to sons, and protect them from the devil, whose evil influence he, Motolinía, and other friars found to be real and omnipresent.

Zumárraga, too, accepted predominant notions concerning social and political organization, and on more than one occasion employed similes then in vogue attesting to a habit of corporate thinking. He also compared the *república*, the political body or state, of New Spain to the human body. Its head was the monarch, the Spaniards its arms. "The head must give strength to the arms and they must defend the head and body of the republic." The Indians, here implicitly part of that organism but with their anatomical position unidentified, should know that the king loved them as a lord and father, just as he did the Spanish, and that he treated them as true vassals. The bishop, like other royal appointees, intended to make certain the Indians knew they were royal subjects rather than vassals of resident Spaniards.

As did his brother Franciscans, Zumárraga initially took inspiration from current European social ideals—from the resurgence of faith in man's natural propensity to good and in the efficacy of education, and from how closely Indian life conformed to mendicant ideals. His outlook, mirroring those of Gante and Motolinía, was Christian, ecumenical, and sanguine. In 1539 he urged the Spanish monarch, who complied, to seek out Vitoria's pupils for missionary work in Mexico.[45] He praised as virtues Indian poverty, simplicity, and malleability and sanctioned the friars' use of native languages and indigenous customs to further morality, loyalty to the monarch, and conversion to Christianity. He was an elitist but no racist, as evidenced, for example, by his request that Christianized Moslem artisans be sent to Mexico from Spain.

In the last years before the schism of Western Christianity brought Roman Catholicism to a more rigid doctrine and a defensive stance, Zumárraga is a striking example of those Spaniards who introduced in Mexico adaptations of religious ideas and practices later forbidden but in the 1520s most closely associated with the Christian humanism of northern Europe then in vogue in Spain, where it was most popularly disseminated in the writings of Erasmus. The bishop, like Gante, had faith in the power of all intellects. Initially he wanted the Bible translated into Mexican and distributed to the populace. And whether he wrote or simply sponsored them, his name appeared on the title pages of the *Doctrina breve*, written to instruct priests, and the *Doctrina cristiana*, a catechism for Indians, both published in Mexico in the 1540s. At a time when Erasmism was suspect in Spain, all of the manual and the second part of the catechism were unacknowledged selections from the *Enchiridion* and the *Paracelsis* of Erasmus. Taken from Spanish versions, these excerpts were even more selective. Clearly Zumárraga admired Erasmus' literary style and his reforming spirit. He approved of the emphasis on return to the orthodoxy of a Christlike life and faith. These manuals repeated Erasmus' favorable opinion of the doctrine of interior Christianity, and denounced as he did the poor quality of the scholasticism then dominant in education. But the Mexican books did not reproduce the passages deriding the mendicants, condemning excesses in practices and ceremonies, or accepting classic philosophers within Christian tradition.[46]

The borrowings were in accord with the Spanish tendency to temper Erasmian insistence on the godlike nature of man with the more traditionally Christian view of the corruption of human nature offered by Augustine; they were also consonant with Aquinas' softening of the doctrine of original sin toward a concept explaining human weakness. Even so, Protestant emphasis on faith and interior Christianity, the discussions at Trent, and Inquisitional activity in Spain, cast suspicion of heresy on individuals who read the Scriptures or who attempted to find their own relationship with God.

The Lutheran movement in Charles' northern lands had begun to bring official reaction in Spain in the mid-1520s. There the liberal and reforming Christianity of Erasmus, its emphasis on individual belief and on both meditation and intellectualism, its advocates, and its contiguity to German schismatics, came under scrutiny of the Inquisition. Zumárraga left Spain at the height of the vogue for Erasmus and before the doctrinal climate stiffened. Yet in Mexico he, too, parted ways with Erasmus and the liberal Christianity he represented. In Zumárraga's case it was where Spanish interests and humanistic universalism diverged. In addition the bishop came on occasion to sanction the use of physical coercion decried by the Dutch humanist.

In the years from 1545 to 1563, during which the Council of Trent sat, ideas that would come to be suspect, at the least, and books stating them, circulated relatively freely in Mexico. The full machinery of the Inquisition was not introduced until 1571; before that time friars and then bishops included it among their functions. This relative freedom in comparison to the situation in Spain indicated less a more liberal intellectual climate with a positive commitment to freer thought than an understanding that idolatry, as the principal threat to Catholicism in Mexico, required different remedies than did heresy in Europe. It also reflected the more optimistic spirit and greater moral commitment of some Spaniards placed in a new and simpler setting, one still institutionally fluid, to improve all society by persuasion—if possible and before resorting to force.

Through his commission as Inquisitor, Zumárraga kept in line fractious natives and Europeans as well. Through public example—by sentences for blasphemy, bigamy, concubinage, sorcery, and sexual deviance from Spanish norms—he warned both those who did and those who would that respect for the sacred and the moral, and for the authority upholding them, was a social imperative. In this spirit, for example, he restrained the erring clergy—among them one Diego Díaz, parish priest at Ocuituco who had come to Mexico with Cortés on his return from Spain in 1530. Díaz had the bad sense, as cleric in the bishop's own encomienda community, so to conduct himself as to be called before the Inquisition three times, charged with solicitation of women in the confessional and with bribing witnesses to accuse the local cacique of idolatry. Zumárraga also brought to trial twenty cases of sorcery, fifteen of them against women of various ethnic backgrounds. He heard accusations of divination, of dispensing potions to attract lovers and husbands, of practicing medicine mixed with black magic and astrology, all attesting to a thriving climate of superstition and folk religion within the Christian façade of all sectors of Mexican society. His sentences were relatively lenient. Díaz was at first allowed to return to his parish, and the sentences for sorcery—limited to combinations of penance, whippings, fines, prison, and banishment—were mild for the period. Zumárraga also tried, and fined, a self-proclaimed reader of Erasmus, but only for making unorthodox remarks. These penalties reflect a worldly-wise understanding of human foibles and an intent to admonish rather than to punish harshly, to keep smooth the surface of a Spanish Christian society rather than vainly attempt to maintain a rigid conformity.[47] By its presence the Inquisition attested to official sanction for public ceremony and conformity, and to a desire to discourage private searchings for God.

Zumárraga tolerated elements of various cultures but only one faith. As Inquisitor on occasion he prosecuted Europeans as Judaizers or Lutherans and, as time went on, he tended increasingly toward a counter-Reformation mentality. He feared particularly Indian paganism and traditional sexual practices, and he came to see in the persisting advocacy by Indian leaders of the cults of the old gods and the old customs not simply backsliding but a growing threat to both the faith and Spanish control. His attitude is a reminder that the Inquisition functioned in Mexico, as it had in the Spain of Isabella and Ferdinand, as a political instrument within an ideological climate where patriotism and orthodoxy were inseparable. Initially, he wrote of and treated Indians in general as tender plants, susceptible to disease from within and without—that is, from Indian paganism and Spanish vices. But he came to look on some of the plants as baleful weeds, to excoriate the continuance of the old habits and their propagation by chieftains. To the crown he lamented the caciques' immoral and lascivious behavior, especially their habit of taking as many young girls as they wished for sexual and domestic service. In his customary caustic fashion he admitted to stalemate in moral reform: "I see no other remedy except possibly to hang most of the caciques, who today do worse in secret than before they heard of the Catholic faith and the gospel."[48]

In 1539, aware of poor crops, the resurgence of the cult of the rain god, Tlaloc, and fearing the possibility of an Indian conspiratorial network and widespread native revolt, Zumárraga made an example of an aristocratic idolator, Don Carlos Chichimecatecuhtli (Ometochtzin), tlatoani of Texcoco and scion of its great kings, Nezahualcoyotl and Nezahualpilli. Although he had been raised in Cortés' household and educated by Gante and at the Franciscan colegio at Tlatelolco, that prince now had the additional and unhappy distinction of becoming one of the very few Indians in Mexico, and the last one, to be burned at the stake on sentence of the Inquisition.[49]

The illustrious cacique was accused of idolatry and stirring up Indians in the region around the city of Mexico, of insisting that friars were licentious, given to concubinage, and prone to punish Indians for things they allowed to Spaniards. Concubinage he declared a true Indian tradition. His brother's widow, María, testified Carlos had fitted practice to theory in forcing her to have sexual intercourse with him. Most germane to his unusually harsh sentence, he was said to have attacked Spanish authority in Mexico and to have declared himself and other indigenous leaders true señores, saying, "This is our land and our treasure, our jewel and our possession, and dominion belongs to us."[50] His sentence by Zumárraga was approved by Mendoza; his execution was a public spectacle.

Zumárraga was bishop of Mexico until 1547, when he was named archbishop. He died in 1548. Initially he had brought liberal Christian theory of the sort associated with Erasmus to bear in Mexican society. Yet at the same time, and increasingly, his activities and correspondence reflected a strong current of reforming Spanish Franciscan tradition including elements of mysticism and violence.[51] At bottom, his was the militant faith expressed in the fortified sixteenth-century Franciscan monasteries, uniquely Spanish and constructed to endure. Spanish, too, was his insistence that to him temporal situation mattered less than eternal salvation. He chided friars who put attachment to earthly patria above the greater and more permanent rewards of life eternal. He insisted that, if they would achieve fame and glory, they must first face death working for the name and glory of Christ. As archbishop-elect, at eighty, he vainly sought royal permission to sail to China as a missionary friar.

Zumárraga's avowed patriotism was otherworldly, his loyalty to the Spanish monarch intense. Again, the Cisnerian type of mentality makes what now may seem an inherent contradiction understandable. He referred to Charles V as king and lord and, in 1544, he wrote to Prince Philip of Charles as "champion of the Catholic faith and the reform of the Church. . . . Under his *imperio* barbarous nations will be removed from the señorío of the Devil and placed beneath the Christian standard."[52] The statement encompassed his political thought. Zumárraga not only assumed that royal and religious purposes were identical but also sought to effect both through his own simultaneous religious and civil administration. Thus in 1532 he wrote that he had sent visitadores to investigate Spanish mistreatment of Indians "so that God and Your Majesty may be served and the land and natives conserved in your justice."[53] Elsewhere, he stated the friars thought it better that Indians and Spaniards appeal to royal protection rather than to arms, so that the land become pacified, Roman Catholicism augmented, and the populace controlled. In short, Zumárraga's administration helped to impart a theocratic, imperial cast to Mexican institutions in their formative period.

How little distance separated all civil and religious administration in terms of royal policy was demonstrated in 1536 when a layman, lawyer, and member of the second audiencia, Vasco de Quiroga, was named first bishop of Michoacán. Quiroga was a living compendium of the prominent, more liberal currents of his period. We have noted his work as an oidor. More attention to his attitudes and activities will be instructive in delineating Mexican adaptations of renaissance Christianity, and their limitations. As we have seen, shortly after his arrival in Mexico, Quiroga founded the hospital village of Santa Fe on the outskirts of the capital. There hundreds of Indians were housed, cared for, indoctrinated, and educated, much as in Gante's school, in skills and as interpreters and aides to missionaries. In Michoacán Quiroga sponsored another hospice community near Pátzcuaro. On both villages he imposed regulations adapted from the description of ideal communal life in *Utopia*, recently published by Erasmus' friend and fellow humanist, Thomas More, counselor to the king of England and steadfast Catholic. Quiroga had borrowed the 1518 edition, bound with Erasmus' *Epigrammata,* from Zumárraga.[54]

Quiroga stated views concerning the Indians similar to those of the Franciscans. He extolled their natural simplicity, compared it to that of the primitive church, and declared that they lacked only the faith to be true and perfect Christians. He condemned Spanish slave-raiding and established his Pátzcuaro community of Sante Fe de la Laguna to resettle Tarascans who had fled from Nuño de Guzmán's expedition there. In his ordinances for "la República del Hospital" he decreed common ownership of property, integration into large "families," a six-hour working day, no luxuries, distribution of the fruits of common labor according to need, and a *principal* to be chosen from members of every four extended families. This *pater familias* was to govern through persuasion and love, not rigor and fear, yet to enforce a moderate regimen of work. In writing to the crown, Quiroga reiterated the oft-stated conviction of Spaniards in Mexico that Indians must be made to work in order to correct a laziness resulting from easy living in a rich land. As oidor he had striven to counter this tendency, and paganism and vagabondage as well, by conscripting natives to construct his first hospital-village. As bishop he followed the same procedure, and in Pátzcuaro he also had Indians labor on the cathedral which, with sublime disregard for local needs and abilities, he attempted to construct on a plan similar to Saint Peter's in Rome.

In brief, Quiroga endeavored to civilize Indians in accord with ideals associated with Christian humanism, of combined classical and Christian derivation, and inspired in part—as were the friars—by how closely communal Indian life conformed to that of the primitive church, the Christian golden age. It is not surprising that contemporaries compared his Michoacán hospital-village to a combined monastery and nunnery; More's *Utopia* has received similar comment. Quiroga's purpose was to provide natives with a social organization and a practical economic base derived from European ideals and in harmony with Indian customs, as he perceived them. Apparently he succeeded, for the villages became self-supporting, even prosperous. We have seen that, as oidor, he had also sought to preserve Indian usage where he thought Spanish law unsuitable or in accord. As bishop he founded in Michoacán the Colegio de San Nicolás, primarily as a seminary to educate both Spaniards and Indians. Its graduates were to disseminate Roman Catholicism, its rector to be Spanish and to exercise supreme authority over the hospital-villages. The community of Laguna was to, and did, support the rector and also several priests graduated from that school.

Quiroga respected Indian culture but subordinated it to Spanish. By mid-century he was also among the majority of clergy favoring a general repartimiento of Indians. Essentially, he remained as he began, a royal administrator, until he died in 1565 in (at least) his late eighties. As bishop his memory was, and it remains, revered by Indians in Michoacán, where as Tata Vasco he came to exemplify the patriarchal image his work helped to attach to Spanish authority. (In this century he has come from regional to national historical importance as a humanitarian figure ennobling the

Spanish past in Mexico, in part because put forth as a corrective to the tendency of nineteenth-century liberals, and of supporters of the Revolution of 1910, to deprecate the peninsular heritage.)

The continuing confluence of religious interest in Indian welfare, of belief in Indian abilities, and of humanistic idealism, allied to royal service and religious purpose, was further exemplified in the career of the relative latecomer, Alonso de la Vera Cruz, a secular priest and former student of Francisco de Vitoria who, at the age of thirty, took the Augustinian habit shortly after arriving in Mexico in 1537. His work indicates how the liberal Christian tradition, and the pro-Indian stance it supported, flowed into and was displaced by a revitalized scholasticism in Mexico as in Spain, and how on both sides of the Atlantic philosophers protecting Indians also thought and acted in strong support of Spanish imperial monarchy and culture.

Vera Cruz first taught reading and writing to Indian and Spanish boys in the Augustinian school in the capital, conforming to royal orders to teach Castilian, then founded a colegio for higher studies, primarily for seminarians, in Michoacán, at Tiripitío, in the 1540s. In 1542 he took charge of that episcopal see in the absence of Quiroga. He learned Tarascan, founded monasteries, refused a bishopric, and probably graduated from his school several Indians who became Augustinians. When the University of Mexico opened in 1553, he taught Thomistic theology there, lecturing on the Epistles of Paul, a text esteemed by Christian humanists, to students from Spain and from various sectors of Mexican society. He returned to Spain in the 1560s to argue at court, with success, that Indians were beset by economic woes and should not be tithed. There, that is, he carried on, in the tradition of Las Casas and Vitoria, in behalf of American natives. [55]

A comparison of Vera Cruz with the earlier pro-Indian religious is illustrative of more general changes in both Spanish liberal and royal mentalities. Vera Cruz brought to New Spain a reforming zeal, connected both to scholastic revival and humanistic ideals, a zeal he later vented within a framework of renovative Aristotelian philosophy and theology. Not only schooled by Vitoria but also a Thomist in his own right, he relied on both experience and systematized thought to find solutions for the problems of the new Mexican society and its relations to Spain. In a sermon in 1554 he went beyond Vitoria in asserting, concerning the Spanish monarch's dominion over the country and the Indians, that the sole royal title lay in the fact that "Indians want to be subordinate [to the Spanish crown] and consider it an honor." [56] This statement implicitly opposed encomienda, Indian slavery and personal service to Spaniards, Spanish title based on papal donation, and individual Spanish claims to dominion by right of conquest or because of a religious or civilizing mission. His argument not only reflected the advance made in subjugating Indians to royal authority but also gave the crown support for a more secular-based theory justifying imposing direct political authority over the native populace, and to Spaniards an attendant obligation to free such fellow subjects and treat them well. Vera Cruz was in the forefront of a hardening climate of religious and political thought, manifest under Philip II in renascent, self-assured scholasticism and a more consolidated imperial outlook, and firmly resting on earlier hypotheses of right, now become ideological certainties—but this is to get ahead of ourselves.

Instead, a general survey of relations of the clergy in Mexico with society and ideology during Charles' reign is in order. Although from 1530 until mid-century the clergy and royal officials in New Spain in a broad sense reinforced one another's authority, from the 1520s on there was some dissension between the two groups and among the clergy themselves. In the fissiparous 1520s churchmen at times moderated between contending factions of Spaniards. Thus Juan (or Julián) Garcés, bishop of Tlaxcala, attempted to mediate between Cortés and Velásquez.[57] They also on occasion took sides, as we have seen. Tensions between Franciscans and Dominicans centered on loyalty to Cortés in this decade but were also in part attributable to competition in delimiting areas for conversion, an ongoing cause of friction. Moreover, members of the two orders differed in attitudes toward Indian abilities and treatment. Disagreement on questions of Indian intelligence, especially, had definite religious and political implications in Mexico as in Spain, for on their answers, it will be recalled, depended the more specific issue of whether or not the natives were competent to be Christians and royal subjects.

Las Casas was thus a prominent example, but only a single one, of ways in which the debate on Indian rationality spanned the Atlantic. Franciscans as a group thought and insisted that Indians were inferior to Spaniards only because of environment and the work of the devil, not naturally inferior through innate character or lack of ability. Dominicans ranged widely in opinion, from Las Casas who insisted upon the natives' rationality and right to local self-government (under the crown), to the leader of the first Dominican contingent in Mexico, Tomás Ortíz, who is said to have declared, "I will affirm that God has never created a race more full of vice and without the least mixture of kindness or culture. . . . The Indians are more stupid than asses and refuse to improve in anything."[58] Initially, too, the first Dominican Provincial, Domingo de Betanzos, insisted the natives were beasts, not men, an opinion that brought him afoul of the second audiencia.[59]

Most of the clergy appreciated Indian abilities but also Spanish needs. Thus Las Casas was among the few who supported in toto the New Laws of 1542, the other bishops and the orders favoring royal control rather than abolition of encomienda.[60] His contrary stance irritated some of the others, particularly, once again, Motolinía: "Truly, for the few canons Las Casas has studied, he presumes a great deal, and his disorder seems very great and his humility small, and he thinks that everyone else is wrong and that he is right."[61] Yet we have seen that, whatever their internal disputes, the regular clergy in Mexico strongly supported the Spanish crown.

Moreover, in the 1530s and thereafter, the regular clergy themselves gained increasing religious and civil power and administrative authority over Indians. Each order staked out definite areas and communities to supervise, independent of the regional bishops.[62] In addition, most of the bishops appointed under Charles were themselves friars. Usually supported by the bishops, by royal policy, and by papal fiat, and allied with native officials, the friars became virtual governors of numerous Indian villages, directing their societies and economies. By mid-century, the religious had become established and had gained power and often its material accoutrements. The initial mendicant zeal for austerity and reform was waning. Large numbers of regular clergy had arrived in the 1540s, and secular clergy were arriving, uneducated—as was customary before the Council of Trent decreed seminary training mandatory. Although at first relatively few, these secular priests gained notoriety for their lack of missionary enthusiasm and of devotion to duty. Not only Las Casas but Mendoza, too, complained of them. Zumárraga thought their morals deplorable. Martín de Hojacastro, a Franciscan and bishop of Tlaxcala in the 1540s, declared them ignorant, listless, and greedy "idiots and fugitives."[63]

Other bishops, Vasco de Quiroga among them, by the 1550s were also on occasion censuring the arrogance and independence of the regular clergy. José López de Zarate, bishop of Oaxaca, in 1551 complained the Dominicans were "virtual lords" who did not respect his authority, so that neither did their Indian charges.[64] In 1554 the archbishop, Alonso de Montúfar, a Dominican, correctly accused regular clergy of taking the funds of certain Indian communities and of impeding official church receipts of Indian tithes.[65]

At mid-century, conflict between bishops and friars centered on this key issue of episcopal tithes. Spaniards paid some tithes. The bishops, of course, again including Vasco de Quiroga, wanted tithing imposed directly upon Indians. The crown had so ordered in 1543–44. Zumárraga had collected some tithes from caciques. But friars, and particularly some of the older religious vehemently opposed it, among them Motolinía and Alonso de la Vera Cruz, Motolinía and other Franciscans insisting Indians could not support the tax, pointing to their decreased numbers and poverty, and censuring civil and ecclesiastical officials for permitting their continuing exploitation. Vera Cruz in 1555 in his *De Decimis* argued Indians should not pay tithes for there was no need of bishops in the New World, that the royal vicarate as exercised through regular clergy sufficed. Montúfar, who was also at odds with more liberal Dominicans, declared Vera Cruz a heretic and, in 1558, denounced him to the Inquisition. The Augustinian's effective appeal at court in the 1560s was not hurt by his strong argument buttressing royal authority.[66] Meanwhile, friars denounced Montúfar for opposing the visita of Diego Ramírez and, where they had praised the second audiencia, now accused oidores of abusing Indians.[67] They supported Velasco in his dispute with the audiencia. The viceroy, nonetheless, did join the oidores in complaining of mendicant power over Indians, of friars meddling in civil affairs and launching outsized building programs.[68]

The crown reacted to both mendicant and episcopal affluence, decreeing in the New Laws that churchmen were not to hold encomiendas, and, in a cédula of 1549, ordered the Franciscan bishop of Oaxaca to cease troubling natives with his flocks and ranches.[69] In 1557 the outline of Philip's policy could be discerned in a royal decree designed to increase episcopal authority and to limit religious construction. It stipulated that bishops must approve new mendicant establishments.[70] Yet although the crown sought tighter and more hierarchical church organization in New Spain, the royal alliance with the regular clergy held. When bishops, angered by the refusal of friars to collect tithes, attempted to place secular priests in mendicant jurisdictions, the crown issued a restraining order.[71]

By the end of Charles' reign, then, as institutions solidified, missionary zeal dwindled, Spaniards increased and Indians declined, cooperation had lessened and competition risen within the clergy as well as among lay officials and between churchmen and civil appointees. Yet the squabbling of clergy among themselves and with civil authorities and lay Spaniards, and despite royal attempts to circumscribe their growing affluence and autonomy, perhaps also strengthened royal power by increasing reliance of churchmen on the monarch as mediator in their quarrels as in all social problems. And the friars and bishops never forgot to address the king as effective source of their power and prerogatives.

Regardless of such social friction, churchmen and particularly the regular clergy became and remained a potent force in maintaining Spanish dominance in New Spain. A royal order of 1528 commended to the clergy in Mexico what it was then shouldering, a joint responsibility with the civil government for the Indians.[72] Zumárraga and the religious were not slow to exercise their authority. The friars moved outward from the capital, keeping pace with, and sometimes leading, lay Spanish explorers and conquerors, their very presence a reminder of the interconnection of Spanish domination and Christianity. By 1530 one bishop appointed the Mexican audiencia and another presided over it. Ecclesiastics sat with officials in consultative, policy-making juntas. Encomenderos were ordered to have clerics in their pueblos, each cabecera to have a church, and the first administrative division of New Spain was made in the form of bishoprics. Four Church provinces were then designated: Mexico, Tlaxcala (including

Puebla), Michoacán, and Oaxaca.[73] Until the late eighteenth century the regional authority most in evidence remained that of the church; civil government in New Spain lacked similar subdivision. Mexicans became accustomed to say that they lived in such and such a (church) province.

The friars had little direct control, in relation to later church influence in all Mexican society, on the first generation of Spanish settlers. For the most part they impinged upon it only indirectly, through relations with Indians. It should be recalled, however, that friars, including the bishops Garcés and Zumárraga, in the 1520s played roles in the factional disputes among Spaniards. In the 1530s, regular clergy offered primary education to Spanish children, sometimes together with those of Indians and, in the 1550s, at the opening of the University of Mexico, founded primarily for American-born Spaniards, Alonso de la Vera Cruz and other religious were among the first professors. A few conquistadors were sufficiently influenced by religion to become friars, among them Alonso de Aguilar and Jacinto de San Francisco. The latter arrived with Cortés, gained an encomienda and over five hundred slaves, and then, after a narrow escape from hostile Indians, joined the Franciscans and urged that natives be converted by persuasion only.[74]

Spaniards of the conquest generation did pay tithes, usually in pigs and sheep, and were also made aware of clerical authority at church, at public ceremonies and festivals, and through hospitals and the prominence of religious foundations. Perhaps they felt most poignantly the ministrations and authority of the bishops—particularly when exposed to ecclesiastics functioning as Inquisitors. Friar-Inquisitors, too, stand as exceptions to the general lack of direct relations between regular clergy and Spaniards. Even immediately after the conquest the Inquisition exercised by friars touched a few Spaniards and undoubtedly influenced many more. Under the Domincan Inquisitor Vicente de Santa María, in 1528 two partisans of Cortés were burned as Judaizers. A year before, under Betanzos, the wealthy octogenarian Rodrigo Rangel (or Rengel)—another supporter of Cortés, a leading conquistador, and a regidor of the ayuntamiento of Mexico, recently enriched after a campaign against the Zapotecs and suffering from advanced syphilis—was denounced as a dirty old man and found guilty of blasphemy, having been indiscreet enough as, for example, to have called the Virgin a *puta* or whore.[75] Such cases perhaps best illustrate Dominican enmity toward Cortés, the pitfalls of wealth, and the fact that the swearing of oaths has usually accompanied military activity— particularly among men afflicted with painful syphilitic tumors. Zumárraga, although he used the tribunal in a less partisan manner, also wielded it as an instrument of church and state control of resident Europeans.

Bishops, too, were community-makers. Quiroga's Indian hospital-villages are a case in point, as is the sponsorship by Bishop Garcés, in conjunction with Motolinía and the audiencia, of the mixed Spanish and mestizo settlement of Puebla.[76] But friars were the founders par excellence of new towns planned to recongregate Indians, and thereby able to support Spanish settlement as well. Friars mediated in local government and society, and also between Indians and encomenderos or corregidores or both. Within Indian villages, they acted as royal representatives and watchdogs, periodically informing the monarch of the state of affairs, as we have seen, assuming it their duty "to guard the royal conscience."[77] Although on occasion causing or supporting Indian factionalism, they more often, at least at first, taught the concept of Christian brotherhood in an effort to allay divisiveness.[78] Frequently having gathered the Indians for indoctrination into villages, these missionaries then became the true local political authorities and overseers of economic life. Thus they acted as intermediaries between Indians and the government, introducing the natives to Spanish administrative organization and giving the king and his officials selected information on their flock. As the conquest expanded, it was the clergy who continued to settle and hold the frontiers in this fashion. Ultimately, their protection and Christianizing of Indians, preserving the work force, enabled Spanish settlement and continuing dominion. By mid-century it was evident, too, that Charles thought of the clergy, rather than the encomenderos, corregidores, or alcaldes mayores, as the most trustworthy royal agents at local level in the Indies.

The clergy, however, like the crown, evidenced no desire to integrate Spanish and Indian communities. Many of the friars came to believe mixed towns would expose Indians to Spanish vices and preferred to unite Europeans and natives only theoretically, as royal subjects. They worked to keep Indians socially and politically apart from Spaniards—although seeing to it that elements of Spanish culture pervaded almost every aspect of Indian life. One early exception to the church stand for segregation, however, was an insistence that Spaniards living with Indian women marry them.[79] And friars schooled offspring of Spanish and Indian unions. Thus, despite official church and state political theory, in culture and bloodlines Spanish-Indian intermingling, *mestizaje,* begun with the conquest, was initially sanctioned by specific church ordinances.

The friars, nuns, and women associated with religious orders had a monopoly on Indian schooling, and most of them vigorously pursued formal education of Indians in Christianity, in Spanish ways, and in obedience to the crown.[80] We know friars staffed schools for boys, some for boys and girls, and that most outstanding of all such early schools were Gante's San José and the Colegio de Santa Cruz. At the Tlatelolco school, a unique and continuing process of cultural interchange took place. Indian boys, entering at ages eight to fourteen, learned Latin, rhetoric, logic, and philosophy, as well as religion, some gaining the equivalent of a European secondary and humanistic education. At the same time, they helped friars to preserve prehispanic indigenous tradition and history. The Franciscans Andrés de Olmos and Bernardino de Sahagún, among others, there taught Latin to Indians and learned Nahuatl from them. With the aid of students they also gathered and set down information on native life and history and on the Indian view of the conquest.

Olmos, who had investigated reports of witches with Zumárraga in Pamplona and had come to Mexico with him in 1528, learned to speak possibly ten indigenous languages and wrote, taught, and preached in them. In 1530, on the request of Ramírez de Fuenleal and Martín de Valencia, he founded a mission in Pánuco, among peoples devastated by Spanish slavers. Olmos wrote a huge book concerning Indian antiquities, its purpose to know Indian tradition in order better to refute what appeared evil in it to Spaniards, and to ascertain what Indian customs were worth preserving. Thus, although some friars and bishops, including Zumárraga, destroyed many Indian manuscripts in their initial zeal to eradicate the old faith and its foundations, some also preserved indigenous traditions and histories, if through a Spanish filter. Olmos also wrote books, including grammars and dictionaries, in Mexican, Huastecan, and Totonacan to aid in explaining Spanish religion to Indians, and he translated the Epistles and gospels into Mexican. His chronicle was based on pictographs belonging to Indian leaders of Mexico, Texcoco, and Tlaxcala, and on conversations with native elders. Although now lost, it served as a basis for nearly all subsequent accounts. Sahagún, arriving in 1529, by mid-century was embarked on what would be a mammoth compendium of native civilization and its conquest.[81]

Extremely important to the sort and degree of impact that the clergy made on Mexican society were the attitudes toward non-European peoples exhibited by the missionaries and early bishops. Here, as evidenced by Gante, Zumárraga, Motolinía, Ramírez de Fuenleal, Olmos, and Quiroga, among others, the clergy's exposure to certain concepts characteristic of renaissance Europe shaped the form and content of their work. They came to New Spain within a mental world in part patterned by exposure to Christian reform, to humanistic studies, ideals, and techniques, to a concomitant renaissance optimism concerning human nature, and to notions of universal Christian brotherhood favored by humanists, especially Erasmus, and consonant with older Spanish legal and political theory which assumed a single human society subdivided into peoples or nations. Their own backgrounds helped to shape the way in which clerics of Christocentric faith perceived and indoctrinated Indians. Franciscans and some Dominicans and Augustinians viewed Indians as, though pagan and barbarian, yet noble through innocence, in many ways purer and less corrupt than Spaniards, and living proper communal lives. Indigenous circumstances, to men accepting the world view of Christian universalism, appeared miraculously appropriate, with some education in faith and morality, to the formation of a new and better Indian society and to its incorporation into Christianity under clerical supervision and imperial aegis. It was in this frame of mind that Gante taught, Motolinía proselytized and wrote, and Zumárraga reportedly observed that while some Spaniards in Mexico stank, the Indians gave off a heavenly aroma.[82] This outlook encouraged friars to preserve Indian languages and traditions, and humanism provided critical techniques abetting writing catechisms and presenting scripture in native tongues often reflecting liberal Christian beliefs. It also fostered an intellectual curiosity conducive to what has been called the collecting instinct—to gathering information on preconquest life and history and on Mexican flora and fauna. The ecumenical frame of reference aided their own adaptation to a new environment and non-European peoples. Many of them came to admire and even love both. It also contributed greatly to cultural syncretism. And although Christian liberalism and humanism came into disrepute by mid-century, the alliance between regular clergy and Indians continued, supported by the traditional millenary ideals predating Spanish liberalism and advocated by some of the older Franciscans such as Gerónimo de Mendieta.[83] And among the older friars, ties developed with land and peoples through long residence.

The presence of non-Spanish missionaries, particularly among the early Franciscans, assured the continuing contact of Spanish friars and of Indians with men bringing broader European norms and values to bear on spiritual and imperial consolidation. In addition to Gante and his two companions, outstanding were the Frenchmen, their names hispanized to Jacobo de Testera (or Tastera), Juan de Gaona, and Juan Focher or Fucher, the Fleming Nicolás de Witte, and Jacobo de Dacio or Daciano, a Dane. All were prominent as linguists, teachers, and missionaries. Witte and Dacio, as was Gante, were reputedly of royal blood. Dacio, learned in Greek and Hebrew, a refugee from the Protestants, was active among the Tarascans by 1525. Witte was an Augustinian and friend of Las Casas who worked on the frontiers. Gaona and Focher taught at the colegio at Tlatelolco when it opened in 1538. Both held doctorates from the University of Paris, where Gante's mentor and companion, Juan de Tecto, had been a professor of theology for fourteen years, and where Francisco de Vitoria had studied and lectured. Gaona, according to Motolinía, was an excellent Latinist and rhetorician, a good preacher and very deep theologian, and he knew some Greek. The library Gaona left in Burgos when he came to Mexico in 1538 included those humanistic staples, the Bible, Plato, and Erasmus. Focher lived in Mexico for over forty years. Lay and ecclesiastic authorities consulted him frequently on church law, to the point that his opinions established distinct Mexican norms concerning legal doctrine and procedure, especially in resolving conflicts between Indian and Spanish inheritance laws. Focher, and apparently most of the other non-Spanish friars as well, enthusiastically supported royal authority—most of them had come from Charles' Habsburg dependencies—Focher maintaining that royal decisions in ecclesiastical matters ought to be obeyed equally with those of the pope.[84]

By 1550 some disillusionment had set in and a withdrawal from the more radical spirit and ideals connected with Christian reform. Friars were less certain of the positive aspects of human nature and the limitless efficacy of education. Also apparent was growing clerical affluence in land, buildings, and requisition of native goods and services. Mendicancy was obviously diminishing. The clergy were discovering that conditions of tutelage impose their own limitations, and that human goodness does not preclude human weakness. Many strongly emphasized the importance to social cohesion of ceremony and conformity. A majority opposed the New Laws. Zumárraga in the 1540s found what he considered Indian lasciviousness ineradicable, and similar Spanish tendencies, coupled with arrogance, impeding God's work. He suggested that the Tlatelolco colegio be converted to a hospital, since even the best young grammarians—"boys of highest intellect"—would not learn sexual continence. Just as bad, he observed Indian girls taught by beatas being rejected, by males raised by friars, as lazy and disinclined "to serve husbands in customary ways." Here he found Castilian beatas at fault, for they refused to remain secluded, to lead pious lives of good example, or to obey their bishop. The world was too much with them all.[85]

Closely related was the changing attitude of the clergy to training a native priesthood. In Tlatelolco initially a few Indians began studies for the clergy. Zumárraga and other Franciscans then agreed with the decision of the 1538 council of bishops to ordain the most able Indians and mestizos, some few of whom became priests. In 1555, however, a Mexican church council, in accord with current sentiment at Trent, opposed a native clergy. Mendieta then spoke for the pro-Indianists, who obediently accepted official policy against a clergy of indigenous stock. He reflected a humanitarianism now able to distinguish individual differences among both Spaniards and Indians, coupling acceptance of the duality of human nature with a narrower, stricter belief in the necessity of countering evil by instilling principles of absolute submissiveness to authority. He was an example of a mentality coming to the fore at mid-century, one well-suited to perpetuating authoritarian institutions.[86]

Other decisions of the 1555 Mexican church council support the same conclusions. It ordered all printed matters to be examined, resulting in Inquisition censure and prohibition of Zumárraga's treatises and of the Tarascan grammars of the French Franciscan Maturino Gilberto.

Yet, a confluence of initial conditions—although changing by mid-century—had allowed the king to delegate combined civil and religious authority to clergy zealous for reform and exposed to the more mystic, pietistic, and liberal Christian currents of the day. This unique ambience had enabled missionaries who were intensely loyal both to the crown and to the ideal of a single human community made up of countless subdivisions to assume priestly functions and responsibility for bringing Indians under Spain. Parallels between European ideals and Indian reality had facilitated retaining much Indian social and political coherence while including the natives within an extended, essentially Spanish, political system. Spanish empire could and did encompass numerous nations. The missionaries greatly helped it to do so, aiding relatively few Spaniards—although often competing among themselves for authority over Indians—to control perhaps millions of Indians by teaching and maintaining submission to all authority. More specifically, the clergy introduced natives to Spanish imperial political organization as intrinsic to the world view of Christianity. "Blessed are the poor in spirit, the meek, the peaceful, and those who suffer for justice," read a popular catechism, obviously useful in instilling attitudes harmonious with belief in submission to the monarch as keeper of peace and purveyor of justice.[87]

The clergy carried out a broad cultural mission for Spain, introducing Spanish civilization, as they interpreted it, over but not in place of the indigenous cultures, keeping alive a variety of plural society and contributing to cultural syncretism. Through formal education the friars trained young natives in Spanish religion, morality, way of life, and government. But it was largely through informal education, through precept and regulating communal life, that the early churchmen reached all levels of Indian society and carried out royal orders to indoctrinate Indians in "our manner of government and good customs."[88] In short, by these means and through Spanish influence, observable in Indian dress, foodstuffs, and construction, in books, plays, social structure, and activity, in warfare, in economy, and in law, the church in Mexico sped cultural mestizaje.[89] Moreover, what the clergy did and how they did it set precedent and established tradition in Mexico. Mentally equipped with an ideology formed of the confluence of a centralizing Spain with Christian renaissance, they introduced and implanted theories and practices delineating and supporting social and political relationships within Mexico and with Spain. And perhaps equally important, Gante, Las Casas, Motolinía, Zumárraga, Quiroga, Vera Cruz, and others themselves became part of that Mexican tradition. By mid-century they were becoming founding fathers of an emerging, syncretic culture unique in Spanish America.

6

Spaniards into Spanish Americans

"I say that the least of the conquistadors"—wrote one of them, Alonso de Aguilar—"merited great reward, for at his own expense ... he gave the king so great a world as this."[1] Another, Bernal Díaz del Castillo, agreed, comparing the exploits of the Spanish conquistadors in Mexico to those of Alexander the Great and Julius Caesar.[2] Both men stated opinions reflecting attitudes common among the Spanish conquerors. They believed that having at the risk of their lives and fortunes placed the land under royal authority, as its conquering heroes they would continue to defend it and, in return, were entitled to control it and reap a goodly share of its material advantages. They were, they thought, its new *señores*. Seeing themselves in this light, after the fall of Tenochtitlán in 1521 the victors immediately began to construct their Spanish city of Mexico on the Aztec foundations and to seek gold—guided by Motecuhzoma's tribute rolls to those areas of highest yield.[3] By the 1530s, they had found gold scarce, silver mining and raising wheat and livestock potentially more profitable, but that, whatever the form of the spoils of conquest, wealth could be gained only through use of Indian labor. They also began to see that they and the crown differed on specifics of what political and social relationships should be among Indians, Spaniards, and the king.[4]

Cortés set the general tone for Spanish relations with Indians. Typical of the conquistador rationale was his report to the king that the natives of the Guanajos Islands, off Honduras, after thanking him for protecting them from Cuban slavers, "offered themselves to me as subjects and vassals of Your Highness. They asked me to decree how they might serve you. I commanded, in your name, that at present in these lands they should do much work, because in truth they can serve in no other way."[5] In this spirit, too, he introduced the institution of encomienda. Falling back on the traditions of reconquest Spain and of the Spanish Caribbean, and also citing Aztec precedent, Cortés, although unauthorized to do so, bestowed in the name of the crown provisional grants of Indian chiefs and their communities upon individual Spaniards. His grants said nothing of how encomenderos were to use Indian labor within them. He only told the recipients to contract with caciques, thereby avoiding the issue of whether or not such Spaniards were entitled to tribute and service, legally the prerogatives of señores. In practice, however, Spaniards assumed they were señores, and acted accordingly, collecting goods and services from Indians. By 1528, the king had accepted encomienda, and decided to focus on exercising royal authority juridically and directly over all Spaniards and Indians, and to reinforce that authority through alliance with religion. The church, under royal supervision, imposed tithes, most of them paid by encomenderos on Indian tribute received but not on services. The contest for power between king and Spaniards in Mexico went on, but it no longer involved encomendero right to Indian tribute. Royal policy was now to regulate tribute, to separate it from service, and to abolish the (untaxed) latter. King and Spaniards agreed on the need for Mexican prosperity; both wanted it in order to increase their own.

In his Ordinances of 1524, Cortés said he sought to organize New Spain as an ongoing concern, to preserve Indians, and to ensure permanent Spanish residence. Noting that many of the conquerors were homesick and talking of returning to Spain, he stipulated that encomenderos had to marry and to reside in New Spain for at least eight years in order to retain their grants of Indians. They should see to it that their Indians raised livestock, wheat, sugar, mulberry trees for silkworms, that is, they should develop crops and cattle for internal Mexican use and for export. He prodded other Spaniards to successful enterprise in all of these endeavors by taking the lead himself. By the 1530s, under the direction of encomendero-entrepreneurs Mexico was producing sufficient surplus to provision the Peruvian expedition, sending horses, ships, sugar, meat, "and twenty other things."[6]

Yet through the 1520s a military mentality bent on living off spoils of conquest predominated. Exports to Spain, aside from sugar, consisted largely of goods taken from the Indians—feathers, cotton, cochineal, and precious metals.[7] To the Caribbean islands, the leading item of trade was initially the Indians themselves. As governor of Pánuco, Nuño de Guzmán developed the illegal but profitable slave trade he found underway there, originally organized by Spaniards disappointed in their search for booty and mines.[8] From Pánuco slaves were sent to the Antilles in exchange for horses and cattle, or to the city of Mexico. Many encomenderos, including

Cortés, operated mines, either singly or in partnerships, and everywhere they collected from their encomienda communities either slaves held by Indians themselves or luckless maceguales (commoners) and children designated as such. They also purchased slaves captured in organized raids in Pánuco and elsewhere. Indian slavery was common, despite Cortés' ordinances forbidding indiscriminate slavery and decreeing that only prisoners of war and natives held as slaves by other Indians could, after being licensed and branded by his government, legally be held by Spaniards.[9] Cortés himself took mine slaves from his villages and sent Andrés de Tapia slave-raiding for more.

In this period the distinction between slaves and Indians in encomienda was usually one less of use than of circumstance. Although Cortés authorized encomenderos to negotiate with caciques for whatever commodities and services their people could reasonably provide, the first encomenderos instead wrested from their towns whatever they could, nor did they care how the burden was divided within the Indian communities.[10] Centering their energies on getting gold and later silver—although Cortés had stipulated that slaves were to work mines and Indians in encomienda were to labor to sustain them—encomenderos often ordered their Indian dependents to the mines, not to maintain other workers but to join mining gangs.[11] Encomenderos, forbidden to reside in their pueblos and usually preferring to live in the city of Mexico, placed over their Indians a general administrator or foreman, a *calpixque*. He was to collect "tribute" in foodstuffs, clothing, and labor, to make Indians sow, and to have them transport goods and produce, usually to mines, cattle ranches, or the city. Mining operations were under a salaried *minero*, herds initially left to the care of one or two Spanish *mozos*, or lads. Individual Spaniards, Cortés among them, counted from the outset on Indians to provide them with food and clothing for sale or estate use, and with labor in fields, on houses, and as *tamemes* (carriers). Cabildos, royal officials, and churchmen used Indians to build towns, churches, monasteries, roads, and to make up military levies.[12] Encomenderos can be viewed as entrepreneurs, employing other Spaniards often as managers and living on the wealth generated by encomienda enterprise.

Spanish life, government, and culture centered in the city of Mexico. Encomenderos, wherever their grants, sought to maintain a residence there. So did royal officials, most clergy, merchants, artisans, and emigrants from Spain in general. Spaniards marked off the central portion of the city for themselves, and from the four Indian *barrios*, districts, on its periphery and from the surrounding Valley of Mexico demanded labor to construct their capital. By 1525 there were 150 Spanish houses, by mid-century over 1500. In a city where Indians outnumbered Spaniards ten to one, the Europeans built turreted urban fortresses, with artillery embrasures, arches, and crenellations—proper dwellings for conquerors in residence. Untold numbers of urban Indians "paid tribute" until the 1560s by embellishing the Spanish city with private and public construction. A magnificent and grandiose urban center resulted, its private dwellings palatial, its public buildings initially more modest, the whole accurately reflecting the self-image of the conquerors of the Kingdom of New Spain.[13] They maintained horses, arms, and large households and thought of themselves as holders of the land primarily in a military sense, as a functioning aristocracy like that of the reconquest, when the people or nation was synonymous with "an army or pool from which the army could be mustered."[14]

A few Spanish women arrived with the conquistadors. Others came in the 1520s—with officials, among the early settlers, or when encomenderos, as ordered, sent for their wives or got new ones. When Cortés and Pedro de Alvarado married Spanish noblewomen in the mid 1520s, their wives brought other women "of gentle birth" to Mexico with them.[15] Among these ladies were seekers after encomendero-husbands and beatas, uncloistered "holy women," supposedly of lay but exemplary lives, affiliated with the Franciscans as a teaching sisterhood. The empress had dispatched them to teach Christian doctrine and household arts to aristocratic Indian girls. By mid-century, some women were among the Spanish vagrants.[16]

Cortés, the crown, and the church agreed that wives and teachers were necessary to stabilize and perpetuate this quasi-military, traditional society, that the family, in an extended sense, was its core unit, and that education was important in maintaining the mentality supporting social arrangements. The orders of Cortés and the crown to encomenderos to marry or send for wives are a case in point. And as the postconquest marriages of Cortés and Alvarado attest, aristocratic wives in their names and persons were a most important social link, that of one family to another, in the literal sense of joined forces. In such marriages, both husband and wife were aware that the standing enjoyed by a woman and her family had much to do with determining who a man was, with fixing his status and with generating esteem in the society that mattered to him.

Women in Spain and Spanish America in this period had few legal rights. Vitoria found the jurisdiction of husband over wife equivalent to that of monarch over subject and parents over children. They were by law dependent upon fathers and husbands, akin to minors. This juridical attitude is at least partially explained in terms of the perceived needs of a military society. Thus in the 1530s the crown ruled that although encomiendas could be inherited by women, the heiresses had to be married within the year so that their husbands when required could fulfill the encomendero duty of military service.[17] To a greater extent, however, lack of women's legal rights was a consequence of resurgent Roman law in the peninsula. Marriage in medieval Hispano-Christian law had formed the basis for society, and man and wife had equal rights in it. Residues of this tradition in custom during the early sixteenth century allowed more real latitude than law indicated.[18] Moreover, in a hierarchical society where all people were circumscribed by their birth, women enjoyed a good deal of their own status and esteem and undoubtedly those who were wives, mothers, or teachers, shared a sense of doing work important to the (highly valued) family, the community, and, ultimately, God. The memory of Isabella, militant exemplar, faithful wife, sagacious ruler, and devout Christian, provided rather exceptional but stimulating precept. In the same spirit, though less of a winner, was María de Mendoza, the comunero heroine who was the viceroy's sister. The best-known and most popular models for emulation were probably the idealized biographies of saints.

Wives of propertied Spaniards in Spain and Mexico often acted as administrative assistants caring for estates and, at times, as seconds in command. For such women the royal court set the standard. There, for example, in the absence of Charles from Spain, Mexican correspondence and appointments were overseen by his wife, the empress, Isabella of Portugal. The European wives of the less well-to-do often assisted their husbands at work. When the first printer in Mexico, Juan Pablos, died in 1540, his Andalusian widow, Jerónima Gutiérrez, carried on the family business. Spanish women in Mexico, however, were relatively few in the first decades after conquest, liaisons between Spaniards and Indian women frequent, but marriages rare, and recognition of offspring sporadic—of this, more later.

From 1525 to 1538 all Charles' European subjects could enter the Indies with royal license, and Flemings and Germans were permitted entry until 1549. Most non-Spaniards outside of the religious orders came as merchants. In addition, although excluded from New Spain by law, among them at mid-century were also a few Genoese, Portuguese, Englishmen, and at least one Scot—most with ties to merchants of Seville. Until then most foreigners were tolerated and prospered, with relatively little official hindrance or persecution for nonconformity. Moreover, by 1532 there were a number of unlicensed foreigners in the region. In that year Ramírez de Fuenleal asked the Inquisition to take steps against the increasing number of foreign merchants and corsairs, many engaged in smuggling in and out of ports, including San Juan de Ulúa and particularly ports on the Pacific and in Central America. Franciscans made the same request in 1552.[19] Yet under Charles very few non-Spanish Europeans were called in by the Holy Tribunal, although several of the Flemings involved in commerce and silver mining at Sultepec were tried for blasphemy and heresy by Zumárraga in 1540. One Juan Banberniguen, for example, a reader of Erasmus and the New Testament, confessed to heresy in admitting that he had denied the existence of purgatory and the real presence of Christ in the Eucharist. His sentence was lenient: penance and a fine. With Montúfar as Inquisitor, however, the climate changed, as evidenced by the trial and harsh sentence of the Englishman Robert Tomson, who had come to Mexico in 1555, for Lutheranism three years later.[20]

In the directing sector of early Mexican society, too, were men and women born in Spain but not fully accepted as Spaniards because of Jewish ancestry. New Christians were prominent at the court of Charles V in the 1520s and came to Mexico as clergy, lay men and women, and royal officials. Most of these conversos appear to have been true converts. They were frequently accepted socially by wealthier and better-educated Old Christians, less often by commoners.[21] The distinction of *New* Christian was in the main an emotional one, the Jewish ancestor often at least several generations back. Ferdinand, after all, had had Jewish forebears, and therefore so had Charles. In Mexico the royal treasurer, Alonso de Estrada, as a bastard son of Ferdinand was also of converso extraction. Cortés was associated with a number of New Christians in Mexico. Bernal Díaz stated Cortés was related to the commercially prominent converso Nuñez family.[22] And through his mother, Mendoza, too, was of Jewish descent.

Throughout Charles' reign, however, statutes were enacted, and increasingly enforced, requiring proof of "purity of blood" for positions in government, the church, and the universities. They were directed specifically against people of Jewish and Moorish descent. Although many prominent Spaniards of converso lineage continued to hold office, these ordinances demanding limpieza de sangre became increasingly popular in high places. These statutes gained force in tandem with intellectual retreat, from aspirations to Christian universalism, into the counter-Reformation climate of ever more rigid social and national conformity and exclusivity. As true social mobility decreased, the sense of social prestige attached to being Old Christian inflated that condition, equating orthodoxy-over-time with honor and even knighthood. Statutes of limpieza and Inquisition trials for backsliding received increasing concurrence from the nobility and the monarch. It is impossible to determine how many conversos so charged were true Judaizers. Probably very few practicing Jews remained in Spain by the 1520s, or came to Mexico.

Mexican Inquisition records indicate that none of those accused in the 1520s of practicing Judaism were doing so—or at least they were not doing so correctly. Rather, they appear not to have conformed to any faith, although it is possible that they may have thought what they were doing was within Judaism. But if they were Christians at all, they were certainly irreverent ones, prone to round oaths and at times to kicking, beating, and urinating on crosses, and attracted to what Christian and Jewish society viewed as sexual promiscuity and perversion. Two Spaniards of Jewish extraction were burned at the stake as Judaizers in the 1520s. One was Hernando Alonso, in his sixties, the blacksmith who had arrived with Narváez, had worked on the brigantines Cortés used against Tenochtitlán, then grown rich as a miner, meat merchant, and slave dealer; the other, Diego de Morales, was a wealthy and trusted merchant. The Dominican Santa María sentenced them in 1527. What set them apart from another two who were spared—one of whom was Morales' brother, Gonzalo—was their loyalty to Cortés.[23]

At least one encomendero-entrepreneur, Gonzalo Gómez, was known to have been a *reconciliado*, that is, he had confessed and repented practicing Judaism, in an auto de fé in Seville. Does that mean that he was in fact a Jew, or simply that he had confessed to being one? We cannot be certain. Gómez was denounced and tried again in the 1530s in Mexico. Zumárraga sentenced him leniently, for blasphemy only, although relapsed penitents in Spain were burned at the stake. His *proceso* (trial record) brought out, among other things, that Gómez was an enemy of Zumárraga's foe, Nuño de Guzmán. Moreover, by then it was clear to officialdom that the Inquisition had been employed previously in Mexico as a factional instrument contributing to social divisiveness rather than to cohesion. Thereafter in New Spain, until the 1570s, Protestants, lumped together as "Lutherans," were the prime targets of a relatively sluggish Inquisition and *judaizantes* were left in salutary neglect. For under Charles, welcome or not—and usually not—Jewish heritage was recognized by many of the educated and well-placed to be integral to Spanish society and through it to Mexican society.

Also present in Mexico in these years were individuals and usages representing the other Spanish heritage becoming officially unacceptable, the Moorish. Zumárraga had requested Moorish artisans for Mexico. Mendoza, the product of a Granada upbringing, stimulated in New Spain the silk industry, a Moorish monopoly in Spain. Moorish elements had been incorporated into Spanish material and physical life, into Castilian, and undoubtedly into the Iberian mentality. Spanish mosques become churches inspired church architecture in Mexico, the mosque of Córdoba an obvious inspiration for Gante's San José. Some moriscos (Moslems accepting Christianity) were reported in Mexico, most often mentioned as slaves. The encomendero of Yanhuitlán was depicted in the 1540s wearing a turban.[24]

The presence of non-Spaniards and of heterodox Spaniards in Mexico testifies to a more open society in the first half of the century, even than officially sanctioned. And Charles permitted more diversity initially, and always more than did Philip II. Further, it was easier for a Spaniard in the early years to combine military and political activities with commercial and extractive pursuits. According to the conquistador rationale, conquest had been a private and expensive enterprise, and now to defend the land required wealth. Wherewithal was to be had, not only from putting Indians to building and to producing commodities, and specie, but also from trading products of native labor. Moreover commerce per se was not only the province of foreigners. Spanish merchants had come to Mexico with the conquistadors. One Spaniard in 1529 wrote to a merchant of Burgos residing in Seville that "trade is the true mines of this land."[25] Trade on a large scale was also engaged in by some conquistador-encomenderos, Cortés once more outstanding among them. In agreement with Genoese merchants in Seville he shipped sugar in return for Negro slaves. Pedro de Alvarado contracted with Francisco de los Cobos to import African slaves.[26] Royal officals with private interests also allied with Cobos in commercial ventures. Prominent among them were Rodrigo de Albornoz and Antonio de Mendoza.[27] The Indian slave trade, both internal and to the islands, is a further case in point. Although not in conformity with the avowed ideals of a military aristocracy—the status claimed by the conquerors—nevertheless commerce was a true obsession of many of the first Spaniards in Mexico.

The keys to wealth, and its indicators, to all Europeans in New Spain, whatever their background or condition—with the exception of some of the friars—were "many towns and mines."[28] Encomenderos and other Spaniards, after Indians ran out of metals and jewels on hand, turned to mining and supportive ventures. Initially they showed little interest in direct titles to land, taking for granted that encomienda included practical control of village lands.[29] Royal decrees, however, soon explicitly recognized the right of Indians to their individual and communal lands. All other land the crown understood, within Castilian tradition, to be under royal stewardship, some to be ceded to the vecinos of new Spanish towns, other specified allotments to be bestowed as mercedes (kindnesses for services rendered) by the king and his officials. Inhabitants of new towns received individual household and garden plots. Ownership, as royal orders stipulated, was contingent upon at least four years' residence. Encomenderos also were granted land by town and royal officials, to encourage raising wheat and cattle. Subsoil and water everywhere was reserved to the crown.[30]

From the beginning, however, Spanish immigrants thought land their due and paid little attention to the, to them, fine distinction between use and ownership. Thus Cortés again epitomized an attitude common to Spaniards in Mexico when he reputedly boasted, "If I have much land, I had to work hard to get it."[31] We know that, as guardian of the young son of the tlatoani of Cuernavaca, he arranged to come into outright possession of much of the best land there, although these arrangements may or may not have been what he meant by work.[32] Other Spaniards as well, through subterfuge or collusion with chiefs or at times purchase, from the 1520s on came to hold Indian lands directly. New arrivals also continued to receive grants of vacant lands and of town plots and to appropriate or purchase land from Indians, sometimes from those in encomienda. Particularly after the famine and plague of 1531, and again after those in 1545, large amounts of Indian land came into Spanish hands by these means as well as in lieu of service, and through Indian deaths and abandonment, and by squatting—that is, through preemption for crops and cattle. And Mendoza granted lands liberally. In the 1540s, as Spaniards and cattle multiplied, and word of Coronado's fiasco to the north turned Spanish attention to central Mexico, Spaniards increasingly sought lands there, assuming Indian labor to work them contingent on holding land rather than, as they had calculated previously, the other way around. In formation at mid-century were the great latifundia, the haciendas based on landholding, which would come to dominate the countryside and its centers of population, for Indian villagers were then tending to be employed on the estates of hacendados, who held or controlled Spanish town offices.[33]

From the outset the first conquerors resented the presence of Spaniards who had arrived after them. Witness the animosity felt by Cortés' followers for those of Narváez. Subsequent resentment of both groups for later arrivals was heightened by competition for spoils. When Cortés gave choice encomiendas to some of the better-connected Spaniards, including royal officials, who appeared after the conquest, both previous factions denounced the receivers of such *resabios señoriales*, "morning-after lordships." Bernal Díaz complained of those latecomers who without fighting a battle had been preferred in lands, honors, and Indians.[34] And Jerónimo López, who had come with Narváez, throughout his lifetime wrote letters of advice to the king, repeatedly scoring those "whom the land cost nothing."[35] Although Cortés showed favoritism to relatives and retainers of Spanish nobles—as well as to his own—he himself epitomized the conquistador-become-settler attitude toward more recent immigrants when in 1524 he reported that the majority of new arrivals were vice-ridden sinners of low birth, and that he would trust Indians sooner than such Spaniards.[36] Each successive individual or group arriving in Mexico met animosity of some sort, and usually either compounded by resentment of preference in patronage or by disdain for lack of it, but, like those who preceded them, they also looked to the king, who, as patriarch, mediator, and judge, they expected would protect or advance their private interests. As Mexican society evolved under Spanish domination, individuals and groups expressed closest ties to others in terms of a common reliance on the crown.

Most of the Spaniards, we have noted, and nearly all of the wealthiest and more powerful, resided in the city of Mexico. There an ayuntamiento (town council) formed, following the Spanish tradition initially introduced by Cortés in Vera Cruz. Composed of propertied Spaniards who immediately claimed preeminence above all other towns of New Spain,[37] its members continued to act as spokesmen for all the kingdom. Its history helps to illuminate the formation of settler attitudes toward the crown and royal officials, and to chart the deterioration of the earliest seignorial aspirations in Spanish Mexico.

Its first members were appointed by Cortés or by his lieutenants annually until 1526, when the principle of royal appointment was introduced by the king's naming of two councilmen in perpetuity.[38] In the 1530s all of them held office by royal appointment, that is, by crown approval. During the 1520s the cabildo, in its deliberations and correspondence, spoke of itself as the effective governing body and center of royal administration for all New Spain. It then asserted a combining of those functions traditional to Spanish cabildos—regulating local daily activities in a predominantly pastoral and agricultural society with those rights and duties that in Spain had evolved from being functions of military councils to being prerogatives of the Castilian cortes during the late medieval period of weak kingship.[39] These pretensions appeared with dominance, first by Cortés and then by coalitions headed by the initial royal appointees, the treasury officials and the first audiencia.

The first *regidores* wrote to the crown, in terms reminiscent of those used by the Vera Cruz cabildo, asking that Cortés be named governor of New Spain.[40] Then, on rumor of his death in 1525, the council reflected the power shift in declaring the treasury officers, Peralmindez Chirinos and Gonzalo de Salazar, legitimate royal subdelegates to be obeyed in his stead. These officials and later Nuño de Guzmán, as president of the audiencia, joined its meetings. Salazar used the council to call a meeting of procuradores, representatives, of the handful of other Spanish towns of New Spain, as did Guzmán later—in Salazar's case to add weight to his petition to the king to exile Cortés from the kingdom.[41] From the beginning, therefore, its members despite their pretensions did no more than share authority with royal governors, real or aspiring.

Whatever faction controlled it, in its petitions to the crown the cabildo continued to request the privileges and preferences it felt belonged to the resident aristocracy by right of conquest. Under Cortés, it asked that all government appointments (still thought of in Fernandine terms as sinecures) go to conquistadors and their sons, and that all lawyers (generally assumed to act as royal agents abetting centralism) be barred.[42] Under

Salazar, procuradores of the Spanish towns of Medellín, Coatzacoalcas, Pánuco, and Colima met with the ayuntamiento of the capital to draft an appeal to the crown in the name of all New Spain. In their petition to the king of 1525, and in those of 1528 and 1529 drawn up under Guzmán, deputies and the cabildo of the capital made what would come to be classic pleas of propertied Spaniards and their American-born, or creole, offspring. They asked for encomiendas in perpetuity, for an unlicensed slave trade, and that all ports of Spain and the Caribbean be opened to commerce. They complained of Franciscan interference with what they considered to be their right to exercise civil and criminal jurisdiction over the Indians. In 1529 they wanted principal native cities bestowed on conquerors, Cortés' holdings to be distributed among Indianless conquistadors in perpetuity, with regidores preferred, and that oidores also be granted Indians. Here their emphasis was on assuring direct control of Indians by Spaniards in Mexico. A notable omission was a request for government offices; later petitions would reintroduce it. These petitioners of 1529 in explicit, and impolitic, allusion equated Indians held by Spaniards in encomienda to vassals serving Castilian lords.[43]

As the petitioners realized, royal aquiescence would have made New Spain a near-autonomous region, nominally under the crown but effectively organized in smaller seignories. They sought to gain through royal mercedes a political system in Mexico which in the same period was being made more and more anachronistic in Spain, in part as a result of Mexican conquest. There the comunero revolt had made the new king wary of representative bodies. Moreover, wealth from America had begun to increase royal independence and to make the calling of the Spanish cortes to gain funds unnecessary. Throughout Charles' reign the members of the ayuntamiento of Mexico ignored these and other signs of real political change. Instead, they preferred to assume an intransigent seignorial stance, soon to be largely an impotent one. The tenor of their petitions in conjunction with their role in factional strife makes it more understandable that the king, who in 1526 had been well disposed toward conquerors' receiving offices and encomiendas and becoming a controlling military aristocracy in Mexico, as his instructions to the visitador Luis Ponce de León and to the first audiencia corroborate, by 1528 was convinced of "the base instincts" of most Spaniards in Mexico, and of their greed, anarchic behavior, and possible separatist tendencies.[44]

With the coming of the second audiencia in 1530, the ayuntamiento of Mexico and propertied Spaniards in general began to understand themselves to be less governing than governed. The new oidores came directly to office from outside the country and were those most distrusted of men, lawyers, presided over by a friar-bishop of the sort now meddling with their Indians. The settlers, including cabildo members, soon saw the audiencia take measures to recall some encomiendas, limit others, break up the largest, impose its jurisdiction over Indians, regulate and limit that of Spaniards, attack slavery and personal service, and effectively make of many Indians direct royal, tribute-paying subjects. Several of the oidores also expressed disdain for the majority of Spaniards in New Spain. One immediate result of audiencia activity was that 150 Spaniards left central Mexico to join Nuño de Guzmán in slave-raiding in Jalisco, and that perhaps 500 more simply departed the kingdom.[45] Others who stayed, including the regidores of Mexico, continued to protest to the king against the new magistrates.[46]

The Mexican ayuntamiento complained to the monarch of audiencia edicts against slaving and forcing Indians to work mines. It anguished over oidores revoking encomiendas granted by their predecessors to married conquistadors and putting them instead under corregidores, who had even forced the old holders to remove their cattle from village lands. It appealed to now stock arguments in again requesting encomiendas be granted in perpetuity. It concluded that caciques prospered and new-comers got wealth and Indians while the original conquerors went poor and hungry.[47] The council also found extremely disconcerting its displacement in ceremony, complaining of the fact that in 1533 the audiencia had usurped its place of honor in the annual Corpus Christi procession.[48] The aggrieved regidores appealed to the crown to reestablish their public preeminence and received in return a cédula giving the audiencia permanent precedence, which in company with other recent decrees should have indicated to the cabildo the tenor of royal policy.

Nevertheless this corporation, as well as other prominent Spanish groups and individuals in Mexico, continued to appeal and report to the monarch, seeing disliked ordinances and public slights less as royal measures than as personal actions of local officials. The regidores not only literally took back seats to the oidores but also came off second best in altercations with them and then lamented their ill-use to the crown. For example, they complained that when they reported in 1534 that Augustinian and Franciscan sermons stirred up Indians and caused social discord and scandal, the oidor Vasco de Quiroga had insulted them by retorting that their injudicious language and actions were more apt than were the friars to cause an uprising.[49] Other oidores, too, held most resident Spaniards in small regard. Ramírez de Fuenleal, president-oidor of the second audiencia, gave further evidence of the more general official opinion in acridly reporting that of the more than 100 corregidores most were isleño-conquistadors who robbed their Indian charges.[50] And yet another oidor, Salmerón, scored old soldiers and recent arrivals as well, writing to the king:

You can not imagine the avarice, disorder, and laziness of Spaniards in this country. Those who have encomiendas only think of making the greatest possible profit out of them, not bothering in the least about the welfare or religious instruction of the Indians. Those who have none complain impudently to us and demand something to live on. If told that they are young and well able to work, they answer arrogantly that they took part in such and such a conquest.[51]

Disdain for the majority of Spaniards in New Spain continued to be exhibited in private, and sometimes in public, by many royal officials there, and resident Spaniards, including those of the cabildo of Mexico continued to complain of it to "the impartial judgement" of the monarch.

When Mendoza as royal surrogate arrived in 1535, the ayuntamiento and other prior settlers initially looked to him for relief from audiencia measures. It was a time of increasing competition by all manner of Spaniards for wealth, power, and authority. Large numbers of Spaniards had immigrated to Mexico and only relatively few of them had gained Indians or land, although those who did claimed large amounts of both. At his arrival 180,000 Indians in the central valley were under only 30 encomenderos.[52] Many of the propertied soon found their allotments of land and Indians reduced by viceregal action, but were soothed by Mendoza's promulgation of royal orders of 1536 extending their encomiendas for another life, and by his appearing to temporize on curbing their use of Indian labor. The viceroy, while progressively extending royal jurisdiction, by his lenience in enforcing royal decrees appeared to resident Spaniards to be favoring their interests. He appeased Spaniards, too, by patiently hearing their appeals, judiciously making some additional grants of Indians and lands, continuing to employ conquerors as corregidores, and granting to the more needy ones or their widows outright pensions. In addition to Mendoza's gaining Spanish adherents through adroitly dispensing justice and patronage, a number of Spaniards prospered when, at his urging, they sent their rapidly growing sheep herds north. And under his generalship many of the more affluent Europeans, at the head of their own forces, took part in the Mixtón Wars against the Chichimecas of Jalisco, thereby signifying their acceptance of the viceroy as supreme military leader in New Spain. The success of that campaign and Mendoza's recruitment of 600 men to fight for their king in Peru in 1547, although the need passed and the volunteers never embarked, were measures increasing a general Spanish pride in defending the realm and serving the crown under viceregal command. Thus in the 1540s viceregal prestige and the self-esteem of many resident Spaniards, derived from simultaneously serving king, patria, and self-interest—and, in the Mixtón campaign, also the faith and the extension of Spanish civilization—increased together.[53]

At the same time the viceroy ingratiated himself with these Spaniards, he restricted more drastically both Spanish use of Indian labor and the political prerogatives of Spanish residents, including those of the Mexican cabildo. Under Mendoza, in 1539, its jurisdiction was restricted legally to 15 leagues around the city of Mexico in principle, and to a smaller area in practice. He personally monitored its business, reviewing all its enactments, occasionally intervening in its quarrels, meeting with it monthly, and putting an oidor into all its sessions. He confined its twelve regidores largely to such necessary offices as "judge of the sheepwalk." Such was his power over the ayuntamiento that simply at his request Francisco Vázquez de Coronado was installed as regidor in 1538 and, after Coronado's expedition failed and he had subsequently disgraced himself in abominably governing Nueva Galicia, Mendoza recalled him from that post but reinstated him to the Mexican cabildo.[54] The viceroy's attitude toward that council, reminiscent of the second audiencia's, was summed up in his observation to the king (in 1549) that Coronado was not fit to fill a government position.

As the cabildo found itself more and more tightly confined to regulating local and ceremonial affairs, and as its prerogatives, in step with the fortunes of many of the conquerors, waned, its arrogance and pretensions waxed. In the year of the New Laws, 1542, its members again repeated the arguments used by Cortés, much as if they were articles of faith, in seeking encomiendas in perpetuity, now for the American-born sons of the old settlers. They requested that this new generation be preferred in all benefices and dignities, that such posts be hereditary, that lands of the Indian towns surrounding the capital be granted to Spaniards, and that the king not heed the advice of friars and like-minded individuals in Mexico. Above all, he should not listen to Bartolomé de Las Casas. In short, the ayuntamiento continued along its (pre-Quixote) quixotic path, citing Spanish precedents of the reconquest in asking it be granted further privileges as first city of the kingdom.[55] That council did affect official decisions, but mostly indirectly, through the influence of some of its members on governing Spaniards, or through individual reports to the crown.[56]

At mid-century, although the cabildo and the encomenderos it spoke for were fighting a rearguard action, encomenderos retained much real power over Indian communities, especially over those well beyond the capital. Slavery and personal service continued to thrive in such frontier regions as Pánuco, Guatemala, Yucatán, Nueva Galicia, and the northern mining provinces.[57] Despite royal orders to the contrary, many encomenderos also continued to negotiate with Indian principales for both tribute in kind and service.[58] Yet the approaching demise of encomienda as the outstanding institution controlling Indians was apparent, just as its death as a de facto local political unit was a concomitant to expanding royal authority and contracting native population. Although encomenderos were not necessarily conquerors, encomienda's flourishing had paralleled that of the generation of the conquest, now dwindling in numbers and emerging as a subject for nostalgia. Bernal Díaz bemoaned how few conquistadors remained and recalled how the encomienda of Chiapa granted him by Cortés, its people his own property, was taken away from him eight years later and reassigned to settlers of the new, nearby town of Ciudad Real. The Dominican Diego Durán, although overstating, documented the passing of giants: "the conquerors have become wretches and their sons poor beggars."[59]

Other Spaniards and other institutions supplanted the early encomenderos. And that most Spaniards in Mexico were not part of a military aristocracy, as their descendants—real and aspiring—would claim, is apparent, for there were also perhaps 3,000 to 4,000 Spanish vagrants.[60] They lived from hand to mouth, often coercing Indian communities to sustain them. A generation of newcomers now literally held much of the land and, occasionally, encomiendas—thus Motolinía reported shoemakers and blacksmiths in New Spain became encomenderos, and that common European laborers in Mexico began as *mayordomos* (managers of estates) and soon became landowners. Among the more prosperous and socially potent, however, remained some earlier arrivals and their descendants.

Outstanding but illustrative of one sort of more recent Spanish emigrant was Alonso de Villaseca, a younger son of a well-connected Spanish family, who was in New Spain by 1540. There he married a wealthy woman, Francisca Morón, and then made more money. He came to have livestock and agricultural haciendas in Hidalgo, Guanajuato, Zacatecas, Vera Cruz, and Mexico, numerous houses in the capital, mines in Zacualpan, Zacatecas, Pachuca, and Ixmiquilpan, and to be one of the ricos sponsoring cultural and charitable institutions—he founded the chair of theology at the University of Mexico, supported the royal hospital, and in the 1570s made possible the Jesuit foundation—and preserving the peace. He is reported to have, at the head of 200 horsemen, put down a riot in the city of Mexico.[61]

At mid-century encomenderos also included official and viceregal retainers and relatives. Joining the propertied gentry of New Spain were such aristocratic couples as Mendoza's niece, María de Ircio y Mendoza, married to Velasco's son, Luis, who would himself become viceroy there.[62] Coronado, other, more successful conquistadors of outlying regions, and poorer Spanish immigrants as well, also tended to marry earlier arrivals' daughters dowered with Indians and land—as did Villaseca.[63] Such marriages also mark what became a salient characteristic of Mexican society, alliances in every generation between heiresses—soon American-born heiresses—and young men come from Spain.

Landed Spaniards now raised cattle, wheat, and sugar not only for export but also for an internal market inflated by the decrease of Indians and the expansion of silver mining. They profited by the royal orders of 1549 instituting the cuatequil system of forced salaried labor, for it made more of the dwindling labor supply available to those with more land than Indians. The decree undoubtedly reflected existing conditions, among them increased Spanish wealth, more mines, fewer slaves, vastly expanded Spanish landholding, an attendant decrease in Indian land, and more and more hiring out of Indians under both the crown and the encomenderos. To relatively recent arrivals often belonged the estancias and haciendas tending to replace encomienda as the Spanish institutions controlling Indian labor.[64] In addition, cheap meat made it profitable to raise cattle only on a large scale, so that small holders were discouraged and latifundia promoted.[65]

As the reign of Charles V drew to a close, so did the lives, power, and property of the remaining conquistadors. They continued to remind the king, however, as did the cabildo of Mexico, of what they had gained for him through tremendous labor and bloodshed. They begged he provide for their sons, and occasionally their daughters, born in the land.[66] Preeminent among those Spaniards who in old age canonized the conquest was, once again, Bernal Díaz del Castillo, his account a trifle heightened and gilded, polished over time. In the history he wrote he recorded the attitudes of the Spaniards who took Mexico, thereby preserving their outlook for Mexicans yet to come. He informed a new generation that "our heroic deeds were never surpassed in any age, and no men ever subdued so many kingdoms and *señoríos* as we, the true conquerors, took for our king and lord."[67] Complaining of eking out his last years with more battle scars than Indians, he looked back on the taking of Mexico as a joint endeavor of Spanish warriors engaged in a civilizing and Christianizing mission.[68] The conquest, he explained, was a blessing to the Indians. The conquistadors had brought the faith before the friars arrived. Because of conquest, sons of distinguished chiefs had learned Spanish. All Indians had been taught prayers and trades, orderly ways, justice, and proper civil government, as well as to tilt, hold tournaments, and appreciate bullfights. They now had cattle, fruit trees, fine towns, and bishops. The Spaniards who had conquered the land and introduced its peoples to Christianity and civilization deserved to govern it. The land and Indians were by right, and in a seignorial sense, their possessions.

Bernal Díaz spoke for the old conquistadors and their Mexican-born heirs in continuing to identify his own interests with royal ones. He praised the second audiencia and Mendoza, and wrote approvingly of Cortés' suggestion—also made by Motolinía—that the land was so good it should be bestowed on an *infante*, or royal prince, thereby expressing both loyalty to the imperial dynasty and great regional pride.[69]

In the same spirit, the ayuntamiento of Mexico, continuing to disregard real political arrangements, in 1549 again addressed the crown as seignorial overlord, its members expressing themselves as dependent señores. As second-life grants to encomiendas were running out, it pressed for royal permission for conquerors to cede their Indians to their children, grandchildren, nieces, or nephews.[70] In 1555, the regidores thanked the king for extending present holdings for a third lifetime—a token success of their campaign, in league with encomenderos, Mendoza, and Vasco de Quiroga, for a general division in perpetuity of all Indians in New Spain.[71] It was fitting that, in 1554, this stronghold of privilege-past voted gifts to Juan Ginés de Sepúlveda, the opponent four years earlier of Las Casas. Sepúlveda, it will be recalled, had also assumed that the conquest had been the achievement of heroic Spaniards bent on civilizing barbarians.[72]

Two related aspects of ayuntamiento attitudes and derivative activities are also important here. The cabildo began to reinforce the conquistador mentality, publicly and almost immediately, in instituting by 1529 the annual celebration of Saint Hippolyte's Day, 13 August, commemorating the capture in 1521 of the last Aztec ruler, Cuauhtémoc, and the fall of Tenochtitlán to the Spaniards.[73] Its members, as the highpoint of their ceremonial activities, each year led through the city the parade of the flag—the *paseo del pendón*—at the head of Spanish and Indian notables, but behind the viceroy, and vied with one another for the privilege of carrying the Spanish battle standard. Throughout the colonial period the annual *paseo* remained a visual reminder to its participants and to the general populace of the conquistador concept of the conquest as an official one, and the basis for social preeminence for domiciled men and women of Spanish lineage. In addition, the council quickly fell into the habit of justifying its views in customary Spanish manner, by appeal to older usages, and to Mexican precedent as well as to Spanish. Thus as early as 1531 it assured the crown that it was the custom in New Spain to employ slaves in the mines.[74] Taking pride in the recent Mexican past, the ayuntamiento assumed legality for a body of part European, part American, but uniquely Mexican regional tradition.

Upon news of the death in 1558 of Charles V, the regidores sponsored ceremonies fully reflecting the now institutionalized conquistador mentality. The celebration of the funeral honors in general, and the depictions and inscriptions on the huge cenotaph erected for the occasion in particular, exuded a sense of aristocratic pride in New Spain as an outstanding region of the Spanish empire and gave visual representation to the heritage now claimed by Spaniards and their offspring in Mexico.

The monument was decorated with a heroic-looking figure of Fernando Cortés, and with Indians against a background of fallen, burning idols "on their knees thanking God because in the reign of Charles and through the intervention of Cortés they were led from darkness."[75] Francisco Cervantes de Salazar, who saw and described this *tumulo imperial*, reported it also depicted the Catholic emperor's victory over the Protestant princes at Muhlenburg. Christendom, it misleadingly implied, remained intact. The author echoed this monument's theme in characterizing New Spain as "a microcosm of both worlds, the old and the new."[76] His description, and the cenotaph, presented Mexico as a distinct and outstanding region, with syncretic traditions, and within the orthodox and universal Christian imperial system of *gran España*.

The ayuntamiento had commissioned Cervantes de Salazar to describe the funeral ceremonies, and also to write a history of Mexico to counter the account of the conquest praising Indians and damning Spaniards set down by Las Casas. He accommodated, his chronicle based on, and in spots paraphrasing, the history eulogizing Cortés written down by the conqueror's old secretary, Francisco López de Gómara.[77] He also borrowed from Motolinía and Bernal Díaz. Cervantes de Salazar had studied the humanities and canon law in Spain and taught rhetoric (Latin grammar) there. He had admired the Latin prose of the Renaissance scholar, thinker, friend of Erasmus, and Spanish exile, Luis Vives, and commented on Vives' ideas of education. He had also written on such fashionably humanistic themes as the evils of idleness, the worth of work, and in 1546 had dedicated to Cortés a dialogue on the dignity of man. Cortés had induced him to go to Mexico where he initially stayed with the conqueror's son, the second marqués, Martín Cortés, and where he first taught Latin privately, then acquired the chair of rhetoric at the new university, and also pursued the higher studies of philosophy and theology under Alonso de la Vera Cruz. In 1555 he became a priest. The wealthy and enterprising Alonso de Villaseca was his cousin.

To provide Mexican students with a text of proper Latin constructions, Cervantes de Salazar emulated Vives' use of dialogues, writing a series of them describing the capital in 1554. Published there in that same year, they imparted pride in Mexico and admiration of both major components of its populace. His dialogues and the funeral cenotaph, in their respective fields, were Mexican constructions of integral Renaissance form.[78] In 1554 humanism gave his writing a classic flavor and a temporal and tolerant veneer. He then displayed a highly developed sense of cultural relativity, having one Spaniard mention how strange to him were Indian names for foods, and another respond "as ours are to the Indians."[79] In addition, he reported that in the school of Tlatelolco the Indians have "a teacher of their own nation named Antonio Valeriano ... in no way inferior to our grammarians.... How admirable," he exclaimed, "is the variety of nature."[80] Yet the qualities he found most admirable in Mexico were those officially favored in contemporary Spain: "Discipline and virtue," he commented approvingly, "appear to have been born Mexicans."

Within the corpus of his work in Mexico can be seen a shift from an initial tendency to observe as a humanist to one reflecting Spanish counter-Reformation attitudes and a full-blown imperial outlook. Throughout, he wrote of Spain as homeland to an empire, of Spaniards in Mexico as empire-builders, contributing mightily to the domain of their monarch in adding to it the magnificent region of New Spain. Charles he termed heir to the Roman Caesars and glory of the Spains, the most powerful of all earthly monarchs. Spain itself was heir to Roman imperial greatness and New Spain was the most outstanding region of greater Spain.

Yet in explaining in his history the relationship between crown, conquerors, and Indians his previous tolerant outlook largely disappeared. He did extol the grandeur of Motecuhzoma, investing that Aztec ruler with attributes borrowed from accounts of kings and emperors in histories of the classical antiquity of Europe. But he attributed even more glory to Cortés, his conqueror. To be a great hero one needs a great adversary. Moreover, it is not surprising that in writing a history commissioned by the Mexican ayuntamiento Cervantes de Salazar should express Sepúlveda-like views, stating that the emperor held a right and just title to New Spain through the conquest, for the coming of the Spaniards gave the Indians true liberty. He claimed the Aztecs were barbarians, slaves by nature, who slavishly obeyed rulers, some of whose orders were against natural law, unjust, allowed no appeal, and were therefore tyrannical. The conquerors had freed them from this tyranny and begun a civilizing mission still carried on by Spaniards. To him the city of Mexico was *la república* of the kingdom's Spanish nucleus, and at the top of its society he discerned a nobility of Spanish conquerors and of their American-born heirs, whom he termed "Mexicans." As for contemporary Indians, in his later writings he declared them inferior to Spaniards, not capable, for example, of being ordained, or of using Latin well. He suggested Tlatelolco be made a Spanish school. Clearly, in the late 1550s the ayuntamiento found an ideal chronicler for its own interpretation of Mexican history.

By the end of our era, then, individual conquistadors, the cabildo of Mexico, and its historian believed in the existence of a Mexican aristocracy of Spanish lineage, its title based on conquest of the old Mexican empire, on defense of the land, and on an ongoing religious and civilizing mission to the conquered. These Spaniards also claimed as their own Mexican heritage a past combining the ancient histories of Europeans and Indians. It must be kept in mind, however, that although men of conquistador mentality praised some of the old Indian heroes and material achievements, they condemned others and found in them justification for conquest. The European heritage remained to them the superior one. Mexico they continued to describe as composed of two repúblicas, the Spanish and the Indian.[81]

Thus, as conquistador-encomenderos died out, they achieved an immortality of sorts, passing from flesh and blood into regional tradition. We have seen that the conquistador mentality was becoming general property of all Spanish inhabitants and their creole offspring, and that Cervantes de Salazar was among the later Spanish arrivals who took as their own, as self-styled heirs to the conquerors, the right to Mexican aristocracy. The conquistador mentality was in fact metamorphosing into the spirit of *criollismo,* one justifying Mexican domination by all propertied inhabitants of "Spanish" descent. These were the maturing children of Spanish lineage, including some of mixed ethnic background and some born out of wedlock, who, whatever the date of parental appearance in New Spain, would come to be called creoles and continue to claim to deserve the fruits of the conquest as descendants of its perpetrators.

Criollismo had been adumbrated, almost immediately, by the resentment expressed by the first wave of Spaniards in Mexico for all subsequent arrivals. It included an element of prior claim intensified by the notion that we who have gained the land, or whose forebears did, are rightfully its masters, in a seignorial sense. Friction with peninsular officials and later immigrants heightened among the Mexican-born Spaniards seignorial pretensions, self-assertion, and, beneath it, an undercurrent of felt inferiority to Europeans. In addition, in the early years of Spanish consolidation after conquest, in order to ensure permanent settlement, royal policy had encouraged psychological attachment to the land. In this vein, Motolinía reported Puebla was founded to settle Spanish vagrants so that they should come "to love the land."[82] To Velasco's discomfiture, many had. Moreover, by mid-century Puebla had attracted small farmers, merchants, artisans, shopkeepers, and others of middling means, making it the second largest city. Some of them wrote to Spain of how good life was in their new home compared to the lack of opportunity in their old.[83] Spain was their past, Mexico their future.

We have seen Spaniards urged, by material inducements, to grow crops and raise cattle, marry and have families, even forbidden to leave New Spain without official permission. Yet in its effort to ensure permanent Spanish settlement the crown succeeded too well, just as it had in reinforcing the belief among propertied Spaniards that they constituted a military aristocracy in New Spain. By the 1550s both attitudes had come to be shared by many less wealthy and even vagrant Spaniards, by poverty-ridden conquistadors and by those more fortunate, and also by later arrivals who had acquired wealth and property and resented increasingly stringent government regulations and the officials from overseas seeking to impose them. As the Mexican ayuntamiento had stated in its petition in 1549, the propertied wanted above all else to make certain their children inherited what they had gained. In that year a conspiracy was reported against governing officials, and, although the conspirators appear to have been few and unimportant, in commenting on the plot Alonso de la Vera Cruz, Velasco, and others warned the crown that Spaniards far from court cared only for their own advancement and that of their families.[84] These fears tell at least as much of official, as of resident, Spanish attitudes.

The majority of immigrants continued to assume themselves to be in accord with the crown on the nature of the relationship of New Spain to Spain although in fact, from the conquest on, they never were. Many of the conquerors wanted manorial estates in the New World and thought their ties to the monarch akin to those of the señores of the reconquest. They saw themselves as military lords of a frontier kingdom. Retainers, indeed lordly retinues, palatial residences, rich dress, and a mania for coats of arms proclaimed their self-image. They posed as hidalgos or cavaliers and did indeed function as a military aristocracy in expanding conquest, leading the sort of private armies now superseded more and more in Spain itself by mercenary troops.

Nevertheless, Spaniards in Mexico looked to Europe for cultural and intellectual guidance. The conquerors read the chivalric romances then in fashion, and some laymen in Mexico read Erasmus. Books influenced by Erasmian notions were still arriving in New Spain at mid-century.[85] At the same time there, as in Spain—though to a lesser extent—a narrowing and more exclusively Spanish intellectual climate affected all inhabitants. Students, readers, churchgoers, and in fact the general public encountered books, teachers, preachers, and public ceremonies disseminating concepts supporting a world view, and a society, less pluralistic, more imperially Spanish. In philosophy and matters of faith humanistic ideals and methods were giving way to a reinvigorated Aristotelian scholasticism, as evidenced, for example, in the works of Vera Cruz. Comparison of Cervantes de Salazar's humanistic dialogues of 1554, stressing cultural relativism, with his later writings emphasizing Spanish might illuminates the change. In the early years, schools for Spanish children were begun by the Mexican cabildo.[86] In Michoacán, young "Spaniards" attended the Augustinian colegio at Tiripitio and Quiroga's Colegio de San Nicolás. The University of Mexico opened in 1553 to preserve and extend the Spanish variety of European letters, philosophy, and theology. Vera Cruz and Cervantes de Salazar taught there. Another of the first professors,

Dr. Frias de Albornoz, of the old contador's family, employed his prodigious memory in writing a tract against Las Casas and in training young Mexicans through disputation, entirely by scholastic method. Such teachers educated, in the main, sons of businessmen eager to rise to the level of nobles, and some sons of poor conquistadors and of other early arrivals seeking professional training. Most students received no more than the equivalent of a secondary education. A maturing, largely American-born generation, taught to vie in quickness of intellect within a scholastic set of assumptions concerning the universe, encouraged in pomp and display, especially in literary contests, tended to emerge as a ceremonial aristocracy or as professionals, deferential and seeking patronage.

Even so, alongside the preservation of Old World Spanish high culture, a new syncretic folk culture was developing. Indian words and new syncretic terms were drifting into Spanish speech, as Gante's letters, Bernal Díaz's history, and Cervantes de Salazar's dialogues demonstrate.[87] And a thriving substratum of superstition and sorcery permeated all reaches of society and its content and practitioners crisscrossed ethnic lines. Conquistadors employed sorcerers from Spain to find gold and consulted Indians learned in medicinal and amoral lore. Cultural mestizaje was quickly observable in everyday Spanish life in New Spain.[88] In reaction to the growing sentiment of Spanish and Spanish-American attachment to Mexico, the crown forbade, much as it had squelched Sepúlveda's pro-encomendero treatises, the sending to New Spain of the eulogistic life of Cortés by his old secretary, Francisco López de Gómara.[89] Again to little avail, for Cervantes de Salazar, we have seen, wrote a Mexican history largely based upon it.

An outstanding historian has observed, "the remarkable feature of encomienda is that royal law prevailed."[90] An extenuating circumstance, of course, is that in New Spain often royal law was accepted as a guiding ideal but not enforced.[91] Yet it is now clear that royal law was *the* wedge used by the crown, in New Spain as in Spain, to insert its authority; and it did so especially through publicizing and practicing its traditional right to jurisdiction. Once Spaniards recognized this right in Mexico, much of the game of autonomy was up. Moreover, encomenderos like other early Spanish residents failed to realize how deeply their political outlooks diverged from royal views, that as another historian puts it, the king's purpose was to be the only encomendero[92]—although activities of the second audiencia made clear the crown proposed to strengthen royal jurisdiction, treat Indians as direct royal subjects or vassals, and define and limit Spanish relations with Indians. In Spain, provisional grants similar to encomienda had often become hereditary over time. Only with the New Laws did propertied Spaniards in Mexico become fully aware of the nature of royal policy. Even then, as Mendoza astutely softened the blow, the cabildo of the capital refused to assimilate their full significance and restated old seignorial assumptions in a petition to the king. Royal authority prevailed because encomenderos, other Spaniards, and their creole offspring never ceased to look to the crown to mediate in their society during their ongoing contest through institutions other than encomienda for control of Indians, and thus for wealth based on their labor.

Although royal policy and officials, and the Indian tendency to die off, were closing down slavery, encomienda, tribute, and personal service as effective avenues of private Spanish exploitation of Indians, at mid-century estancia, hacienda, and cuatequil offered viable alternatives. Yet as the first generation of Spaniards in the land dwindled, so too did Spanish settlers' hopes of exercising any sort of direct and formal political power as part of the Spanish administrative system. Instead, those with lands and Indians retained much effective local power and were a faction in the balance-of-power politics then pertaining. With royal authority to do justice, tax, and oversee defense now taken for granted, and royal patronage much desired, they showed great deference to the monarch and engaged in the practical business of finding ways to evade his officials. A maturing second, creole generation now joined the families of the conquerors and of some postconquest arrivals in acting as a military and social aristocracy, and they too looked on the heritage of the conquest as their own. These Spanish Americans were politically unconnected to Spain except through its monarch. They felt a sense of community with peninsular Spaniards only through a shared faith and a culture even then beginning to diverge. Their present and future was their stake in the land and their dominance over the other inhabitants in New Spain, or Mexico, that is, in *their* patria and region of Spanish empire. They were, as Cervantes de Salazar indicated, Mexicans.

7

The Indians under Spain

Among the Indians, Spanish policies and activities after conquest facilitated the further development of the sorts of attitudes toward the authority of the Spanish monarch initially reported by Cortés to be in the process of formation. We have seen that Charles regarded the natives as vassals in a state of tutelage who were to pay tribute, become Christian, and be gainfully employed but not abused. Although the first officials and oidores misused their commissions, Cortés successfully employed encomenderos, friars, and forceful relations with Indian leaders to begin the business of imposing and maintaining public and private Spanish authority and control over a subject population of many millions.[1]

Cortés perceived and used similarities between Spanish and Indian political organization. He replaced the overlordship exercised by Motecuhzoma II by that of the Spanish crown, ruling as governor while acknowledging the Spanish monarch as his political superior. He abolished central Indian authority, posed as champion of Indian welfare, saw to it that the natives respected the friars, and that in turn the clergy imposed Spanish religion on the general populace and instructed Indian children, particularly the sons of the indigenous leaders, in the faith and in European concepts of culture. Largely owing to his efforts, in the decade after conquest the Indian chieftains of central Mexico acknowledged the Spanish king to be their señor universal, encomenderos and friars functioned effectively as intermediaries between crown and natives, and Indian leaders on behalf of their peoples treated with these Spaniards.

Within this seemingly smooth transition, however, as Cortés noted in a remarkable understatement, the Indians had "received some vexations from our people because of the change of masters."² He referred to the years of Spanish expansion immediately after the conquest. In the aftermath of victory the Indian attempts at resistance, termed revolts by the Spaniards, were harshly quelled. Most of the highest native lords died. Many other less important chiefs were displaced. And slaving was so widespread that encomienda can be viewed as protecting numerous communities from total bondage and dispersion. Tribute and service by Indians in encomienda in the 1520s was usually a euphemism for enslavement.

The tremendous ecological disruption occasioned by Spanish conquest climaxed in famine and epidemics, first in 1531 and 1532 and again between 1545 and 1548. In both periods, the immediate cause of Indian deaths may have been typhus or yellow fever and measles.³ Whatever the exact nature of the great plagues, the most careful estimates to date are of a preconquest population, of perhaps 25 million in 1519 in central Mexico alone—shrunk by mid-century to one-fourth that number.⁴ Motolinía described the Indian decline attendant upon what Cortés termed the change of masters as a series of catastrophic plagues in the broader, biblical sense, as afflictions visited by God on New Spain. He recorded that millions of Indians died, and more suffered, from sickness, starvation, and overwork, forced to labor for encomenderos, government, and friars.⁵ Building the city of Mexico alone engaged more workers, he was certain, than had Solomon in the Temple of Jerusalem. Other Indians gave Spaniards all their gold and, when pressed for more, got it by selling their lands and their children to merchants. And, he lamented, thousands died as a result of the slave trade, and on mining gangs. Recalling the wholesale sacrifices of prehispanic days, he attributed them to the work of the devil. The postconquest horrors, however, were God's punishment of the natives for idolatry and for vices such as polygamy and sodomy. Yet within the context of divine wrath, he reported Indian misery and death caused by Spanish greed. Whatever our standards of historical objectivity, we should not forget that although Indian society endured at the communal level, if with its institutions altered, less potent, and acculturated, many millions of Indians did not.

In the 1520s, moreover, the "change of masters" extended to an immediate replacement of the native leaders in many communities. Encomenderos intervened in town politics to depose old chiefs too powerful or too obstinate, and raised new ones, sometimes maceguales, more amenable to negotiation and direction. At a higher level, Cortés and the crown began to make of the remnants of the old aristocracy a ceremonial elite, largely superseded in function by royal officials. Cortés carefully picked the more acquiescent from among the competing noble aspirants to replace their dead lords. He chose the postconquest successors to Motecuhzoma in Mexico, as well as those to many other great and lesser native rulers, being careful to appoint as legitimate chieftains men from within indigenous ruling families who were also open to Spanish supervision. Other early royal officials, and encomenderos, less circumspect, elevated commoners to leadership, and in 1528 in the process of accruing wealth and power and of countering Cortés, the first oidores stripped away grants of lands and peoples the conqueror had made to his noble indigenous allies and to the daughters of Motecuhzoma. The second audiencia subsequently restored some of these grants. The events of these years, in turn, impressed upon native aristocrats that the new Spanish señores could be controlled only by the king and his European governors and upon native communities that their most potent immediate allies were the regular clergy.

Although old usages were given the guise of continuity, as in Cortés' ordinances to maintain preconquest norms of tribute paid in slaves, by 1530 it is clear that society in native towns in encomienda was not functioning as it is so often said to have, that is, much as before conquest. In these decrees and in many surviving indigenous customs and institutions, change was apparent within seeming continuity; hispanizing was underway by the time ordinances of the second audiencia presented it as official policy in the 1530s. Then titles earlier applied to native rulers, *rey* and *señor*, were forbidden and reserved to the Spanish sovereign alone.[6] The chieftain or *tlatoani* thereafter tended to be referred to by the Spanish importation, the Caribbean term *cacique*. Other communal leaders remained known as *principales*. The cacique was often but not always appointed governor—*gobernador del rey*—and *regidores* were chosen usually from among the *principales*. When caciques were not also governors they frequently appeared on municipal payrolls for reasons of hereditary status alone.[7]

In one sense, a general acceptance of the separate but parallel nature of Indian and Spanish town governments was evidenced when in the early 1530s Indian and Spanish town representatives met in a general assembly to make formal complaint against Nuño de Guzmán.[8] Yet that meeting, and others held to advise the second audiencia on the state of the kingdom, demonstrated at most that the parallel structure allowed greater reach for royal officials. In these juntas Indian nobles sat as native political equivalents to less aristocratic, Spanish vecinos. In authority, too, Indian cabildos were more limited than their Spanish counterparts, especially through undergoing supervision by Spaniards soon notorious for rapacity, the corregidores, and, from Mendoza on, also alcaldes mayores. Immediately after the conquest we saw that old chiefs found their functions as military and spiritual leaders eroding, that new men, some commoners among them, often sought communal power and wealth through Spanish intervention. An official attempt was made in the 1530s to support or to reinstate the old tlatoanis and their children in positions of leadership, but it failed, for many of the old lords at all levels had lost position along with real power in the social ferment accompanying the Spanish takeover.[9] Whatever his background, now the greatest responsibility of the native governor was assessing and collecting from his community tribute agreed upon with the encomendero or corregidor. Thus placed in a pivotal position and deprived of ultimate responsibility for their decisions, Indian caciques tended to emulate their Spanish superiors. Many of them added large personal charges of goods and services to the tribute imposed initially by encomenderos and later by government schedule. Many collected food and clothing for themselves in the name of the corregidor, the encomendero, or the friars; and many demanded women, held slaves, and sold communal lands as their own. And they continued to do so. In periods of lowered tribute assessment some still charged their people the old rate and appropriated for themselves the "tribute leftovers."[10]

The Spanish conquest affected the upper strata of native society in other ways as well. Many Indian leaders sought to imitate the aristocratic European way of life, adapted Spanish dress, valued arms and horses highly, affected retinues, and made it generally known that they esteemed Spanish modes above their own. Chieftains were baptized. Some gave their daughters to Spaniards, sometimes under the mistaken impression they would marry them. Noble children received Christian instruction from friars. We have seen that some of the heirs-apparent of Indian lords, or at least boys represented as such, attended Gante's school at San José and the Franciscan colegio in Tlatelolco. Many such Indians, educated by the religious, came to consider it a great honor to serve them, including several boys who became Christian martyrs as a result of ferreting out relatives given to idolatrous backsliding. As one scholar has concluded, for Indian leaders "hispanization was both a symptom of authority and a method of maintaining authority."[11]

Some of the highest and most capable of Indian leaders, however, were also among the most anti-Spanish. Continued opposition was the cause given by Cortés and other Spaniards for the execution, on the expedition to Honduras, of some of the most prestigious of Indian princes. Among them was Cuauhtémoc of Mexico (who had succeeded his uncle, Motecuhzoma II) and his nephew, Coanacochtzin (baptized as Pedro de Alvarado), son of Nezahualpilli and ruler of Texcoco. Soon thereafter another of Nezahualpilli's sons, Hernando Ixtlilxochitl, a protégé of Cortés, became tlatoani of Texcoco. Ixtlilxochitl was the initial host to the first Franciscans, Gante and his two companions, and he helped the Spaniards, as a labor foreman extraordinary, to build their city of Mexico.[12]

Throughout the 1520s and 1530s in nominally subjugated areas, there were still Indian leaders who contested Spanish authority over their peoples. During Cortés' absence in Honduras, for example, Spaniards had to suppress risings in Oaxaca and elsewhere. Numerous native leaders also fought back by keeping alive their old morality and religious practices. Secret adherence to traditional ways of life and to the old gods was both their creed and one of the most effective counterattacks possible to all forms of Spanish control. Cognizant of the true nature of the threat inherent in the old faith and morality, friars continued to burn manuscripts, smash idols, tear down temples, and insist on monogamy and Christian sexual standards. The Inquisitors, in turn, rooted out and publicly punished native leaders bent on perpetuating the old order. Yet burning at least four Indians at the stake for heresy in the 1520s did little to mitigate a general Spanish fear of Indian insurrection which persisted throughout the 1530s. Thus in 1532 on rumor of an Indian rising the oidores chose to call into the city of Mexico the then exiled Fernando Cortés, with an armed force, preferring to risk civil war rather than revolt by the native majority. Church and state felt most threatened by aristocratic Indians who remained unintimidated by Spanish might and unimpressed by Spanish culture, and Spanish officialdom continued to fight political insubordination as inseparable from moral and religious backsliding. Political disaffection was frequently countered by employ of religious institutions, a process culminating in the execution in 1539 of another descendant of the old rulers of Texcoco, its current tlatoani, Don Carlos.

Other, lesser caciques who resisted Spanish religion and culture, but not so explicitly Spanish rule, were sentenced by Zumárraga only for bigamy and blasphemy.[13] Like Carlos, these others would not give up the prerogatives of numerous wives, of sexual relations with close relatives, and the old cults. Indians who claimed to be priests of the old gods were arraigned as simple sorcerers. One Tacatetl of Tanacopán (in present-day Hidalgo), for example, was accused by an encomendero of training boys for the priesthood, hiding idols in a cave, insisting he had a daughter by a goddess, and of being thought able to turn himself into a jaguar. On trial he admitted to being baptized a Christian but to having recently made human sacrifices to Tlaloc, the rain god, when drought threatened his people. He also admitted collecting tribute for the gods, having two wives, and two children by his daughter.

A similar potpourri of un-Spanish behavior also appeared in the trial of Ocelotl, a nomadic priest who had once been imprisoned by Motecuhzoma for predicting the coming of the Spaniards and the downfall of the Aztecs, and again in that of Mixcoatl, who gathered a following of believers who thought him to be a doctor and a magician, a combination of Christ and the brother of Tlaloc—that is, a native messiah, of the kind now better known to have flourished in periods of bad weather and poor crops in the arid northeast of Brazil. The punishment of these two was largely for public instruction. Their hair shorn, Ocelotl and Mixcoatl were stripped to the waist, tied to burros, paraded, and flogged. They repented, embraced Christianity publicly, and went into exile. Their crimes were not advertised as against their fellows, but as harmful to God, the state, and civilization. Through such object lessons Indians in all walks of life were shown something of the nature and advantages of complying with Spanish ideology.

Also effective in the process of acculturation, and usually somewhat more cheerful, were church services, religious instruction, and attendant ceremonies. Sometimes thousands of Indians were involved in plays written for holy days by friars for the enjoyment and edification of their native charges, and of neighboring Spaniards as well.[14] Some of these spectacles fostered both imperial identity and Christian virtue. The temptation of Christ enacted in 1539 fulfilled a double function of presenting all material wealth in a bad light while declaring the riches of Spain and Mexico as the best of the worst. This rather ambivalent piece and others, beginning in the 1520s, became annual traditions in Indian towns by the late 1530s. They continued to promote cultural and political mestizaje, as did the Spanish practice of affixing the names of patron saints to each Indian community.

In the capital the festival of Corpus Christi included a procession in which both Indian and Spanish artisans marched in separate groups and by trades. These Indians, parading in their own subdivisions of shoe-makers, blacksmiths, stonemasons, carpenters, barbers, silversmiths, and tailors, demonstrated a degree of specialization, often in Spanish skills, that was even then dying out. And by the mid-1540s Spaniards had begun to fear Indians were assimilating too many Spanish practices. Jerónimo López and Motolinía were unhappy about Indians riding horses and carrying Spanish arms. Zumárraga found the natives sadly undiscriminat-ing in their adaptations, or worse, more attracted to less admirable Spanish proclivities. He banned the Corpus Christi celebrations, he said, because during them, masked men dressed as women did lascivious dances, "embarrassing even to improper persons." Such things, he said, although done in other lands were not to be tolerated in this new church, for Indians who watched the Spaniards were quicker to imitate their profane vanities than their Christian customs. They even equated such scandalous behav-ior with their own old rites and believed that it too was sacred.[15]

The bishop sought unsuccessfully to select and to limit aspects of Spanish behavior and belief Indians would emulate. His complaint also indicates that Spanish influence on religion was only an indicator of more pervasive change. For viewed in its broadest possible context, Spanish domination immediately brought real change in all Indian life, if within seeming institutional continuity, for it shattered the old indigenous world view. Lives, balanced for maintenance in the traditional prehispanic societies, were knocked askew. Slavery was more burdensome and experienced by many more people; tribute exaction was far heavier. Work, which before had been invested with religious and social purpose and therefore had some chance of being psychically rewarding, now was in general longer and harder and had little meaning to the laborer, just as the old positions of leadership were now associated with relatively little responsibility. Opportunism now more often replaced a sense of *noblesse oblige* attendant on pride in ascribed social position. Death was more commonplace, and played a large part in communal disruption. Hope, when it appeared, was likely to be expressed as an appeal to higher authorities against injustices done by lower and closer ones. Indians usually complained of abuse by corregidores or by the mayordomos of encomenderos, and they did so to the clergy, to the audiencia, to the viceroy, and, ultimately, to the king.[16] In this manner Spanish exploitation also served to deepen Indian dependence on the crown. As we have seen, with religious instruction came teaching of obedience to, indeed near veneration of, the Spanish monarch. Indians learned theory supporting Spanish political relations and many came to rival Spaniards in the degree to which they held trust in the king and in royal justice as an article of faith.

With Mendoza came increased royal regulation of all spheres of Indian life. In the 1540s, too, church establishments in areas of native concentration proliferated. More friars arrived to swell the great missionary thrust of the 1530s and 1540s. Decrease in the Indian population of central Mexico paralleled Spanish expansion and the increase of livestock, particularly sheep. From the 1530s on, Indians lost much of the usable land. On frontiers, Indians continued to be incorporated into the labor force, in encomienda or as slaves. Viceregal government exerted its right to license and regulate Spanish-Indian relations, setting tribute to be paid by each Indian community to encomenderos, limiting slavery, discouraging personal service, regulating mine work, and revoking, granting, or extending encomiendas. It also intervened more actively in all Indian communities, imposing Spanish governing institutions including the cabildo, royal overseers, and appointing native officials. And, despite an avowed official policy of retaining old chieftains, it increasingly sanctioned the appointment to community offices of new men who were often commoners and, by the 1540s, frequently mestizos.[17]

These Spanish-style magistrates increasingly usurped the eroding, traditional authority of the old principales and, at times, of the tlatoani. As gobernadores they curried favor with encomenderos and friars and gained affluence and power. With the maturing of a new, postconquest generation, conflict increased in claims to legitimate succession, real and spurious, as did competition among such opportunists themselves and, with it, appeals to Spanish justice.[18] Lawsuits among Indians had earlier caused Vasco de Quiroga to associate native justices to his court. Friars also became involved in these internal squabbles, sometimes bringing suit on behalf of native factions. All these appeals for arbitration not only reinforced the native habit of litigating but also royal authority and the prestige of the king.

In the ongoing Spanish conquest some Indians of the central valley themselves became conquistadors expanding the royal domain. Tlaxcalans under their leaders had marched with the Spaniards against Tenochtitlán. Bernal Díaz reported that 3,000 Indians of Mexico, Tacuba, and Michoacán had accompanied Cortés to Honduras.[19] Others went to Jalisco with Nuño de Guzmán. Still others aided Cortés' lieutenants in subjugating unconverted tribes and in settling frontier areas, including Querétaro, as buffer regions. By the 1540s the earlier military alliance with Spaniards had become indigenous tradition. Following this precedent, Christianized Mexican, Tlaxcalan, and Otomí chieftains and their people—perhaps 40,000 strong—went north with Mendoza and the Spanish encomendero captains in the Mixtón Wars to subdue Chichimecas and unconverted Otomí, who were rising under native priests in response to Spanish slaving and expansion into their lands. These indigenous leaders, allowed horses and weapons, and during the campaign permitted to enslave captured Indians and awarded military honors, all much to the discomfiture of some Spaniards, remained loyal allies of the viceroy and his king. Some of them stayed to settle towns strategically located on the silver route to the north.[20]

The opening of the north in 1540s and "pacification" to the south in Yucatán and Guatemala meant more slaving in frontier areas, more pressure on encomienda Indians everywhere to produce and transport food and clothing in order to sustain mining expansion and to construct roads, dwellings, and the many ecclesiastical foundations built in that decade. It also meant greater inroads on village lands and labor by more Spaniards raising more livestock and wheat. And more effective government and taxation put a greater burden of tribute and tithes ultimately on Indian laborers. In central Mexico the boom in agriculture and stock-raising meant communal lands were increasingly overrun or acquired by Spaniards through collusion with pliant caciques or with corregidores. After famine and plague from 1545 through 1548 left perhaps only six and a half million Indians in central Mexico,[21] caciques responsible for maintaining pre-epidemic levels of tribute payment made yet heavier demands on the remaining maceguales. Government directives briefly lowering tribute in the 1550s often resulted in caciques collecting the old levies and keeping the difference, some of them receiving more tribute than their encomenderos.[22] In communities and between communities the initial Spanish impact ensured that some Indians profited at the expense of others, and also that maceguales usually bore the brunt of ongoing conquest.

As mid-century approached, unsuccessful revolts—of the Mayas in Yucatán in 1546, of natives in Oaxaca in 1547, and among the Zapotecs, Guachichiles, and Guamares in 1550—indicated last gasps of organized Indian resistance, mostly in areas where Spaniards were relatively well-established.[23] In regions under Spanish control, the imposition of the cuatequil system forced Indians to work for wages after 1549. More Spanish competition for the labor of fewer Indians chiefly benefited Spanish non-encomendero agricultural and mining interests, Spanish construction, and also Indian caciques. It signified an attempt by the crown to direct Indian labor and to garner its fruits at the expense of encomenderos, rather than improved labor conditions for Indians. Legislation by the late 1550s required each Indian to be paid for his work, then in turn to pay a head tax or fixed tribute in maize and money directly to treasury officials, who were to apportion it to local Spanish and Indian authorities.[24] This policy must be interpreted as both a desire to increase royal supervision of Indian affairs and a comment on the limitations of a central government unable to trust its local appointees—as well as an acknowledgment of the failure of Indian leaders to deal equitably with either native communities or the authorities.

In the 1550s many of the old abuses survived, though sometimes in altered form. Tribute assessment and its application continued to vary widely, encomenderos and caciques still to concert on rates rather than adhere to audiencia schedules. More encomiendas were directly under the crown, and Indian slavery was dying out in the central area; yet while it has been estimated that by 1555 only 4,000 native slaves remained in the central valley, there were many more in outlying regions, particularly in the new mines to the north. In the central valley in the 1550s Indians previously sentenced for crimes to slave labor in the mines were sent instead to workshops, for as sheep replaced people in central Mexico more labor was needed to loom wool cloth.[25] Some encomenderos residing in the city of Mexico continued, illegally, to force their Indians to carry tribute to them. And Tello de Sandoval reported in 1545 that 20 leagues outside the capital little or no recourse to the king's justice was usually permitted, that "the Indians have for kings their señores and encomenderos and know no others."[26] Seven years later Diego Ramírez made much the same observation.[27]

At mid-century, then, royal law prevailed in theory, but in practice in Indian communities it was diluted by immediate indigenous and Spanish authorities. Yet although the observable impact of royal authority was greatest near the capital and at the upper levels of Indian society, the reverberations of Spanish domination were felt throughout. For the commoner the labor and tax load increased. Society within native communities was simplified into two classes, Indians and chiefs. The old distinctions of *mayeques* (serfs), maceguales, skilled artisans, merchants, and the complex upper stratum of principales with specialized functions were disappearing along with the legitimate tlatoani. In the first post-conquest generation many communities were simply divided into overseers and work gangs, a phenomenon apparent, for example, among the previously powerful Texcocans, 20,000 of whom may have labored to build the city of Mexico under their supervisor-prince, Ixtlilxochitl.[28] Among the survivors, the members of the old aristocracy had proved their adaptability, the maceguales their own endurance. All other categories of society were becoming extraneous. Population was down, new men in command, lands preempted, diversity in production and fine craftsmanship diminishing, the specialization which marks civilization disappearing. Such change was gradual, allowing Indians and Spaniards to experience and record the slow dismemberment of the old Indian order and, as it disappeared in real life, to enshrine it in Mexican tradition as both a glorious past and a utopia that might have been.

The Indian impact on some of the early Spaniards, conversely, is responsible for sustaining certain indigenous usages. Early Spaniards recognized and preserved a certain amount of Indian diversity. Cortés commented on the wide differences between Indian groups and treated them to some extent accordingly. Quiroga judged partially on the basis of preconquest custom. Mendoza informed his successor and the crown that he had governed Indians with local conditions in mind. Cortés, Zumárraga, the second audiencia, and Mendoza all consulted as precedent prehispanic tribute rolls. And charges imposed on entire native communities through their chiefs, although onerous, helped maintain group cohesion and individuality. Friars aided in preserving, because they used them, certain preconquest indigenous political divisions. Thus, although encomenderos did not, friars working among natives outside the capital understood and employed the old cabecera-sujeto relationship, establishing themselves in the principal town and visiting its dependencies.

Friars also recorded for posterity indigenous traditions, customs, and languages, accounts of Indian environment before and after conquest, and the natives' reaction to the initial Spanish invaders. As we have noted, churchmen, primarily motivated to report the progress of Indians in Christianity, or to explain indigenous ways to other missionaries and royal officials, wrote of prehispanic and nonhispanic aspects of Mexican life as they disappeared. Some of the friars, although they destroyed with the old temples most of the written records of the native past, and much of the stimulus to remember it as well, were also largely responsible for what was subsequently salvaged of the remnants of written and oral indigenous history. Their accounts would influence all subsequent views and verdicts on Indian civilization. The histories of Motolinía and Olmos, in particular, directly or indirectly became a basis for the work of most future historians of Mexico. In their chronicles it is important to recognize that they presented native cultures through a Spanish filter, if of a special sort. And, putting oral and written memories, as (among others) Sahagún did, into a Nahuatl written in a Spanish alphabet was itself an aspect of general acculturation then occurring.[29]

The process of compiling these seminal histories, too, indicates ways European culture affected Indians. In this process, the Franciscan Colegio de Santa Cruz de Tlatelolco served as an outstanding center for accultura- tion of both friars and Indians. Each group came to admire aspects of the other's way of life, but the Spanish component was the dominating one. To Olmos and Sahagún the caciques and principales of Mexico, Texcoco, and Tlaxcala yielded up what remained of the old pictographs, encour- aged to do so by the friars' students at Tlatelolco, who also aided them in questioning native elders. From the colegio at Tlatelolco, too, came another sort of book perpetuating the native heritage, even more inter- twined with the European, and more illustrative of a process underway throughout Indian society. Martín de la Cruz, a mestizo doctor practicing in the school, compiled a Mexican herbal in his mother's language, Nahuatl. It was translated into Latin by a lecturer there, Juan Badiano, an Indian of Xochimilco. The book presented indigenous medical lore and practices organized in European fashion, and in the terminology of Pliny. It was dedicated to Mendoza's son, Francisco.[30]

Such works, and lists of books in the library at Tlatelolco, as well as our earlier inventory of the backgrounds of some of the friars who taught there, indicate that young Indians encountering the conquerors' mental world at Tlatelolco were exposed to some outstanding European minds in relatively pristine form, or at least to men who had been exposed to them. The school had on its shelves at mid-century the Bible and books by Plutarch, Virgil, Cicero, Luis Vives, and Erasmus, all texts favored by Christian humanists. It also had Aristotle's *Logic*, so important in Spain to renascent scholasticism, which in turn supported a religious and political hewing to dogma and orthodoxy.

Although the majority of Indians were little touched by such literary activities and exposure, a directing elite were. Graduates of the school, having been instructed in Christianity, and some in an advanced Euro- pean curriculum, returned to their communities to positions of leadership or worked in posts bridging the two societies—as interpreters for the audiencia, as secretaries and clerks to native governors, judges, and other officials, as teachers of native languages to friars, or as instructors in the colegio itself. Santa Cruz de Tlatelolco was a Spanish experiment born of combined currents of Christian humanism and reform and, like them, of brief vitality but lingering presence in Mexico. Like them, too, by mid-century the school was in decline. Many of its most able students had died during the plague years. Thereafter, within its walls enthusiasm waned, while Spanish administrative rigidity increased and official favor retreated—the school's fate reflecting the more general situation in Spain.[31]

Indian social organization remained formally separated from Spanish. Officials continued to distinguish between the two repúblicas, the Indian and the Spanish. Royal policy and Mendoza's decrees stipulated that Spaniards were to reside outside of native villages, and in a distinct district in the capital. Yet by 1550, despite this official policy of segregation, Spanish impact was much in evidence in the mixture of the two cultures—a mestizaje indeed abetted by royal officials, as well as by the clergy and other individuals. Old Indian usages had become diluted by Spanish practices introduced with the conquest. Such changes intensified, serving to erase or blur cultural lines. Spanish elements appeared in Indian religion, language, political forms, manuscripts, dress, domestic arrangements, social structure, and crafts. Native economies were integrated to Spanish demands. Indians became accustomed to new sorts of work, to Spanish plows, draft animals, pig and sheep herds, and construction techniques. Natives experienced Spanish impact in medicine and magic, and more and more frequently in physiognomy as well.[32] The presence of the mestizo was only the most visible result of the Spanish conquest. Deeper and broader were varying degrees and sorts of mestizaje in culture and in ideology. Native leaders, particularly, now looked up to Spanish religion and civilization. They acquiesced in the official Spanish, Christian, and imperial concept of numerous distinct social communities (repúblicas) or peoples (naciones) as microcosms of a single, unified political entity, the umbrella-like kingdom of New Spain. This theory supported the cultural and political subservience of Indians to Spanish domination, and fostered in them a sense of imperial belonging.

Friars had taught Indians respect for the Spanish crown along with Christian doctrine. At the same time, the crown furthered control of the Indian population of Mexico by successfully eliciting the respect and avowed loyalty of Indian leaders. This it did largely through the mechanism of confirming positions of aristocracy, through encouraging appeals to royal justice, and through gaining recognition of the royal origin of the tribute system. The treasurer Albornoz had early recommended that taxes be levied directly on Indians in order to impress them with where sovereignty lay, as well as to collect revenue. The second audiencia reported it had, in clarifying tribute rates, strengthened loyalty to the crown through letting Indians know from whence reform had come. Similarly, the New Laws had been in part a bid for Indian favor, stating that the king wanted all Indians to know "our will to relieve them," by granting them tribute assessments below preconquest levels. In 1555, we recall, Motolinía wrote that Indians then understood the tribute system very well. The previous year Alonso de la Vera Cruz had taken for granted, as the basic assumption of his argument justifying royal dominion, that the Indians wanted to be royal subjects and considered it an honor.

Possibly because of the tribute system, from the 1530s on, Indian leaders in and outside royal towns had direct contact with royal officials, and perceived royal supervision by oidores, visitadores, or their agents, in examining, reevaluating, and registering tributes. The visita of Tello de Sandoval, the numerous visitas between 1547 and 1550, and the tour of Diego de Ramírez in the early 1550s demonstrated to natives how long was the royal reach. Although caciques, and certain Spaniards, had found the system initially profitable, in the last years of Charles' reign the copious decrees flowing from Spain regarding tribute put them on notice that their role was to be circumscribed and their share of tribute to be regulated by the crown. At mid-century three-quarters of the Indians of central Mexico were directly under the crown, and tribute policy succeeded in ever more pointedly having individual Indians pay a tax to king's men. By then most Indian aristocrats had lost not only their communal revenues and rents but also their exemption from paying tribute, although the chiefs and their elder sons remained exempt.[33]

By the end of Charles' reign, the greatest nobles of central Mexico, recipients of honors, lands, and pensions from the monarch, had intermarried, or were themselves the products of, native liaisons with Spaniards and were acculturated and still powerful but dependent upon Spain. In the 1550s Doña Leonor Cortés Montezuma, a daughter of Fernando Cortés and Motecuhzoma's daughter (baptized as Isabel Montezuma), married the wealthy founder of Zacatecas, Juan de Tolosa. They had three children: Juan, a mineowner and cabildo member; Isabel, who became the wife of Juan de Oñate, adelantado of New Mexico, and Leonor, who wed another latterday conquistador, Cristóbal de Zaldívar Mendoza. To such people, whatever their station, belonged both European and indigenous heritages, and these mestizo aristocrats, among the more important Mexican residents, were now linked also in common subservience to the Spanish monarch. Royal efforts of the early 1550s to ameliorate tribute were short-lived. Growing bankruptcy caused the crown to press Indians for funds. Yet native leaders, like resident Spaniards, tended to blame only local officials for their increased tax burden.

In 1556 central Mexican Indian princes, led by Don Antonio Cortés, legitimate tlatoani and designated gobernador of Tacuba, responded to the worsening plight of their own people, and to their own problems, by repeatedly petitioning the crown, appealing to royal justice, certain that "only the king can help us."[34] And upon news of the death of Charles V, over 200 Indian caciques and principales joined the commemorative parade and took part in funeral observances held in Gante's church of San José.[35]

As Philip II began his reign, Indian leaders had generally accepted Spanish dominion and an imperial ideology, disseminated in accord with royal policy. Commoners too were exposed to it in sermons, in other contact with respected friars, and in public ceremonies. The result was not only token acceptance by Indians of a new dominant religion and ruler but also a deeper process of cultural change within a drastically shrunken Indian society. And among the survivors many practices and institutions appearing to be continuities of prehispanic indigenous life were now in fact hybrid accommodations to the impositions of new masters. Yet despite changes, many elements of prehispanic culture endured, often in combination with Spanish practices, as common habits and observances. Native religion passed into folk religion and prehispanic art into folk art, often simplified and putting new Christian façades on old sacred objects. Tradition survived as folklore. Although accommodating to Spanish dominion and absorbed through their leaders into the Spanish political system, Indian societies, although partially hispanized, maintained a sense of separate identity, and retained ways of life distinct from the Spanish. They would, as entities, continue to attest to diversity as a Mexican characteristic.[36]

8

Mexico, Imperial Region:
Toward a New Society

New Spain, as one writer has accurately described it, at mid-sixteenth
century was a kingdom possessed of a certain autonomy within an empire
resembling a solar system.[1] Royal policy, successful in making it a
component region of empire, regulated its internal social arrangements,
its relations to Spain, and, through the metropolis, to the wider world. It
also directed trade between imperial regions. Government in Mexico
strove to ensure that the Mexican economy met what the crown construed
to be its own financial requirements. In theory and practice, New Spain
was incorporated into the crown of Castile—now become that of imperial
Spain—and it was managed in patrimonial fashion for the ultimate
benefit of the royal treasury.

Accordingly, official policy in Mexico endeavored to develop the
region's economy to sustain settlement and, ultimately, to supply bullion
to the royal treasury. All Mexico was encouraged to engage in activities
abetting the production of gold and silver, for as Mendoza reported, most
royal revenue there came from taxes on mining production. Also of
importance, he added, were Indian tributes, import duties, and the sale of
monopolies, among them licenses to import Africans as slaves.[2]

Royal economic regulation was based on political policy. The government encouraged trade and extractive and agricultural industry primarily
for its own income and to supply settlers. Commercial interests were
secondary. The idea of capital development belongs to a later age;
bullionism dominated whatever Spanish economic thought there was at
the time, and it determined royal practice. Charles' goal was specie from

New Spain, or goods convertible to it. Such mercantile notions as protection of national manufactures and favorable balance of trade, which would mark incipient capitalism in England and France, were foreign to Spanish policy. New Spain, from Cortés' first treasure shipments, suffered from the outflow of specie to Spain, from where much of it was reshipped to purchase goods, or pay royal debts and expenses, into the Lowlands, Italy, and, to a lesser extent, France and England. Some Mexican products received the same treatment, the cochineal trade a case in point. As Mexico was dependent upon Spain, Spain itself was an economic colony increasingly dependent upon the more developed nations of Europe.[3]

The crown ensured monopoly of Atlantic trade and limited the supply of goods. From 1529 all commerce between Europe and Mexico could only flow between Vera Cruz and ten Spanish ports, and Seville had to be first port of call on the return voyage. In Seville the Casa de Contratación regulated all shipping. In was joined in 1543 by the Seville *consulado,* a private municipal merchant guild, regulated by the government, turning over certain taxes to the state, and bound to it in common cause.

Traditional Castilian economic practices were introduced into Mexico, official ordinances and activities reflecting royal policy and its lack of sense of economics per se. In New Spain, piecemeal and minute regulation occurred, designed—to employ modern terminology—to allocate social resources and to maintain commodity supplies. We have mentioned decrees intended to control wages and working conditions—in fact, by mid-century to regulate the entire spectrum of Indian labor. Others set limits to prices, amounts, and sorts of commodities produced.[4] Spanish town councils, functioning as local administrative units, controlled production and distribution of basic commodities. They enforced government orders and decreed and administered prices and amounts, for example, of grains and beef sold. Cabildo activities and Mendoza's ordinances can be viewed as measures to maintain Mexico as a going concern producing royal income. The viceroy's mining ordinances, his encouraging the building of roads, raising merino sheep, weaving cloth, and growing silk, his establishing a mint and standardizing weights and measures, all can be seen as means to feed and clothe the ordinary inhabitants of Mexico, support mining and expansion, increase taxable commodities and, ultimately, fill the treasury. Interest in Indian welfare, too, in guaranteeing resources and labor, made economic sense. However, such measures as Mendoza's setting of limits to the amount of silk individual towns were to spin perhaps partially stemmed from his own desire to monopolize silk manufacture in Mexico.[5]

His economic activities provide outstanding examples of both the impulse given and the effective limitation placed upon Mexican prosperity by governing officials. We have seen that, at the same time Mendoza acted for the crown, he often took opportunity to profit privately, investing in herds, cloth workshops, commerce with Spain, and exploration. In Mexico he apparently handled economic affairs much as Cobos did at court, combining public concern with patronage and private gain, granting specific monopolies to favored individuals, seeking to produce royal revenue while ensuring his own equitable share of profits—which he judiciously conceived of as a comfortable but not excessive sum.

Court and viceroy set precedent in economic notions and practices pervading Mexican officialdom. The first treasury men from Spain had emulated Fernandine practices, devoting themselves to private gain while setting aside a portion for the crown, and the first audiencia had followed their lead. Mendoza, like Cobos, appears to have reversed this process. Oidores, with a few notable exceptions, especially among members of the second audiencia, continued to engage in private enterprises, but with some sense of discretion. A sense of responsibility to the monarch, and of how far they could safely indulge themselves, curbed entrepreneurial tendencies among higher officials. Holders of lesser posts, however, particularly the corregidores and alcaldes mayores, expected to receive a living from legal fees and sustenance from Indian communities, and were usually unhampered by a similar sense of proportion, many of them instead following the rapacious example set by encomenderos in the 1520s.

Conquistadors and other early settlers had displayed private initiative and enterprise in conquest and, afterwards, some continued to do so in business and commerce. What they wanted, as we have noted, was not simply wealth but objectives realizable through wealth. Their goal was seignorial status, and the means necessary to achieve and maintain a lordly way of life. Their mercantile endeavor of itself was not supported by ideology. But while making money was not a prestigious activity, playing the *rico hombre* was. Theirs was a fundamentally military mentality, reminiscent of the reconquest. By mid-century it had become one of a ceremonial military aristocracy, and was strongly influenced by attitudes at court. Wealthy Spaniards in Mexico then strove to emulate the peninsular aristocracy and, above all, the monarch, including his economic attitudes and sumptuous style of living. Official and individual attitudes infused activities conducive to an essentially static economy providing luxuries as their due and as indicators of their status to leaders and defenders—thus, ran the argument, preserving society.

Yet beginning in the 1520s, individual Spaniards seeking fortunes downward in the earth, and outward in peripheral areas, did spur, to support their endeavors, production of food, simple clothing, and household goods, and they stimulated economic interaction and exchange involving much of New Spain, particularly as expansion opened areas initially incapable of self-maintenance under Spanish-style exploitation. Thus, the needs of mining communites such as those in Colima and, later, Zacatecas, and the impetus early mining gave to the general economy, encouraged a very rudimentary but discernible economic interdependence among subregions of New Spain.

These Spaniards mobilized men, women, and goods to support mining towns and way stations to them, and, to a lesser extent, to produce for their individual profit sugar, hides, and dyes for export, primarily to Europe. The outstanding example of economic enterprise is to be found in the integrated activities of the scattered towns and areas held by Cortés. Money was scarce, credit expensive. It proved advantageous to him and to other Spaniards—singly or in partnerships or groups, to become involved directly in as many facets as possible of production, exchange, and distribution—for encomenderos and officials sold commodity tribute in Spanish towns. Often the same people were encomenderos, mine-owners, and stockmen, integrating all aspects of metal extraction and supportive enterprises. They had close ties to energetic merchants who controlled exchange between regions, where encomenderos did not, and across the Atlantic. Aiding commerce, Indians as the labor force constructed roads, cities, and dwellings and carried goods and ore, thereby also facilitating both settlement and the opening of outlying areas producing goods (through Indian labor) for export. In short, within the confines of crown-centered regulation a limited but recognizably regional economy was developing within Mexico.

The capital was its core, hub of economic and also social, political, and intellectual activities, seat of the viceregal court, and residence of most Spaniards. Nearly all who could, wherever their encomienda or properties, maintained houses there. Whereas in 1525 the city had perhaps 150 houses of Europeans, by the 1550s they numbered between 1,500 and 2,000 and were in the central area, while in four major native barrios lived over 80,000 Indians. A majority of resident Spaniards then lived in the capital, Indians in the countryside. Spaniards also settled in the other European towns. Puebla, second largest, had approximately 600 Spanish households, Oaxaca perhaps 500 Spaniards.[6] In Spanish towns Indians provided most of the labor. They also mixed with less affluent Europeans and other peoples to make up what classically minded contemporaries referred to as the *plebe*.

As Spain grew ethnically more homogeneous, in Mexico ethnic variety increased, and was at first not officially impeded. The government and church, to uphold Christian morality, initially favored Indian-Spanish marriages as preferable alternatives to informal cohabitation. In 1529 Zumárraga asked grave penalties be exacted of Spaniards living with Indian women without benefit of clergy. In 1537 the bishops of Oaxaca and Guatemala joined him in requesting that the crown insist Spanish bachelors living with Indian women marry them. Church pressure led to numerous mixed marriages, and to legitimizing many mestizos born out of wedlock. In Puebla in 1534, of the 80 male settlers 20 had Indian wives.[7]

Mestizo children, especially when recognized as legitimate heirs by their Spanish fathers, became members of Spanish society in Mexico. And official policy allowed the mestizo offspring of highborn Indian women to receive their legacy of wealth and position, although not real power. They sometimes wed Spaniards. We have seen Leonor, a daughter of Cortés and Isabel Montezuma, although mestiza and illegitimate, married Juan de Tolosa and founded a northern dynasty.[8] Informal unions, such as that of Leonor's parents, were more common. Las Casas observed that Indians often gave their daughters to Spaniards in good faith, believing they would marry them, but that mestizos were usually illegitimate. A 1533 decree, as did Zumárraga, expressed patriarchal concern for impoverished mestizo "orphans."[9] To house, Christianize, and acculturate them, Spaniards founded the school of San Juan de Letrán for boys and a convent for girls. Such children, usually born to macegual mothers, so proliferated that by the 1550s *bastardo* meant mestizo.[10]

As this new generation matured, it included mestizos who lived among Indians. Some mestizos, we have seen, tended to claim legitimately, or to usurp, local headship, to govern native communities, and to act as mediators between Indians and Spaniards. Some probably became priests.[11] Each year a few outstanding graduates of San Juan de Letrán were authorized to attend the University of Mexico. Other mestizos, footloose, caused official exasperation. Outside all organized society, exempt from tribute, unemployed, propertyless, they harassed Indian communities or in various ways gained influence in them. Velasco reported such vagabonds numerous and "evilly inclined."[12] A royal order of 1523 had required Spaniards to send their mestizo sons to Spain, probably reflecting a hope to assimilate them.[13] By mid-century, the official attitude had changed permanently. The government, seeking to preserve what it termed "social equilibrium"—that is, to ensure a stable, static society—attempted to discourage the production of children of mixed lineage. Too late. Individual Spaniards and Indians had, by and large without premeditation, ensured the appearance of a new, distinctly Mexican generation, with many of its members of mixed background included within Spanish Mexican society.

Spaniards had guaranteed Mexico further ethnic complexity. A few Negroes had come from the Antilles with Cortés and subsequent expeditions. Black slaves from Spain had been introduced in Española by 1503, and under Ferdinand an organized trade developed. He is known to have authorized the treasury to ship 100 or 200 Negroes on several occasions, for sale to colonists. He also licensed other shipments of them and allowed individuals to take slaves with them to the Indies.[14] And in Española his government had black slaves, whom it employed in mining and constructing fortifications.

Assured by Spanish residents that blacks would relieve Indian laborers, Las Casas, as had Dominicans previously, supported black slavery, and in 1517 requested that each Spaniard be allowed to bring in twelve Negro slaves. He later regretted the decision, admitting that Indians continued to be abused and now blacks were too, beginning with what he now realized was their usually unjust enslavement by the Portuguese in Africa to fill the demand in the Spanish Indies. Blacks sent to the Indies then came largely from Africa by way of the slave market in Seville.[15] Thus, Las Casas and other Spaniards, while they saw Indians being unjustly enslaved—in that they were neither taken in war nor cannibals nor prior slaves—could believe the origin of Negro servitude legitimate, that is, in accord with Iberian custom and Christian principles, until they were disabused by evidence to the contrary—one explanation for why many Spaniards opposed to Indian slavery accepted black servitude.

Cisneros during his regency forbade issuing permits to ship Negroes.[16] When Charles came to Spain, Gattinara and Adrian, heeding Las Casas, ordered Fonseca's House of Trade to determine what number of blacks were needed in the islands. They were told 4,000. In 1517 Charles granted an eight-year monopoly over shipping blacks to America to a Flemish favorite, who sold it to a Genoese-controlled firm in Seville.[17] The Genoese shipped some slaves and resold numerous licenses at great profit—to whom, and for how many blacks, is unclear. Private licenses were also granted, to Cobos among others. Large numbers of Negroes began to be sold in the Indies from 1518 on, and, ultimately, the Portuguese factories in Africa supplied black slaves to Spanish America. Las Casas, known for his generous statistics, wrote in the 1550s that 30,000 Negroes had been shipped to Española, and more than 100,000 to all Spanish America.[18]

Early royal officials, and probably most Spaniards of wealth and position, brought black slaves from Spain to Mexico in their entourage. Estrada, for example, was licensed to bring twelve, and twelve more are known to have come with the first oidores.[19] Zumárraga and Quiroga, although opposed to Indian slavery, held Negro slaves.[20] Other blacks, slave and free, continued to arrive from the Caribbean and the peninsula, and slaves, increasingly, direct from Africa. Some enterprising Spaniards in the Antilles reportedly lived by training Negro slaves as artisans, then selling them on the mainland.[21] In Mexico male Negroes worked as herders, farmers, teamsters, artisans, at weaving textiles, on construction, and in sugar mills and mines, some with trusted positions as overseers of Indians.[22] Black slaves were both privately and government held. Of two who arrived with Narváez, one is known to have been a jester, another to have brought smallpox to Mexico.[23] A black claimed to have been the first to sow wheat in New Spain.[24] One Juan Valiente ran away from a Puebla master and became a conquistador of Chile.[25]

Data on Negroes in our period are spotty but indicate that black slaves were introduced by Spaniards in Mexico for their own prestige, labor, and profit. The junta of Mexican cabildo representatives convoked by Salazar and Chirinos, on 10 November 1525 asked the king that no monopoly be granted to ship black slaves to Mexico, that the trade be free.[26] Nevertheless, on 15 November 1527 Cobos and Dr. Diego Beltrán of the Council of the Indies each received licenses to export 200 slaves to the Indies. A month later they contracted with Pedro de Alvarado to form a company to export slaves to work Guatemalan mines. And in 1528 Charles issued a permit to two German agents of his Welser bankers for shipping to America 4,000 black slaves in four years and continued to grant other licenses for private use.[27] From 1532 on, the government contracted all such commerce directly, heightening competition and increasing the number of blacks shipped.[28] In 1533 the audiencia of Mexico reported the arrival of 131 Spaniards bringing with them many Negro slaves.[29]

Black slaves in Mexico were valued by Spaniards above their Indian counterparts. In the 1530s they were relatively few compared to the numbers then in the Caribbean, and expensive compared to Indian slaves. Motolinía then reported a letter written by a black slave in Mexico to another in Spain or Española:

> Friend Fulano, this is a good land for slaves. Here the black has good food. Here the black has a slave who serves him, and the black's slave has a *naboría,* that is, an [Indian] boy or servant. Arrange to have your master sell you so that you may come to this land, for it is the best in the world for blacks.[30]

Motolinía added, however, that all slaves, if they proved lazy or vicious, or ran away two or three times, had to wear a collar.[31]

In the 1530s individuals in Mexico receiving permits to bring in slaves for sale included Mendoza, who as of 1542 had not used the privilege. Two Seville merchants paid, in 1537, for a license to ship 1,500 blacks to America.[32] By the 1540s the expanding economy, the hardening of royal policy against Indian servitude, the royal need for funds, Indian decimation, and the belief that one Negro worker was worth up to four Indians, had stimulated the import of probably thousands of blacks. In 1542, for example, in return for a loan, Charles granted two Genoese a permit to ship 900 Negroes to America. Many were sent to Vera Cruz, and most were sold to Cortés for his sugar mills. The marqués, it will be recalled, signed a contract to exchange sugar for slaves, a practice becoming general and making of both trades a single enterprise. After his death, his son Martín, the new marqués, made a similar contract in 1550, again with Genoese in Seville.[33]

Blacks as well as Indians died of the plague, further intensifying demand in the mid-1540s. In 1545 the visitador Tello de Sandoval, commenting on the situation to Prince Philip, revealed current assumptions, and something of official attitudes, concerning Negro slaves. He reported that royal cattle were harming Indian crops and that their black slave herders were subject to plague, and suggested selling both herds and Negroes.[34] In the same year Jerónimo López, in his periodic report to the king, mentioned that 14 of his slaves had died and asked permission to import 50 blacks duty free.[35] And in 1545 the ayuntamiento of Mexico asked and obtained a license to introduce 3,000 Negro slaves for mine work.[36] Velasco was granted a permit to bring in 100 Negroes in 1549. At mid-century legal black slave imports continued to rise as a result of royal licenses, urged on merchants in return for forced loans or confiscated American bullion. In 1552, Prince Philip reportedly sold 23,000 slaving licenses. Blacks were also prime contraband.[37]

Free blacks also appeared early in New Spain. There were blacks with Montejo in Yucatán, others with Alvarado in Guatemala, and some 200 of them in his Peruvian expedition, their status unclear. Yet it is reasonable to assume all were not slaves, since free Negroes were numerous in Seville, and known in the Antilles and Mexico. From at least 1530, some slaveholders in New Spain followed the Spanish practice of freeing slaves in their wills, among them Zumárraga and Quiroga. The story is told of Juan, a Negro freed by Alonso de Estrada by 1531, who was also given a pig farm in the valley of Otumba; through friendship with a neighboring Otomí principal he then secured the labor of a village of 1,000 Indians, "who served the Negro as lord and master until he died."[38] Escaped black and Indian slaves, free in fact, lived in the mountains separating the valleys of Mexico and Toluca, and by the 1530s were raiding Indian houses and fields. At mid-century free blacks were among the vagabonds scored by the government.[39]

An early royal cédula yields insight into Spanish attitudes conducive to emancipation and related to prevailing assumptions regarding human nature. In order that Negroes should not hide or run away, but settle, marry, work, "and serve their masters with more goodwill . . . it would be well that they should receive their freedom and have it confirmed after serving a certain time" and paying a stipulated sum.[40] The royal suggestion followed practice among at least some Spanish slaveholders in Seville and the Caribbean. Spanish belief that promise of freedom at some future time would induce hard work and good behavior among black slaves undoubtedly accounts for the presence of many free Negroes. Further, there is evidence that some slaves were given holidays from work during which they could make money to buy their freedom.

Little information is available on female Negroes. They appear infrequently in contemporary accounts, which by their nature may distort the overall situation. Black women were mentioned as slaves in wills left by Spaniards, and in the records of Zumárraga's Inquisition and those of later ones they appear as domestics and concubines to Spaniards, and somtimes free, living on the fringes of society, charged with sorcery, practicing folk magic, and in general engaging in sub rosa activities.[41] They were less desirable merchandise than males; so the crown stipulated that one female must be shipped for every three males.

Although estimates vary widely, blacks and part-blacks probably outnumbered Spaniards in New Spain by the 1540s.[42] In 1553 Velasco reported 20,000 Negroes.[43] The contraband trade in blacks made population estimates even more difficult. Whatever their number, while valued individually they were feared collectively. Negroes joined Indians rioting in the city of Mexico in 1533. In 1536 Negroes in a reputedly widespread conspiracy plotted, with Indian complicity, to kill all Spaniards in New Spain and set up a black king. The arrival of more blacks in the 1540s, coupled with Spanish dread of Negro rebellion, reinforced by more uprisings and reported Negro plots in that decade, encouraged retention of a military mentality on the part of settlers and officials. One result was restriction of Negro movement and activity, such as had earlier taken place in the Caribbean. Blacks were not to carry arms, assemble, be out at night, buy wine or pulque, and were subjected to stiffer penalties for crimes they committed. Mendoza suggested fewer of them be sent to Mexico. Velasco expressed the same opinion and, in 1553, established a Santa Hermandad, a constabulary on the Castilian model, to protect the countryside from vagrants, including blacks. Fear, too, was a factor in repeated and largely futile directives to keep Negroes and Indians apart.[44]

Importation at the customary three men to one woman ratio, and proximity in daily work, ensured mingling of blacks with Indians and especially with mestizos. Children born in New Spain of mixed black and Indian parentage, then termed *zambaigos* or *zambangos*, and of white and mulato parents, described as *negros criollos* or *mulatos* or *moriscos*, were much in evidence by mid-century.[45] Mulatos and moriscos also came from Spain. Quiroga had a mulato slave.[46] According to one chronicler, a *mulata*, Beatriz de Palacios, married to the soldier Pedro de Escobar, was with Cortés during the conquest and performed soldier's duties.[47] Another mulata, named Ana, freed by a Sevillian aristocrat, emigrated to New Spain in 1537.[48] According to House of Trade registers, many other freed blacks or part-blacks emigrated to the New World, most of them single men and women but some married and with families.[49] In this period the term criollo meant only mulato.[50] Although by the eighteenth century accepted as pertaining to all Mexican-born "Spaniards"—that is, as synonymous with whites, criollo may have retained traces of its prior meaning.

Marriage between Negroes and Indians at first was unusual, unacculturated non-Spanish peoples showing little interest in that Spanish institution, and the government and Spanish masters frowning on such unions. A cédula of 1527 urged black men who would marry to do so with black women "in so far as possible."[51] It was reissued in 1538 and 1541. An order of 1551 stated the more usual arrangement, "we understand that many Negroes have Indian women for concubines."[52] It appears that, as in Spain, in Mexico Negroes were church members, forbidden ordination but allowed marriage. The Siete Partidas and Spanish custom gave masters absolute control of slaves but allowed slaves legitimate marriage, including to nonslaves—the Partidas stating slaves might marry whom they chose—but not freedom because of marriage. In contradistinction, in Mexico slave marriage at times apparently brought freedom but at others was arranged and forced by masters, who justified such union as a device for moral-religious ends and employed it to increase tractability as well as the number of their slaves. Children of more casual liaisons between free Indian women and black male slaves were usually raised free, those of female slaves usually remained enslaved.[53] A royal cédula of 1538 noted that a Mexican regidor, Bartolomé de Zarate, informed the crown that when male Negro slaves arrived they lived with Indian and black women in and out of their masters' houses. When masters made such couples marry "to rid them of sin," the slaves thereupon insisted that they were free. The decree repeated an order of 1527 stating that Negro slaves and Indians might marry with the consent of their masters but "they will not be free."[54] The ayuntamiento published it in 1541. Yet rather than have slaves wed Indians or partners of their own choice, some masters preferred to force them to marry other slaves they held, countering resistance with violence. A few appeals to the church and the courts are known to have succeeded in divorce, or in mitigating abuse of slaves.[55]

There is evidence of Spanish-mulata marriage by 1540, as well as of numerous unsanctified liaisons between Spanish men and black or part-black women, often their slaves. Of five Negro women tried by Zumárraga for sorcery and superstition in 1536, two were slaves, accused of buying aphrodisiacs from an Indian to administer to their Spanish masters in order better to please them sexually. One said she wanted to forestall her owner's seeking relations with other women and thus, through monopoly, to secure better treatment, gifts, and freedom.[56]

A first generation of offspring, usually born of black fathers to free Indian women and so often free themselves, at mid-century were finding employ much like that of mestizos, in pivotal positions between Spaniards and Indians, in what anthropologists neatly term societal interstices. The men who worked included overseers of Indian field labor, known as *calpixques* or *estancieros*, workshop foremen, laborers or supervisors in sugar mills and mines, and herdsmen.[57] Mulatos as well as mestizos were replacing traditional Indian rulers at mid-century.[58] Mulatas labored in fields, mills, and as household servants. Many mulatos also were vagrants, part of the urban plebe or living off Indian villages. Free blacks and part-blacks, employed or not, remained on the edges of society, legally excluded from membership and generally feared by its members proper, by the government, and by the clergy. A royal decree of 1541 insisted that all Negroes attached to encomiendas should have no trade, communication, or habitation with Indians, and characterized blacks as "very prejudicial to Indian towns, aiding and inciting vices and bad customs, hurting the royal treasury, and doing other harm."[59] Motolinía included calpixques and blacks among his ten plagues visited on the Indians, and in 1555 warned the crown of yet another Negro plot.[60]

In sum, Spaniards tended to lump mestizos, mulatos, and free blacks as undesirables, especially as their numbers increased by the 1540s. Known as *castas*, all were excluded from the priesthood in 1555, from the trade guilds beginning to organize in Mexico in the 1540s and, as far as possible, from all social position.[61] They did not officially enjoy, as did Indians, even segregated status. They had no legitimate position in Mexico, unless as slaves, and no place in the imperial scheme. Yet being beyond the pale had its compensations, for mulatos and mestizos paid no tribute until 1580.[62] Blacks and part-blacks, excluded from Mexican society under Habsburg rule, have since been assimilated into it but largely ignored as a component of its population and an element in its history.[63]

Cultural syncretism, where the input was Spanish and Spanish superiority was understood, was officially encouraged as an effective means of controlling the indigenous populace and all non-Spanish and part-Spanish peoples. Miscegenation, on the other hand, went counter to the dominant Spanish Christian view of society vigorously fostered under Isabella and Ferdinand and now official tradition.[64] It went against increasingly important notions of racial purity, and it caused official irritation partially, as reports to the crown imply, because attesting to a certain irremediable sloppiness in the Spanish imposition of order in Mexico. For by 1550 in New Spain an accepted, imperial ideology upheld by law and the church delineated the relationship of (only) Spanish and Indian societies to the monarch, regulated their internal structures, but encouraged only labor relations between them, and assumed Spanish superiority. Slaves had an ascribed, legal position, described in the Partidas as "a contemptible one," at the bottom of the social hierarchy.[65] Free blacks and all new peoples recognized as of mixed parentage, however, had no place in the dominant ideology and appeared socially obtrusive to its adherents in theory, and increasingly frequently so in person. Yet, by hindsight, the Mexican future belonged to such a mixture of peoples.

9

Reflections on an Era

The roots of much Mexican history since the Spanish conquest are discernible in both material and mental aspects of the years during which Spain established domination. Prevalent conditions today—government by one party and government or party as mediator among social factions, constitutionalism, the survival of peasant communities, mestizo control and caciquismo in many towns, indigenismo, the strength of Mexico City, of central government there, and of central control of funds, as well as other remnants of the past which have only recently lost their potency or altered their forms—especially the traditional economic and landholding arrangements—all were visible in the initial period of Spanish and Indian encounter. And important to that period, in turn, were the peninsular backgrounds of the Spanish conquerors and the preconquest life of the native peoples.

What Spaniards did in and concerning Mexico was influenced by conditions there and by Spanish interaction with the new environment. Spaniards' perceptions of the peoples, the country, and of their own situation within it, however, had been conditioned by the society from which they had come. Ways of life and institutions that took root under Spanish domination were bounded by the life and institutions of the immediate past. Conversely, the new situation affected selection and adaptation of older usages.

Spaniards brought to Mexico not only ways of life but also assumptions about morality, social order, and ultimately, human purpose, corresponding to a stock of knowledge they thought of as common sense and in accord with Christian principles of universal application. This broadly

Christian outlook on the world proved well suited to overseas expansion and empire. The concept of a universal community with numerous subdivisions made excellent sense to Spaniards, and later to Mexicans, of the great diversity among groups in New Spain. They could see all organized groups as included ultimately within a universal order transcending human differences. And they could find that order reflected in the imperial system. A ruler whose attributes could be thought of as mirroring the divine ones of father, judge, and protector could be endowed with great political authority. Knowing that their souls were equal, men and women could accept the idea of a hierarchical society in which function justified position. *Don Quixote* could not have been written in, or of, the early sixteenth century, when social structure and function appeared harmonious, practical, useful, and right—that is, when social conditions were more or less compatible with individual consciousness of social reality.

The relative ideological harmony induced by Isabella and Ferdinand, particularly in Castile, and its importation to America helps to explain certain specific long-standing apparent historical discrepancies, important to Mexico and all Spanish America. First, we now better understand how concepts later systematized by the Jesuit Francisco Suárez earlier had become part of a Spanish American mentality. His corporatism was native to medieval Spain, as was his idea of a pact between community and ruler. Both notions had been long employed in Spain as oligarchic or royal devices advancing seignorial domination. They continued to be used for the same purposes in both Spain and America. So much for the anachronistic assertion that "Suárez lies hidden beneath the Latin American encomienda."[1] Second, and related, has been a too strong assumption among scholars and others that Thomism shaped Spanish political and legal thought. Rather, it reinforced traditional tendencies on both sides of the Atlantic. Third, although Spanish national integration was beyond the horizon in 1519, Spanish national identity was not. Finally, Spain was not, nor has ever been, a corporate entity. Certain corporations have been powerful there and in America, but corporatism was not a political system among Spaniards; instead, it was a way of thinking order into diversity. Fundamentally, corporatism was a theory employed by central authority to facilitate control. Such theoretical centralization was successfully imposed and did its work, up to a point. In Spain and Mexico under Charles V, corporate and universal Christian principles, embedded in language and religion, were accepted by leaders of all segments of society, and were reinforced by the joining of Spanish monarchy to Holy Roman Empire and by being connected with mystical and humanistic reform movements.[2]

Under such an ecumenical umbrella much diversity could exist. Men

145

and women had only to acquiesce to the authority of crown and church, and to the superiority of Spanish civilization. They could with impunity hold views which only by hindsight appear contradictory to official ideology. Seemingly dissonant belief in unofficial values such as individual experience and opportunism, or in social mobility through military achievement or wealth, did not conflict with the official world view. These values, rooted in popular Spanish tradition and in oligarchic custom had received a certain official cachet in being associated with the reconquest, and during conquest in America they could be seen as military adjuncts not threatening established central authorities. Afterwards, however, continuance of a military mentality caused friction among Spaniards, was allied to resistance to royal power, and was successfully contained by the crown. This mentality, surviving among resident Spaniards and as a component of criollismo throughout the colonial period, subverted official values, such as respect for authority and deference to it, but for 250 years it did not challenge adherence to the sacrosanct concepts of the crown, church, and culture. The stubborn persistence of this mentality is visible today in effective power arrangements, discernible in local and regional power structures, in military governments, and in widespread military strength and influence. Related is one explanation for seeming discrepancies between authoritarian political practices and much constitutional theory in Spanish America, for theory often remains an umbrella, indicating where political and moral authority ultimately reside, while real power is vested in more immediate and de facto authorities. This arrangement itself is a traditional one.

Connected, too, is the tendency of many observers of Spain and Spanish America, whose own background is Anglo-American, to assume institutions in the United States and in Latin America are, or should be, parallel in structure, function, and potency. Yet institutions involving almost every facet of life introduced in Mexico under Charles V reflected habits quite different from those connected with Anglo-American settlement later. In addition, institutions introduced even a generation later in South America differed from their Mexican counterparts. The strong belief of Mexican conquistadors in the interlocking nature of military values and Christian ecumenism may well have been a factor in easing introduction of greater royal authority in Mexico than even was present in Spain, and in discouraging the kind of challenge to royal power accompanying civil war in Peru.[3] The very powerful Cortés, and clerics and lawyers, and Mendoza—raised in the afterglow of the fall of Granada, during a period of royal prestige, aware of classic political and legal thought, their concepts of patriotism and public service reinforced by Greek and Roman examples, and proudly subject to *the* Christian emperor—combined royal cause, Christian reform, and self-interest to give to Mexican institutions a stamp unique in America. In the years during which these Spaniards organized Mexican institutions, the Spanish background allowed them to put high value on education of all peoples as a means to social reform and harmony, and on rational activity and a well-spent life as approaches to God. It also sparked heroic endeavor placing a high emphasis on glory, the gaining of eternal renown through great works. In a new and exotic setting, these early Spanish administrators initially took an optimistic view of human nature and expended tremendous energy in implementing their plans for bettering the human condition.

The Spanish ambience also makes more understandable the ability of relatively few Spaniards to conquer and control millions of Indians. Conquistadors' feats were acts of will based on their conception of Spanish military norms and on an unswerving purpose reinforced by classic and chivalric ideals. They conquered with Indian aid, through superior technology, but also, and largely, owing to a superiority of intangibles, among them political assumptions of a universal applicability and an optimistic and militant faith that God was on their side. Mexico was won through high courage, endurance, and nerve, and also through using perceived similarities in Spanish and Indian power arrangements—enabling adroit handling of Indian allies and Motecuhzoma and afterwards, in the same vein, the establishing of encomienda.

Spanish domination of New Spain was built not simply on Spanish usages, but upon use of both traditional Spanish and Indian institutions, as Spaniards saw them. Spaniards continued political consolidation begun by Aztecs and Tarascans. They elaborated upon indigenous systems of tribute, slavery, landholding, social organization, and upon acceptable custom. They brought Indian communities into the Spanish political system through manipulating native leaders and through the interim device of encomienda—a negotiated compromise between conquerors and crown. But they established more lasting habits through successfully syncretizing Spanish to older native usages, through imposing Castilian political ideas, especially the notion of the monarch as *señor universal,* and by acculturating natives through religion. Today, indigenous communities, where they have survived, are of a postconquest hybrid culture geared to European domination.

In connection with Spanish conquest, these further points are worth emphasizing. First, although the conquistadors introduced their own, essentially anachronistic, version of a traditional Spanish seignorial system, the crown quickly asserted its authority as overlord to squelch political practices tending to autonomy, but it did continue to support a propertied Spanish elite as a key to holding the land and its peoples. Second, encomienda approximated slavery in the 1520s, which helps to explain why Indian slavery was not more widespread. Third, the crown vigorously discouraged what outright Indian slavery there was, as a result of the Caribbean experience—that is, both because of Indian decimation and because Indian slavery was found to undercut royal authority and the concept of Indians as royal vassals or subjects, as encomienda, limited tribute regulation, and right of appeal, did not. Encomenderos—according to the royal policy—could enjoy stipulated fruits of Indian labor but must view holding Indians as a privilege of delegated payments and services due the king. Black slavery, conversely, was favored because it did not challenge royal authority, because it was thought of as just, and because it was construed as a measure to preserve royal subjects (the Indians) and increase royal revenue. Lastly, the conquest was essentially a private military endeavor, booty included repartimientos of Indians and, immediately afterwards, was often invested in private enterprise. But mentality and situation were not propitious to the development of an economy wherein private capital increased through investment. Capitalist elements were present but the system prevailing by mid-century was a limited seignorial one, derived from prior Caribbean and peninsular practices.

Reinterpretation of the Spanish struggle for justice during expansion into America assures the importance of the principle of justice to the history of Spain in America, but changes some of the reasons why. Las Casas was a sincere reformer, schooled in law and theology, exposed to humanism, an idealist of universal Christian persuasion. He had a natural ally in the king, particularly since his arguments provided justification for royal rule and damaged conquistador rationales for their own seignorial dominion in America. He, and Cisneros, equated royal dominion with moral concern for the Indians. Vitoria, a transitional figure—that is, a scholastic previously influenced by the humanist Erasmus—coupled traditional Spanish and revitalized scholastic theory with humanitarian concern. In delivering their opinions on the New World and its inhabitants, Las Casas and Vitoria supported monarchy and abetted development of a Spanish imperial ideology suitable for American domination. The two friars could do so in the first place because the concept of justice was central to religion, and to royal and ecclesiastic legal and political theory. Justice had become a prime royal instrument. The Spanish struggle to impose justice was a royal project, and it successfully contributed to legitimating and expanding effective monarchical authority in Mexico.

An increasing understanding of relations between crown and conquerors indicates that it will not do simply to categorize conquerors as revolting against superior authority, or to identify them as royal agents—two scholarly tendencies that have muddied the history of the conquest and its consolidation, making unintelligible social relations and political theory and practice.[4] By hindsight the conquistadors were working much more for the government than they imagined, but much less than the crown desired. Although by mid-century official royal theory explained the conquest as opening the Indies to royal domination, crown and conquerors both believed Mexico was theirs. The conquerors felt it was theirs to enjoy the fruits of victory as its immediate lords, while to the crown the military conquest was only, when viewed in its best light, a first step to introducing royal authority.

Subsidiary here is the dispute concerning the nature of the Indians; attitudes toward Indians were related to factional interests in the tug-of-war for power in Mexico. Thus, the Indian if capable of rational activity could be a royal subject and a Christian; if not, he could be relegated simply to brute labor for individual Spaniards. Many Christian humanists and friars honestly believed in Indians as rational beings and members of the human community, but even most of the more optimistic of them thought of Mexican natives, since they lacked European standards of civility, as minors or wards to be educated; Indians also, ran this line of thought, had to be made to work, that is, to perform their ascribed (ultimately religious) social function. The discussion of the natives as slaves by nature, the men-or-beasts dispute, and other kindred issues can now be viewed not only as theoretical considerations but also as indicators of the interlocking relationship of events, activities, and ideas.

The intense Spanish concern with law and legalism and interest in justice, transported to Spanish America, can be better understood when seen in network relationship to politics and ideology. Written law in Castile was the king's justice, and respect for it of great political value. Law was sanctified as embodying ideals, derived from religion, of Christian morality. Its practice was a means to preferment and prestige, and perhaps also wealth, and a source of royal income as well as of authority. Respect for law was related to the high value placed on an ordered and static society. Peace, order, and law were interdependent concepts, all reflecting the divinely regulated and harmonious universal scheme. Thus the formal, abstract, and logical nature of Spanish codes, and a reason why royal decrees, couched in patriarchal tone, frequently appealed to general moral principles in resolving particular situations. Thus, too, the seeming gap between the literal and the generally understood senses of law, for it was expected that royal legislation was at times a moral desideratum, not necessarily an imperative, and at others an overlay on or interpretation of local custom, to be imposed by officials where, and to the extent, possible—allowing for human weakness and without rupturing consensus. Although acknowledging customary usage, it was, as the Laws of Toro stated, to be the royal interpretation of it that counted. What had begun as a royal wish under Isabella and Ferdinand had come to be

149

viewed in Castile as a higher sort of law, a harmonizing device by which to review custom. Spanish law cannot be compared to that of English precedence literally, or without taking into account its milieu and the way it worked. And within this context, argument over whether or not the monarch in Castile was above the law makes little sense. As one historian has observed, "those who devise the rules are likely, in the last round, to win the match."[5]

Government control was imposed and worked out in Mexican society by trial and error, with the help of the clergy and under royal guidelines. A state apparatus of audiencias and a viceroy replaced Indians and Spaniards functioning in Mexico as political lords. Although at local level much effective political power remained to encomenderos and especially to large landholders, three real brakes curbed their power: the spiritual and institutional strength of the church, the right of appeal to royal courts, and the royal right to regulate and receive taxes. This political situation, its foundation stone the strengthened concept of royal authority, would prevail for 250 years.

Conquerors had brought their religion in militant form as the victorious faith, but the regular clergy, in tremendous missionary enterprise, were responsible for its domestication and endurance. A victory of proselytizing zeal and humanistic ideals over physical reality was the ability of early sixteenth-century European friars to see in American Indians a reflection of the first Christians. Roman Catholicism and its propagators secured a near-monopoly on education and introduced in Mexico the most effective ongoing institutions and personnel maintaining popular support for Spanish imperial control. Mendoza could well have said, as he reportedly did, "the monasteries of the friars were bulwarks and castles defending the land, their example and missionary work the sturdiest parapets of the king."

Religious schism in Charles' German lands from the 1530s on deeply affected Spanish policy in Mexico, rendering inappropriate concepts of an ecumenical world order and of universal Christian brotherhood, accentuating problems of religious deviance, and increasing royal pressure on Mexican revenues. By mid-century, in Europe and Mexico closer conformity to a narrower, more dogmatic Spanish Christianity was seen as essential to the faith and the monarchy. More strictures were put on interior Christianity and more importance attached to outward observance. The government supported a more inflexible and structured church. The same forces shaping decisions made at Trent influenced policies in Mexico. Secular, individual study and rational inquiry were discouraged. Orthodoxy narrowed and, as Cervantes de Salazar remarked, the virtues of humility and obedience naturalized. In Spain the lingering vitality of other faiths and sects was being crushed and all cultural plurality discouraged. The optimistic spirit earlier observable in official circles had evaporated with Charles' defeat in Germany. In Mexico, Spanish disenchantment was fed by persisting idolatry. There an earlier optimistic appraisal that the human potential was realizable through faith and rational activity had shrunk to a perceived need to direct all behavior and to have it conform to established social principles.

Philip II came to the throne of a Spanish imperial complex now only (but strongly) a dynastic one. He was supported by no universal Christian title but rather by Spanish consensus concerning the worth to Christendom of Spanish domination. Effective in making sense of the new political situation was revived scholastic philosophy, now still employed for justification—but of maintenance, not reform. Now, at last, appeared its eminent political systematizer, Francisco Suárez, who with other Spanish Jesuits in Europe and America reinvigorated and perpetuated ideological components reinforcing empire.[6] In Mexico as Charles' reign ended, nostalgia had set in. For the crown, the problem of the acceptance of royal authority over New Spain had been solved. Control of Spanish officials and the new young native-born aristocracy was more pressing. Passed was the spirited period of experiment, of gaining experience, and of establishing workable institutions. Many of the problems the clergy and the crown had thought solvable still remained—paganism, greed, abuse of Indians, official peculation, seignorial tendencies, immorality—all appearing to bear witness to human weakness, the potency of the irrational, and human inability to realize ideals. The gray and lackluster but diligent Philip was left the problems of social regulation, and treasury deficits. Spaniards in Mexico had begun to look back upon the initial era of Spain in Mexico, although it had been no bed of roses, as a golden age. Whatever their specific complaints, all lamented the passing of their own earlier, relatively sanguine state of mind. Public ceremonies and chronicles now glorified the reign of Isabella and Ferdinand, eulogized Mexican government and church under Charles, and sanctified men and institutions of that earlier day. Friars, including Mendieta and Sahagún, extolled it as the golden age of the church, embroidering upon the deeds and piety of the early missionaries. One conquistador in particular, old Bernal Díaz del Castillo, fuming at the Cortés-centered account of conquest published by López de Gómara, countered it with his reminiscences of the exploits of all the conquerors. Indians and part-Indians recounted previous glories of indigenous peoples.[7] Governors of more practical stamp and more limited vision lacked Mendoza's style and opportunity. Velasco grew prematurely old and sick trying to arbitrate among Méxican factions and succor Spain's bankrupt treasury, not so much mediating in society as juggling competing interests and seeking social harmony not through encouraging concepts of unity but through balance of power among its components.

Yet in fact a Mexican society had appeared, formed immediately after conquest in mentality and ethnic mixture. It included Spaniards, other Europeans, conversos, Indians, blacks, and probably a few Moors and Asiatics. By mid-century Mexican particularism had appeared in literature, law, religion, language, and physiognomies. The mestizo increment was notable. Large numbers of blacks arrived and began to be assimilated, eventually to be lost sight of within the Mexican population.

Underway at mid-century in Mexican society was a loss of useful function by Spanish Americans. Chivalric ideals valued by young caballeros replaced a more functional military mentality and erupted in tourneys, horsemanship, and other games. Regidores pompously carried the old battle standard of the conquerors once a year. Education was less and less concerned with developing other rational qualities than memory. Greater official emphasis on form, protocol, and ceremony reinforced outward social compliance. Appearances became increasingly important, norms of dress and behavior more elaborate. Officials, unlike Mendoza, paid less attention to specific situations and more to creating a façade of administrative uniformity. A false consciousness of social reality, fostered by officialdom, gained ground among Spanish Americans. In Mexico as in Spain Don Quixote was now becoming possible. The aristocratic young Spanish Americans who plotted an uprising to put New Spain into the hands of Martín Cortés were worthy precursors of Cervantes' impractical, seventeenth-century exemplar of the cleavage between social ideals and social situation, and especially of Quixote's chivalric self-image and devotion to outmoded values.[8] In New Spain, effective institutions continued for two hundred years to undergo more or less spontaneous adjustment to changing conditions. Much power and vitality persisted throughout the colonial period within structures now indigenous to the region, notably in the hacienda and in social and political arrangements among powerful residents and with laborers.[9]

Persisting, too, and gaining sanctity through time, was a strong sense among creoles of their own Mexican-ness. When Charles V died, the commemorative cenotaph and ceremonies sponsored by government and church, and participated in by the populace of the capital, had indicated a developing sense of a composite Mexican history, and of a Mexican identity. Spanish and Indian groups separately and formally paid homage to the memory of the monarch. Civil and church dignitaries, displaying their joint eminence conducted ceremonies. The ability of the faith to transcend social distinctions was evident as Spaniards and Indians attended funeral services held in Gante's San José chapel. The monument—the *túmulo imperial*—and numerous pageants graphically depicted the indigenous Mexican heritage and the ancient history of Europe as the twin antiquities of all New Spain.

Participants, events, and decoration reflecting the cultural syncretism taking place also provided additional, and public, evidence supporting the commonly held political assumption that *gran España* encompassed many disparate nations and territorial entities, and that nation and patria need not be mutually self-limiting. That is, Mexico, a distinct territorial region of empire having a unique historical heritage, was the patria of all those born on its soil. This populace included numerous "nations," the Spanish and their American-born children composing the dominant one. *Nation,* in the 1550s retained its biblical meaning, connoting a community with common ancestry, religion, and history.[10]

Cervantes de Salazar, humanist and scholastic, Spaniard and resident Mexican, described the process underway by presenting Mexico as a microcosm of both worlds, the old and the new, Europe and America. Thus although Spanish exclusivism was exported to Mexico and perpetuated there in the idea of two repúblicas, plurality lingered in their joint incorporation in the Kingdom of New Spain, as well as in the fact that within each were many individuals genetically belonging to both. Moreover, the Indian commonwealth was spoken of, by Motolinía for example, as itself being subdivided into many repúblicas. The tendency to think and to speak of these disparate societies in corporate terms and as numerous microcosms of *the* overriding república, and finally the joining of the Spanish and Indian commonwealths in one kingdom, allowed a sense of ultimate social cohesion within real differences.[11] More than one society could, within the ideology and language supporting monarchy, exist in one kingdom and under a ruler who wore numerous crowns; thus the societies making up the Spanish empire had coalesced under Charles, king of Spain and also *the* medieval temporal lord, the Holy Roman Emperor. Only Cortés had the grandeur of vision to see Mexico as another empire for his monarch. Other Mexican residents took pride in New Spain as their region of *gran España*—distinct, important, and in theory subservient to the ruler alone. Spaniards and their Mexican-born children claimed as their heritage, through Spain and Christianity, Europe's classical antiquity, that of imperial Rome in particular, together with the more immediate Spanish past, including the Christian conquest in Spain and America. The two repúblicas did not remain segregated either mentally or physically. Some of the new Spanish Americans were in fact doubly mestizo, endowed with two genetic and historical heritages.

All inhabitants could—although all did not—share a sense of Mexican belonging, its elements including, by 1550, birth in a common patria for Spanish Americans and other peoples, and a single king, an intertwined history, and one faith. Moreover, in advocating at mid-century the cult of the Virgen de Guadalupe, the Dominican archbishop Montúfar sanctioned a syncretic madonna symbolizing divine approbation to Mexicans. Her shrine at Tepeyec, on a site long sacred to the indigenous goddess,

Tonantzin, where the Christian Virgin of Guadalupe was said to have appeared miraculously to the Indian Juan Diego, attracted devotees of all backgrounds despite the disapproval of early Franciscans. Spanish adherence to the cult may well have emanated from a devotion to the peninsular Virgin of Guadalupe, such as was shown by their Catholic majesties and Fernando Cortés. Spanish devotees may have been responsible for her sobriquet, *de Guadalupe*, and for having fostered Christian worship at a site revered by native tradition. In her cult, what were probably elements of two folk cultures converged effectively and gained popularity until, in the eighteenth century, Mexicans succeeded in having their Virgin of Guadalupe named *patrona* of New Spain. She was a symbol of religious syncretism, cultural mestizaje, and regional identity throughout the colonial period. Her image became a unifying device among insurgents in the nineteenth-century struggle for independence.[12]

Yet, although all peoples with social legitimacy were by virtue of it connected to the Spanish monarchy and religion, among many the sense of effective community was much more restricted, and confined to ethnic and class affiliations. And outside of all community lived numerous blacks and castas, many seeking social admittance wherever possible, and some gaining it. A thin but compact top layer of Spaniards and part-Spaniards now governed in the capital, held the countryside, and vented a spirit of Mexican belonging compounded of social exclusivity, taking pride in (often self-proclaimed) aristocracy based on conquest, hostility to newcomers from Spain, superiority to Indians, disdain for castas, and an equating of blacks with slaves. A first generation of Spanish Americans, some of them mestizo, all later to be known as creoles, no matter of what condition or economic level, tended to accept these assumptions as part of their birthright, and Mexico as their patria. Spanish traditions and social theory, royal policy, and their own proclivities had succeeded in providing form and substance for many of their attitudes relating to Mexico. They had come to love the land. By the seventeenth century their sense of belonging to Mexico, and its belonging to them, would be identified with *criollismo*, essentially a conservative cast of mind, later highly visible in those who were either for or against independence, characteristic of many nineteenth-century oligarchs, and endemic among defenders of the old regime during the twentieth-century Mexican Revolution.

A more complete national identity in Mexico had to wait until the appearance among creoles in the later eighteenth century of a modern sense of nationalism, one including ideas of popular participation in government, citizenship, constitutional government, and, most important, the fundamentally secular concept of a nation composed of a society united principally by birth, geography, and history, and also by language, government, and sense of purpose. The sovereign nation, that mystical and corporate entity, then took on many of the attributes of earlier empire but insisted, as empire did not, on geographical and historical unity and popular—if corporate—government.[13]

The patterns of political thought in both countries tended to remain as static as the theory they embodied until nation and patria became synonymous in the latter part of the eighteenth century, until men put forth the nation as a proper basis for, and as the limits of, political sovereignty, and until the Bourbon regime in Spain itself rent the ideological web binding Mexico to Spain—until under Charles III (1759–88) Christian monarchy was dropped in favor of reason of state.

Although the monarchy had encompassed numerous nations and communities, and common habits of thinking about society, political authority, and the universe had unified Mexico ideologically and connected it for three centuries to Spain, this is not to say that all inhabitants subscribed to dominant beliefs. Myth and magic persisted as a refuge against ideologies imposed by dominant groups, but within folk practices some elements of broadly Mexican character, often associated with Christianity, contributed to a new syncretic folk culture.

Conversance with early Habsburg Mexico provides a better basis for evaluating changes introduced under the Bourbons, especially under Charles III and thereafter. Most important then to upsetting traditional political assumptions was the official substitution in the 1760s of Spain as *la nación* for Spain as empire. It proved a blow to regional particularism at one end of the political spectrum and imperial belonging at the other. Not surprisingly, Mexicans found it at least difficult to view themselves as Spanish nationals. The Bourbon regime, espousing and introducing measures to promote reason and progress—for Spain—and decreeing obsolete the traditional, static, religiously based, and heretofore official social and political ideology, disavowed many of the traditional supports of Spanish domination in Mexico, weakened some of the old corporations—notably the church—and banished a religious order most effective in maintaining popular adhesion to Spain, the Jesuits. Bourbon reforms, which were instituted with unchanged economic objective—that is, treasury receipts—but with increased efficiency, were combined with a rhetoric equating individual and social happiness with national well-being and demonstrated to Mexicans the advisability of seeing to their own national progress. Under Charles IV, some royal counselors invoked what they termed, Montesquieu-like, the medieval constitution of Spain as a national one. One response was that Americans took interest in their own constitutions and in Suárez the republican. Creoles, invoking Mexican history to legitimate their Mexican nationality, had much recourse to the accounts by sixteenth-century chroniclers, and later ones based upon them.[14] Miguel Hidalgo and José María Morelos, insurgent leaders, had a historically based sense of Mexican nationality. Their movements, and a new seignorial reaction among landed creoles in Mexico, at length succeeded, in the 1820s, in capturing the land for Mexican nationals.

A number of elements later associated with Mexican nationalisms were present by the mid-sixteenth century. Spanish Americans took Mexico as their patria and thought of themselves as *the* Mexicans. Genetic mixture, friars' chronicles and documents, and official political theory, helped to maintain the dual heritage, Indian and Spanish, as a living Mexican tradition, one which became an element of criollismo. Creoles displayed great pride in Mexico as a region of empire; and that regionalism was a direct progenitor of Mexican national identity. Symbols associated with the nation during the wars for independence, then part of a syncretic folk culture also combining elements of the two heritages, had meaning by 1550. In evidence by 1550 was not only the Virgin of Guadalupe, but also nascent pride in the Aztec legacy, signified in 1810 by the eagle on the cactus—symbol of a sign to Mexicas long ago to settle in the valley of Mexico. The royal mystique, which lingered after 1808 in the image of the savior-king, Ferdinand VII, *el deseado*, was firmly fixed by 1550 in popular consciousness, and slow to be detached from patriotism, as much subsequent history demonstrated.

The Mexican experience is a reminder that national particularism can, and did, develop within an imperial situation, and—although regionalism was manifest in power struggles with the monarchy—with no initial conflict between concepts of nation and empire. In the Mexican case, Spanish-introduced Christian universalism infused social and political ideals and attitudes conducive both to imperial belonging and to the growth of Mexican national identity and a sense of Mexican cohesion. Ironically, it was largely from Spain, too, that in the eighteenth century a new secular universalism was exported to Mexico, a view of a world made up of sovereign nations, an outlook incompatible with domination from overseas. Here Spain, unmindful of the effectiveness of the old rules, changed them—and lost the match.

In sum, the history of Mexico under Charles V was one of dynamic process, of an initial, mutual impact upon one another of two societies, both in a state of flux at time of contact, and of proto-national beginnings. It indicates something of the continuing interaction between people and environment, of how institutions come into being or are redirected, and of how ideologies arise, alter, and relate to society. It illuminates ways in which ideas and beliefs general in one society infused institutions, then lost their initial vitality, much moral impetus, and their more liberal and sanguine content. Some of the concepts themselves underwent revision or changed emphases, and came to be used by a new generation to reorient institutions and to reinterpret old values. Exceptionally important for Mexico subsequently was not only what happened there during the reign of Charles V but who was doing what, that is, the nature and activities of the individuals who introduced Spanish control. Most important, a sense of the vast potential of millions of people found in a wondrous land elicited near-superhuman effort from members of a generation uniquely qualified to think in grand terms. Reformers putting ideals to work had limited success and mixed motives but lasting renown—born of their attempt, in the sort of postconquest milieu generally not propitious to concern for subjugated peoples, to implement some of the more humanitarian aspects of their belief in human community, and to bring to bear in an extremely difficult situation profound commitment to human dignity.

Notes

Full citations to sources are given only at the first appearance of each. References to first citations are listed in the Index.

PREFACE

1. Denys Hay, *The Italian Renaissance* (Cambridge: Cambridge Univ. Press, 1961), p. 26.

2. For analogous framework I refer readers to Peter Berger and Thomas Luckmann, *The Social Construction of Reality* (Garden City, N.Y.: Doubleday, 1966), and to Berger's *The Sacred Canopy* (Garden City, N.Y.: Doubleday, 1967).

3. Berger, *Sacred Canopy*, pp. 10-11.

4. Eric Wolf, "Aspects of Group Relations in a Complex Society: Mexico," in Dwight B. Heath and Richard N. Adams, eds., *Contemporary Cultures and Societies of Latin America* (New York: Random House, 1965), p. 86.

5. Erik H. Erikson, *Young Man Luther* (New York: Norton, 1958), p. 22. See Berger and Luckmann, pp. 3-12; Jorge Carrión, *Mito y magia de mexicano* (Mexico: Porrúa y Obregón, 1952); Karl Mannheim, *Ideology and Utopia: An Introduction to the Sociology of Knowledge* (New York: International Library of Psychology, Philosophy, and Scientific Method, 1936; Harvest paperback, n.d.), tr. Louis Wirth and Edward Shils.

6. Berger and Luckmann, p. 113.

7. *América como conciencia* (Mexico, 1953), p. 106.

8. A prime weakness of the study of Latin American history in the United States in the past has been an insistence on separating and at times appearing to quarantine the notion of ideas as operative in history. See Howard F. Cline, ed., *Latin American History: Essays on Its Study and Teaching, 1898-1965*, 2 vols. (Austin: Univ. of Texas Press, 1967), and the run of the *Hispanic American Historical Review* for evidence of this general trend. Exceptions to the trend exist, but not many in the history of the early sixteenth century, and most of those treating ideas within too narrow limits, or too simplistically.

9. *Sacred Canopy*, p. 107.

10. Thus, for example, Herbert Bolton, the borderlands historian, in evolving mentally, from an ambience of anti-Spanish mid-American isolation, to stressing Spain's positive features, was a liberalizing influence in his society, and so he is described in Cline's *Latin American History*. Today, in a climate where imperialism of all sorts is once more under attack (although the ideological antagonists have changed), Bolton, among others, may be viewed as an exponent of the white legend cleansing Spain of across-the-board cruelty to American Indians. Further discussion of Spanish cruelty to Indians in theory and practice, and of its interpreters, will appear throughout this book.

11. Cf. Wolf, in Adams and Heath, p. 96: "It seems possible to define 'national character' operationally as those cultural forms or mechanisms which groups involved in the same over-

all web of relationships can use in their formal and informal dealings with each other. . . . in modern Mexico the behavior patterns of certain groups in the past have become the expected forms of behavior of nation-oriented individuals. These cultural forms of communication as found in Mexico are manifestly different from those found in other societies."

12. Garrett Mattingly, in Cline, p. 100.

CHAPTER ONE

1. Bernal Díaz del Castillo, *Historia verdadera de la conquista de la Nueva España,* ed. Joaquín Ramírez Cabañas (Mexico: Porrúa, 1968), 6th ed., 1:437. A few conquistadors were not Spanish. One who was, Alonso de Aguilar, in his *Relación breve de la conquista de Nueva España* (Mexico: Porrúa, 1954), p. 25, recorded, among his fellows, men from Venice, Greece, Sicily, and Portugal. Aguilar became a friar and changed his first name to Francisco, as it appears on his chronicle.

2. Bernal Díaz, 1:183.

3. Pascual de Gayangos, ed., *Cartas y relaciones de Hernán Cortés al emperador Carlos V* (Paris: A. Chaix, 1866), pp. 558, 568.

4. Robert S. Chamberlain, "The Concept of *Señor Natural* as Revealed by Castilian Law in Administrative Documents," *Hispanic American Historical Review* (hereinafter *HAHR*) 19 (1939): 130–37.

5. See Jean Hippolyte Maríejol, *L'Espagne sous Ferdinand et Isabelle* (Paris, 1892), tr. as *The Spain of Ferdinand and Isabella* by Benjamin Keen (New Brunswick, N.J.: Rutgers Univ. Press, 1961); Stanley G. Payne, *A History of Spain and Portugal* (Madison: Univ. of Wisconsin Press, 1973), vol. 1, chaps. 7–11; J. H. Elliott, *Imperial Spain, 1469–1716* (London: Arnold, 1963); Alfonso María Guilarte, *El regimen señorial en el siglo XVI* (Madrid: Instituto de Estudios Políticos, 1962); Mario Góngora, *El estado en el derecho indiano: Epoca de fundación, 1492–1570* (Santiago de Chile: Instituto de Investigaciones Historico-Culturales, Facultad de Filosofia y Educación, Universidad de Chile, 1951); José Cepeda Adán, *En torno al concepto del estado en los reyes católicos* (Madrid: Consejo Superior de Investigaciones Científicas, Escuela de Historia Moderna,1956); Jaime Vicens Vives, *Approaches to the History of Spain,* tr. Joan C. Ullman (Berkeley and Los Angeles: Univ. of California Press, 1970), pp. 68–95, 171; and Vicens Vives, "Estructura administrativa estatal en los siglos XVI y XVII," in *Rapports des XIe Congrés International des Sciences Historiques* vol. 4 (1960); José Antonio Maravell, "The Origins of the Modern State," *Journal of World History* 6 (1961): 789–808. Aragon and Castile were not unified in law, taxes, money, or trade. The Basque provinces were autonomous. Some of Isabella's reforms were attempted by her predecessor and uncle: see William David Phillips, Jr., "Enrique IV of Castile, 1454–1474," Ph.D. dissertation, New York Univ., 1971.

6. See Machiavelli, *The Prince,* xxi; Ramón Menéndez Pidal, *Los reyes católicos según Maquiavelo y Castiglione* (Madrid: Espasa-Calpe,1952). Francisco Guicciardini, ambassador to Ferdinand's court, 1512–13, observed in "Relación de España," in Antonio Maria Fabié, ed., *Viajes por España . . .* (Madrid, 1879), that Isabella was largely responsible for governing Castile and that she had successfully caused her subjects to love and fear the monarchy (p. 211), and that Ferdinand appeared to listen attentively to all opinions, then went ahead and did what he had planned to do in the first place (p. 213).

7. Antonio Domínguez Ortiz, *The Golden Age of Spain, 1516–1659,* tr. James Casey (New York: Basic Books, 1971), p. 174.

8. See Marvin Lunenfeld, *The Council of the Santa Hermandad* (Miami: Univ. of Miami Press, 1970). In 1480 royal revenues came from export-import duties, internal customs, the *alcabala* (sales tax), *diezmos* (tenths) on commerce, mines, and salt, the *servicio cruzada,* and *tercios reales* (two-ninths of ecclesiastical tithes). The war against Granada also provided justification for extraordinary royal taxation. See Maríejol, pp. 209 ff.; Jaime Vicens Vives,

An Economic History of Spain, tr. Frances M. López-Morillas (Princeton: Princeton Univ. Press, 1969), pp. 291-314, and Payne, 1:178-83. Guicciardini (p. 127) says the most profitable war tax was income from bulls of crusade.

9. The crown thus limited the nobles by providing vassals with recourse from seignorial courts. The chancellería of Valladolid dates from 1485 and that of Granada from 1505. See Maríejol, 146.

10. See Ricardo del Arco y Garay, *La idea de imperio en la política y la literatura españolas* (Madrid, 1944).

11. In *Los códigos españoles concordados y anotados* (Madrid, 1848-51), vols. 2-4; tr. into English by Samuel Parsons Scott (Chicago, 1931). And see José Antonio Maravell, "Del Regimen feudal al regimen corporativo en el pensamiento de Alfonso X," in *Estudios de historia de pensamiento español: Edad media* (Madrid: Ediciones Culturales Hispanicas, 1967), pp. 89-140.

12. In 1248, the year Castile took Seville, Vincentius Hispanus, a canonist, insisted Spain was the greatest of all provinces and an empire. He assumed the Spaniards possessed a national character, proudly stating that while the French use words, the Spanish act. See gloss in *Decretales,* 1.6.34, Gaines Post, ed., *Speculum* 29 (1954): 206; Post, "Two Notes on Nationalism in the Middle Ages," *Traditio* 9 (1953): 308; and Post, *"Blessed Lady Spain*—Vincentius Hispanus and Spanish Nationalism in the Thirteenth Century," *Speculum* 29 (1954): 198-209. These are collected in Post's *Studies in Medieval Legal Thought* (Princeton: Princeton Univ. Press, 1964).

13. Gifford Davis, "The Development of a National Theme in Medieval Castilian Literature," *Hispanic Review* 3 (1935): 149-61; and see below, n. 16. Davis comments on Isidore of Seville's *De laude Spaniae,* and its imitation during following centuries.

14. Vicens Vives (*Approaches,* pp. 22-27, 158-59) argues persuasively that the Visigothic influence in Spain did not long outlast the Visigothic monarchy there (in the sixth and seventh centuries), itself a graft on Roman institutions: "The Visigoths constituted only a superstructure of power," he concludes, discounting any artistic, juridical, or ethnic Visigothic legacy in Castile and thus refuting theories of another eminent historian of medieval Spain, Claudio Sánchez-Albornoz. Yet Vicens Vives concedes that the Goths "did bequeath an important principle: political unification under a monarchy." It was an elective one as well. Visigothic kings also attempted to reconcile custom, Roman law, and Germanic law in the *Liber judiciorum,* later known as the *Fuero juzgo,* which, like the Partidas, was stymied by supporters of local custom. See Samuel P. Scott, tr., *The Visigothic Code* (Boston, 1910). Here we discuss only perceived heritages, not those very much there but unacknowledged, the Islamic and the Jewish. Also see P. D. King's *Law and Society in the Visigothic Kingdom* (Cambridge: Cambridge Univ. Press, 1972), where, however, little attention is paid to Roman influence on Visigoths. And cf. Davis.

15. *Partidas* I:1:1, 2.

16. Ibid. II:1:13. See J. A. Maravell, "La idea del cuerpo místico en España antes de Erasmus," *Boletín Informativo del Seminario de Derecho Político* (Salamanca), May-October 1956; Maravell, *Estudios*; and Maravell, *El concepto de España en la edad media* (Madrid, 1954); Juan Beneyto Pérez, *Los origenes de la ciencia política en España* (Madrid, 1949). Participation in any corporation was, by extension, felt to be participation in society at large. Cf. R. W. Carlyle and A. J. Carlyle, *A History of Medieval Political Theory in the West,* vol. 6, *Political Theory from 1300 to 1600* (New York: Barnes and Noble, 1936; reprint, 1962); David Knowles, *The Evolution of Medieval Thought* (paperback; New York: Random House, 1962); Walter Ullmann, *A History of Political Thought: The Middle Ages* (Baltimore: Penguin, 1965); Post, *Studies;* Fritz Kern, *Kingship and Law in the Middle Ages,* tr. S. B. Chrimes (reprint of 1939 ed., New York: Barnes and Noble, 1968); E. H. Kantorowicz, *The King's Two Bodies: A Study in Mediaeval Political Theory* (Princeton: Princeton Univ. Press, 1957); E. N. Van Kleffens, *Hispanic Law until the End of the Middle Ages* (Chicago:

Aldine, 1968); and Carl J. Friedrich, *The Philosophy of Law in Historical Perspective,* 2d ed. (Chicago: Univ. of Chicago Press, 1963).

17. "Leyes de Toro," in *Los códigos españoles,* 6:557-67. Their compilation underway before Isabella died, they state that in civil and criminal cases not covered by that code, or by fueros, "mandamos que se libren por las leyes de las Siete Partidas que el Rey D. Alfonso nuestro visabuelo mandó ordenar." Further, the Laws of Toro where applicable were to take precedence over fueros. See also Juan Beneyto Pérez, "The Science of Law in the Spain of the Catholic Kings," in Roger Highfield, ed., *Spain in the Fifteenth Century, 1369-1516* (New York: Harper & Row, 1972), pp. 276-95; and Van Kleffens, who, however, presents these Spanish codes as having the high purpose of unification and does not mention their use for royal power.

18. *Partidas* II:8:1.18, 32. The Laws of Toro assert ". . . al Rey pertenesce, y ha poder de hacer fueros, y leyes: y de las interpretar, y declarar, y emendar donde viere que cumple." They do, in effect, put in force the Partidas (as Alfonso X could not do).

19. *Partidas* II:1:1.5.

20. Ibid. II:1:1.9.

21. Ibid. IV:25:1.5; also II:10-15; and above, n. 11.

22. Ibid. IV:25; also II:10, 12, 13:2.

23. Vicens Vives notes that "feudalism" never developed fully in Castile, but did in Catalonia. Domínguez Ortiz concurs. I have preferred not to use the term at all. Cf. Elizabeth A. R. Brown, "The Tyranny of a Construct: Feudalism and Historians of Medieval Europe," *American Historical Review* (hereinafter *AHR*) 79 (1974): 1063-88. It should be noted that in the fifteenth century, in the face of aristocratic and regional strength and of royal weakness, Juan II, Isabella's father, and Enrique IV, her half-brother, and their chanceries advanced ever more grandiose theories of royal sovereignty and of the monarch's absolute power; see Luis Sánchez Agesta, *El concepto de estado en el pensamiento español del siglo XVI* (Madrid: Instituto de Estudios Políticos, 1959), app. III, pp. 169-82; and Elena Lourie, "A Society Organized for War: Medieval Spain," *Past and Present* 35 (1966): 54-76. Under Isabella and Ferdinand, what had been fantasies of political control came closer to fact. Aragonese history is not stressed in this résumé, for, although important, in Spanish Mexico under Charles V Castilian history and influence were more important. Catalonia, Aragon, the Basque provinces, Navarre continued to have a good deal of autonomy under Trastámaras and Habsburgs.

24. Carlyle and Carlyle, vol. 6; Vicens Vives, *Approaches,* pp. 74-75, 84; Joseph F. O'Callaghan, "The Beginnings of the Cortés of León-Castile," *AHR* 74 (1969): 1503-37; Payne, vol. 1.

25. Beneyto Pérez, *Origines,* p. 148; Carlyle and Carlyle, 6:186-87. On 5 July 1465 outside of Avila Isabella's brother, Alfonso, was proclaimed king and Enrique IV stripped of his regalia in effigy—by disaffected nobles in public ceremony. Alfonso died at sixteen in 1468—and to Isabella, then seventeen, fell his claim to the throne.

26. See Albert Sicroff, *Les controverses des statuts de "pureté de sang" en Espagne du XVᵉ au XVIIᵉ siècle* (Paris, 1960); and for the most recent general treatment of ethnic and religious policies and attitudes see Henry Kamen, *The Spanish Inquisition,* (New York: New American Library, 1968); Kamen is, however, wrong in playing down the political uses and advantages, in this period, of the Inquisition and of all activity against non-Old Christians, and too simplistic in presenting the Holy Office primarily as an instrument of class warfare, although right in suggesting that it materially benefited an oligarchy. When religion is *the* unifying factor, and "racial purity" a concomitant, other peoples appear as outside threats and those within the faith feel a sense of solidarity, in this case social, political, and religious.

27. A bull of 1486 granted their majesties the right of general or universal patronage in Spain. Bulls of 1493, 1501, and 1508 gave them dominion of the Indies, a monopoly on Christianizing Indians, American tithes, and universal patronage there. These bulls appear, in Spanish, in Bartolomé de Las Casas, *Tratados* (Mexico and Buenos Aires, 1965), vol. 2,

app. I, pp. 1277-90. See W. Eugene Shiels, S.J., *King and Church: The Rise and Fall of the Patronato Real* (Chicago: Loyola Univ. Press, 1961); John Lloyd Mecham, *Church and State in Latin America,* rev. ed. (Chapel Hill: Univ. of North Carolina Press, 1966).

28. A. G. Dickens, *The Counter Reformation* (New York: Harcourt, Brace & World, 1969), pp. 45-50 (the title is misleading—the first half is on Catholic reform before schism); Herbert Holzapfel, O.F.M., *The History of the Franciscan Order,* tr. Antonine Tibesar, O.F.M., and Gervase Brinkmann, O.F.M. (Teutopolis, Ill., 1948), pp. 91-125. The Dominican order, too, was undergoing reform. See José García Oro, *La reforma de los religiosos en tiempo de los reyes católicos* (Valladolid, 1969); Vicente Beltrán de Heredia, O.P., *Historia de la reforma de la provincia de España (1450-1550)* (Rome, 1939); and P. Tarsicio de Azcona, *La elección y reforma del episcopado español en tiempo de los reyes católicos* (Madrid, 1960). But the clergy in general were unreformed: Guicciardini, pp. 223-24.

29. Kamen, p. 103.

30. The converso scholars were Alfonso de Zamora, Pablo Coronel, Hernán Nuñez, and Antonio de Nebrija. The ultra-benevolence toward Spanish humanism appears in the work of such scholars as Aubrey F. G. Bell and Rudolf Schevill, among others, and most recently in Kamen. Cf. Stephen Gilman, *The Spain of Fernando de Rojas: The Intellectual and Social Landscape of La Celestina* (Princeton: Princeton Univ. Press, 1972); Dickens, pp. 46-50; Myron P. Gilmore, *The World of Humanism, 1453-1517* (New York: Harper & Row, 1952); and Paul Oskar Kristeller, *Renaissance Thought: The Classic, Scholastic, and Humanist Strains* (Cambridge, Mass: Harvard Univ. Press, 1955; paperback, Harper Torchbook, 1961).

31. Nebrija, *Gramática castellana,* ed. Pascual Galindo Romeo and Luis Ortiz Muños (Madrid: Edición de la Junta del Centenario, 1946), 1:5. Nebrija was evoking a concept derived from the *Elegantiae* of the Italian humanist Lorenza Valla and reiterated earlier in Spain, in 1490, by micer Gonzalo, a jurisconsult to Ferdinand; see Eugenio Asensio, "La lengua companera del imperio," *Revista de Filología Española* 43 (1960): 399-413. Earlier, in Spain, Alfonso X had deliberately established Castilian as the language of his kingdom. Cf. Dickens on relationships of humanism and nationalism. Nebrija also made a lexicon of the civil law (Vicens Vives, *Economic History,* p. 286).

32. Editions of his works include: *Epistolario,* 4 vols. (Madrid, 1953-57); *De orbe novo,* tr. into English by F. A. MacNutt, (New York and London, Arthur H. Clark, 1912), 2 vols.; and *Decadas del Nuevo Mundo,* ed. Edmundo O'Gorman (Mexico, 1964). For Peter Martyr d'Anghiera, see Howard F. Cline, ed., *Guide to Ethnohistorical Sources.* Pt. 2 of *Handbook of Middle American Indians* (Austin: Univ. of Texas Press, 1973) (hereinafter *HMAI*) 13:46-47. Also Maríejol, p. 308.

33. Kamen, p. 105.

34. Cf. Nicholas G. Round, "Renaissance Culture and Its Opponents in Fifteenth-Century Castile," *Modern Language Review* 57 (1962): 204-15; Gilman (p. 305), cites Juan de Lucena, the royal chronicler: "When the king used to gamble, we were all gamblers, but now that the Queen studies, behold us all turned into students."

35. Quoted in Elliott, *Imperial Spain,* p. 87. Gilman (p. 301) cites Diego Hurtado de Mendoza, recalling that Ferdinand and Isabella put government in the hands of *letrados,* "people of middle strata between the great and small, without offending therefore one or the other. . . . They lived without bad habits, neither visited nor received gifts nor had close friends, nor dressed in costly finery, and were moderate and humane in their dealings." Cf. Maravell, *Estudios,* pp. 347-80.

36. Mario Góngora, "Regimen señorial y rural en la Extremadura de la Orden de Santiago," *Jahrbuch für Geschichte von Staat, Wirtschaft und Gesellschaft Lateinamerikas* 2 (1956): 17-18.

37. See above, n. 27; Manuel Giménez Fernández, "Las bulas alejandrinas de 1493 referentes a las Indias," *Anuario de Estudios Americanos,* app. I-III (Seville, 1944), pp. 343-69; Antonio de Herrera y Tordesillas, *Historia general de las hechos de los Castellanos en*

las islas i tierra firme del mar océano, 4 vols. (Madrid, 1601-15), I:4:7. The *patronato real* in the Indies allowed the crown to select and send missionaries, prescribe liturgical norms and precepts for the regular clergy, collect tithes, create and apportion dioceses, and present candidates to all ecclesiastical posts.

38. The text of the *requerimiento*, dated 14 August 1513, appears in Juan Manzano Manzano, *La incorporación de las Indias a la corona de Castilla* (Madrid, 1948), pp. 43-46. For Ferdinand and America: Manuel Giménez Fernández, *Bartolomé de Las Casas*, 2 vols. (Seville, C.S.I.C., Escuela de Estudios Hispano-Americanos, 1953, 1960); Troy S. Floyd, *The Columbus Dynasty in the Caribbean, 1492-1526* (Albuquerque: Univ. of New Mexico Press, 1973).

39. Rafael Altamira, "El texto de las Leyes de Burgos de 1512," *Revista de Historia de América* (hereinafter *RHA*), 4 (1938): 5-79; and R. D. Hussey, "The Text of the Laws of Burgos," *HAHR* 12 (1932): 301-27. See Antonio Ybot León, "Juntas de teólogos asesoras del estado para Indias, 1512-1550," *Anuario de estudios americanos* 5 (1948): 397-438; Venancio D. Carro, *La teología y los teólogos-juristas españoles ante la conquista de América*, 2 vols. (Madrid: Escuela de Estudios Hispano-Americanos de la Universidad de Sevilla, 1944). Juan Lopez de Palacios Rubios, *De las islas del mar océano*, and Fray Matias de Paz, *Del dominio de los reyes de España sobre los Indios* (bound together), intro. by Silvio Zavala (Mexico and Buenos Aires: Fondo de Cultura Económica, 1954). Palacios Rubios also had a large part in preparing the Laws of Toro and the *requerimiento*.

CHAPTER TWO

1. Bernal Díaz, 1:109. For a general account of the conquest of Mexico, see the Bernal Díaz history, the dispatches of Cortés, and W. H. Prescott's *History of the Conquest of Mexico*, all available in numerous editions. A large literature on the conquest exists; here we are concerned only with certain aspects of it.

2. Bernal Díaz, 1:84.

3. Ibid., 1:42.

4. *Historia de las Indias*, 2d ed., ed. Agustín Millares Carlo (Mexico, 1965), lib. III, cap. 114:3.

5. Francisco López de Gómara, *Cortés: The Life of the Conqueror by His Secretary*, tr. and ed. Lesley B. Simpson (Berkeley and Los Angeles: Univ. of California Press, 1966), p. 10.

6. Ibid., p. 7; Las Casas, *Historia*, lib. III, cap. 27; Bernal Díaz, 2:328-29. See Góngora, "Regimen señorial," pp. 1-29, for regional background; cf. Lourie, "A Society Organized for War," and see John H. Elliott, "The Mental World of Hernán Cortés," *Transactions of the Royal Historical Society*, 5th ser., 17 (1967): 47-48.

7. For life in Salamanca in these years, see Gilman, pp. 267-353. Introductory Latin texts then in use there included that of Nebrija. Salamanca was above all a law school. Its graduates were among the top royal bureaucrats (p. 300). Elliott notes similarities between expressions used by Cortés and *Celestina*, whose author, Fernando de Rojas, was at Salamanca the year before Cortés; Rojas drew on much local literary convention and material there, according to Gilman. The question of how much ambience, how much direct influence again arises. Cortés and the other conquerors also knew and were influenced by romances of chivalry: see Irving Leonard, *Books of the Brave* (reprint of 1949 ed; New York: Gordian, 1964).

8. Gayangos, pp. 567-68.

9. 30 October 1520, ibid., p. 52.

10. Bernal Díaz, 1:67.

11. Ibid., 1:121. Also see the letter of the cabildo of Vera Cruz to the crown, 10 July 1519, in Mario Hernández Sánchez-Barba, ed., *Hernán Cortés: Cartas y documentos* (Mexico: Porrúa, 1963), pp. 11-16. Cf. A. R. Pagden, ed., *Hernán Cortés: Letters from Mexico* (New York: Grossman, 1971).

12. Las Casas (*Historia*, lib. III, cap. 120) asserted that the Indians did not understand

Cortés nor he the Indians. Although probably right regarding Catholicism, Las Casas undoubtedly underestimates the chieftains' political acumen, particularly since Motecuhzoma had familiarized them with much the same system.

13. 30 October 1520, Gayangos, pp. 99–100.

14. See Charles Gibson, *The Aztecs under Spanish Rule: A History of the Indians of the Valley of Mexico, 1519–1810* (Palo Alto: Stanford Univ. Press, 1964); R. H. Barlow, *The Extent of the Empire of the Culhua Mexica* (Berkeley and Los Angeles: Univ. of California Press, 1949); Friedrich Katz, *The Ancient American Civilizations,* tr. K. Lois Simpson (New York: Praeger, 1972).

15. Letter to Charles V, 3 September 1526, Gayangos, p. 491; also 30 October 1520, ibid., p. 68.

16. Bernal Díaz, vol. 1, passim. By his arrival in Tenochtitlán, Cortés had adopted a more politic policy of waiting to smash idols until the populace was subdued; see his letter of 30 October 1530 in Hernández Sánchez-Barba, pp. 74–75.

17. Cabildo of Vera Cruz to the crown, 10 July 1519, ibid., p. 12.

18. Fernando Cortés, *The Last Will and Testament,* ed. G. R. G. Conway (Mexico, 1939), xix, pp. 8, 33. It includes a facsimile and paleographic version of the original, dated Seville, 11 October 1547. Cortés named two churchmen, Juan de Zumárraga, a Franciscan and archbishop-elect of Mexico, and Domingo de Betanzos, Dominican provincial of Mexico, among the administrators (lxiv, pp. 18, 43). See L. Redonet y López-Doriga, "El latifundia y su formación en la España medieval," *Estudios de Historia Sociedad de España* 1 (1949): 202–3, for customary bequests by Spanish nobility.

19. Hernando Cortés, *Ordenanzas del buen gobierno (1524)* (Madrid, 1960), pp. 14–15; also in *Colección de documentos inéditos de Indias* (hereinafter *DII*) (Madrid, 1876), 2d ser., 26:135–49.

20. 10 July 1519; Hernández Sánchez-Barba, p. 20. See the declaration made to the crown by Francisco de Montejo and Alonso Portocarrero, representatives (*procuradores*) of the Vera Cruz cabildo, 29–30 April 1520, in Francisco del Paso y Troncoso, *Epistolario de Nueva España, 1505–1818,* (Mexico, 1939), 1:44–50. Las Casas, who was not present, states convincingly (*Historia* lib. III, cap. 123) that Cortés masterminded the entire business at Vera Cruz. Also see Bernal Díaz, 1:137–68. The plural *highnesses* refers to Charles V and his mother, Juana, hereditary queen of Castile.

21. Hernández Sánchez-Barba, p. 23. See John T. Lanning, "Cortés and His First Official Remission of Treasure to Charles V," *RHA* 2 (1938): 5–29. For Spain see the very important article by Robert S. Chamberlain, "Castilian Backgrounds of the Repartimiento-Encomienda," *Carnegie Institute of Washington Publications* 509 (1939): 19–66; and Payne, vol. 1.

22. See Manuel Giménez Fernández, "Hernán Cortés y su revolución comunera en la Nueva España," *Anuario de estudios americanos* 5 (1948): 1–58; and Giménez Fernández, "El alzamiento de Fernando Cortés," *RHA* 31 (1951): 1–58. Victor Frankl, "Hernán Cortés y la tradición de *Las Siete Partidas,*" *RHA,* June 1962, pp. 9–74, argues from similarities that Cortés and his men knew the Partidas. Cortés' direct knowledge of those laws was possible but not necessary to account for his beliefs or for the process of town founding. Cortés had been a *regidor* and a notary in Cuba, and much of the political and legal theory in the Partidas was in 1519 part of more recent Spanish statutes and codes and also of the Spanish mentality. Cf. Elliott, "Mental World," and his essay in Pagden's edition of Cortés' letters. Elliott relies too heavily on Frankl here. Also see Payne, 1:46–47, 59.

23. Chamberlain, "Castilian Backgrounds."

24. Silvio Zavala, *Ensayos sobre la colonización española en América* (Buenos Aires, 1944), p. 140. Royal cédula of 15 October 1522, *DII* 26:59–65, named Cortés governor and captain general.

25. *Ordenanzas,* pp. 17–18; *DII* 26:145. Chamberlain, in "Castilian Backgrounds," says

that similar grants in Spain although made for only up to one lifetime tended to become perpetual.

26. Royal concession, 6 July 1529: Hernández Sánchez-Barba, pp. 599-600; *DII* 12: 291-97. Grant of 23,000 vassals, 30 June 1529; in Vasco de Puga, *Provisiones, cédulas, instrucciones de su magestad, ordenanzas de difuntos y audiencia para la buena expedición de los negocios y administración de justicia y gobernación de esta Nueva España, y para el buen tratamiento y conservación de los Indios desde el año de 1525 hasta este presente de 63,* ed. Joaquín García Icazbalceta (Mexico, 1878), 1:129-36. In fact, Cortés continued to hold many more than 23,000 Indians. For a summary of his political fortunes in these years, see Charles W. Hackett, "The Delimitation of Political Jurisdiction in Spanish North America," *HAHR* 1 (1918): 40-70, and below, chaps. 4, 6.

27. Clement VII granted Cortés patronage, but the king and Council of the Indies prevented his exercising it. See for his holdings as marqués, Gibson, *Aztecs,* pp. 59-61; Peter Gerhard, *A Guide to the Historical Geography of New Spain* (Cambridge: Cambridge Univ. Press, 1972), pp. 8-9; also François Chevalier, *Land and Society in Colonial Mexico,* ed. Lesley B. Simpson (Berkeley and Los Angeles: Univ. of California Press, 1963), pp. 127-30; G. Micheal Riley, *Fernando Cortés and the Marquesado in Morelos, 1522-1547* (Albuquerque: Univ. of New Mexico Press, 1973); Bernardo García Martínez, *El marquesado del Valle: Tres siglos de regimen señorial en Nueva España* (Mexico: Colegio de México, 1969), pp. 93, 114; and Juan Friede, "El privilegio de vasallos otorgada a Hernán Cortés," in B. García Martínez, et al., *Historia y sociedad en el mundo de habla española: Homenaje a José Miranda* (Mexico: Colegio de México, 1970), pp. 69-78. *Partidas* II, tit. 1, 1.11, explains: "*Marqués* means the lord of some great district which is included in the territory of a kingdom."

28. After his return from the expedition to Honduras in 1526, Cortés may have considered ousting the royal officials in New Spain and closing the land to further Spanish immigration, but it is doubtful that he was prepared to declare independence from the Spanish monarchy. Rather, if he did plan a move it was more likely, in the spirit of his Vera Cruz tactic, to regain for himself effective authority in New Spain. Henry R. Wagner, in *The Rise of Fernando Cortés* (Berkeley: Cortés Society, 1944), presents Cortés as a *condottiere.* Wagner underrated his political acumen and qualities of leadership, but not the complexity of his personality. Peter Martyr d'Anghiera (*De orbe novo,* II, 350-51), gives evidence of Cortés' loyalty. Cf. Las Casas, *Historia,* lib. II, cap. 28. Also see *Relaciones de Fernando Cortés a Carlos V sobre la invasion de Anáhuac,* ed. Eulalia Guzmán (Mexico: Libros Anáhuac, 1958); and Archivo Mexicano, *Documentos para la historia de México: Sumario de la residencia tomado a don Fernando Cortés* ... 2 vols. (Mexico, 1852-53).

29. Las Casas, *Historia,* lib. III, cap. 27; Gómara, p. 10. On *hidalgo*: "This word had of old been loosely applied to all nobles; but it was now limited to the 'squirearchy,' who differed in standing from the peasants, but could not claim antiquity of family. There was at first a formal hidalgo class, but entry was never closed, and by the end of the sixteenth century it had come rather to represent a set of principles and a way of life ... a state of mind." Harold Livermore, *A History of Spain* (New York, 1958), pp. 274-75; cf. Payne, I; Lourie. Apparently in the course of the sixteenth century, *caballero,* previously divided into *caballeros hidalgos* and *caballeros villanos*—that is, noble and non-noble—simply came to be equated with *hidalgo.* Thus aristocracy, if not formal nobility, was thought a concomitant of, or derived from, mounted military service. And see Góngora, "Regimen," p. 19.

30. Bernal Díaz, 1:178. Cortés sent the culverin in 1524.

31. 30 October 1520, Hernández Sánchez-Barba, p. 33.

32. Guicciardini, p. 204.

CHAPTER THREE

1. Cited by Arco y Garay, p. 42; and see Payne, 1:37, 57.

2. Hernández Sánchez-Barba, pp. 33, 242.

3. Cited by Arco y Garay, pp. 133–34.

4. On 30 November 1519 Gattinara instructed that Charles be addressed as "Sacra Cesárea Católica Real Majestad." Hayward Keniston, *Francisco de los Cobos* (Pittsburgh: Univ. of Pittsburgh Press, n.d.), p. 57.

5. See Otis H. Green, *Spain and the Western Tradition* (Madison: Univ. of Wisconsin Press, 1965), vol. 3; and Hans G. Koenigsberger, *The Habsburgs and Europe, 1516–1660* (Ithaca: Cornell Univ. Press, 1971), p. xii, chap. 1.

6. Ibid., p. xii; see Jaime Vicens Vives, "Imperio y administración en tiempo de Carlos V," in *Charles-Quint et son temps* (Paris, 1959), p. 9–21; Domínguez Ortiz, *Golden Age,* pp. 45–46.

7. In 1535; Koenigsberger, p. 1. Keniston, p. 170, states that in 1535, reviewing his forces in Barcelona, Charles unfurled a banner of Christ crucified and cried, "This is your captain-general! I am his standard bearer!"

8. 6 May 1543, in José María March, ed., *Niñez y juventud de Felipe II: Documentos inéditos ...* (Madrid, 1942), 2:23–24. Maravell, "Regimen," p. 124, notes the thirteenth-century shift from vassal to subject and ties it to the bourgeois culture of the epoch. The Partidas use both terms; see above, chap. 1.

9. Ferdinand had raised Charles' younger brother, also Ferdinand, in Spain, while Charles grew up in the Habsburg court. His mother, Juana—mentally deranged, it was thought—was confined to a castle at Tordesillas. Charles was seventeen. His initial position was not strong.

10. Cédula of 14 September 1519, in *Recopilación de los reynos de las Indias,* 4th ed. (Madrid, 1791), III:1:1. Manzano, pp. 300–301, includes text from Diego de Encinas, *Libro primero de Provisiones ...* (Madrid, 1596), p. 59, and argues that the text appearing in the *Recopilación* is incorrect, containing later additions. Also see Ernst Schäfer, *El Consejo Real y Supremo de las Indias* (Seville, 1947), 2 vols.; and cf. Demetrio Ramos, "El problema de la fundación del Real Consejo de las Indias y la fecha de su creación," in presentación por el Dr. Luis Suárez Fernández, *El Consejo de las Indias en el siglo XVI* (Valladolid, 1970), pp. 11–41.

11. Cédula of 22 October 1523, Paso y Troncoso, I, 46.

12. Cédula of 15 October 1522, *DII* 26:69. One of the officials was Alonso de Estrada, treasurer, an illegitimate son of Ferdinand who had been raised in his court and had been regidor of Ciudad Real. Estrada had fought for Charles in the comunero rising and was sent to New Spain "after a serious encounter with some caballeros, resulting in deaths and disgraces." See Francisco Fernández del Castillo, "Alonso de Estrada: Su familia," in *Memorias de la Academia Mexicana de la Historia* 1 (1942): 402; and Norberto de Castro y Tosi, "Verdadera paternidad de Alonso de Estrada," *Revista de Indias,* 8 (1948): 1011–26. The others were Gonzalo de Salazar, *factor,* another anti-comunero; Rodrigo de Albornoz, *contador;* and Pedro Almindez (Peralmindez) Chirinos, *veedor.* See Francisco A. de Icaza, *Conquistadores y pobladores de Nueva España* (Madrid, 1923), I, 89–90; Silvano García Guiot, *Rodrigo de Albornoz, contador real de Nueva España* (Mexico, 1943); and Bernal Díaz and chaps. 4, 6 below, for their activities in Mexico. Most responsible for choosing these men was Francisco de los Cobos, the royal secretary, who administered Spanish affairs in Charles' absences from 1530 to 1547 and who in our period was *fundidor mayor* of New Spain and an increasingly important member of the privy council. Salazar and Chirinos, especially, were Cobos' men, Chirinos possibly being related to him by marriage (see Keniston, p. 83). All were loyal and experienced officials, but of Fernandine cast, as their subsequent Mexican activities attest.

Charles inherited an embryonic bureaucracy from Ferdinand. Juan Rodríguez de Fonseca, bishop of Burgos, was responsible, as head of the Casa de Contratación, for American affairs—note that they were centered in a board of trade. Lope Conchillos, Ferdinand's principal secretary, had from 1508 on as his chief accountant Francisco de los Cobos. All grew wealthy in royal service, and were capable officials. Under Ferdinand in governing the Indies they took what they could and had their own commercial interests there (Herrera II:2:4). On that king's death, Cobos went to Charles in Flanders, became secretary for the Indies, then in 1519 transferred that post to Juan de Samano but supervised him. That year Cobos, as protégé of both Fonseca and Gattinara, replaced Conchillos as principal royal secretary and was also named treasurer of Mexico (and later Peru), to be paid 1 percent on metals assayed and minted. Keniston, pp. 54-55, notes, "this single appointment became the chief source of his ultimate wealth." Diego Velásquez had ties to the Fernandine group, headed by Fonesca and opposed by Diego Colón (Columbus), Las Casas, and Gattinara. Cobos, however, gained responsibility and power as that of his old confederates eroded, and remained always more circumspect. Charles eased out Fonseca and imposed a more direct royal control over American affairs and their overseers by founding the Council of the Indies. In 1524 its first head was his confessor, the Dominican García de Loaisa, who in 1530 received a cardinal's hat and was sent to Rome, leaving Cobos in effective charge of the council. It was Cobos to whom Charles in 1525 gave the cannon sent him by Cortés. Cobos had it melted down. His grants in the Indies also included licenses to export black slaves. He contracted with Pedro de Alvarado to ship them to Guatemala. Alvarado married in succession two sisters, distant relatives of Cobos, who also had business arrangements with the first viceroy, Antonio de Mendoza. Both had been procuradores to court from Granada in 1515. Cobos and Loaisa sat on the commission to draft the New Laws of 1542, and Cobos survived Charles' investigation of the Council of the Indies in that year, a consequence of denunciations by Las Casas and resulting in removal of two members and implicating them all in accepting bribes. Loaisa was replaced by Sebastian Ramírez de Fuenleal. Cobos died in 1547. Thus court officials and factions strongly influenced royal rule in Mexico, with Cobos setting the tone, one adroitly combining Fernandine opportunism with a new moderation perhaps best described as consonant with a more bureaucratic and professional government, wherein position depended on continuing royal favor. But they did so within broad policies set by the king, ultimate mediator among official factions as in society. See Las Casas, *Historia*, lib. III, cap. 100 ff.; Manuel Giménez Fernández, *Las Casas*; Clarence Haring, *Trade and Navigation between Spain and the Indies* (Gloucester, Mass.: Peter Smith, 1964); Haring, "Ledgers of the Royal Treasurers in Spanish America in the Sixteenth Century," *HAHR* 2 (1919): 174; and Góngora, *Estado*.

13. Bernal Díaz, 1:44; and royal cédulas of 22 October 1523; Paso y Troncoso, 1:51-57.

14. For decrees regarding the royal fifth and tithes: nn. 10, 11 above; for tribute and tithes, *Recopilación* VI:4:1, 4, 21, 22, 24, 27, 28, 31-34; for mining, ibid., IV:19:1-3, 9; IV:22:1, 3; see also Haring, *Trade* and Haring, *Spanish Empire in America* (New York: Oxford Univ. Press, 1947); and cédula to Cortés of 15 October 1522; for instruction for governing, *DII* 26: 65-70; for orders to Cortés of 1523, *DII* 23:353-68; and for royal income chap. 4, n. 5.

15. *DII* 23:358.

16. See above, chap. 1, nn. 27, 37; Herrera II:2:4.

17. Instructions to Cortés, 26 June 1523, Hernández Sánchez-Barba, pp. 585-92; *DII* 23:353-68.

18. See Silvio Zavala, *Las esclavos indios en Nueva España*, (Mexico: El Colegio Nacional, 1968), chap. 1.

19. See Koenigsberger; Karl Brandi, *The Emperor Charles V*, tr. C. V. Wedgwood (London: Cape, 1939). Note, too, Charles' use of churchmen in high government posts, among them in Spain Ruiz de la Mota, Fonseca, and Loaisa. For trenchant discussion of Spanish crown-papal relations, see Dickens.

20. Cédula of 15 October 1522, Hernández Sánchez-Barba, p. 582.

21. See Manzano; Góngora, *Estado*; Giménez Fernández, "Cortés"; Las Casas, *Historia*, lib. III, cap. 149, 151; Herrera II:4:2-5.

22. See above, n. 17. Yet in royal instructions to the *visitador,* Ponce, in 1525, nothing was said against slavery. Instead, he was to see about using Indian slaves in gold mines. Zavala found the first prohibition of enslaving free Indians in New Spain dated 9 November 1526.

23. See Herrera II:2:3; Giménez Fernández, *Las Casas;* Carro; Ybot León; Juan Friede and Benjamin Keen, eds., *Bartolomé de Las Casas in History* (De Kalb: Northern Illinois Univ. Press, 1971), for a sampling of Lascasiana and also for the short biographical essay by Giménez Fernández.

24. See Giménez Fernández, *Las Casas.*

25. *Tratados* 1:10–11.

26. Ibid. 1:8–9; and see 1:461–500, and 2:915–1233.

27. Ibid. 1:490–91.

28. Ibid. 1:482–83.

29. Bartolomé de Las Casas, *Apologética historia sumaria,* ed., Edmundo O'Gorman (Mexico, 1967), chaps. 187–88, 199.

30. Bernice Hamilton, *Political Thought in Sixteenth-Century Spain* (New York: Oxford Univ. Press, 1963), pp. 171–75. See Francisco de Vitoria, *Las relecciones de Indis y De iure belli . . .,* ed. Javier Malágon Barceló (Washington, D.C.: Pan American Union, 1963); James Brown Scott, *The Spanish Origin of International Law* (Oxford, 1924), pp. 84–85; Manzano, pp. 63–83; José Miranda, *Vitoria y los intereses de la Conquista de América* (Mexico: Colegio de México, 1947); and Carro, pp. 286–87, who notes that the University of Paris was a center of conciliar ideas and that there John Mair or Maior, a Scot, Dominican, and nominalist, first raised the Indies question in a book of 1510, stressing the civil origin of authority; cf. J. H. Parry, *The Spanish Theory of Empire in the Sixteenth Century* (Cambridge: Cambridge Univ. Press, 1940), and Vicente Beltrán de Heredia, O.P., *Francisco de Vitoria* (Barcelona, 1939).

31. ". . . in the forum of the conscience a man is bound to base his judgement not on his own sentiments but on demonstrable reason or on the authority of the wise; else his judgement is presumptuous." Vitoria, cited in Scott, p. iii.

32. First *relectio,* xxxiii (Scott, app. A).

33. Ibid., *De potestate civili,* lxxii–lxxxv; and *De jure gentium,* passim (Scott, app. C, E).

34. Second *relectio,* lii (Scott, app. B).

35. Ibid., lii–liii, lxix, lv; *De jure gentium.*

36. Cf. *Las Siete Partidas:* natural law: "which men and also other animals which have sense possess naturally in themselves," and which is responsible for the family; *jus gentium:* common law of all nations, suitable for men and not animals, established by reason as well as force because men could not live properly with one another in concord and peace if all did not observe it. By it men know what territory is theirs, and city limits. It requires them to praise God and obey parents and the government of their country (patria), and it permits self-defense against dishonor and violence (*Partida* I, tit.1, 1.2). Vitoria, *De jure gentium,* lxxviii.

37. "The Indian aborigines are not barred from the exercise of true dominion. This is proved from the fact that the true state of the case is that they are not of unsound mind but have, according to their kind, the use of reason. This is clear because there is a certain method in their affairs, for they have politics which are orderly arranged and they have definite marriage and magistrates, overlords, laws, and workshops, and a system of exchange, all of which call for the use of reason; they also have a kind of religion . . ." First *relectio,* xiii.

38. ". . . the aborigines undoubtedly had true dominion in both public and private matters, just like Christians, and that neither princes nor private persons could be despoiled of their property on the grounds of their not being true owners. It would be harsh to deny to those, who have never done any wrong, what we grant to Saracens and Jews, who are persistent enemies of Christianity." Ibid.

39. Ibid., xxxiv; also second *relectio,* liii; *De potestate civili,* xl; *De jure gentium,* lxi–lxv.

40. First *relectio,* xli, xxxvi-xlvi.
41. Ibid., xxxvii, xlv.
42. Ibid., xlvi; *De jure gentium,* lxi.
43. The New Laws abolished slavery and encomiendas held by officials and prelates, reduced those thought to be too large, levied a tax on tribute paid to all encomenderos, forbade new encomiendas, and ordered old ones to revert to the crown on the death of their holders. The last clause was repealed in 1546. See Antonio Muro Orejón, comp., "Las leyes nuevas (1542-43)," *Anuario de estudios americanos,* 2 (1945): 809-36—a facsimile reproduction; Henry Stevens and Fred W. Lucas, eds. *The New Laws of the Indies* (London, 1892).
44. Manzano, pp. 139-48, 208-10, 227.
45. Sepúlveda, *Democrates segundo o de las justas causas de la guerra contra los Indios* (Madrid: Consejo Superior de Investigaciones Científicos, Instituto Francisco de Vitoria, 1951), in Latin and Spanish, ed. Angel Losada, p. 33; also see Losada, "Hernán Cortés en la obra del cronista Sepúlveda," in *Estudios cortesianos* (Madrid, 1948), pp. 127-69; Losada and Giménez Fernández in Keen and Friede; Manzano, p. 157; and *Handbook of Middle American Indians* 13:71.
46. P. 35.
47. See Silvio Zavala, *Servidumbre natural y libertad cristiana según los tratadistas españoles de los siglos XVI y XVII* (Buenos Aires, 1944); Góngora; *Estado;* Carro; Ybot León; and Las Casas, *Apologética historia.*
48. First *relectio,* xlv-xlvi; Hamilton, p. 133.
49. Manzano, pp. 173-75, includes participants. Sepúlveda, influenced by Cortés and García de Loaisa, president of the Council of the Indies, in the mid-forties wrote *Democrates alter.* Las Casas says that when the Council of the Indies rejected it, Sepúlveda appealed to the Council of Castile. Las Casas, arriving at court in 1547, complained against it, so that council referred it to the universities of Alcalá and Salamanca in 1548. The disputants appeared before the Valladolid junta in 1550. For Soto, see Hamilton, pp. 176-80.
50. Lewis Hanke, *The Spanish Struggle for Justice in the Conquest of America* (Philadelphia, 1949; reprint, Boston: Little, Brown, 1966); Hanke ignores the fact that it was normal to place political theory and policy within a moral and religious context in western Europe at the time. Also see Silvio Zavala, *Las instituciones jurídicas en la Conquista de América,* 2d ed. (Mexico, 1971); and Zavala, *Servidumbre.* See Edmundo O'Gorman, "Lewis Hanke on the Spanish Struggle for Justice in the Conquest of America," *HAHR* 29 (1949): 563-71; the exchange: Benjamin Keen, "The Black Legend Revisited: Assumptions and Realities," *HAHR* 49 (1969): 703-21; Hanke, "A Modest Proposal for a Moratorium on Grand Generalizations: Some Thoughts on the Black Legend," ibid., 51 (1971): 112-27; Keen, "The White Legend Revisited: A Reply to Prof. Hanke's Modest Proposal," ibid., 51 (1971): 336-51, is all somewhat off the issues.

In 1555 Cano drew up a *parecer,* or opinion, at the request of Charles V, concerning royal differences with Paul IV, in which he argued that if the Spanish monarch yielded to it, the Roman curia could destroy the church with its avarice, that Charles was more religious than was that pope; see Henry Charles Lea, *Chapters from the Religious History of Spain connected with the Inquisition* (Philadelphia, 1890), pp. 124-25.
51. Charles, in confirming Fernando Cortés as royal deputy in Vera Cruz, for instance, agreed with that town's council in equating imposition of royal authority with exercise of jurisdiction and did appoint him "to be our Judge, Governor, and Captain General, to perform our Justice in those kingdoms ..." 15 October 1522, Hernández Sánchez-Barba, p. 582; and see p. 587.
52. The first royal decrees for Mexico, as noted, concerned finances, opposed grants of encomienda and indiscriminate Indian enslavement, and urged good treatment of Indian vassals. See Puga; *Recopilación* IV, VI, etc. Subsequent policy then elaborated law on the same general principles, in interaction with events in New Spain and other parts of Spanish America. Spaniards succeeded Incas in Peru by 1535; subsequent legislation often was

directed to both viceroyalties. Thus, for example, the New Laws of 1542 were in the main a reaction to the newer situation in Peru but were drawn for Mexico as well (Schäfer, 2:268–69). By and large, legislation was designed principally for New Spain from 1522 until the late 1530s, later often tending to be addressed specifically to a particular problem in one locale. Cédulas were also drawn, in the absence of the king, by the queen, Isabella of Portugal, in the king's name by the Council of the Indies and, increasingly, toward mid-century by Prince Philip. Schäfer notes a divergence in outlook between the king and council members on occasion. In this account care had been taken to cite Charles' policy where they differ. See the pertinent works of Rafael Altamira—for example, "La legislación indiana como elemento de la historia de las ideas coloniales españolas," *RHA* 1 (1938): 1–24; and José María Ots Caqdequi, *Historia del derecho español en América y de derecho indiano* (Madrid: Biblioteca Juridica Aguilar, 1969).

53. My thanks to Charles Gibson for raising this point (letter of 21 April 1973). Las Casas said that Sepúlveda, in basing the royal right on force, would make the king a tyrant, that the right should instead be based on the royal duty to extend Christianity.

54. First *relectio*, xiv–xlvi.

55. See above, chap. 1.

56. To Mendoza, 25 April 1935, in *Colección de documentos inéditos relativos al descubrimiento, conquista y organización de las antiguas posesiones españoles de Ultramar* (Madrid, 1885–1932) (hereinafter *DIU*), 10:243 ff.; to the audiencia of Mexico, 28 October 1548; Puga, 2:8–13.

57. Arthur S. Aiton, *Antonio de Mendoza, First Viceroy of New Spain* (Durham: Duke Univ. Press, 1927), p. 39; cédula of 22 February 1549 permitting cuatequil; *Recopilación* VI:12:1. Also see Silvio Zavala, *La encomienda indiana* (Madrid: Centro de Estudios Historicos, 1935), pp. 115–17, and Zavala, *Esclavos*, pp. 135–36.

58. Orders to Cortés, 26 June 1523, see above, n. 17.

59. To Luis Ponce de Léon, 28 April 1526, Puga, 1:17–18.

60. 12 September 1530, Puga, 1:164, *Recopilación* V:11:22.

61. 21 September 1551, *Recopilación* I:22:1; Puga, 2:87–88. To Mendoza, 14 July 1536, *DII* 23:454–67. To Augustinians, 7 June 1550, *Recopilación* VI:1:18, states that natives were to learn Castilian so that it would be easier to indoctrinate them in "our" policy and good customs. Cf. Laws of Burgos which see Castilian as a means to religious indoctrination only. By 1550 the broader desire to acculturate was apparent. Also cédula of 17 June 1550, *Recopilación* VIII:1:6, and Edmundo O'Gorman, comp., "Enseñanza del Castellano como factor político colonial: Mediados del siglo XVI y finales del XVIII," *Boletin del Archivo General de la Nación* (hereinafter *BAGN*), 17 (1946): 163–71. And cf. Nebrija (above, chap. 1), who endorsed language as an instrument of empire, to be used by Isabella.

62. See above, n. 43; and below, chaps. 4, 6.

63. *Recopilación* IV:19:1; cf. Góngora, *Estado*, p. 23, for distinction between king's *senorío* and private estate.

64. See Haring, *Trade and Navigation;* Ramón Carande, *Carlos V y sus banqueros*, 2 vols. (Madrid, 1943, 1949); William P. Glade, *The Latin American Economies* (New York: published by Van Nos Reinhold; Krieger, 1969); M. Colmeiro, *Historia de la economía política en España* (Madrid, 1963), vol. 2.

65. See above, no. 12.

66. See Kamen; Sicroff; Marcel Bataillon, *Erasmo y España* (Buenos Aires and Mexico, 1950), 2 vols.; Leonard, pp. 81–82; Dickens.

CHAPTER FOUR

1. Cortés, *Ordenanzas* of 20 May 1524, letters to the king of 15 October 1524 and 3 September 1526, and instructions to Hernán de Saavedra, 1524–25, *DII* 26:160–94.

2. Bernal Díaz, 1:321–26.

3. Motolinía to Luis de Velasco, 27 August 1554, in Mariano Cuevas, S.J., *Documentos inéditos del siglo XVI para la historia de Mexico* (Mexico, 1914), p. 230. Writing so many years later, Motolinía may well be paraphrasing rather than quoting Cortés.

4. Letter of 15 October 1524, Hernández Sánchez-Barba, p. 241.

5. Ibid. Cortés asserted that if Spaniards received Indians as their own, with rights of tribute and jurisdiction, they would treat them as now only he did! For how his and other Indians were treated, see below, chap. 7.

Royal income came, theoretically, from "the royal fifth" levied on spoils, and from tribute, duties, receipts, fines, and confiscations. And under patronato real, the crown was also in charge of church monies. Greatest initial income, of course, was from the royal share of booty, including slaves (Haring, *Spanish Empire*, etc.; Lanning; Zavala, *Esclavos*, p. 5). Enforcement of the fifth on mining was not strict. To encourage output it varied from a fifth to a tenth. An import duty, the *almojarifazgo*, was in force by 1532, when a royal order noted attempts to avoid it (Puga, 1:175). Although Haring ("Ledgers," p. 177) states it was first levied in Mexico in 1524, royal instructions of 5 April 1528 to the audiencia, asking the oidores to investigate the possibility of imposing it, indicate it was not then in effect (Puga, 1:74). After 1550, revenue was also derived from the *juzgado de bienes de difuntos* and forced loans (Aiton, *Mendoza*, pp. 70-74). And see above, chap. 3, nn. 12, 14, 64.

6. *Ordenanzas*, pp. 17-18.

7. Bernal Díaz, 2:164-72; Zavala, *Esclavos*, p. 6. In some towns Cortés did specify encomendero exactions and attempt to regulate duration of native service and sorts of labor and produce exacted. (See García Martínez, *Marquesado*, and Riley, *Cortés*.) Charles Gibson, in *Tlaxcala in the Sixteenth Century* (Palo Alto: Stanford Univ. Press, 1967), pp. 170-81, discusses the general meaning of tribute, a very elastic term, and notes it was paid in money, kind, and labor to the church, the government, Indian principales, and as military service. Tlaxcala, directly under the crown, provided various sorts of tribute. Cf. José Miranda, *El tributo indígena en la Nueva España* (Mexico: Colegio de México, 1952).

8. Albornoz to the king, 15 December 1525, in Joaquín García Icazbalceta, ed., *Colección de documentos para la historia de Mexico*, (hereinafter *CD*), 1 (Mexico, 1858): 484. Albornoz was answering the conquistadors' charge that the crown needed them to turn tribute paid in goods and services into cash. Also see Zavala, *Encomienda;* Lesley B. Simpson, *The Encomienda in New Spain*, rev. ed., (Berkeley and Los Angeles: Univ. of California Press, 1966); and above, chap. 3, n. 12.

9. Gayangos, pp. 369-76; see Bernal Díaz, 2:179-254. Gibson, *Tlaxcala*, p. 63, notes misuse of royal funds by treasury officials.

10. Luis Ponce de León died (shortly after arrival in the spring of 1526), as did his successor, Marcos de Aguilar, leaving the commission to Alonso de Estrada. For details see Bernal Díaz, 2:255-87, and Hackett.

11. Miranda, *Tributo*, p. 61.

12. Royal cédulas creating the audiencia of Mexico: 29 November 1527, 13 December 1527; *Recopilación* II:15:3. The audiencia formally convened on 1 January 1529. Nuño de Guzmán was friendly with Albornoz, and probably also a Cobos protégé.

In 1525 New Spain extended from Colima to Salvador on the South Sea (the Pacific Ocean) and from Pánuco to Honduras on the Atlantic. Then the crown gave Pánuco and adjoining Vitoria Garayana as a governorship to Guzmán, put Honduras under Diego López de Salcedo, and in Yucatán and Cozumel made Francisco de Montejo governor and captain-general for life. In 1527 Guatemala was declared a separate entity under Pedro de Alvarado. These and "all provinces between the Cape of Honduras and the Cape of Florida" were put under the first audiencia of Mexico, excluding political jurisdiction in Honduras, Guatemala, and Pánuco. See Hackett; Donald Chipman, *Nuño de Guzmán and the Province of Pánuco in New Spain, 1518-1533* (Glendale, Calif.: A. H. Clark, 1967); Hubert Howe Bancroft, *History of Mexico*, vol. 2 (San Francisco, 1883); Simpson, *Encomienda*, pp. 66-76; and Gerhard.

13. Puga, 1:41-129. It was also to take the *residencia*—that is, to make public inquiry concerning the conduct in office—of the treasury officials and to send them to Spain. Morality was to be safeguarded, pretensions to aristocratic behavior limited by making sumptuary laws, and gambling prohibited. Oidores were to list mines, call an advisory council including prelates, friars, and native dignitaries, report on the land, and reserve lands for future settlers. The oidores were not to hold encomiendas, or become involved in commerce, and they were to see to the welfare of the Indians.

14. Miranda, *Tributo,* p. 65.

15. For private interests of the oidores, see Enrique Otte, "La Nueva España en 1529," in Bernardo García Martínez et al., *Historia y sociedad en el mundo de habla española. Homenaje a José Miranda* (Mexico, 1970), p. 96. The oidores clashed with Juan de Zumárraga, bishop-elect of Mexico, over the bounds of their respective jurisdictions, and because of their abuse of Indians. See below, chap. 5.

16. Bernal Díaz, 2:288-309. The second audiencia was appointed by the bishop of Badajoz at the request of the empress and the Council of the Indies, in the absence of the emperor. Four lawyers were named in August 1529: Juan de Salmerón, Alonso Maldonado, Francisco de Ceynos, and Vasco de Quiroga. See Aiton, *Mendoza,* pp. 22-24.

17. Instructions of 12 July 1530; Puga, 1:154-85. Order of same date, repeated 20 March 1532, that no encomiendas be granted to clergy; *Recopilación* VI:8:12. Also see Zavala, *Encomienda,* p. 71.

18. Puga; Zavala, *Esclavos,* pp. 30, 40-41. Payne, vol. 1 for corregidores in Spain.

19. Puga, 1:266-74, 281-85; Zavala, *Esclavos,* p. 89, n. 109.

20. Opinion to crown (1532), in García Icazbalceta, *CD,* 2:165-89; also see Francisco Ceynos to crown 22 June 1532; ibid., pp. 158-64.

21. Document on participants in this junta published by José A. Llaguno, S.J., *Personalidad jurídica del indio y el III Concilio Provincial Mexicano* (Mexico, 1963), pp. 151-54.

22. Audiencia to empress, 11 May 1533, Paso y Troncoso, 3:91-92; García Martínez, *Marquesado,* pp. 59-72; Simpson, *Encomienda,* pp. 98-100; see also *Procesos de residencia instruidos contra Pedro de Alvarado y Nuño de Guzmán,* ed. J. F. Ramírez (Mexico, 1847); and Cortés' residencia, *DII,* vols. 26-29.

23. See pertinent documents in Paso y Troncoso, vols. 2, 3; *DII,* 13:206-23; Zavala, *Encomienda,* p. 73; Góngora, *Estado,* p. 202; Miranda, *Tributo,* pp. 80-81; and Toribio de Motolinía, O.F.M., *Memoriales,* ed. Luis García Pimentel (Mexico, 1903), pp. 197-98.

24. Ceynos to crown, 1 March 1565, in García Icazbalceta, *CD,* 2:237-43; and see Zavala, *Esclavos,* pp. 30-31, 42, 45, 64; Bancroft, 2:331.

25. Aiton, *Mendoza,* p. 58. Maldonado was scored, in his residencia, for proclivities to race horses and play *pelota.* He swore that the ball playing was on doctor's orders. In 1543 he became president of the new Audiencia de los Confines in Guatemala and governor there. Fuenleal and Salmerón returned to Spain, Fuenleal to become bishop of Cuenca and president of the Council of the Indies and Salmerón a member of it. Ceynos was a Mexican oidor until 1565. Quiroga became first bishop of Michoacán (ibid., p. 101).

26. In García Icazbalceta, *CD,* 2:165; and see Miguel León-Portilla, "Ramírez de Fuenleal y las antigüedades mexicanas," *Estudios de Cultura Nahuatl* 8 (1969): 9-49.

27. Salmerón to Council of Indies, 13 August 1531, cited in Simpson, *Encomienda,* p. 95.

28. See Rafael Aguayo Spencer, ed., *Don Vasco de Quiroga, Documentos* (Mexico, 1939); Nicolas León, ed., *Documentos inéditos referentes al ilustrisimo señor Don Vasco de Quiroga* (Mexico, 1940); Silvio Zavala, *Recuerdo de Vasco de Quiroga* (Mexico: Porrúa, 1965); and Fintan B. [J. Benedict] Warren, *Vasco de Quiroga and His Pueblo-Hospitals of Santa Fe* (Washington, D.C.: Academy of American Franciscan History, 1963). The ordinances of these hospital-villages appear in Aguayo Spencer and as an appendix to Juan José Moreno, *Fragmentos de la vida del venerable don Vasco de Quiroga . . .* (Mexico, 1776; 2d ed., Mexico, 1940). John McAndrew, *The Open-Air Churches of Sixteenth-Century Mexico* (Cambridge: Harvard Univ. Press, 1965), pp. 622-23, states: "A number of large and hand-

some charity hospitals had recently been built in Spain under the patronage of Ferdinand and Isabella. The Aztecs had had big hospitals before the Spaniards came." In Mexico Cortés' Hospital de Jesús was first, then others built by religious orders. "Even in a land so rich in hospitals, the two founded by Vasco de Quiroga were exceptional. . . . each hospital was a model Christian socialist colony, a school for vocational and humanistic studies, an orphanage, old people's home, and hospital in the modern sense."

29. León-Portilla, "Fuenleal," connects the president to the early and influential account of Indian life written by Andrés de Olmos, now lost but drawn on previously by a number of other chroniclers; and see below, chap. 5.

30. Fuenleal reported to the empress that the audiencia had arranged for Franciscans in the city of Mexico to teach Indians "romance grammar." 8 August 1533, Paso y Troncoso, 3:118. See below, chap. 5; and cf. above, chap. 3, Vitoria's argument for the royal right to enter the Indies was based on Matthew: "Teach all nations . . ."

31. Erika Spivakovsky, *Son of the Alhambra: Don Diego Hurtado de Mendoza, 1504–1575* (Austin: Univ. of Texas Press, 1970), includes pertinent family background of the humanist's brother, the future viceroy of New Spain (pp. 4–8). Also see intro. by Robert Brian Tate, ed., to Fernando del Pulgar, *Claros varones de Castilla* (Oxford: Clarendon, 1971); Aiton, *Mendoza*, pp. 1–16; Ciríaco Pérez Bustamante, *Don Antonio de Mendoza, Primer Virrey de la Nueva España* (Santiago de Compestela, 1928); Emilio Meneses García, ed. *Correspondencia del Conde de Tendilla*, vol. 1 (1508–1509) (Madrid: Real Academia de Historia, 1972); Dickens, p. 49.

32. Pérez Bustamante, p. 105, n. 1. Many moriscos were only nominal Christians, retaining a largely Moorish way of life.

33. Aiton, *Mendoza*, pp. 36, 48. He also exercised supervisory authority over the Mexican Inquistion; see below, chap. 5.

34. Ibid., pp. 52, 137; Edmundo O'Gorman, ed., "Una instrucción secreta a Don Antonio de Mendoza," *BAGN* 9 (1938): 588; and C. H. Haring, "American Gold and Silver Production in the First Half of the Sixteenth Century," *Quarterly Journal of Economics* 39 (1915): 433–79.

35. See Puga, 1:351–79; Aiton, *Mendoza*, pp. 34–42; Miranda, *Tributo*, pp. 90–92. Mendoza's instructions in *DIU*, 10:242, 245–62, were signed by the empress.

36. Mendoza to Velasco, in *Instrucciones que los vireyes de Nueva España dejaron a sus sucesores*, 2 vols. (Mexico, 1873), 1:28; Aiton, *Mendoza*, p. 87.

37. Mendoza to Velasco, 1:23; Antonio de Mendoza, *Ordinanzas y compilación de leyes: Obra impresa en México, por Juan Pablos en 1548 . . .*, facsimile ed. (Madrid, 1945); A. S. Aiton, ed., "Ordenanças hechas por el Sr. Visorrey, don Antonio de Mendoça, sobre las minas de la Nueva España. Año de M.D.L.," *RHA* 14 (1942): 73–95; Paso y Troncoso, vols. 3–5, passim; and Edmundo O'Gorman, ed., "Mandamientos del Virrey D. Antonio de Mendoza," *BAGN* 10 (1939): 213–311.

38. See Miranda, *Tributo*, p. 96; Ceynos to crown, 1 March 1565, in García Icazbalceta, *CD* 2:237–43; Silvio Zavala, *Encomienda*, pp. 82–83, *Esclavos*, pp. 103, 122–24, and "Los encomiendas de Nueva España y el gobierno de Don Antonio de Mendoza," *RHA* 1 (1938): 59–75.

39. A. S. Aiton, "The Secret Visita against Viceroy Mendoza," in *New Spain and the Anglo-American West* (Los Angeles, 1932), 1:1–22; and Aiton, *Mendoza*, p. 159. On 17 April 1535 the crown authorized Mendoza to restrict Cortés and commend *cosas de guerra* to others, at his discretion (Puga, 1:357–58, and *DIU* 10:242–43). Cortés was ordered not to use the office of captain-general except on order of the audiencia (16 April 1535, text in Pérez Bustamante, p. 138). On 30 November 1537, Mendoza directed that Cortés' Indians be counted (Paso y Troncoso, 3:227). The text of Cortés' petition to have Mendoza's residencia taken is in Pérez Bustamante, p. 185.

40. Mendoza opened wagon roads from Mexico to Acapulco, Oaxaca, Tehuantepec,

Huatelco, Michoacán, Colima, Jalisco, Pánuco, to the mines of Taxco and Sultepec, and repaired the road to Vera Cruz. The roads reflect Spanish expansion, decreasing Indians, and the desire to protect them by replacing *tamemes,* or carriers, with carts and beasts of burden. See Vicente Riva Palacio, *México á través de los Siglos* (Mexico, n.d.), 2:358. Also López de Gómara, pp. 405-6; Aiton, *Mendoza,* p. 109; García Icazbalceta, *CD,* 2:72-140; Andrés Cavo, S.J., *Los tres siglos de Méjico . . .,* ed. Carlos María de Bustamante (Mexico, 1852), pp. 36-45; Miranda, *Tributo;* and Miranda, *La función económica del encomendero en los orígenes del régimen colonial (Nueva España, 1525-1531)* (Mexico: Universidad Nacional Autónoma de México, 1965), pp. 26-27; William H. Dusenberry, *The Mexican Mesta: The Administration of Ranching in Colonial Mexico* (Urbana: Univ. of Illinois Press, 1963); Woodrow Borah, *Silk Raising in Colonial Mexico* (Berkeley and Los Angeles: Univ. of California Press, 1943); Miguel Othón de Mendizábal, *Historia económica de México* in *Obras completas,* 6 vols. (Mexico, 1947), 6:312-496.

41. See Miranda, *Tributo,* pp. 93-108; Aiton, *Mendoza;* Gibson, *Aztecs;* Zavala, *Encomienda.*

42. Mendoza eulogized the school's progress to Velasco; see J. Ignacio Rubio Mañé, "Apuntes para la biografía de don Luis de Velasco, el viejo," *RHA* 3 (1941): 48; Francis Borgia Steck, "The First College in America: Santa Cruz de Tlatelolco," *Catholic Education Review* 34 (1936): 449-62; Aiton, *Mendoza,* pp. 36, 52, 69, 91; and below, chap. 5.

43. See Joaquín García Icazbalceta, "Education in the City of Mexico during the Sixteenth Century," tr. Walter J. O'Donnell, in *Historical Records and Studies* 20 (New York, 1931): 16-17; and chap. 3, n. 61.

44. *Ordinanzas;* O'Gorman, "Mandamientos"; Paso y Troncoso, vols. 3-5; Puga, vol. 1.

45. Aiton, *Mendoza,* p. 94.

46. *Ordinanzas;* Spivakovsky, p. 73; Simpson, *Encomienda,* p. 101; Zavala, "Mendoza," p. 60; Aiton, *Mendoza,* pp. 104-9.

47. Spivakovsky, p. 99.

48. López de Gómara, pp. 405-6; Juan de Torquemada, *Monarquía indiana,* 4th ed., 3 vols. (Mexico: Porrúa, 1969), 1:611; Prince Philip to Tello de Sandoval, 9 September 1545, Paso y Troncoso, 4:209-35; Aiton, *Mendoza,* pp. 48-50.

49. Spivakovsky, p. 98. Keniston, p. 45, states that Antonio de Mendoza and Cobos were the two representatives from Granada at the cortes of 1515. They were, therefore, old acquaintances.

50. Mendoza to Velasco, 1:23; Aiton, *Mendoza,* pp. 10, 99. For divergences in this period between Mendoza's policy and royal legislation, see also Zavala, *Esclavos,* pp. 121-26; Zavala, *Encomienda,* pp. 115-20; and Chevalier, *Land,* pp. 91-92.

51. Francis Bacon, *Works* (London, 1869), 13:337.

52. Cited by Aiton, *Mendoza,* p. 51. On 20 June 1544 Mendoza wrote to the crown: "Never was justice so feared . . . as in my time nor Spaniards so harmonious nor natives so well treated" (*Instrucciones . . . vireyes,* 1:50).

53. Rubio Mañé, pp. 50-56.

54. Prince Philip to Velasco, 1552, in Cuevas, pp. 170-75. See also Bancroft, 2:564; Manuel Rivera Cambas, *Los gobernantes de México* (Mexico, n.d.), 1:34; Miranda, *Tributo,* pp. 110-12.

55. Zavala, *Encomienda,* pp. 129-34, and *Esclavos,* pp. 121-38, 167, n. 246; Miranda, *Tributo,* pp. 103-7.

56. Sherburne F. Cook and Woodrow Borah, in *Essays in Population History,* vol. 1, *Mexico and the Caribbean* (Berkeley and Los Angeles: Univ. of California Press, 1971), p. 80, note the greatest indigenous population loss occurred between 1532 and the 1550s in the central valley. They indicate 16.8 million Indians in 1532, 6.5 million in 1548, and 2.65 million in 1568. Also see Gibson, *Aztecs,* pp. 448-49; and below, chap. 7.

57. Miranda, *Tributo;* Gibson, *Aztecs,* pp. 62-63, 354; Puga, 2:108-249; Velasco to

empress, 21 February 1552, Paso y Troncoso, 6:139–42; Ceynos to crown, 1 March 1565, García Icazbalceta, *CD,* 2:237–43; Cavo, pp. 49–53; Simpson, *Encomienda,* pp. 129–34; and Walter V. Scholes, *The Diego Ramírez Visita* (Columbia: Univ. of Missouri Press, 1946). Under Mendoza, between 1547 and 1550, a number of visitas were made to determine tribute policy, etc., and a résumé collated, the *Suma de Visitas,* used as a basis for mid-century changes in the system. Above, chap. 1, n. 8, for hermandad.

58. Velasco to king, 21 February 1552, Paso y Troncoso, 6:139–43.

59. Velasco to Philip, 7 February 1554, Cuevas, *Docs.,* pp. 183–218; 1 February 1558, ibid., pp. 244–45; Zavala, *Encomienda,* p. 131, and *Esclavos,* p. 134.

60. García Icazbalceta, "Education," pp. 38–39.

61. Velasco to Philip, 7 February 1554, Cuevas, pp. 207–11.

62. Velasco to Philip (1554), cited by Zavala, *Encomienda,* p. 134; Rubio Mañé, p. 59.

63. Gibson, *Aztecs.* pp. 27, 382. Archbishop Montúfar complained of the influence of *frailes* on Velasco. Ernest J. Burrus, S.J., in *The Writings of Alonso de la Vera Cruz* (Rome and St. Louis, 1968), 1:76, notes that many of the viceroy's letters are in the same hand as a manuscript he attributes to Vera Cruz. Velasco may well have supported the Augustinian's defense of the Indians. See below, chap. 5, for Vera Cruz.

64. Velasco reported as corrupt, and frequently tangled with, the more pro-settler and rancher audiencia of Mexico. The crown in 1555 told oidores it was well aware of their obstructionist tactics (W. Scholes, pp. 48, 81); Rubio Mañé; Puga, vol. 2; Zavala, *Esclavos,* p. 157; Simpson, *Encomienda,* p. 79; Chevalier, *Land,* pp. 99–101.

65. Cortés also had, with his second wife, Juana de Zúñiga, a legitimate son named Martín who became the second Marqués del Valle de Oaxaca. Cortés' father, it will be recalled, was also named Martín.

66. Rubio Mañé; Cavo, p. 53; France V. Scholes and Eleanor B. Adams, eds., *Cartas del licenciado Jerónimo Valderrama y otros documentos sobre su visita al gobierno de Nueva España, 1563–1565* (Mexico, 1961), pp. 48–56, 60, 89, 96.

67. See above, n. 64; Rubio Mañé, p. 55. Chevalier (pp. 118–24) states that by mid-century the royal treasury officials of the twenties, Albornoz and Chirinos, were landed gentry; although the crown revoked their encomiendas shortly after 1550, Chirinos had become land wealthy. Gonzalez de Salazar, too, held Indians in encomienda, in the 1540s gained title to lands purchased from the Taximaroa Indians, and began a highly successful sugar refinery in Zitácuaro. Public offices and the law were some of the earliest sources of capital in Mexico. Many officials became cattle barons, and many oidores and others returned to Spain wealthy. Alonso de Estrada died in 1530, but one of his daughters, Beatriz, married Francisco Vazquez de Coronado, the conquistador, and another, Luisa, married Jorge de Alvarado, Pedro's brother, and also joined the Mexican aristocracy; see *Colección de documentos inéditos para la historia de Ibero-América,* 14 vols. (Madrid, 1937–32) (hereinafter *DIA*), 1:362; Fernández del Castillo, "Estrada," pp. 402–4. Also see Constance A. C. Carter, "Law and Society in Colonial Mexico: Audiencia Judges in Mexican Society from the Tello de Sandoval Visita General, 1543–1547," Ph.D. dissertation, Columbia University, 1971; and below, chap. 6, nn. 62, 63.

68. Aiton, *Mendoza,* p. 13. For private interests of the first audiencia, above, n. 15.

69. Ibid., p. 184.

70. Puga, 2:138–40. The crown also raised the salaries of the viceroy and oidores in 1551 and again ordered those officials to refrain from commerce, stockbreeding, and demanding personal service of Indians.

71. Aiton, *Mendoza,* pp. 47, 66–67.

72. The second audiencia had ordered corregidores' salaries to be paid in kind and as part of tribute; Miranda, *Tributo,* p. 81. Gibson, in *Tlaxcala,* pp. 67–79, indicates that in Tlaxcala corregidores were paid from tribute and also given other sustenance, that

some were royal officials of professional stamp, and that some had a genuine interest in Indian welfare, as they understood it.

73. Tejada to king, 11 March 1545, Paso y Troncoso, 4:183-89; Diego Ramírez to emperor, 4 April 1551, ibid., 6:36-40; emperor to D. Ramírez, 3 August 1551, ibid., 6:59-60; Aiton, *Mendoza*, p. 178; J. H. Parry, *The Audiencia of New Galicia in the Sixteenth Century* (Cambridge: Cambridge Univ. Press, 1948); Woodrow Borah, "Los tributos y su recaudacíon en la audiencia de Nueva Galicia durante el siglo XVI," in García Martínez, *Miranda*, pp. 27-48. The audiencia of Nueva Galicia had jurisdiction over what is now parts of the states of Jalisco, Guanajuato, Nayarit, Sinaloa, and Zacatecas. See also Robert S. Chamberlain, *The Conquest and Colonization of Hondouras, 1502-1550* (Washington, D.C., 1953), Chamberlain, *The Conquest and Colonization of Yucatán, 1517-1550* (Washington, D.C., 1948); Zavala, *Encomienda*, p. 144 (concerning Colima); Carl. O. Sauer, *Colima of New Spain in the Sixteenth Century* (Berkeley and Los Angeles: Univ. of California Press, 1948); Zavala, *Encomienda*, pp. 148, 174-75 (Yucatán), p. 152 (Guatemala); Zavala, *Contribución a la historia de las instituciones coloniales de Guatemala* (Mexico, 1945); William L. Sherman, "Indian Slavery and the Cerrato Reforms," *HAHR* 51 (1971): 25-50 (Guatemala); William B. Taylor, *Landlord and Peasant in Colonial Oaxaca* (Palo Alto: Stanford Univ. Press, 1972); Gerhard; Murdo J. MacLeod, *Spanish Central America* (Berkeley and Los Angeles: Univ. of California Press, 1973). Throughout New Spain lawyers staffed audiencias, litigation and appeal to royal justice replaced much preconquest warfare, and it is very understandable why Cortés, the conqueror, asked Charles very early to send no lawyers to Mexico.

74. Second audiencia to empress, 30 March 1531, Paso y Troncoso, 2:35-64; Ramírez de Fuenleal, Opinion of 1532, García Icazbalceta, *CD* 2:178-82; audiencia to crown, 2 January 1535, Paso y Troncoso, 3:175; Aiton, *Mendoza*, pp. 113, 184; and see below, chap. 8.

75. Cavo, p. 53; Rivera Cambas, pp. 35-36; and see below, chap. 8.

CHAPTER FIVE

1. Juan de Zumárraga to Prince Philip, 2 June 1544, in Cuevas, *Docs.*, p. 121.

2. Joaquín García Icazbalceta, ed., *Nueva colección de documentos para la historia de México: Codice Franciscano. Siglo XVI* (hereinafter *CF*) (Mexico, 1941), pp. 99-121; and see Francisco Mateos, S.J., "La iglesia americana durante el reinado de Carlos V, 1517-58," *Missionalia Hispanica* 15 (1958): 356.

3. See Pius Joseph Barth, O.F.M., *Franciscan Education and the Social Order in Spanish North America, 1502-1821* (Chicago: published Ph.D. diss., Univ. of Chicago, 1945), p. 121. In 1528 on Cortés' request, the empress sent to Mexico sixteen women, including nine nuns, to instruct Indian girls. In 1529 Zumárraga mentioned two Spanish beatas—who instructed "many single and widowed women, daughters of señores and principales, and others who want to come"—cloistered at Texcoco, in a large walled house (J. García Icazbalceta, *Don Fray Juan de Zumárraga, primer obispo y arzobispo de México* [Mexico, 1947] 2:199). In 1530 the empress sent to Mexico with the Marquesa del Valle six women, recruited through requests "to Salamanca and elsewhere," to teach "womenly offices" to Indian girls (Herrera IV:VI:4). Only one of them was still doing it by 1544 (García Icazbalceta, *Zumárraga*, 4:177-78), and the bishop had found nuns to be more tractable. See also Gil González Dávila, *Teatro eclesiástico de la primitiva iglesia de las Indias Occidentales* (Madrid, 1649-55), vol. 1; Torquemada, *Monarquía indiana;* Isidro Felix de Espinosa, O.F.M., *Crónica de los Colegios de Propaganda Fide en la Nueva España*, ed. Lino G. Canedo, O.F.M. (Washington: Academy of American Franciscan History, 1964); Bernardo de Lizana, *Historia de Yucatán* (Mexico, 1893); Agustín Dávila Padilla, O.P., *Historia de la fundación y discurso de la Provincia de Santiago de México* ... (Mexico, 1596; 2d ed., Brussels, 1625; reproduced in facsimile, 1955, ed. Agustín Millares Carlo); Antonio de Remesal, O.P.,

Historia general de las Indias Occidentales y particular de la gobernación de Chiapa y Guatemala (Guatemala, 1932, reissue of 1619 ed.); Mariano Cuevas, S.J., *Historia de la iglesia de México*, vol. 1 (El Paso, 1928); and Robert Ricard, *The Spiritual Conquest of Mexico*, tr. Lesley B. Simpson (Berkeley and Los Angeles: Univ. of California Press, 1966)—Ricard does not specifically put the missionary endeavor within the more general context of Spanish conquest. The better edition is the original: *La "conquête spirituelle" du Mexique* (Paris, 1933), with scholarly apparatus. And consult *HMAI*, vol. 13.

4. Gerónimo de Mendieta, O.F.M., *Historia eclesiástica indiana*, ed. J. García Icazbalceta, 2d facsimile ed. (Mexico, Porrúa, 1971); Fernando de Alva Ixtlilxochitl, *Obras históricas de ...*, ed., Alfredo Chavero (Mexico, 1891-92), abridged in English as *Ally of Cortés: Account 13 of the Coming of the Spaniards and the Beginning of the Evangelical Law*, tr. and with foreword by Douglass K. Ballentine (El Paso: Texas Western Press, 1969), pp. 74-77; Bernal Díaz, chap. 171. By his will Cortés endowed several religious institutions in Mexico and ordered others constructed. For a rather general account, see Fidel de Lejarza, "Franciscanismo de Cortés y Cortesianismo de los Franciscanos," *Missionalia Hispanica* 5 (1948): 43-136. Undoubtedly Cortés recognized as estimable the religious zeal of the friars, but also that full ecclesiastical religious organization would challenge his authority.

5. Mendieta, pp. 310-13. Motolinía (Toribio de Benavente), O.F.M., *History of the Indians of New Spain*, tr. and ed. Elizabeth Andros Foster (Berkeley and Los Angeles: Univ. of California Press, 1950), p. 196. Cf. Fray Toribio de Benavente Motolinía, *Memoriales o libro de las cosas de la Nueva España y de los naturales de ella*, ed. Edmundo O'Gorman (Mexico: Universidad Nacional Autónoma de México, 1971).

6. Tomás Ortiz headed the first Dominican twelve. In Mexico five of them died and others returned to Spain. Only Domingo de Betanzos and two companions remained to establish the province. See García Icazbalceta, *CD* 2:xxxvi-viii; Richard E. Greenleaf, *The Mexican Inquisition in the Sixteenth Century* (Albuquerque: Univ. of New Mexico Press, 1969), pp. 11-26; and above, note 3.

7. See above, chap. 4. They met with hostile reception by the cabildo of Mexico. Las Casas was, briefly, imprisoned in chains by the Dominicans there, the Santa Maria group hostile to Cortés and the second audiencia. (Giménez Fernández in Keen and Friede, pp. 83-85).

8. The bishopric of Chiapas was erected in 1539. The first bishop, named in 1540, was an old companion at Alcalá of Ignatius Loyola, Juan de Arteaga y Avendaño, member of the Order of Santiago and a professor of theology. He died in Mexico City in 1541 and Las Casas succeeded him, named bishop on 19 December 1543. Las Casas resided *poco tiempo* in his bishopric and renounced it in 1550 (González Dávila, 1:187; Schäfer, 2:573).

9. Joaquín García Icazbalceta, *Bibliografía mexicana del siglo XVI* (hereinafter *BMS*), ed. Agustín Millares Carlo (Mexico, 1954), pp. 90-104; Pedro de Gante, *Cartas de ...*, ed. Fidel de J. Chauvet, O.F.M. (Mexico: Provincia del Sto. Evangelo de México, 1951); Gante letter of 1522 in *Cartas de Indias* (Madrid: Ministerio de Fomento, 1877); Gante, *Catecismo de la doctrina cristiana* (Antwerp, 1528?; facsim. ed. Madrid: Dirección General de Archivos y Bibliotecas, 1970); Mendieta, passim; Mateos, p. 358; McAndrew; *HMAI*, vol. 13. García Icazbalceta identifies Gante (Peter of Ghent, originally van der Moere or Pedro de Mura) as a close relative of Charles V and cites him as saying that from childhood he had worked to serve the crown. His companions were Juan de Tecto (Van Tacht) and the elderly Juan de Aora (Mateos conjectures van Aar). Tecto had been professor of theology for fourteen years at the Sorbonne, guardian of the Franciscan monastery at Ghent, and confessor to Charles V. The three went first to Texcoco, there accepted the hospitality of its ruler, Ixtlilxochitl, learned Nahuatl, and baptized Indians, then three years later moved to Mexico. (See Alva Ixtlilxochitl.) Tecto and Aora were jointly responsible with Gante for introducing missionary methods; they died on Cortés' expedition to Honduras.

10. See Gante to Philip II (1558), García Icazbalceta, *CD* 2:220-28. Mendieta, p. 609, states that at his death Gante was held in greater esteem than the archbishop.

11. Gante to Philip II (1558). In 1532 he wrote that he had 500 to 600 children in his charge. His *Doctrina* was published in Antwerp in 1528, in Mexican and Latin, and in Mexico City in 1547 and 1553. See above, n. 9; García Icazbalceta, *BMS,* pp. 94-99; also Alva Ixtlilxochitl, p. 74; and Mendieta, pp. 408-9, 607-11. Gante was also responsible for the building of churches in the four Indian barrios, wards, of Mexico City (García Icazbalceta, *CF,* p. 6).

12. Gante to Philip II (1558); Torquemada, 3:221. He guided Indians, said Mendieta (p. 608), "not only in spiritual matters concerning the salvation of their souls but also in temporal ways of human industry, in order to open the eyes of understanding of the *rudos* so that spiritual matters might enter, for as the apostle said, *Prius quod animale, deinde quod spirituale.*" (Paul, 1 Cor. 15). McAndrew, p. 388, finds Gante's San José was modeled on the mosque of Córdoba.

13. Gante to the Franciscans of Flanders, 27 June 1529, *Cartas,* p. 12.

14. Augustine, *City of God* 19:17.

15. Letters of 1529, 1532, 1558. By 1529 he had overcome an initial homesickness for Flanders. Mendieta (p. 610) reported it had been a temptation of the devil.

16. Gante to Charles, 20 July 1548 and 15 February 1552, *Cartas,* pp. 25-26, 28.

17. To Philip (1558), García Icazbalceta, *CD,* 2:203-9.

18. Gibson, *Tlaxcala,* pp. 34-36. Valencia destroyed idols and had executed, in 1527, four Tlaxcalan chiefs. For Motolinía, see Mendieta, p. 211; he also stated that all of the first group went barefooted and had only the clothes they wore (pp. 254-55). See also Motolinía's writings; George Kubler, *Mexican Architecture in the Sixteenth Century,* 2 vols. (New Haven: Yale Univ. Press, 1948), 1:4-8; Torquemada; Ricard, passim; and *HMAI* 13:144-45.

19. Cf. Gilmore, pp. 204-5.

20. Holzapfel; and see above, chap. 1. Cf. José Antonio Maravell, "La Utopia político-religiosa de los Franciscanos en Nueva España," *Estudios Americanos* 1 (1949): 199-227; Maravell emphasizes the influence of Savonarola and the earlier Italian apocalyptic tradition on friars in Mexico, including Martín de Valencia, but underemphasizes other currents in the Spanish millieu. Also cf. Dickens; and John L. Phelan, *The Millennial Kingdom of the Franciscans in the New World,* 2d ed., rev. (Berkeley and Los Angeles: Univ. of California Press, 1970).

21. Mendieta, pp. 571-96; O'Gorman-Motolinía, pp. 175-87, 196-201; Kubler, 1:8. The Twelve were sent through the influence of Fray Francisco de Quiñones, Charles' confessor (Mateos, pp. 359-60).

22. See above, n. 20.

23. Motolinía to Charles, 2 January 1555; García Icazbalceta, *CD,* 1:253-77; Simpson, *Encomienda,* p. 243. In 1537 Motolinía declared nine million Indians baptized (Foster-Motolinía, p. 133).

24. Ibid., pp. 234-43; and García Icazbalceta, *CD,* vol. 1.

25. García Pimentel, ed., *Memoriales,* pp. 18-27. Motolinía opposed the New Laws; see his letter of 1555; and Zavala, *Esclavos,* p. 6.

26. Francis B. Steck, ed., *Motolinía's History of the Indians* (Washington, D.C.: Academy of American Franciscan History, 1951), pp. 171, 188, 148, 251.

27. Barth, p. 236.

28. O'Gorman ed., pp. 106-15; J. García Icazbalceta, intro. to Fernán González de Eslava, *Coloquios espirituales y sacramentales y poesías sagradas* (Mexico, 1877) pp. xvi-xxii.

29. (1555), Simpson, *Encomienda,* p. 240. For miscegenation, see below, chaps. 6-8.

30. He was close to Gante and Zumárraga, supported Mendoza and Velasco, and was generally respected. See Motolinía to Velasco, 27 August 1554, Cuevas, *Docs.,* pp. 228-32.

31. See O'Gorman ed., intro.

32. Ibid., pp. 207-8.

33. See below, chap. 9.

34. O'Gorman ed., p. 222.

35. Steck ed., pp. 87, 245, 248.

36. Ibid., p. 281; O'Gorman ed., p. 222.

37. Steck ed., pp. 260, 265–66. Mexico City was comparable in size and population to larger European capitals.

38. There is some evidence of a joint conspiracy of Franciscans—including Motolinía, Gante, and two others—and Cortés, before December 1528, to take over the government of New Spain, to recognize the Spanish king but to allow no more Spaniards in. See O'Gorman ed., intro., p. cv.

39. Martín de Valencia et al. to Charles V, January 1533, García Icazbalceta, *CF*, pp. 161–69; Kubler, 1:9. For biography, see García Icazbalceta, *Zumárraga*; Alberto María Carreño, comp., *Don Fray Juan de Zumárraga . . . (Documentos inéditos)* (Mexico, 1950); Richard E. Greenleaf, *Zumárraga and the Mexican Inquisition, 1536–1543* (Washington, D.C.: Academy of American Franciscan History, 1961). Also see Zumárraga's letters in Cuevas, *Documentos*. If Zumárraga, as evidence indicates, lived modestly, he did not live as a mendicant for he held slaves and encomiendas. See below, n. 43.

40. Zumárraga, Ordinances of 1532, in García Icazbalceta, *Zumárraga*, 4:110–12; Zumárraga to Cortés, 13 December 1530, ibid., 4:105; letter to the crown, 1531, Cuevas, *Docs.*, p. 51; Mendieta, pp. 629–32; Zavala, *Esclavos*, pp. 12–13, 19, 31, 98, n. 161.

41. Miranda, *Función*, pp. 44–45, and *Tributo*, pp. 63–64. The tasaciones, dating from 1528 to 1531, were few and calculated to show good faith in protecting Indians.

42. Zumárraga to Council of the Indies, 24 November 1536 and 8 February 1537, García Icazbalceta, *Zumárraga*, 4:119–23, 142–52; to his nephew, Sancho García de Larraval, 23 August 1539, and 18 August 1541, García Icazbalceta, *CF*, pp. 263–71; and the regulations for the Colegio de Santa Cruz de Tlatelolco, ibid., pp. 62–69; Torquemada, 3:113–15; Kubler, 1:219–23.

43. In his will, Zumárraga freed two married Negroes and all his Indian slaves, including an East Indian cook from Calcutta (Zavala, *Esclavos*, p. 64). Also see Zumárraga to Prince Philip, 4 December 1547, Cuevas, *Docs.*, pp. 135–53; Mendieta, p. 539; Hamilton, p. 174; Las Casas, *Tratados*, pp. 672–73.

44. Zumárraga et al. to Charles, 4 October 1545, García Icazbalceta, *Zumárraga*, 3:231–39. The same simile was used by Domingo de Betanzos in an undated opinion to the crown, García Icazbalceta, *CF*, pp. 190–97.

45. Hamilton, p. 175.

46. *The Doctrina Breve* (1544), facsimile ed., ed. Thomas F. Meehan (New York, 1928); *Regla Cristiana Breve*, ed. José Almoina (Mexico, 1951); García Icazbalceta, *CF*, pp. 275–82; Kubler, 1:10–11; appendix to Bataillon, *Erasmo*; William B. Jones, "Evangelical Catholicism in early Colonial Mexico: an analysis of Bishop Juan de Zumárraga's Doctrina cristiana," *The Americas* 23 (1967):423–32; José Almoina, "La primera 'doctrina' para indios," *RHA* 53–54 (1962): 75–98; Greenleaf, *Zumárraga*, pp. 38–41. Zumárraga also owned Froben's 1518 edition of Erasmus' *Epigrammatica*. The *Doctrina breve* included chapters on remedies for vices from the *Enchiridion*. Its conclusion from the *Paracelsis* followed the modified translation of the Spanish Franciscan Alonso Fernández (see Bataillon, *Erasmo*, 222). The first part of the *Doctrina cristiana* was an abridgment of the *Suma de doctrina* of the Spanish Erasmist and confessor to Charles V, Constantino Ponce de la Fuente, which insisted on primacy of faith over works. Ponce was posthumously charged with Lutheranism by the Inquisition, his bones dug up and burned in an *auto de fé* of 1558. Bataillon (appendix) notes that in the first half of the sixteenth century, reading the Bible in the vernacular was recommended. It was then forbidden, as was the *Enchiridion*, in the 1559 Roman and Spanish indices. For Gante's interest in having the Bible read, see García Icazbalceta, *BMS*, p. 104. For the Spanish reform movement and its relation to Protestantism, see Dickens; and Antonio Márquez, *Los alumbrados* (Madrid: Taurus, 1972).

47. See Julio Jiménez Rueda, ed., "Proceso contra Francisco Sayavedra por erasmista [sic] 1539," *BAGN* 18 (1947): 1–15; Greenleaf, *Inquisition*, pp. 122–23; and Greenleaf, *Zumárraga*, pp. 85–86, 109–21; Bataillon, *Erasmo*, appendix. José Miranda, in *El erasmista mexicano, fray Alonso Cabello* (Mexico, 1958), concludes, from Inquisition evidence, that of those charged with Erasmism, only Cabello in the 1570s was a true Erasmist. Alfonso Reyes, in "Reseña sobre el erasmismo en América," *RHA* 1 (1938): 53–55, notes that numerous copies of works of Erasmus circulated in Mexico, but that Erasmism was also "in the atmosphere of the century." As Bataillon documented of Spain, in Mexico Erasmism was also a literary fashion in the 1520s. When, from the end of that decade on, Erasmus was suspect as heterodox, "Erasmism" was at times used as a catch-all in denunciations and by Inquisitors for a jumble of unorthodox beliefs, as was the more serious *Luteranismo*. Diego Delgadillo, in a letter from Mexico to Juan de la Torre, a merchant of Seville, of 21 March 1529, orders "some books of the works of Erasmus" (Otte, "1529," p. 102), probably implying curiosity concerning a prestigious fad on the part of this colleague of Nuño de Guzmán—and also cultural lag. Zumárraga's borrowings show the continuing if indirect influence of Erasmus' writings and ideas on at least one educated reformer who had left Spain before Erasmian notions came into disfavor. It should be mentioned, however, that Erasmus in stressing the ideals of St. Paul and the primitive church served to reinforce reforming trends within the Franciscan order, trends appearing to the early missionaries paralleled in Indian life and character. Erasmism in Mexico is thus important as illuminating a more general and complex intellectual ambience, compounded of both Erasmian liberalism and traditional, radical Franciscan mysticism—the whole strongly valuing interior Christianity; cf. Maravall, "Utopia," and above, n. 20.

48. Zumárraga to Council of Indies, 24 November 1536, García Icazbalceta, *Zumárraga*, 4: 122; and to Francisco Tello de Sandoval, 12 November 1547, Cuevas, *Docs.*, p. 127. Zumárraga's appointment as Inquisitor was for the province of Mexico only, as its bishop and in conformity with the delegation of Inquisitorial power to all bishops in the Indies made in 1517 by Cisneros, as Inquisitor General of Spain. For 1536 to 1543—when Tello de Sandoval arrived with inquisitorial powers—Greenleaf (*Zumárraga*) states he found records of 152 *procesos*, or recorded denunciations, including 56 for blasphemy, 5 for Lutheranism, 19 *Judaizantes* (backsliding conversos or descendants of conversos, of which 12 were investigated), 14 for idolatry and sacrifice, 23 for sorcery and superstition, 8 for heretical propositions, 20 for bigamy, and 5 trials of clergy. In all, 19 of these were against Indians. Only one accusation of Lutheranism appears valid; the others attached the label to moral deviation and reformist sentiment. See below, chap. 6; *Procesos de indios idólatras y hechiceros* (Mexico, 1912), in Publicaciones del Archivo General de la Nación (PAGN); and Greenleaf, *Zumárraga*, pp. 64–66, for denunciations of several lecherous caciques.

49. *Proceso inquisitorial del cacique de Texcoco* (Mexico, 1910) in PAGN, vol. 1. A cédula (Council of the Indies to Zumárraga, 22 November 1540, García Icazbalceta, *Zumárraga*, 4:172–73) reproved him for executing Don Carlos, arguing that moriscos in Spain were "not used with similar rigor" and that the Indians, scandalized, believed the cacique had been burned for his property, which his heirs should have. Zumárraga, instead, should have moved against the Spaniards who had sold idols to Indians! The cédula also transferred the Inquisitional commission to Tello de Sandoval, who did little with it, so that in effect the tribunal was inconspicuous during the remaining years of Charles' reign. Earlier, Valencia had executed four caciques for idolatry (above, n. 19). Diego de Landa was still at it in Yucatán in the 1560s.

50. *Proceso . . . cacique*; and Greenleaf, *Zumárraga*, p. 70.

51. See pp. 91–93.

52. 2 June 1544, in García Icazbalceta, *Zumárraga*, 4:175–78; Cuevas, *Docs.*, pp. 120–21.

53. Ordinances of 1532, García Icazbalceta, *Zumárraga*, 4:108.

54. Quiroga was closely related to, and friendly with, Bartolomé Carranza, archbishop of Toledo and advocate of Erasmian principles who was a member of the Valladolid junta of 1550 and was later, under Philip, held for Lutheranism by the Inquisition, but supported by his

friend, Las Casas. Quiroga was also friendly with Bishop Juan Bernal Díaz del Luco, a member of the Council of the Indies, a reader of Carranza and Erasmus, and also a friend of Las Casas. Quiroga, however, in a letter of 13 April 1553 to Luco, sent a copy of his own treatise *De debellandis indis*, backing the doctrine of Sepúlveda. See Marcel Bataillon, "Vasco de Quiroga et Bartolomé de Las Casas," *RHA* 33 (1952): 83–95. Sepúlveda was, of course, a fellow humanist, and Quiroga's flock then included both Spaniards and natives. Note that it would be a mistake to suppose humanists were necessarily pro-Indian, scholastics not, or even that those two methods of education and their products were antithetical—rather, they were complementary in Spain; see Gilman. Nor are humanist and humanitarian necessarily synonymous.

See Zumárraga to Council of Indies, 28 February 1537, in Cuevas, *Docs.*, pp. 76–77, praising Quiroga; Zavala, *Recuerdo*; Warren; Ernest J. Burrus, S.J., "Cristóbal Cabrera (c.1515–1598), First American Author: A Checklist of His Writings in the Vatican Library," *Manuscripta* 4 (1960): 67–89; Burrus, "Cristóbal Cabrera on the Missionary Methods of Vasco de Quiroga," ibid., 5 (1961): 17–27; and above, chap. 3.

55. Juan de Grijalva, O.S.A., *Crónica de la Orden de N.S.P. Agustín en la provincia de la Nueva España, 1533–1592* (Mexico, 1624; 2d ed., 1924); Diego Basalenque, O.S.A., *Historia de la Provincia de San Nicolás de Tolentino de Michoacán del Orden de N.P.S. Agustín* (1st ed. 1673; Mexico: Jus, 1963, intro. José Bravo Ugarte). Basalenque states the Augustinian's original name was Alonso Gutiérrez. See also Burrus, *Vera Cruz*; Arthur Ennis, O.S.A., *Fray Alonso de la Vera Cruz, O.S.A. (1507–1584)* (Louvain, 1957: offprint from *Augustiniana*, vols. 5–7 1955–57). Ricard, passim, notes that the order founded a colegio to teach Spaniards and Indians in the capital to read and write, before 1537, and also a hospital, an elementary, and a trade school; also see Cuevas, *Docs.*, pp. 86–88. García Icazbalceta (*BMS*, 107–8) states that the first book by Vera Cruz, published in Mexico in 1554, was on the dialectics, logic, and natural philosophy of Aristotle. Oswaldo Robles, in *Filosofos mexicanos del siglo XVI* (Mexico: Porrúa, 1950), finds him, although advocating clarity, to be dry, monotonous, and too dependent on authority.

56. Burrus ed., 1:76–87.

57. Bancroft, *Mexico,* 2:262; Garcés was of Aragonese nobility and was in his seventies when he took his bishopric in Tlaxcala in 1529. The first to be named a bishop in Mexico (1525), he was a Dominican and a professor of theology and was eulogized as a Latinist by Nebrija. He had studied in Paris and had been Fonseca's confessor and the first bishop of Cuba (Herrera, Dec. II, lib. III, cap. 2). Mateos, p. 334, notes he was also "deservidor del Rey en tiempo de Comunidades." He had a major responsibility for Paul III's bull Sublimis Deus, of 1537, stating Indians were rational human beings. See Gibson, *Tlaxcala,* pp. 54–56.

58. Martyr, 2:274–75.

59. Audiencia to the queen, 11 May 1533, Paso y Troncoso, 3:87–93, argued that Betanzos was wrong in saying the Indians were incapable—that is, not rational. Betanzos is said to have retracted this opinion on his deathbed (Hanke, *Struggle,* p. 12). Also see audiencia to queen, 1 May 1532, Paso y Troncoso, 2:125, favoring the Franciscans; Luis de Fuensalida, Franciscan guardian, to the audiencia, against Betanzos, 29 June 1533, ibid., 2:93; Franciscans to queen, 1 May 1532, ibid., 2:125; and Ricard, pp. 339–63, on the dissensions in general. Lino Gómez Canedo, O.F.M., in "¿Hombres o Bestias?" *Estudios de historia novohispana* (Mexico, 1966), pp. 29–51, noted that the argument essentially concerned whether or not Indians were capable of receiving Christian doctrine. It also, as explained above, chap. 3, bore on royal dominion since this was allied to Christianizing.

60. Bernal Díaz, 2:370–74. A few encomiendas were held by the bishops and orders (Kubler, 1:18, 138–39). All the orders also sanctioned Negro slavery; see Zavala, *Esclavos,* passim, and Riva Palacio, vol. 2, chap. 27.

61. See above, n. 24. Motolinía collected manuscript copies of Las Casas' guide to

confessing Spaniards (*confesionario*) in 1549, and turned them over to Mendoza, who had them burned (O'Gorman-Motolinía, p. cxvi). Las Casas deplored Motolinía's lax methods of conversion.

62. See Elena Vázquez Vázquez, *Distribución geográfica y organización de las ordenes religiosas en la Nueva España (siglo XVI)* (Mexico, 1965).

63. Cited by José J. Bta. Merino Urrutia, *Fray Martín Sarmiento de Ojacastro, O.F.M.* (Madrid: Cultura Hispanica, 1965), p. 92. See Simpson, *Encomienda*, p. 116; Gibson, *Aztecs*, p. 124; Ricard, p. 250. Mendoza to Velasco, 1:47, and Kubler, 1:55-58, note much building by the orders in the 1540s, and a great increase in their numbers. In 1541, 150 Franciscans arrived. By 1559 there were 210 Dominicans in New Spain, with 40 convents (*casas*), and the Augustinians had 46 convents.

64. Cited by Taylor, pp. 165-66.

65. Montúfar to Council of the Indies, 15 December 1554, Paso y Troncoso, 7:311.

66. Burrus; Miranda, *Tributo*, pp. 126-28. In 1544 crown ordered Indians tithe only on products not of the land—livestock, silk, wheat. In 1557 it overrode the decision of the 1555 Mexican church council to have Indians tithe. See Motolinía and Diego de Olarte to Velasco, 27 August 1554, Cuevas, *Docs.*, pp. 231-32, against Indian *diezmos;* Haring, *Empire*, pp. 265-67; Georges Baudot, "L'Institution de la dîme pour les indiens du Mexique: Remarques et documents," in *Mélanges de la Casa de Velázquez* (Paris), vol. 1 (1965); and for excellent discussion of the institution in Mexico, and bibliography, see Woodrow W. Borah, "Collection of Tithes in the Bishopric of Oaxaca during the Sixteenth Century," *HAHR* 21 (1941): 386-409.

67. For example, Witte to Las Casas, 24 August 1555, Cuevas, *Docs.*, pp. 242-44.

68. Rubio Mañé, passim.

69. Aiton, *Mendoza*, p. 113; Borah, "Tithes," p. 394.

70. Kubler, 1:20. In 1559 a royal cédula ordered tithing imposed on Indians "as in the time of Zumárraga"; see Borah, "Tithes," pp. 401-3.

71. Until the 1570s, when Philip ordered secular clergy to replace regular in Indian parishes; see R. C. Padden, "The *Ordenanza del Patronazgo*, 1574: An Interpretative Essay," *The Americas* 12 (1956): 334-54. Also, for ongoing royal support of regular clergy, and vice versa, Peggy K. Liss, "Jesuit Contributions to the Ideology of Spanish Empire in Mexico," ibid. 29 (1973): 314-33, 449-70.

72. Puga, 1:119-29.

73. Ibid., 1:320-25, 394-95. *Recopilación* VI:8:63, 20 November 1536; also see ibid. XIII:3:39; and Mateos.

74. Jacinto de San Francisco to Philip, 20 July 1561, García Icazbalceta, *CF*, pp. 217-18. For Aguilar, see above, chap. 1, n. 1. Las Casas began as an encomendero in Cuba, then recanted and became a friar.

75. Greenleaf, *Zumárraga*, pp. 89-103, and *Inquisition*, pp. 19-37. But in Betanzos' absence, Motolinía sentenced Rangel only to a stiff fine in money and Indian labor and produce. For Rangel, Bernal Díaz, 2:167-68.

76. François Chevalier, "Signification sociale de la Fondation de Puebla de los Angeles," *RHA* 23 (1947): 105-30. Mendieta credits Motolinía with founding the city (p. 682). Motolinía says that the second audiencia founded it at the behest of the friars (García Pimentel, ed., *Memoriales*, pp. 197-98). Gibson, *Tlaxcala*, states Garcés wanted Spanish settlement in Tlaxcala but got it in neighboring Puebla. Obviously Puebla resulted from the concerted endeavor of civil and religious authorities.

77. Gibson, in *Aztecs*, p. 102, notes that friars also used the old Indian jurisdictions, *cabeceras* and *sujetos*, as *doctrinas* and *visitas*, thus preserving indigenous political and administrative units, rather than recognizing newer arrangements under encomenderos. See Zumárraga to Council of Indies, 8 February 1537, García Icazbalceta, *Zumárraga*, 4:146-50;

Motolinía to Velasco (1554), Cuevas, *Docs.*, pp. 228-32; Dominicans to the emperor, 4 May 1539, ibid., pp. 88-89; Franciscans to Charles, 20 May 1552, García Icazbalceta, *CF*, pp. 199-201.

78. See Zumárraga, *Regla Cristiana Breve;* Dickens; José Miranda, "La fraternidad cristiana y la labor social de la primitiva iglesia mexicana," *Cuadernos americanos* 24 (1965): 148-58.

79. See Delfina López Sarrelangue, "Mestizaje y catolicismo en la Nueva España," *Historia mexicana* 23 (1973): 1-42.

80. Above, passim. In a letter to the emperor, 15 December 1537 (Cuevas, *Docs.*, pp. 86-88), the Augustinians stated they had just been left an estate by a Spaniard, Bartolomé de Morales, in order to teach reading, writing, and grammar to Spaniards and Indians. They said they planned to open the school and had formed a *cofradía* to sustain it. Greenleaf (*Zumárraga*, pp. 50-52) mentions that when Tacatetl, an Otomí priest of Tanacopan (near Tula), in 1536 was found guilty by the Inquisition of having incestuous relations with his daughter María and children by her, María was sent to live with the nuns of Santa Clara "for instruction." For Tacatetl, see below, chap. 7.

81. Olmos sent his manuscript and three or four copies to Spain, where they disappeared. Sahagún taught with him, however, and Mendieta, who arrived in 1554, talked to Olmos at length and saw a summary of his work. See Mendieta, García Icazbalceta, *BMS;* León-Portilla, "Fuenleal," for both men; Bernardinó de Sahagún, *Historia general de las cosas de Nueva España*, 4 vols. (Mexico: Porrúa, 1969), ed. Angel María Garibay K., and tr. and ed. Arthur J. Q. Anderson and Charles E. Dibble, as *General History of the Things of New Spain: Florentine Codex*, 13 pts. (Santa Fe, N. Mex.: School of American Research, 1950-69). See *HMAI* 13:186-239, for Sahagún, pp. 72-73 for Olmos, and in general for ongoing influence of early friars. Sahagún's major writing was completed in the latter part of the century, beyond the scope of our inquiry. His introduction to Nahuatl came from his shipmates, returning Indian nobles taken to Spain by Cortés. In 1533 he climbed Popocatépetl and Iztaccíhuatl, to demonstrate the triumph of Christianity over those formidable peaks, sacred to Indians. He taught Latin at Tlatelolco, 1536-40, nearly died of plague in 1545, again taught at the colegio and, until 1566, collected materials on Indian customs and history. His *Historia* was written in Latin, Spanish, and Nahuatl with the aid of native informants and scribes. See Miguel León-Portilla and Angel M. Garibay, eds., *Fuentes indígenas de la cultura náhuatl: Informantes de Sahagún*, vols. 1-3 (Mexico, 1958-61), tr. as *The Broken Spears* (Boston: Beacon, 1962). Other friar-chroniclers include: Martín de Jesús de la Coruña, *The Chronicles of Michoacán*, tr. and ed. Euguene R. Craine and Reginald C. Reindorp (Norman: Univ. of Oklahoma Press, 1970), written between 1539 and 1541 and based on Tarascan oral tradition; and on the Maya, Diego de Landa, O.F.M., *Landa's Relación de las cosas de Yucatán*, tr. in English and ed. Alfred Tozzer (Cambridge: Harvard Univ. Press, 1941; reprint, Kraus, 1968); Pablo de la Purísima Concepción, O.F.M., *Crónica de la Provincia de los Santos Apóstoles San Pedro y San Pablo de Michoacán*, 3 vols. in AGN *Publicaciones*, vols. 17-19 (Mexico, 1932); Francisco de Burgoa, O.P., *Geográfica descripción de la parte septentrional de Polo Artico ... y sitio de esta Provincia de Predicadores de Antequera, Valle de Oaxaca*, 2 vols. (Mexico, 1674, 1934); Burgoa, *Palestra historica ...* (Mexico, 1670, 1934); Espinosa, on Jalisco and Guatemala; Juan González de la Puente, O.S.A., "Crónica de la Orden de San Agustín en Michoacán," in Francisco Plancarte y Navarrete, ed., *Colección de documentos inéditos y raros para la historia eclesiástica mexicana* (Mexico, 1909), vol. 1; Baltasar de Medina, O.F.M., *Chrónica de la Santa Provincia de San Diego de México de Religiosos descalzos de N.S.P.S. Francisco en la Nueva España* (Mexico, 1682); Francisco de Pareja, O.Merc. *Crónica de la Provincia de Visitación de Nuestra Señora de la Merced, redención de cautivos de la Nueva España* (Mexico, 1882-83); Cristobal de Aldana, O.Merc., *Crónica de la Merced de México* (Mexico, 1929,

1953) is taken from Pareja, with additions; Francisco Vásquez, O.F.M., *Crónica de la Provincia del Santisimo Nombre de Jesús de Guatemala,* 2d ed., vol. 1, bk. I, ed. J. Antonio Villacorta C. (Guatemala, 1938-44); and see above, n. 3.

82. Mendieta, pp. 631-32.

83. See above, n. 20.

84. Kubler, 1:12, comments that letters by Martín de Valencia and Zumárraga were published in Toulouse in 1532 at the height of evangelical ideas, religious unrest, and secret Scripture study there by a pan-European student body, and at the moment of most active recruiting for Mexican friars, and suggests research into the European antecedents of Franciscans arriving in Mexico after 1532. More data is also necessary on those who arrived earlier. For Focher, García Icazbalceta, *CF,* pp. xx-xxxvii, xli, 6; Mendieta, pp. 678-79. Juan de Tecto probably began those missionary methods developed by Gante; see García Icazbalceta, *BMS,* p. 92; Mendieta, pp. 187, 268, 605-7. For Dacio, García Icazbalceta, *CF,* p. xvii, and *BMS,* p. 239. For Testera, Mendieta, pp. 380, 385, 665-66; Cuevas, *Docs.,* p. xxvi; Ricard; Fidel Chauvet, "Fray Jacobo de Tastera, misionero y civilizador del siglo XVI," *EHN* 3 (1970): 7-34; Kubler, 1:97, says he came to Mexico from Bayonne in 1529 and in 1543 was accused of encouraging rebellion against Spain during Charles' war with Francis I of France. Gaona taught rhetoric, logic, and philosophy, the last with Francisco de Bustamante and Juan Focher; see Motolinía; Mendieta, pp. 415, 450-51, 489-91; Alfonso Sahar Vergara, "Fray Juan de Gaona y el Colegio de Santa Cruz de Santiago ..." *Filosofía y Letras* 26 (1947): 265-86; and Georges Baudot, "La Biblioteca de los evangelizadores en México: un documento sobre Fray Juan de Gaona," *HM* 17 (1968): 610-17. For Witte, Cuevas, p. xxix. Others were the great Tarascan linguist, the Frenchman Maturino Gilberti (Mendieta, pp. 378, 552; García Icazbalceta, *BMS,* pp. 269-70; Ricard), and the Augustinian Arnaude de Bassac (Arnaldo de Bassaccio or Arnoldo de Basancio), also French, who taught Latin grammar at San José and Tlatelolco, where he was superseded by Olmos and Sahagún. Tello de Sandoval, as Inquisitor, investigated his sermons for having allegedly been critical, as was Gilberti, of the sale of bulls of crusade (Greenleaf, *Inq.,* p. 82). Criticizing the sale of indulgences will be remembered as Luther's first public protest.

85. Zumárraga to emperor, 17 April 1540; Cuevas, *Docs.,* p. 107; Zumárraga to Council of Indies, 24 November 1536, ibid., pp. 55-57; to Prince Philip, 2 June 1544, ibid., pp. 120-23. See Marcel Bataillon, "L'Iñguiste et la Beata. Premier voyage de Calisto à México," *RHA* 31 (1951): 59-75.

86. Mendieta, pp. 438-50; Phelan; García Icazbalceta, *Zumárraga,* 1:110, 3:152-53; Ricard; García Pimentel-Motolinía, *Memoriales,* p. 136, mentions that three or four students at Tlatelolco were given the habit of probation but did not persist in their studies. Ennis finds evidence that the Augustinians did ordain a few Indians. See above, n. 79; and Constantino Bayle, "España y el clero indígena de América," *Razón y Fe* (Madrid), 10 February 1931, pp. 213-25, and 25 March 1931, pp. 521-35. A mestizo, Diego Valadés, born in Tlaxcala in 1533 became a Franciscan in 1550, an outstanding linguist and missionary, and a Franciscan official in the 1570s. See Francisco de la Maza, *Fray Diego Valadés, escritor y grabador franciscano* del siglo XVI (Mexico, 1945); and *HMAI* 13:74.

87. Alonso de Molina, O.F.M., *Doctrina Breve* (1546), published by order of Zumárraga, García Icazbalceta, *CF,* p. 49, and *BMS,* pp. 71-74. It was reprinted in 1570 for general use. Molina came to Mexico as a child immediately after the conquest, and was raised there.

88. Royal cédula to the Augustinians, 7 June 1550, Puga, 2:87-88.

89. For examples: Gibson, *Aztecs;* Ricard, Motolinía, Kubler, etc. For law: Quiroga, Focher, above, and García Icazbalceta, *CF,* concerning publication of Focher's syncretic legal opinions. Quiroga and Zumárraga were among those introducing Spanish plants, crops, and crafts. The Franciscan guardian, Luis de Fuensalida, requested of the queen merino sheep, olives, and plants: 27 March 1531, Paso y Troncoso, 2:33-34. The teaching of

Castilian and Latin, and the use of native languages in missionary activity can be thought of in this context. Some friars at mid-century wanted Mexican retained as a general idiom; see Rodrigo de la Cruz to emperor, 1550 in Cuevas, *Docs.*, p. 159.

CHAPTER SIX

1. Aguilar, p. 88.
2. Bernal Díaz, passim.
3. Ibid., 2:75; Sauer, *Colima.*
4. See *Actas de cabildo de la ciudad de México* (Mexico, 1889), 6:461. The Partidas stated (IV:25:1), "A lord . . . is one who has command of, and authority over, all persons living in his jurisdiction . . . Vassals are those who receive honors and benefits from their lords as, for instance, knighthood, land, or money in return for special services which they are obliged to render them. Every man who is of noble birth is a lord with power to arm and create knights, but a person of his kind is only to be called lord by his vassals and clients."
5. 3 September 1526, Gayangos, p. 478.
6. López de Gómara, p. 404. See Aiton, *Mendoza*, pp. 109–10; Woodrow Borah, *Early Colonial Trade and Navigation between Mexico and Peru* (Berkeley and Los Angeles: Univ. of California Press, 1943); Fernando B. Sandoval, *La industria del azúcar en Nueva España* (Mexico: Instituto de Historia, Universidad Nacional Autónoma de México, 1951); Ward Barrett, *The Sugar Hacienda of the Marqueses del Valle* (Minneapolis: Univ. of Minnesota Press, 1970); Riley, *Cortés;* Miranda, *Función;* and the *Relación* of the Puebla cabildo, 20 April 1534, Paso y Troncoso 3:137–44. Concerning Spanish homesickness, both Las Casas and Motolinía observed that an oath common to conquistadors was, "May God carry me to Castile!" A number returned to Spain, some rich; see Motolinía to the king, 1555, García Icazbalceta, *CD*, 1:253–77, and app. to Simpson, *Encomienda;* and Martín de Hojacastro to the king, 1 June 1544, García Icazbalceta, *CF*, pp. 171–76.
7. In exchange, from Spain came iron, arms, paper, fine cloth, books, wine, olive oil, soap, mercury after 1555, and black slaves. See Otte, "1529"; Ruth Pike, *Enterprise and Adventure: The Genoese in Seville in the Sixteenth Century* (Ithaca: Cornell Univ. Press, 1966). Cochineal was a source of valued red dye made from insects which fed on cactus. Some 70,000 of them yielded a pound of dye. The government kept its source a secret. From Spain cochineal was transshipped to the cloth centers of Belgium or Flanders.
8. Zavala, *Esclavos*, p. 7, estimates that 9000–10,000 Indians were sent as slaves to the islands. See Report of the town of Santisteban del Puerto (Pánuco), 9 October 1529, Paso y Troncoso, 1:153–66; Chipman; Franciscans to Charles V, 31 July 1533, Cuevas, *Docs.*, pp. 13–16.
9. See Cortés, *Ordenanzas*, 20 March 1524; Bernal Díaz, 2:384–90; Zavala, *Esclavos*, pp. 2–29.
10. Motolinía and Olarte to Velasco, 27 August 1554, Cuevas, *Docs.*, p. 230; Gibson, *Aztecs*, pp. 196, 413–34; Alonso de Zorita, *Life and Labor in Ancient Mexico: The Brief and Summary Relation of the Lords of New Spain*, tr. Benjamin Keen (New Brunswick: Rutgers Univ. Press, 1963), pp. 201–7 (Zorita probably wrote between 1566 and 1570; earlier, he was an oidor in Mexico); García Pimentel-Motolinía, p. 25; Zavala, *Esclavos*, p. 65.
11. See above, n. 9; Miranda, *Función;* Zavala, *Esclavos*, p. 29; Sauer; Berta Ulloa Ortíz, "Cortés Esclavista," *HM* 16 (1966): 239–73. The first mines were placers of gold and silver in Taxco, Zumpango, Sultepec, the southeastern part of the valley of Toluca, with others in the sierras of Oaxaca, Michoacán, and Nueva Galicia. By 1532 silver mines were being discovered (audiencia to king, 5 August 1533, Paso y Troncoso, 3:111); in the 1540s deep deposits began to be worked in Compostela, northwest of Guadalajara (1543), Zacatecas in 1546, Guanajuato in 1548, and Taxco, Sultepec, and Temascaltepec in 1549. An extraction process using mercury was introduced in 1553. *Actas de cabildo*, 6:461; Torquemada, 1:610–11; Carlos Prieto, *La minería en el Nuevo Mundo*

(Madrid: Revista de Occidente, 1968), pp. 60-64; Henry R. Wagner, "Early Silver Mining in New Spain," *RHA* 14 (1942): 49-71; D. A. Brading and Harry E. Cross, "Colonial Silver Mining: Mexico and Peru," *HAHR* 52 (1972): 545-79.

12. For example, Cortés used Indians from Toluca in the mines of Taxco, from Oaxtepec in sugar mills in Cuernavaca and from Tuxtla in those of Oaxaca, and from La Riconada to construct an inn there (García Martínez, p. 146). He used mining gangs of 28 to 100 slaves each. In 1543 there were 395 slaves in five gangs in his Tehuantepec gold mines, supervised by a Spanish *minero* who got a percentage of the gold. They were maintained by a Tehuantepec encomienda of Cortés which gave 3,200 cotton *mantas*, 800 turkeys, and 800 hens each 50 days; 80 loads of salt, and 80 loads of fish each 40 days, etc. Perhaps five Indians were used to support one in the mines. [J. P. Berthe, "Las minas de oro del Marqués del Valle en Tehuantepec, 1540-1547," *HM* 8 (1958).] See Gibson, *Aztecs;* Miranda, *Función;* Ulloa; Riley; and Kubler, 1:134-41. Encomiendas often included a number of towns and sometimes also only a portion of a particular town.

13. Gibson, *Aztecs*, pp. 68-81, 112; Kubler, 1:198. See Lucas Alamán, *Disertaciones sobre la historia de la república megicana . . .*, 3 vols. (Mexico, 1844-49), vol. 2.

14. Thomas Bisson, "Military Origins of Medieval Representation," *AHR* 71 (1966): 1200. In petitions to the crown, conquistador-settlers repeatedly assert they maintain arms and households, that is, that they are prepared to defend the land and so deserve royal mercedes in return; see Icaza. Cf. *Las Siete Partidas,* II:12 and 15.

15. Bernal Díaz, 1:399, 441; II, 66; Herrera II:X:4; III:I:22; Aña María Ortega Martínez, *Mujeres españolas en la conquista de México* (Mexico, 1945); Peter Boyd-Bowman, *Patterns of Spanish Emigration to the New World* (Buffalo, 1973), pp. 25-26.

16. For seekers after conquistador-husbands, see Garcilaso de la Vega, el Inca, *Royal Commentaries of the Incas and General History of Peru*, tr. H. V. Livermore (Austin: Univ. of Texas Press, 1966), 2:733-34. The importance of women to the religious mission was commented on by Mendieta (Barth, pp. 92-93). The early friars, Zumárraga, and the second audiencia concurred, thus their appeal for beatas and the empress' response. They received the *maestras* warmly, housed them well, put young daughters of principales and caciques in their charge, and only slowly became aware that some of the ladies were tinged with Sevillian illuminism—a form of interior Christianity in Spain coming to be thought of as approximating Lutheranism—and with worldly interests; see Márquez. Bataillon, "Beata," tells of one beata, Catalina Hernández, who had long been intimate with Calisto de Sá, an early friend of Ignatius Loyola. Calisto, acting as a retainer to the group of beatas, followed her to Mexico—much in the tradition of the other Calisto, of *La Celestina*, Bataillon implies. Moreover, Catalina was a close friend of Francisca Hernández, a Sevillian *alumbrada* or illuminist, accused of Lutheranism in 1529 by the Inquisition. In Mexico, officials and the bishop came to realize that this was not the sort of woman they wanted to raise impressionable Indian girls. Zumárraga, especially, was alarmed, then incensed when Catalina berated the oidores for exiling Calisto. As mentioned previously, he complained to Prince Philip (2 June 1544) of indias who, raised by these women, were idle and uninterested in serving husbands. He now wanted only cloistered maestras, who "would not flaunt their lack of obedience or go about in the world, or refuse to go to church with the girls. . . . And I will say no more, but not because I could not . . . (to Council of Indies, 24 November 1536). Zumárraga saw to it that future beatas and nuns (the Clares) were more virtuous, tractable, and supportive of authority. So much for the traditional myth that all early beatas were pious (cf. Agustín de Vetancourt, O.F.M., *Teatro mexicano* [Mexico, 1697-98], II, 342.)

García Icazbalceta ("Education," pp. 17-18) cites a royal order to Mendoza that Spanish girls, "who like magdalenes wander throughout the land," be schooled by virtuous women. Mendoza was to favor these girls with money or employ men who would marry them.

17. *Recopilación*, VI:11:1, 2, 13; Vitoria, *De potestate civili,* lxxxiii Bernal Díaz, 2:383. Catalina Montejo inherited and exercised the post of adelantado in Yucatán. Her case was

exceptional, however; and inheritance possibilities by women were more circumscribed by the government toward mid-century; Ots Capdequí, *Derecho*, pp. 216-26. Spanish women appear to have made most of their imprint on early Mexican history indirectly. Thus, the private relationships of some of them with oidores and other royal officials contributed to political complexity, and general turmoil, in the 1520s. A contemporary wrote of the first oidores: "those who command ... are doña Catalina, wife of the contador [Albornoz]. Because of her the president [Guzmán] is going to hell [*anda perdido*].... The other is Isabel de Hojeda y Delgadillo, that oidor's perdition, whose madness is unequaled, nor can I write of her dissoluteness.... If one has to give or take away Indians in this land or present other matters, these women are the ones who order and present to whom they wish. Concerning [oidor] Matienzo with the widow of Fernando Alonso Herrero, who burned, there are also tales ..." Francisco de Terrazas to Cortés, 30 July 1529, Paso y Troncoso, 1:139. The Dominican Inquisitor, Santa Maria, had burned Herrero as a Judaizer. This informed gossip is indicative of important political ramifications of certain social relations, but not necessarily of general tendencies among Spanish women in Mexico; cf. Bernal Díaz; Herrera.

18. Payne, 1:45; Leyes de Toro; Ots Capdequí, *Derecho.*

19. Greenleaf, *Zumárraga,* p. 19; cf. Albornoz to king, 1 March 1533, Paso y Troncoso, 3:38-45.

20. Greenleaf, *Zumárraga,* pp. 76-88. G. R. G. Conway, *An Englishman and the Mexican Inquisition* (Mexico, 1927) includes Tomson's account.

21. Martin A. Cohen, "Some Misconceptions about the Crypto-Jews in Colonial Mexico," *American Jewish Historical Quarterly,* June 1972, pp. 277-93; Antonio Domínguez Ortiz, *Los Judeoconversos en España y América* (Madrid, n.d.). Also see B. Netanyahu, *The Marranos of Spain from the Late Fourteenth to the Early Sixteenth Century* (New York, 1966); Ruth Pike, *Aristocrats and Traders: Sevillian Society in the Sixteenth Century* (Ithaca: Cornell Univ. Press, 1972); *Los judíos en la Nueva España,* PAGN, vol. 20 (Mexico, 1932); and *La vida colonial* PAGN, vol. 7 (Mexico, 1923).

22. Domínguez Ortiz, *Judeoconversos;* Greenleaf. Cortés lived with a cousin married to a Nuñez while at Salamanca. For the Nuñez, Ponce de León, and Guzmán families as conversos, see Pike, *Aristocrats;* Gilman. Las Casas was descended from conversos; see Claudio Guillén, "Un padron de conversos sevillanos," *Bulletin Hispanique* 60 (1959): 80 ff.; Gimenez Fernandez; *Las Casas.*

23. See chap. 5; Cohen; Domínguez Ortiz, *Golden Age,* p. 218. For Alonso, see above, n. 17.

24. See McAndrew, chap. 10; R. Pike, *Aristocrats;* the conquerors compared Indian temples to mosques, and Indian society to Moorish in Andalusia; see Cortés' letters and Bernal Díaz, passim.

25. Juan Peláez de Berrio to Juan de la Torre, 24 March 1529, in Otte, "1529," p. 103; see Miranda, *Función;* Silvio Zavala, *Los intereses particulares en la conquista de la Nueva España* (Mexico: Universidad Autónoma Nacional de México, 1964). Boyd-Bowman, *Patterns,* mentions 179 merchants coming from Spain in the 1530s and 108 more between 1540 and 1559.

26. R. Pike, *Enterprise,* pp. 64-80; and see France V. Scholes, "The Spanish Conqueror as a Businessman: A Chapter in the History of Fernando Cortés," *New Mexico Quarterly* 28 (1958): 1-29. Domínguez Ortiz, *Golden Age,* p. 137, observes that small retailers had no status but bigger merchants did, were oligarchs serving on urban councils, and made noble marriages; that between 1535 and 1575 Castile seemed closest to developing "into a country where trade mattered." Cf. R. Pike, *Aristocrats.* For Negro slavery, see below, chap. 8. For Alvarado: Keniston; Giménez Fernández, *Las Casas;* William L Sherman, "A Conqueror's Wealth: Notes on the Estate of Pedro de Alvarado," *The Americas* 26 (1969): 199-213. While Cortés, Scholes estimates, was worth at his death two and a half million 1958 dollars,

Alvarado, a gambler and lavish spender, died destitute; "only his sheep increased." See John E. Kelly, *Pedro de Alvarado: Conquistador* (Princeton: Princeton Univ. Press, 1932); Sedley J. Mackie, ed., *An Account of the Conquest of Guatemala in 1524 by Pedro de Alvarado* (New York, 1924; reprint, Milford House, 1972); and above, chaps. 2, 4 for Cobos' alliances.

27. See above, chap. 3, n. 12.

28. Jerónimo López to Charles V, 6 February 1542; *DIA* 1:102. López was a conquistador. See below, n. 56.

29. An exception was the royal grant to Cortés, whose marquesado included "23,000 vassals with their lands and villages," but in 1533 that land grant was revoked. See above, chap. 2, n. 26.

30. J. M. Ots Capdequí, *España en América: el régimen de tierras en la época colonial* (Mexico and Buenos Aires: Fondo de Cultura Económica, 1959); Lesley B. Simpson, *The Exploitation of Land in Central Mexico in the Sixteenth Century* (Berkeley and Los Angeles: Univ. of California Press, 1952); Chevalier, *Land;* Góngora; Glade; and above, chap. 3. Royal legislation concerning land in this period in the *Recopilación* includes under lib. IV, tit. 12, the following laws: (1) 18 June 1513, reissued 26 June 1523 and 19 May 1525, that new settlers be given house and garden plots (and encomiendas), and must reside in their towns for four years; (2) 19 May 1525, that settlers with land in one new province should not move and get land in another; (5) 4 April 1532, that regidores should be consulted and preferred in making land grants; that Indian lands should not be disturbed; (10) 27 October 1535, that settlers who receive land must remain in the country and should not sell their land to a church, monastery, or ecclesiastic; (11) 20 November 1536, that settlers must take possession of granted lands within three months, and must plant them; (12) 24 March and 2 May 1550, that since cattle estancias do great harm to Indian maize crops, they should be granted away from Indian fields; (16) 27 February 1531, in grants and sales of land, procedures to avoid harm to Indians; and, under lib. VI, tit. 1:xxx, 14 May 1546, that when Indians die, all their lands go to their communities, and when a pueblo has sufficient lands, those of Indians dying intestate in it fall to the king. Also Martín Cortés to the king, 10 October 1563, *DII* 3:440-62; Puga, 1:242; 16 February 1530, permitting granting lands of Mexico City to its Spanish inhabitants; Miranda, *Función,* Gonzalo Canal Ramírez, *Función social de la propiedad* (Bogotá, 1953).

31. Cited by Juan Friede, *Los gérmanes de la emancipación americana en el siglo XVI* (Bogotá: Universidad Nacional de Colombia, 1960), p. 14.

32. Riley, *Cortés;* Barrett.

33. Steck-Motolinía, p. 196; Gibson, *Aztecs,* pp. 273-75; Simpson, *Land.* Miranda (*Función,* p. 27) states that in 1542-43 Mendoza conceded 218 mercedes of land for various uses, at least 116 of them to encomenderos. In the 1520s the cabildo of Mexico granted lands outside its jurisdiction, as well as innumerable concessions to encomenderos within it. Lands within one encomienda, he adds, were at times granted to others, including other encomenderos. Chevalier (*Land,* p. 299) found the first known entail to have been granted by the crown in 1550, to "one of the first conquerors." Also see Silvio Zavala, *De encomiendas y propiedad territorial en algunas regiones de la América español* (Mexico, 1940); and "Documentos relativos al Virrey Don Antonio de Mendoza," *BAGN* 6 (1935): 1-22. For laws governing the Mesta, or cattlemen's association, signifying the growth of the cattle industry, see *Recopilación* V:5, 1; José Miranda, "Notas sobre la introducción de la Mesta en Nueva España," *RHA* 17 (1944): 1-26; and Dusenberry, *Mesta.* Taylor (p. 158) notes that in Oaxaca by the 1530s landholding and officeholding were intertwined, also that many estates were sold on owners' deaths and that primogeniture was not the rule. He found family prestige rarely ascendant for more than a generation or two, but warns that the Oaxacan situation may have been exceptional because of conflicts between other Spaniards and Cortés, and lack of vacant land. Cf. Chevalier, *Land;* Gibson, *Tlaxcala.*

34. Bernal Díaz, 2:164-72, 255-87, 356-57.

35. For example: Letter of 1 March 1547, Paso y Troncoso, 5:18.

36. Letter of 15 October 1524, García Icazbalceta, *CD,* 1:470.

37. Royal cédula of 4 July 1523, *Actas de cabildo* 1:211-12; ayuntamiento of Mexico to the king, 10 November 1525, Paso y Troncoso, 1:75-89. The city was also granted a coat of arms.

38. Lois K. Dyer, "History of the Cabildo of Mexico City, 1524-1534," *Louisiana Historical Quarterly* 6 (1923): 438. Earlier an unheeded decree of 6 June 1523 had ordered Cortés to have town councils choose their own members (Hernández Sánchez-Barba, p. 590).

39. Duties of the ayuntamiento included civil and criminal jurisdiction within 15 leagues around the city. Appeals were to be heard and acted upon by the audiencia and, later, the viceroy. Council members were to supervise public works and fix prices, etc. (*Recopilación* IV:10:2, 3, 6, 12). They were also theoretically responsible for public education. Each city was to have twelve regidores chosen by vecinos from among their own number; the regidores were not to engage in commerce. These regulations were often breached by both crown and regidores. And see Aiton, *Mendoza,* pp. 54-55, 114-15; O'Callaghan; Bisson; Payne, vol. 1; Fredrick B. Pike, "Public Work and Social Welfare in Colonial Spanish American Towns," *The Americas* 13 (1957): 361-75; William Dusenberry, "Regulation of Meat Supply in Sixteenth-Century Mexico City," *HAHR* 28 (1948): 38-52; "Ordenanzas de gremios de la Nueva España," in *Compilación de Ordenanzas de la Muy Noble Insigne y Muy Leal e Imperial Ciudad de México,* comp. Francisco del Barrio Lorenzot (Mexico, 1920); Manuel Carrera Stampa, *Los gremios mexicanos* (Mexico, 1954). The cabildo regulated guilds from their founding in the 1540s.

40. Bernal Díaz, 2:87.

41. *Actas de cabildo* 1:52-55; 2:10-15; "Junta celebrada en México . . .," 10 November 1525, Paso y Troncoso, 1:78-94; and see Hackett.

42. Bernal Díaz, 2:87-88.

43. Above, n. 41; *Actas de cabildo* 2:133-36; Simpson, *Encomienda,* pp. 85-87.

44. Puga, 1:126.

45. Ayuntamiento of Mexico to the king, 6 May 1533, Paso y Troncoso, 3:80-87; *Actas de cabildo,* 2:179; 3:89-90; Aiton, *Mendoza,* p. 29; Miranda, *Tributo.*

46. Also ayuntamiento to the king, 1 June 1544, Paso y Troncoso, 4:102-4; and see ibid., 2:89, 103, 242; 3:1, 22, 35; Miranda, *Tributo,* pp. 51-52, 77-78.

47. And see Francisco Fernández del Castillo, comp., *Tres conquistadores y pobladores de la Nueva España,* PAGN, vol. 12 (Mexico, 1927).

48. Herrera, V:6:14.

49. *Actas de cabildo* 3:41; 4:16, 188; 5:70.

50. Sebastian Ramírez de Fuenleal to the king, 1532, García Icazbalceta, *CD,* 2:165-89; Francisco Ceynos to the king, 22 June 1532, ibid., 2:158-64; audiencia to empress, 11 May 1533, Paso y Troncoso, 3:87-93; Zavala, *Esclavos,* p. 90, n. 122. These oidores suggested a limited number of *feudatorios* be granted Indians and established as defenders of the land.

51. Quoted in Simpson, *Encomienda,* p. 95.

52. Gibson, *Aztecs,* pp. 61-66.

53. J. López to the king, 1 March 1547, Paso y Troncoso, 5:4-22; Torquemada, 1:610; Aiton, *Mendoza,* pp. 175-77, and passim.

54. A. S. Aiton, "The Later Career of Coronado," *AHR* 30 (1924-25): 298-304; and above, chap. 4.

55. Instruction of ayuntamiento to procuradores, 28 November 1542, Cuevas, *Docs.,* pp. 109-18; Miranda, *Tributo,* pp. 101-2. On 29 December 1552, the cabildo forbade Las Casas' writings on war and Indians to be given to anyone without permission (*Actas* 6:121). It had originally, in 1531, objected to his presence, and that of other Dominicans from Española. On 30 September 1531 it argued against Dominicans in Mexico being put under the authority of those of Española (*Actas* 2:131-32).

56. Thus the visitador Tello de Sandoval listened to the regidor, Alonso de Villanueva, as well as to other Mexican dignitaries, in deciding to delay enforcing the New Laws (Aiton, *Mendoza*, pp. 97–98). The letters of Jerónimo López, the second-wave conquistador who served as secretary to, and wanted a seat on, the Mexican ayuntamiento, catalog the problems of Spanish inhabitants and merchants during the 1540s. See his letters of 20 October 1541, García Icazbalceta, *CD*, 2:141–54 and pp. xxxi–xxxii; of 6 February 1542 (above, n. 28); of 20 January and 25 October 1543, of 25 February, 1 March, and 10 September 1545, and of 1 March 1547, Paso Troncoso, 4:47–51, 64–75, 150–79, 227–33; 5:4–22; also *DIA*, vol. 1; ayuntamiento to the crown of 1 June 1544, Paso y Troncoso, 4:102–4; and Fredrick B. Pike, "The Cabildo and Colonial Loyalty to Habsburg Rulers," *Journal of Inter-American Studies* 2 (1960): 405–20.

57. Diego Ramírez to the king, 1552, *DIA* 1:185–91; and 1557, ibid., 1:195–99; W. Scholes; Borah, "Tributo ... Nueva Granada"; Chamberlain, *Honduras;* Chamberlain, *Yucatán;* Sherman, "Cerrato"; Zorita, p. 208; Aiton, *Mendoza*, p. 184; Zavala, *Esclavos*, pp. 109, 144–75; Zavala, *Encomienda*, pp. 140–55; Sauer; Philip Wayne Powell, *Soldiers, Indians, and Silver: The Northward Advance of New Spain, 1550–1600* (Berkeley and Los Angeles: Univ. of California Press, 1952), pp. 1–54; P. J. Bakewell, *Silver Mining and Society in Colonial Mexico: Zacatecas, 1546–1700* (Cambridge: Cambridge Univ. Press, 1971); and above, chap. 4.

58. Royal order of 18 December 1552, Puga, 2:195–96; Gibson, *Aztecs*, p. 83, and *Tlaxcala*, p. 68.

59. *The Aztecs: The History of the Indies of New Spain*, tr. Doris Heyden and Fernando Horcasitas (New York: Grossman, 1964), p. 295. Durán's manuscript was completed in 1581. There were, in the 1550s, besides the Marqués del Valle, flourishing encomenderos. For example, the Ramírez visita failed to exert royal authority over two of the largest, in present-day Hidalgo. Simpson, *Encomienda*, pp. 145 ff., in a chapter called "The Tamed Encomienda," includes other Franciscan reports supporting Motolinía's that encomenderos then strove to protect their remaining Indians. Cf. Ceynos to the king, 1 March 1565 (García Icazbalceta, *CD*, 2:237–43), where Ceynos requests jurisdiction for encomenderos in order to protect Indians. There is also evidence that at mid-century encomenderos may have treated their Indians better in order to attract others to their towns. See Chevalier, *Land*, p. 143, for J. López, and pp. 138–40 concerning Diego de Ordás, a leading conquistador, influential in the choice of the second audiencia (Enrique Otte, "Nueve cartas de Diego de Ordás," *HM* 53 [1964]: 102–30), whose nephew and descendants prospered through marriage, municipal office, and business—that is, through adaptability. Also García Martínez, p. 57.

60. Velasco to the king, 7 February 1554, Cuevas, *Docs.*, p. 206; Norman F. Martin, *Los vagabundos en la Nueva España, siglo XVI* (Mexico, 1954), p. 65; Magnus Mörner, *La corona española y los foráneos en los pueblos de Indios de América* (Stockholm, 1970); Zorita, p. 212. As early as 1529 Zumárraga (García Icazbalceta, 4:204–5) complained of Spanish vagabonds disrupting Indian village life. Statistics for Spanish immigration are spotty. Boyd-Bowman, *Patterns*, states that, between 1520 and 1559, 22,538 Spaniards emigrated to Spanish America, a third to Mexico. He estimates that between 1520 and 1539 6.3 percent of all immigrants to America were women and between 1540 and 1559 some 16.4 percent. He finds record of 1,150 Spaniards traveling to the city of Mexico: 228 before 1520, 686 between 1520 and 1540, 236 between 1540 and 1559. Cf. Juan Friede, "The *Catálogo de pasajeros* and Spanish Emigration to America to 1550," *HAHR* 31 (1951): 338–48. These figures leave out what must have been a tremendous number of unlicensed immigrants to Mexico. Cook and Borah (*Essays*, 2:180–97) calculate that the 2,000 to 3,000 Spaniards present by 1521 had swollen to over 60,000 by 1568 in central Mexico—"that is, Mexico west and north of the isthmus of Tehuantepec." They add, however, that "if of legitimate birth or of upper class parentage, mestizos could consider themselves Spaniards and so counted since

in dress, education, and way of life they were indistinguishable from Europeans. The category of Europeans or Spaniards, therefore, included a substantial number of mestizos acceptable by the Spaniards as part of their group" (p. 181). Cook and Borah have made the most careful estimates to date, and raise questions obviously meriting further research. For mestizos, below, chap. 8.

61. J. García Icazbalceta, "Un creso del siglo XVI en México," in his *Obras* (Mexico, 1896), 2:435–41; Francisco Javier Alegre, S.J., *Historia de la Provincia de la Compañía de Jesus de Nueva España*, ed. Ernest J. Burrus and Felix Zubillaga (Rome, 1956), 1:273–76.

62. See above, chap. 4; Rubio Mañé, p. 54. For families of the first treasury officials: Icaza and chaps. 3 and 4, nn. 67, 68. Francisco Morales to Philip II, 17 May 1563, *DIA* 1:362, mentions Mendoza's grant of an encomienda of half the Indians of Metztitlan to Alonso de Merida, who came with him as royal treasurer. He is one of the encomenderos mentioned by Simpson (above, n. 59) whom the Ramírez visita could not touch. Oidores, too, although forbidden, acquired Indians and land. See chap. 4; and *DIA* 1:372, and passim, for Maldonado.

63. Morales to Philip (n. 62 above) says both daughters of Alonso de Estrada hold Indians, one through a grant by Mendoza, and mentions one is married to Francisco Vázquez de Coronado. See also chap. 4 and Icaza.

64. See Lesley B. Simpson, *The Repartimiento System of Native Labor in New Spain and Guatemala* (Berkeley, 1938); Simpson, *Exploitation of Land;* Zavala, *Encomienda*. Chevalier (*Land,* pp. 66–67, 88, 96–97) finds that the 1549 royal cédula began the estancia, which included rudimentary property rights and was directed to raising crops and cattle. Clearly hacendados included conquistador-encomenderos and their children, later arrivals granted encomiendas, and those whose holdings had never been anything but land. Thus the hacienda in part developed out of the encomienda, and in part involved new Spanish personnel entirely. The rising cost of living from the 1530s on must have been particularly hard on Indianless old settlers or those on fixed pensions. See Woodrow Borah and Sherburne F. Cook, *Price Trends of Some Basic Commodities in Central Mexico, 1531–1570* (Berkeley: Univ. of California Press, 1958).

65. Chevalier, *Land,* p. 93.

66. See J. López to the king, 1 March 1547, and above, n. 56. For the same complaints by other conquistadors, see Paso y Troncoso, vols. 3–5 passim; and C. Harvey Gardiner, *Martín López, Conquistador Citizen of Mexico* (Lexington: Univ. of Kentucky, 1958; reprint 1974).

67. Bernal Díaz, 2:365.

68. Ibid., 2:358–432.

69. Ibid., 1:366; and cf. Motolinía, chap. 5 (above).

70. 18 October 1549, Paso y Troncoso, 5:195–96.

71. Bernal Díaz, 2:370–74; above, chaps. 4, 5; García Icazbalceta, *Zumárraga,* 1:215–20; Zavala, *Encomienda,* pp. 112–20. In his letter to the king of 1 March 1565 (n. 59 above), Ceynos reported that after the crown extended encomienda for another life in 1555 (*Recopilación* VI:6:13) few encomenderos complained.

72. 2 August 1555, *Actas de cabildo* 6:178.

73. 11 August 1529, ibid., 3:8–9. It also ordered the event be celebrated by a bullfight. Alexander von Humboldt reported holiday and festivities still observed in the early nineteenth century.

74. Zavala, *Esclavos,* pp. 33–34.

75. *Túmulo,* pp. 183–99; see García Icazbalceta, *BMS,* pp. 98–121.

76. *México en 1554,* p. 65.

77. Cervantes de Salazar, *Crónica de la Nueva España* (Madrid, 1914); and see *HMAI* 13:70–71; O'Gorman's intro. to *México en 1554;* Agustín Millares Carlo, *Apuntes para un estudio bibliográfico del humanista Francisco Cervantes de Salazar* (Mexico, 1958); and Jorge Hugo Díaz Thomé, "Francisco Cervantes de Salazar y su Crónica de la Conquista de Nueva España," in *Estudios de historiografía de la Nueva España* (Mexico, 1945), pp. 15–47.

Also cabildo of Mexico to Cervantes de Salazar, 8 February 1554, in *Actas* 6:128. He came to New Spain probably in 1551, where his relative, Dr. Rafael Cervantes, was treasurer of the metropolitan cathedral. He had studied humanities in Toledo and canon law in Salamanca, visited Italy and Flanders, and held the chair of rhetoric at the University of Osuna. He published the *Túmulo imperial* in Mexico in 1560 and dedicated it to Velasco. In 1567 he became rector of the University of Mexico.

78. An attribute Kubler, 1:103, ascribed to the cenotaph. This humanist's chronicles are full of the classical and renaissance admiration of fame and glory.

79. *México en 1554,* p. 53.

80. Ibid., p. 55. Valeriano, who taught Latin grammar at the colegio, worked with Sahagún in his researches into Indian life and history.

81. Ayuntamiento of Mexico to the king, 6 May 1533, Paso y Troncoso, 3:81: corregidores will harm the república and cause Spaniards not to settle permanently. J. López to the king, 1 March 1547, ibid., 5:18: "dos repúblicas, naturales y españoles."

82. Steck-Motolinía, p. 261; Mendoza to Velasco, p. 15, stated that creoles with Latin might become priests, but was unenthusiastic about the prospect, and about creoles. Cf. Cook and Borah, *Essays,* 2:181; Severo Martínez Paláez, *La patria del criollo: Ensayo de interpretación de la realidad colonial guatemalteca* (Guatemala, 1970); and André Saint-Lu, *Condition coloniale et conscience créole au Guatemala* (Paris, 1970).

83. Enrique Otte, ed., "Cartas privadas de Puebla del siglo XVI," *Jahrbuch für Geschichte von Staat, Wirtschaft und Gesellschaft Lateinamerikas* 3 (1966): 10–87.

84. Burrus-Vera Cruz, 1:80; Cavo, p. 48; above, chaps. 4, 5. Apparently the civil wars in Peru had caused reverberations in Mexico. A discussion of the Peruvian situation in a gambling house by a jailkeeper and an Italian, joined by some guards or soldiers, was reported to Mendoza. He sent two spies (one, Dr. Blas de Bustamante, later became a respected teacher of grammar), who hid under a bed, and subsequently arrested six or seven of those present. Under torture they admitted loose conversation but no real intent to revolt. The two leaders were drawn and quartered, a spectacle impressing at least one young Spanish American, Juan Suárez de Peralta, with fear of, and respect for, the government, and at the same time with the innocence of the victims and the rigor and injustice of the sentence. See his *Tratado del descubrimiento de las Indias: Noticias históricas de Nueva España,* ed. Federico Gómez de Orozco (1st ed., Seville, 1580; Mexico: Secretaría de Educación Popular, 1949), pp. 92–93. He was probably between eight and ten years old at the time of the execution, but also probably tended to overstate the innocence of the executed as prelude to his defense of later creole conspirators in the 1560s, including two sons of Cortés. Yet in the light of the unpunished grumblings in the 1530s, the affair indicates a hardening official attitude toward criticism of Spanish authority. Also see José Durand, *La transformación social del conquistador* (Mexico: Porrúa y Obregón, 1953) 2 vols.

85. Peter Boyd-Bowman, "Early Spanish Trade with Mexico: A Sixteenth-Century Bill of Lading," in *Studies in Latin America: A Miscellany,* ed. Albert Michaels, Buffalo Studies 4 (1968):45–56; Francisco Fernández del Castillo, *Libros y libreros en el siglo XVI* (Mexico, 1914); Bataillon, *Erasmo;* Leonard; and above, chap. 5.

86. Millares Carlo, p. 27; García Icazbalceta ("Education," pp. 18–19) says that about 1536 the king appointed a university graduate, Gonzalez Vazquez de Valverde, to teach grammar, that Cervantes de Salazar began private classes, and a third teacher was also at work. Aiton (*Mendoza,* p. 106) mentions a notary, Baltasar de Salto, who taught reading and writing. Beatas, nuns, and Augustinians taught Spanish children, too; see above, chap. 5.

87. Manuel Alvar, *Americanismos en la "Historia" de Bernal Díaz del Castillo* (Madrid, 1970); Juan Clemente Zamora, "Early Loan Words in the Spanish of Mexico and the Caribbean," in *Studies in Latin America* (n. 85 above), pp. 29–42; Chevalier, *Land,* pp. 111–12, mentions as examples the new American word *estanciero,* in use at mid-century, and the new Mexican institution, the *rodeo.*

88. Julio Jiménez Rueda, *Herejías y supersticiones en la Nueva España: Los heterodoxos*

en México (Mexico, 1946); Greenleaf; Gonzalo Aguirre Beltrán, *Medicina y magia: El proceso de aculturación en la estructura colonial* (Mexico: Instituto Nacional Indigenista, 1963); José Almoina, *Rumbos heterodoxos en México* (Santo Domingo, 1948).

89. See Díaz Thomé; Bataillon, *Erasmo.* On 8 February 1554, it will be recalled, the Mexican cabildo voted an award to Sepúlveda (*Actas,* 6:128).

90. Gibson, *Aztecs,* p. 97.

91. For a succinct commentary, see Zorita, p. 216.

92. Simpson, *Encomienda,* p. 87.

CHAPTER SEVEN

1. In general this chapter is based on Bernal Díaz, Motolinía, Sahagún, Mendieta, Zorita, and the research of Miranda, Zavala, and Gibson, including Gibson's "The Transformation of the Indian Community in New Spain," *Journal of World History* 2 (1955): 581-607, and "The Aztec Aristocracy in Colonial Mexico," *Comparative Studies in Society and History* 2 (1960): 169-96. Also Zavala and Miranda, "Instituciones, indígenas en la Colonia," in Alfonso Caso et al., *Métodos y resultados de la política indigenista en México* (Mexico: Instituto Nacional Indigenista, 1954), pp. 29-112. Prehispanic indigenous history of itself is outside the scope of our inquiry. Those interested should read Gibson, *Aztecs,* etc., Friedrich Katz, *Situación social y económica de los Aztecas durante los siglos XV y XVI* (Mexico: Universidad Nacional Autónoma de México, 1966); Katz, *Ancient American Civilizations* (New York: Praeger, 1972); Miguel Léon-Portilla, *Aztec Thought and Culture* (Norman: Univ. of Oklahoma Press, 1963); and Anna-Britta Hellbom, *La participación cultural de las mujeres: indias y mestizas en el México precortesiano y postrevolucionario* (Stockholm: Ethnografiska Museet, 1967).

2. 11 September 1526, Gayangos, pp. 369-76.

3. Gibson, *Aztecs,* pp. 448-49, notes contemporary mentions of the nature of the diseases, and that Humboldt identified the 1540s plague as typhus or yellow fever.

4. Cook and Borah, *Essays;* and see Cook and Borah, *Indian Population of Central Mexico, 1531-1610* (Berkeley and Los Angeles: Univ. of California Press, 1960).

5. García Pimentel-Motolinía, pp. 18-27.

6. Audiencia to crown, 9 February 1533, Paso y Troncoso, 3:22.

7. Royal order of 26 February 1538, *Recopilación* VI:7:v; Gibson, *Aztecs,* p. 155; Gibson, "Aristocracy," p. 178; Delfina López Sarrelangue, *La nobleza indígena de Pátzcuaro en la época virreinal* (Mexico: Universidad Nacional Autónoma de México, 1965), p. 76.

8. Bernal Díaz, 2:298.

9. Zorita, pp. 113-21; Gibson, *Tlaxcala,* p. 65.

10. Ibid., F. Scholes, p. 15; Góngora, p. 205; and López Sarrelangue, p. 95.

11. Gibson, "Aztec Aristocrats," p. 81; see also Gibson, *Aztecs,* p. 121, and *Tlaxcala,* pp. 35-40; Mendieta, p. 255, tells of the cacique, Don Martín of Guacachula, who took it upon himself to supply the friars with clothing. Mendieta, p. 616, also notes that Fray Martín de la Coruña went to Michoacán initially at the behest of its *cacique señor,* or Caltzontzin, who he says had come to Mexico to find missionaries for his people and who returned with this Franciscan, subsequently famed for idol-smashing. And see below, n. 34.

12. Bernal Díaz, 2:24-25; Gibson, *Aztecs,* p. 170; Kubler, 2:152; and Alva Ixtlilxochitl.

13. Greenleaf, *Zumárraga,* pp. 52-71, and above, chap. 5.

14. Bernal Díaz, 2:310-18; and above, chap. 5.

15. García Icazbalceta, intro. to González de Eslava, pp. ix-xxvii. When Zumárraga died in 1548 the ayuntamiento allowed the plays and dances resumed, but when a torrential downpour occurred on the morning of the fiesta the cabildo, understanding it as God's displeasure, revoked the permit. By 1565 the Corpus Christi celebrations were on again.

16. For examples, see above, n. 6, and the letter of Indian principales of Tlatelolco and Xoloc to the king, 1537, *DIA,* 1:83-84.

17. Indian cabildos, like Spanish, had to present notice of appointment by the crown. Gibson (*Aztecs,* p. 169) notes as an exception to new men the continuance from the 1530s to the 1560s of relatives of Motecuhzoma as gobernadores of Tenochtitlán, but also that they were mestizos. Also see Miranda, *Tributo;* and above, chap. 4.

18. Gibson, "Aztec Aristocrats," p. 185; Riley, *Cortés,* pp. 90–91.

19. Bernal Díaz, 2:190.

20. Narrative by Franciso de Sandoval Acazitli, cacique of Tlalmanalco on Mixtón wars, in García Icazbalceta, *CD,* 2:307–33; J. López to the king, 20 October 1541, ibid., 2:141–54; 307–33; Paso y Troncoso, 6:172. See Gibson, *Tlaxcala,* pp. 145–51, 158–59, where the patriotism and pride revealed in the *Lienzo de Tlaxcala* of 1550 are noted; Aiton, *Mendoza,* pp. 177–84; Wigberto Jiménez Moreno, *Estudios de Historia Colonial* (Mexico, 1958); Powell, chap. 1. Indians on such expeditions were exempted from tribute payment, as were Indians founding new towns.

21. Cook and Borah, *Essays,* 1:80; and see Borah and Cook, *The Population of Central Mexico in 1548: An Analysis of the* Suma de visitas de pueblos (Berkeley and Los Angeles: Univ. of California Press, 1960).

22. Royal order of 10 May 1546, *Recopilación* VI:4:xliv; Gante to king, 15 February 1552, *Cartas,* p. 28; Gibson, "Aztec Aristocrats," pp. 182–83; Miranda, *Tributo;* Borah, "Tithes," p. 395.

23. Chamberlain, *Yucatán,* pp. 235–52; Jerónimo López to the king, 1 March 1547, Paso y Troncoso, 5:20–21, notes risings in Pánuco and Jalisco as well as Yucatán. Diego Ramírez, corregidor of Tlaxcala in 1547, told Tello de Sandoval the Oaxaca rising was caused by the lack of missionary work and abuse of Indians (*DIA* 1:163). See also Zavala, *Encomienda,* pp. 174–75; and Cavo, pp. 47–49.

24. Royal order permitting cuatequil of 22 February 1549, *Recopilación* VI:12:i; Gibson, *Aztecs,* pp. 224–27; Simpson, *Repartimiento;* Miranda, *Tributo.* By the mid-1560s the standard poll tax was a peso and a half *fanega* of maize for crown or encomendero, one and a half to two *reales* to the community. Minors, elders, and infirm were exempt; those not married paid half.

25. Motolinía to the king, 1555, app. to Simpson, *Encomienda;* Paso y Troncoso, 5:22; Zavala, *Esclavos,* pp. 140, 144–56; Zorita, p. 178.

26. Letter to Prince Philip, 9 September 1545, Paso y Troncoso, 4:210.

27. *DIA* 1:185–91; and see Ramírez letter of 1557, ibid., pp. 195–99.

28. See above, n. 12; Gibson, *Aztecs,* p. 97.

29. Friars did the same thing in catechisms and Bible translations; see above, chap. 5.

30. An English edition is *The Badianus Manuscript* (*Codex Barberini, Latin 241*), *Vatican Library: An Aztec Herbal of 1552,* tr. Emily Walcott Emmart (Baltimore, 1940). See Aguirre Beltrán, *Medicina,* pp. 116–21; Barth, p. 276. Under Philip II mestizo historians continued to preserve Indian traditions; see *HMAI,* vol. 13.

31. Barth, pp. 243–44, 350–53; García Icazbalceta, *CF,* pp. 62–68; Steck. See above, chap. 6, for Valeriano. An outstanding Spanish historian of Mexico, Juan de Torquemada (1564-1624), studied under Valeriano.

32. See above, chap. 5; and Donald Robertson, *Mexican Manuscript Painting of the Early Colonial Period: The Metropolitan Schools* (New Haven: Yale Univ. Press, 1959); Carrera Stampa, pp. 254–55; and Charles Gibson, "Llamamiento general, Repartimiento, and the Empire of Acolhuacan," *HAHR* 36 (1956): 1–27, concerning a "gradual sixteenth-century departure from precolonial precedents."

33. See above, chap. 5; Miranda, *Tributo,* pp. 66–109. Caciques had been ordered not to sell their subjects as slaves, on 6 November 1538, an order repeated 26 October 1541; another of that date prohibited encomenderos from selling Indians (*Recopilación* VI:2:2, 3). On 16 April 1550, corregidores were forbidden to collect tribute; royal officials were instructed to do it. On 31 January 1552, the government in Mexico was ordered to regulate tribute paid

caciques (Miranda, *Tributo,* p. 114). Again, royal government was most effective closest to the capital, but in our period progressively less effective in an outward spiraling pattern from it. For confirmation of positions of aristocracy, above, n. 7; and for Indian appeals to royal justice, above and chap. 5.

34. 2 May 1556, Paso y Troncoso, 16:64–66. Also see Don Pedro de San Juan, cacique of Ciutepeque, to king (1553?), *DIA* 1:201-2. For Antonio Cortés, see Gibson, *Aztecs,* p. 171. Gibson (*Tlaxcala,* p. 164) tells of Indian nobles going to Spain in 1526 to get encomiendas from Charles; cf. Gibson's "Aztec Aristocracy." Guillermo Fernández Recas (*Cacicazgo y nobiliario indígena de la Nueva Espana* [Mexico: Biblioteca Nacional, 1961]), catalogs Indian aristocrats and mentions that after the Spanish conquest caciques wanted coats of arms and exemption from tribute (p. xviii).

35. Cervantes de Salazar, *Túmulto,* p. 208.

36. See above, n. 1; Aguirre Beltrán, *Medicina;* McAndrew; Robertson; Jorge Carrión, *Mito y magia de mexicano* (Mexico: Nuestro Tiempo, 1952); Eric Wolf, *Sons of the Shaking Earth* (Chicago: Univ. of Chicago, 1959); etc., and such suggestive studies as Lewis Spence, *The Magic and Mysteries of Mexico* (London: Rider, 1930; reprint, Detroit: Blaine Ethridge, 1973); and R. Gordon Wasson, "Ololiuhqui and Other hallucigens of Mexico," in Antonio Pompa y Pompa, ed., *Summa anthropologica: en homenaje a Roberto J. Weitlaner* (Mexico, 1966), pp. 329-48.

CHAPTER EIGHT

1. Octavio Paz, *The Labyrinth of Solitude: Life and Thought in Mexico,* tr. Lysander Kemp (New York: Grove, 1962), p. 117.

2. C. H. Haring ("American Gold and Silver") noted that the Mexican silver yield in 1540-44 was thrice that of the decade preceding and that it almost doubled again between 1544 and 1548. Output increased with the opening of the mines of Zacatecas in 1548 and of Guanajuato in 1558. In 1524-31 the gold to silver ratio was 25:1, in the 1530s, 3:2. Silver surpassed gold from the 1540s on. For taxes see above, chap. 3 and 4, n. 5. At mid-century grain and maize were being produced in Puebla to supply the capital, sugar and indigo in Cuernavaca, salt, maize, cotton, raw silk, and cochineal in Mixteca, and livestock, European foods, maize, and cochineal in Oaxaca.

3. See, for example, the tract by Thomas Mun (1571-1641), *England's Treasure by Forraign Trade or the Ballance of Our Forraign Trade is the Rule of Our Treasure* (London, 1664), pp. 5-23, for seventeenth-century comment on Spanish economic practices under Charles I as a horrible example of national squandering, a verdict on bullionism delivered by a mercantilist. Also Eli F. Heckscher, *Mercantilism,* ed. E. F. Söderlund, tr. Mendel Shapiro, 2d rev. ed., 2 vols. (London, 1955); Stanley J. Stein and Barbara H. Stein, *The Colonial Heritage of Latin America: Essays on Economic Dependence in Perspective* (New York: Oxford Univ. Press, 1970), pp. 3-84; Pierre Chaunu and Huguette Chaunu, *Séville et l'Atlantique, 1504-1650,* 2 vols. (Paris, 1955-60); Vicens Vives, *Economic History;* Glade; Elliott, *Imperial Spain;* F. Braudel and Frank Spooner, "Prices in Europe from 1450 to 1750," in *Cambridge Economic History of Europe* (Cambridge: Cambridge Univ. Press, 1967), 4:374-86; Colmeiro; Carande; Haring, *Empire;* Haring, *Trade;* Earl J. Hamilton, *American Treasure and the Price Revolution in Spain, 1501-1650* (Cambridge, Mass.: Harvard Univ. Press, 1934); and Hamilton, "Spanish Mercantilism before 1700," in *Facts and Factors in Economic History* (Cambridge, Mass.: Harvard Univ. Press, 1932), pp. 214-39; D. C. Coleman, ed., *Revisions in Mercantilism* (London: Methuen, 1969); and see above, chap. 3, nn. 12, 14, 64. For cochineal, see above, chap. 7, n. 7.

4. For example, a royal decree of 24 April 1535, *Recopilación* III:9:22; and see Vicens Vives, *Economic History,* pp. 370-71.

5. Aiton, *Mendoza,* pp. 111–12; and above, chap. 4.

6. Gibson, *Aztecs,* pp. 68–81, 112; Kubler, 1:198; Cook and Borah, *Essays;* Conway, *Englishman.*

7. *Recopilación* VI:1:2, 7; Chevalier, "Puebla," p. 121: C. E. Marshall, "The Birth of the Mestizo in New Spain," *HAHR* 19 (1939): 161–84; Hellbom; López Sarrelangue, "Mestizaje," pp. 3–4. Las Casas, in *Historia,* lib. III, cap. 88 (cf. Herrera II:2:4), states that in his instructions for governing the Indies Cisneros suggested that Castilians marry chiefs' daughters to gain succession to native headship: "porque desta manera muy presto podrán ser todos los caciques españoles y a excusarán muchos gastos."

8. Above, chap. 7 Bernal Díaz, passim; Martin, pp. 94–97; Vasco de Quiroga to Council of the Indies, 1542, Paso y Troncoso, 4:46; Puga, 1:316–17; Gibson, *Aztecs,* pp. 166–75; Gibson, "Aztec Aristocracy"; J. López to Charles V, *DIA,* p. 102; Francisco Terrazas to the king, 1544, ibid., p. 120, for conquistador attitudes to mestizo children; and López Sarrelangue, *Nobleza.*

9. Puga, 1:316–17. Cf. chap. 4, n. 46.

10. Gibson, "Aztec Aristocracy," p. 192. San Juan de Letrán was officially founded when a request from Ramírez de Fuenleal brought a royal order of 3 October 1533. Bayle called the school an "especie de reformatorio." Better, it was a preventive measure. Mendoza mentions to Velasco (*Instrucciones,* 1:14) repeated royal orders to collect mestizo sons of Spaniards, "because many of them wander lost among the Indians." As a remedy he has opened "a *colegio de niños* not only for *los perdidos,* but for many others with fathers, so they may learn Christian doctrine, to read, write, and have good customs. There is also a house where *mozas de esta calidad* are placed and *de alla se procura sacallas casadas.* Dr. Quesada is in charge of the girls, Lic. Tejada of the boys, because they asked it as a *merced.* They do good work—necessary, holy, work—for this *república*"—he means New Spain. See Cervantes de Salazar, *1554;* Barth, pp. 88–89. The 1554 dialogues also mention the asylum for mestizo girls, where they were closely watched, taught arts proper to womankind, sewing, embroidery, and also Christian doctrine and, when old enough, encouraged to marry. See also above, chap. 3, n. 61, chap. 4, n. 43; and García Icazbalceta, "Education," pp. 16–18.

Cook and Borah (*Essays,* vol. 2, chap. 2) include mestizos living as Spaniards within their estimates of the Spanish component of Mexico. On p. 181 they state that in this period there were a substantial number of Mexicans of mixed Indian-European origin; on p. 199 they say that by 1570 there were few mestizos, meaning few people specifically termed mestizos. They also lump mestizos living among Indians as Indian, and do not discuss Indian-black peoples but by inference put them in their mothers' categories, or among the groups whose way of life they adopted. Nor do they try to assess numbers of mestizos in the Spanish component, or in the others. Was there, as they imply, very little perceived mestizo element per se in Mexico at mid-century? Distinctions between Spaniard and part-Spaniard may have been more subtle than heretofore supposed by historians, but they did exist.

11. Concerning mestizo priests, above, chap. 5, n. 86.

12. To Prince Philip, 7 February 1554, Cuevas, *Docs.,* p. 190; and chap. 5.

13. Herrera III:5:1.

14. [Sir] Arthur Helps, *The Spanish Conquest in America* (London, 1902), 1:155, 173, 340; Haring, *Empire,* p. 203; Carl O. Sauer, *The Early Spanish Main* (Berkeley and Los Angeles: Univ. of California Press, 1966), pp. 206–7.

15. Las Casas, *Historia,* lib. III, cap. 102, 129. Herrera (I:9:5) stated Ferdinand ordered that Guinea [Western Sudanese] males be imported, "for the work of one Negro is more useful than that of four Indians." Isabella had permitted some Christianized slaves brought to the Indies from Spain. See Antonio Domínguez Ortiz, "La esclavitud en Castilla durante la edad moderna," *Estudios de historia social de España,* vol. 2 (1952); R. Pike, *Aristocrats,*

pp. 56–58; Charles Verlinden, "Medieval Slavery in Europe and Colonial Slavery in America," in *The Beginnings of Modern Colonization* (Ithaca: Cornell Univ. Press, 1970), pp. 33–51.

16. When Hieronymite friar-governors asked licenses be given for slaves for the Indies (Sauer, *Main*, p. 207), Herrera (II:2:8) stated Cisneros explained that since black slaves were in such demand in the Indies, the court had to work out a more profitable tax system on the slave trade. Helps (1:350) wrote that Charles, in Flanders, had been persuaded to grant a license for 400 or more, and that Chièvres, the head of his government, had bought 600 and had them sent to America. Cisneros had scored the transaction, saying he feared slave revolt, but Chièvres laid that protest to national jealousy. Charles allowed the shipment; five years later the blacks revolted.

17. Las Casas, *Historia*, lib. III, cap. 102, 129; R. Pike, *Aristocrats*. Gattinara also granted licenses to individuals while still in Flanders. Herrera III:5:8.

18. Ibid.; Helps; Keniston, pp. 46–54. Haring, *Empire*, p. 204, states that 8,000 blacks came to the Indies as slaves between 1520 and 1530. R. Pike, *Aristocrats*, tells of the Sevillian slave market, from whence probably came the first blacks to America, but then, increasingly, directly from Portuguese factories in Africa. She says the Genoese doubled their money, while Helps (II, 13) reports a twelvefold increase, also causing high prices for slaves sold. Herrera (III:5:8) says that the Fleming received a monopoly again in 1523, before the expiration of the first, for 4,000 slaves, in eight years. Herrera cited a royal order revoking that monopoly shortly thereafter, at the request of representatives at court from the Indies. Instead, the crown permitted stipulated numbers of slaves to be sent to various islands; how and by whom is not stated. The order also noted that because there were many more Negroes than Christians [Spaniards] in the islands, the slaves had begun to be insolent; therefore no household should have more than three slaves to each Spaniard. See the only scholarly book-length study of blacks in Mexico: Gonzalo Aguirre Beltrán, *La población negra de México* rev. ed. (Mexico: Fondo de Cultura Económica, 1972); see also Domínguez Ortiz, "Esclavitud" and Domínguez Ortiz, *Orto y Ocaso de Sevilla* (Seville, 1946). Cf. Cook and Borah, *Essays*, vol. 2.

19. Aguirre Beltrán, *Negra*, p. 19.

20. Above, chap. 5, n. 43. For Spain, see Domínguez Ortiz; R. Pike, *Aristocrats*, pp. 58–59. In Seville, retinues of servants and retainers were important social accessories and included black slaves. For Quiroga, see his will in Aguayo Spencer, and cited by Rubén Landa in *Vasco de Quiroga* (Mexico and Barcelona, 1965), pp. 224–25.

21. José Antonio Saco, *Historia de la esclavitud de la raza africana en el nuevo mundo, y en especial en los paises américo-hispanos* (Havana, 1938), 2:9.

22. Peter Boyd-Bowman ("Negro Slaves in Early Colonial Mexico," *The Americas* 26 [1969]: 134–51) gives occupations revealed by notarial records for 1540–56 in Puebla. See also Saco, 1:221–67; 2:12–43—Saco relies heavily on Herrera; and Aguirre Beltrán, *Negra*, pp. 7–25. R. Pike (*Aristocrats*, pp. 135, 150) notes that slaves, freed blacks, and moriscos nearly monopolized unskilled work in Seville, and that artisans hired free blacks and slaves as unskilled labor. Aiton (*Mendoza*, p. 162) mentions that blacks built fortifications at San Juan de Ulúa, did general unskilled labor in Mexico (p. 114), and were in the Spanish forces in the Mixtón campaign (p. 147). Riley, *Cortés*, pp. 53–56. Warren (pp. 63, 67) notes that blacks were used as armed retainers by encomenderos, to retake Indian slaves.

23. Aguirre Beltrán, *Negra*, p. 19.

24. Icaza, 1:98, cites a personal report given to the viceroy between 1540 and 1550 of Juan Garrido, black, apparently free, Christianized in Lisbon. He spent seven years in Castile and was in Santo Domingo and Puerto Rico; in New Spain he took part in the capture of Tenochtitlán. Married with three children, he claimed to be very poor and in need.

25. Boyd-Bowman, "Negro Slaves," pp. 150–51. Valiente, in Chile with Valdivia, received

a land grant and an encomienda, wrote to his master in Puebla asking to buy freedom, and was later killed in battle.

26. Paso y Troncoso, 1:87.

27. Aguirre Beltrán, *Negra,* p. 22; Keniston, pp. 105-6.

28. R. Pike, *Enterprise,* p. 59.

29. 3 August 1533, Paso y Troncoso, 3:112.

30. O'Gorman-Motolinía, pp. 370-71.

31. Ibid. Torquemada cites Motolinía and elaborates: incorrigibles were sold frequently and buyers knew from the number of past sales someting of a slave's temperament. Cf. R. Pike, *Aristocrats,* p. 180, for punishment in Seville. Jerónimo López stated he sold a black male slave who ran away and bought another (in Fernández del Castillo, *Conquistadores,* p. 240). A royal order of 15 April 1540, *Recopilación* VII:5:23, forbade castration ("la pena de cortarles las partes, que honestamente no se pueden nombrar") as a penalty for escaped blacks (*negros cimarrones*), probably in response to practice, but we do not know if it was a Mexican one. See David M. Davidson, "Negro Slave Control and Resistance in Colonial Mexico, 1519-1650," *HAHR* 46 (1966): 235-53, where the references are not always exact but the discussion is generally good, with heavy reliance on Aguirre Beltrán.

32. Helps (3:152) says the price was 9,750 ducats.

33. R. Pike, *Enterprise,* pp. 65-80, and *Aristocrats,* pp. 106-22; Riley, *Cortés,* p. 53. Barrett (p. 78) states that Cortés contracted with the Genoese Leonard Lomélin for 500 Negroes from the Portuguese factory in the Cape Verdes, two males to each female, to be between 15 and 26 years of age. Of the first large shipment of 100 in 1544, Cortés' agent refused 2 and described the other 98 as thin and tired. Pike (*Aristocrats,* pp. 106-7) cites as an example of Seville slave traders the Jorge brothers, conversos, who had as agents in Mexico in the 1540s two members of the family and who employed other, usually converso, agents.

34. 11 November 1545, Paso y Troncoso, 4:235.

35. 10 September 1545, ibid., 4:232.

36. Zavala, *Esclavos,* p. 112.

37. *DIU,* 9:285-88: a royal order of 28 June 1527 stated that many persons without licenses were secretly shipping Negro slaves and others of color, and that some with licenses were shipping many more than permitted. It decreed that smuggled slaves be confiscated; and see cédula of 16 April 1550, *Recopilación* VIII:17:2. Helps (2:151-52) says that Philip sold the seven-year monopoly to one Fernando Ochoa de Ochandiano and with the money from licenses and a duty of eight ducats per slave built the royal palaces of Madrid and Toledo. Helps stated that, at the end of 1552, 2,000 blacks had been shipped legally, and that smuggling was going on at the rate of two to one. Also Saco, 2:36; Aiton, *Mendoza,* pp. 88-89.

38. Herrera (IV:9:14) probably cites the occurrence because it was unusual. See Aguirre Beltrán, *Negra,* p. 20; and above, n. 24. Boyd-Bowman ("Slaves," p. 22) notes numerous freedmen from Europe in Puebla. R. Pike (*Aristocrats,* pp. 189-90) states that many free Negroes and mulatos went to America to improve their status, some of the men with former owners, the women at times as domestics. She also mentions creole slaves who went to Spain, then often returned to America freed. Not all slaves were freed in wills. Jerónimo López, for example, as of 1 June 1549, left to his heirs four male and two female black slaves (in Fernández del Castillo, *Conquistadores,* p. 240).

39. Warren, p. 53. Aiton (*Mendoza,* p. 174) mentions the fear of the Compostela (Guadalajara) cabildo, in 1549, of Negro slaves joining warlike Indian tribes to the north; yet that council still sought a license to import 2,000 more blacks. And see above, chap. 4.

40. Helps, 4:249. A cédula of 15 April 1540 (*Recopilación* VII:5:8) ordered audiencias to hear black men and women held as slaves who claimed to be free. See Frederick P. Bowser in

David W. Cohen and Jack P. Greene, eds., *Neither Slave nor Free* (Baltimore: Johns Hopkins Univ. Press, 1972), pp. 19–58. The Spanish idea that marriage promoted social stability was thus extended to blacks, as it had been in the Partidas (see below, n. 53).

41. Greenleaf, *Zumárraga*, pp. 114–16. Barrett (p. 81) in the marquesado inventory of 1549 found twenty-two black female slaves: eleven under 6 years of age, ten from 16 to 35, and one between 56 and 65. And see R. Pike, *Aristocrats*.

42. Joaquín Roncal ("The Negro Race in Mexico," *HAHR* 24 [1944]: 530–40) gave no evidence but asserted that by the second half of the sixteenth century Negroes and mulatos numbered over 20,000. Aguirre Beltrán concurs. The 20,000 figure may come from Velasco's estimate. Cf. Cook and Borah, *Essays*, vol. 2. They combine Negroes and Afromestizos as *pardos*, a common eighteenth-century term, then find these numbered 22,556 or 25.7 percent of the non-Indian population in New Spain between 1568 and 1570. Including among Europeans acculturated mestizos, they estimate such Europeans numbered 62,866 and made up 71.5 percent of the non-Indian population (p. 197). Not revealed here are how many "Europeans" are mestizo, nor relative numbers of blacks and part-blacks to Europeans and part-Europeans appearing in New Spain between 1556 and 1568, nor for that matter, relative numbers for the 1550s.

43. Saco, 2:34.

44. Directives to keep Negroes from Indian villages: *Recopilación* VII:5:7, 12, 15; VI:9:14. Royal decree of 1552 against blacks carrying arms: ibid. VII:1:15. Boyd-Bowman ("Slaves," p. 148) states that Negroes suffered loss of limb for theft. Cf. Herrera III:4:9, reflecting official fear after a black slave rising in Santo Domingo in 1523. See Torquemada, 1:610; Riva Palacio, 2:227 ff.; Saco, 2:34. Mendoza's request and his report on the conspiracy of 1536: Mendoza to emperor (n.d.), *DII* 2:198–99. Mendoza finds too many blacks arriving, many in Mexico, and reports that another such incident will place the land in jeopardy; he has declared a state of alert. On 5 October 1537, as a result of the conspiracy, Mendoza told the Mexican cabildo that the city should be fortified and no Indian houses permitted within cannon shot of it. The regidores agreed to stand watches and have the city patrolled, provisioned, and fortified (*Actas de Cabildo* 4:98–99; Cavo, p. 44). Aiton (*Mendoza*, p. 173) mentions a 1546 black slave conspiracy in Tlatelolco and Tenocha. Saco (2:15, 35) notes Negro slave rebellions in Honduras in 1548 and 1554, and in Guatemala too in the latter year. Zavala (*Esclavos*, p. 56) says mine conditions for both Negro and Indian slaves worsened at mid-century. For Mendoza's mind change, ibid., p. 50, and Mendoza to Velasco, in *Instrucciones*, 1:21. See above, chap. 4, n. 46.

45. The terms *mestizo, negro, mulato,* and *zambango* appear, for example, in a royal decree of 22 February 1549, *Recopilación* VI:12, 1. Aguirre Beltrán (*Negra*, pp. 159–62) found these terms employed in Inquisition records. Barrett (p. 79) states that *mulato*, when used after 1585, also meant Negro-Indian, but states that in marquesado records the term was not used until then. Cf. Riley (*Cortés*, p. 103), who says that in 1547, the year Cortés died, he had 103 Negro slaves, 1 morisco, and 4 mulatos.

46. Landa, *Quiroga*, p. 224. R. Pike (*Aristocrats*, p. 171) says that numerous *esclavos blancos* were present in Seville who were Moorish or morisco. Most moriscos were from Granada, and were usually women. Aguirre Beltrán (*Negra*, pp. 103–4) states that licenses for "white slaves" were granted in the 1530s and 1540s to Mexican residents and thinks they were destined for prostitution. White slaves came to include Moors, Berbers, and Jews from the Moroccos and Fez.

47. Herrera, III:1:22. She stood sentinel, tended the horses and the wounded, cooked, and "hacía otras cosas como qualquier soldado." Bernal Díaz (2:34) mentions three Escobars, without giving their first names. Pedro was probably not the page, but either the *bachillor*-surgeon or the strong bellicose soldier who was hung.

48. R. Pike, *Aristocrats*, p. 189.

49. Ibid.

50. Aguirre Beltrán, *Negra,* pp. 59-62; and Boyd-Bowman, "Slaves."

51. *Recopilación* VII:5:5. Cf. R. Pike, *Aristocrats,* p. 188; miscegenation in Seville was common. Negroes had full membership in the church and those of the second generation often became sincere and pious Christians. Their cofradías, or brotherhoods, participated in religious celebrations. The church accelerated the process of hispanization of blacks.

52. *Recopilación* VII:5:7. It goes on to state they mistreat these women and ordered a penalty of 100 lashes given publicly for a first offense, if the blacks were slaves, and exile from New Spain for a second. Slaveholders, too, were to be fined for such activity by their blacks.

53. *Partida* IV:5 concerns slavery. *Ley* 1 allows slave marriage but does not specify master's consent needed. Frederic P. Bowser ("The African in Colonial Spanish America . . . ," *Latin American Research Review* 7 [1972]: 77-94) errs in stating that the Partidas had no force in this period; cf. above, chap. 1. See also Aguirre Beltrán, *Negra,* pp. 252-58, and R. Pike, *Aristocrats,* for slave marriages and offspring, including those of clerics and their slaves; and see King, passim, for older Spanish usage.

54. *DIU* 10:430, 10 July 1538. *Recopilación* VII:5:5, 11 May 1527.

55. Aguirre Beltrán, *Negra,* pp. 252-58. Aguirre Beltrán found record of very few, but some, cases of church intervention annulling such marriages. The church did uphold the more liberal old Spanish injunctions (cf. Siete Partidas) against separation of married slaves. Montúfar alone is known, in Mexico in this period, to have stated that black slavery was as unjust as Indian—on 30 June 1560, Paso y Troncoso, 9:53-55; and cf. attitude of Las Casas, above, n. 15. For discussion of church and state attitudes, see Frank Tannenbaum, *Slave and Citizen* (New York: Random House, 1946); David Brion Davis, *The Problem of Slavery in Western Culture* (Ithaca: Cornell Univ. Press, 1966); and for ongoing comment, see Eugene D. Genovese, "Materialism and Idealism in the History of Negro Slavery in the Americas," in Laura Foner and Genovese, eds., *Slavery in the New World* (Englewood Cliffs, N.J.: Prentice-Hall, 1969), pp. 238-55, which includes bibliography. Also see above, chap. 5, n. 60.

56. Greenleaf, *Zumárraga,* pp. 114-16.

57. Gibson, *Aztecs,* pp. 147, 346; above, n. 22. Apparently in Mexico as in Spain blacks and part-blacks, slave and free, did much the same sort of work, mostly in an unskilled capacity.

58. Gibson, "Aztec Aristocracy," pp. 180-81.

59. 17 December 1541, *Recopilación* VI:9:15; and 22 February 1549, ibid. VI:12:1.

60. García Pimentel-Motolinía, p. 22; and Motolinía's letter of 1555 in Simpson, *Encomienda,* p. 241.

61. Aguirre Beltrán, *Negra,* p. 172, says the term *mulato* originally applied to the color of animals only, that the designation was purposely deprecatory, stemming from Spanish racism. Indians, too, were occasionally referred to as "dogs" by the Spaniards; see *Ordenanzas de gremios;* and Carrera Stampa.

62. Gibson, *Aztecs,* p. 205.

63. Roncal; Aguirre Beltrán, *Negra.*

64. A special case is Cisneros' suggestion (above, n. 7) that Castilians could marry chiefs' daughters in order to gain headship succession. This may be a broad-minded statement, but scarcely an open-minded one.

65. *Partidas* IV:5, prologue.

CHAPTER NINE

1. Louis Hartz, et al., *The Founding of New Societies* (New York: Harcourt, Brace & World, 1964), p. 5. Hartz is commenting on the essay in that book by Richard Morse.

2. Cf. José Miranda, *Las ideas y las instituciones políticas mexicanas* (Mexico: Instituto de

Derecho Comparado, 1952); O. Carlos Stoetzer, *El pensamiento político en la América Española durante el periodo de la emancipación (1789–1825),* 2 vols. (Madrid: Instituto de Estudios Políticos, 1966); Silvio Zavala, *Instituciones jurídicas;* and *La filosofía política en la conquista de América* (Mexico, 1947); Fredrick B. Pike and Thomas Stritch, eds., *The New Corporatism* (Notre Dame: Univ. of Notre Dame Press, 1974); and Maravell, above, chap. 1, n. 11.

3. For Peru: Nathan Wachtel, *La vision des vaincus: Les Indiens du Pérou devant la conquête espagnole, 1530–1570* (Paris: Gallimard, 1971); James Lockhart, *Spanish Peru, 1532–1560* (Madison: Univ. of Wisconsin Press, 1968); and *The Men of Cajamarca* (Austin: Univ. of Texas Press, 1972) for recent interpretations. Concerning comparison of colonial Anglo-American and Latin American institutions: Michael Kammen, *People of Paradox* (New York: Knopf, 1972) is a recent example. Kammen's book should be compared with Berger and Luckmann, and with Bernard Bailyn, *The Ideological Origins of the American Revolution* (Cambridge, Mass.: Harvard Univ. Press, 1967), which unscrambles many of Kammen's posited paradoxes.

4. J. H. Parry, for example, in *Cambridge Modern History* 2:588, finds it "a measure of the self-confidence of sixteenth century Spain, and of Spanish respect for liberty and law, that in the days of Charles V . . . a great king and a great autocrat—treatises denouncing the excesses of the *conquistadores* (who, after all, were in a sense the agents of the Crown), treatises criticising the whole enterprise of the Indies, treatises in some circumstances advocating tyrannicide, could be circulated and read without scandal." Cf. above, chap. 3, n. 50.

5. J. H. Elliott in Pagden, p. xxxvii. Lack of understanding of Spanish legal history permeates and distorts many accounts in English regarding Spanish law, as well as the Spanish notion of justice. For one example, and there are many, see Phanor Eder, *A Comparative Survey of Anglo-American and Latin American Law* (New York: New York Univ., 1950); Eder thinks Iberian law rigidly formal, abstract, not worked out on the basis of practice, common sense, and local adaptation. He does not understand the concept of law in Spanish lands, or its origins and purposes, or the fact that the sources of Castilian law—oligarchic custom and royal will—were not closely associated with a national legislature and were insufficiently harmonized to be combined as was customary in England and America, into a composite notion of The Law. Cf. above, chap. 1, n. 15, chap. 3, n. 50.

6. See Liss, "Jesuits."

7. Angel María Garibay K., "Los historiadores del México antiguo en el virreinato de la Nueva España," *Cuadernos Americanos* 23 (1964): 128–47; Gibson, *Tlaxcala,* for Diego Muñoz Camargo; Alva Ixtlilxochitl; León-Portilla, ed., *Broken Spears;* Hernando Alvarado Tezozomoc, *Crónica Mexicana* (Mexico, 1943); *HMAI,* vol. 13.

8. See Suárez Peralta; José Miranda, *España y Nueva España en la época de Felipe II* (Mexico: Universidad Nacional Autónoma de México, 1962).

9. Chevalier; and, for the seventeenth century, Bakewell; and J. I. Israel, "Mexico and the 'General Crisis' of the Seventeenth Century," *Past and Present* 63 (1974): 33–57.

10. See above: Cortés' "nación," chap. 1; Vitoria, etc., chap. 3; Velasco, referring to Spain as "nuestra nación," chap. 4; and, for Indian nations, Mendoza to Velasco (*Instrucciones*): to treat Indians as any other nación (p. 28), and opposing Indians in priesthood until "*esta nación* arrives at the state *de policia* in which we Spaniards are" (p. 15). Also see above, passim, for references repeatedly made by royal officials, conquistadors, and clergy.

11. Motolinía in his letter of 1550 (Cuevas, *Docs.,* p. 161) also included Indians and Spaniards within one república. Zumárraga in a letter of 1543 made the analogy, common in political theory of the time, of the república, the body politic, to the human body (García Icazbalceta, *Zumárraga,* 4:146–50). Diego Ramírez wrote to the king (1552; *DIA* 1:189) of "maceguales y sus repúblicas."

12. Whether or not there was official sanction for the cult before the 1550s is uncertain; see Ricard, pp. 188–91; and Francisco de la Maza, *El guadalupanismo mexicano* (Mexico: Porrúa y Obregón, 1953). Both men deny the popular tradition that Zumárraga fostered the cult, Ricard noting that Franciscans in 1556 denounced it in accord with their general censure of worship of images. Yet in 1544, hoping to get divine relief from the plague, Franciscans organized a procession of children to the Virgin of Guadalupe's chapel. Greenleaf (*Zumárraga*, p. 49) mentions Indians who tended to call God and all Catholic images they saw *Santa María*. Keniston (p. 109) says it was at the shrine of the Virgin of Guadalupe in Seville that Cortés, leaving an *ex voto*, met Cobos' wife, María de Mendoza (not the viceroy's sister). A royal order of 1 May 1551 mentions the well-known devotion of "los Reyes nuestros progenitores, de gloriosa memoria," to her shrine in Spain and permits Spaniards residing in the Indies to form cofradías attached to "la casa de Guadalupe" but prohibits Indians doing so (in Richard Konetzke, ed., *Colección de documentos para la historia de la formación social de hispanoamérica, 1493–1810* [Madrid: Consejo Superior de Investigaciones Científicas, 1953] 1:285–86). The cult gained prominent adherents in Mexico, including Jesuits, throughout the colonial period. The Virgin of Guadalupe was considered *patrona* of Mexico by the eighteenth century, and continued to arouse debate well beyond it. Important here is the appeal of the dark-skinned Mexican *virgen* to all components of Mexican society, beginning in the immediate postconquest period. See *Información que el Arzobispo de México, D. Fray Alonso de Montúfar, mandó practicar . . . acerca de la devoción y culto de Nuestra Sra. de Guadalupe (1556)* (Mexico, 1953); Anna-Britta Hellbom, "Las apariciones de la Virgen de Guadalupe en México y en España," *Ethnos* (Stockholm), vols. 1–2 (1964); Jacques Lafaye, *Quetzalcoatl et Guadalupe: La formation de la conscience nationale au Mexique* (Paris, 1974); and Eric Wolf, "The Virgin of Guadalupe: A Mexican National Symbol," *Journal of American Folklore* 71 (1958): 34–39.

13. See Peggy K. Korn [Liss], "The Problem of the Roots of Revolution: Social Crisis and Intellectual Ferment in Mexico on the Eve of Independence," in Fredrick B. Pike, ed., *Problems in Latin American History* (New York: Harcourt, Brace, 1970), pp.99–132, and "Topics in Eighteenth-Century Mexican Historiography: The Bourbon Reforms, the Enlightenment, and the Background of Revolution," in *Investigaciones contemporáneas sobre historia de México* (Austin: Universidad Nacional Autónoma de México and Univ. of Texas Press, 1971), pp. 159–95; and, most recent, David A. Brading, *Los orígenes del nacionalismo mexicano* (Mexico: Sepsetentas, 1973), a chapter of which appeared as "Creole Nationalism and Mexican Liberalism," in *Journal of Interamerican Studies*, May 1973; also see Brading's "Government and Elite in Late Colonial Mexico," *HAHR* 53 (1973): 389–414.

14. See Garibay K.; Hugo Díaz-Thomé, et al., *Estudios de historiografía de la Nueva España* (Mexico: Colegio de México, 1945); *HMAI*, vol. 13; John L. Phelan, "Neo-Aztecism in the Eighteenth Century and the Genesis of Mexican Nationalism," in Stanley Diamond, ed., *Culture in History: Essays in Honor of Paul Radin* (New York: Columbia Univ. Press, 1960), pp. 760–71; Paz; and bibliography in my "Topics."

Selective Bibliography of Books in English for Further Reading

Aiton, Arthur S. *Antonio de Mendoza, First Viceroy of New Spain.* Durham: Duke Univ. Press, 1927.

Alva Ixtlilxochitl, Fernando de. *Ally of Cortés.* Translated by Douglass K. Ballantine. El Paso: Univ. of Texas at El Paso, 1969.

Alvarado, Pedro de. *An Account of the Conquest of Guatemala in 1524.* Edited by Sedley J. Mackie. London: Milford House, 1972.

Anghiera, Peter Martyr d'. *De orbe novo.* Translated by F. A. MacNutt. 2 vols. New York and London, 1912.

Bakewell, P. J. *Silver Mining and Society in Colonial Mexico: Zacatecas, 1546-1700.* Cambridge: Cambridge Univ. Press, 1971.

Bancroft, Hubert Howe. *Mexico.* Vol. 1. San Francisco, 1883.

Barrett, Ward J. *The Sugar Hacienda of the Marqueses del Valle.* Minneapolis: Univ. of Minnesota Press, 1972.

Barth, Pius Joseph, O.F.M. *Franciscan Education and the Social Order in Spanish North America, 1502-1821.* Chicago, 1945.

Benitez, Fernando, *The Century after Cortés.* Translated by Joan Mac-Lean. Chicago: Univ. of Chicago Press, 1965.

Burland, C. A. *Montezuma, Lord of the Aztecs.* New York: Putnam, 1973.

Burrus, Ernest J., ed. *The Writings of Alonso de la Vera Cruz.* 5 vols. Rome and St. Louis, 1968-.

Cervantes de Salazar. *Life in the Imperial and Loyal City of Mexico ...,* facsimile of *México en 1554.* Translated by Minnie Lee B. Shepard. Introduction by Carlos E. Castañeda. Austin: Univ. of Texas Press, 1953.

Cerwin, Herbert. *Bernal Díaz, Historian of the Conquest.* Norman: Univ. of Oklahoma Press, 1963.

Chamberlain, Robert S. *The Conquest and Colonization of Honduras, 1502-1550.* New York: Octagon, 1966.

———. *The Conquest and Colonization of Yucatán, 1502-1550.* Washington: Carnegie Institution, 1948.

Chevalier, François. *Land and Society in Colonial Mexico.* Translated by Alvin Eustis. Edited by Lesley B. Simspon. Berkeley and Los Angeles: Univ. of California Press, 1963.

Chipman, Donald. *Nuño de Guzmán and the Province of Pánuco in New Spain, 1518-1533.* Glendale, Calif., 1967.

Cline, Howard F., ed. *Guide to Ethnohistorical Sources.* Pt. 2 of *Handbook of Middle American Indians* (vol. 13). Austin: Univ. of Texas Press, 1973.

Cook, Sherburne F., and Woodrow Borah. *Essays in Population Study.* 2 vols. Berkeley and Los Angeles: Univ. of California Press, 1971, 1973.

Cortés, Fernando. *Letters from Mexico.* Edited by A. R. Pagden. New York: Grossman, 1971.

Díaz del Castillo, Bernal. *The True History of the Conquest of Mexico.* Translated by Maurice Keatinge. New York: Robert M. McBride, 1927. (More recent editions are abridged.)

Dickens, A. G. *The Counter Reformation.* New York: Harcourt, Brace, & World, 1969.

Durán, Diego. *The Aztecs.* Translated by Doris Heyden and Fernando Horcasitas. New York: Orion, 1964.

Elliott, John H. *Imperial Spain, 1469-1716.* New York: Mentor Books, 1966.

————. *The Old World and the New, 1492-1650.* Cambridge: Cambridge Univ. Press, 1970.

Floyd, Troy S. *The Columbus Dynasty in the Caribbean, 1492-1526.* Albuquerque: Univ. of New Mexico Press, 1973.

Foner, Laura, and Genovese, Eugene, eds. *Slavery in the New World: A Reader in Comparative History.* Englewood Cliffs, N.J.: Prentice-Hall, 1969.

Friede, Juan, and Keen, Benjamin, eds. *Bartolomé de Las Casas in History.* Northern Illinois Univ., 1971. (Essays of mixed value.)

Fuentes, Patricia de, ed. and tr. *The Conquistadors.* New York: Orion, 1963. (Includes accounts by Juan Díaz, Andrés de Tapia, Cortés, Francisco de Aguilar, the Anonymous Conquistador, Pedro de Alvarado, and García del Pilar.)

Gardiner, C. Harvey. *Martín López, Conqueror Citizen of Mexico.* Westport: Greenwood, 1974; reprint of 1958 ed.

Gerhard, Peter. *A Guide to the Historical Geography of New Spain.* Cambridge: Cambridge Univ. Press, 1972.

Gibson, Charles. *The Aztecs under Spanish Rule.* Palo Alto: Stanford Univ. Press, 1964.

————. *Spain in America.* New York: Harper & Row, 1966.

————. *Tlaxcala in the Sixteenth Century.* Palo Alto: Stanford Univ. Press., 1967.

Glade, William P. *The Latin American Economies.* New York: Van Nos Reinhold, 1969.

Greenleaf, Richard E. *The Mexican Inquisition in the Sixteenth Century.* Albuquerque: Univ. of New Mexico Press, 1969.

————. *Zumárraga and the Mexican Inquisition, 1536-1543.* Washington: Academy of American Franciscan History, 1961.

Hamilton, Bernice. *Political Thought in Sixteenth-Century Spain.* New York: Oxford Univ. Press, 1963.

Haring, Clarence H. *The Spanish Empire in America.* New York: Harcourt, Brace & World, 1947.

Innes, Hammond. *The Conquistadors.* New York: Knopf, 1969.

Kagan, Richard L. *Students and Society in Early Modern Spain.* Baltimore: Johns Hopkins Univ. Press, 1974.

Katz, Friedrich. *The Ancient American Civilizations.* Translated by K. M. Lois Simpson. New York: Praeger, 1972.

Kelly, John E. *Pedro de Alvarado: Conquistador.* Princeton: Princeton Univ. Press, 1932.

Knowles, David. *The Evolution of Medieval Thought.* New York: Random House, Vintage paperback, 1962.

Koenigsberger, Hans G. *The Habsburgs and Europe, 1516–1660.* Ithaca: Cornell Univ. Press, 1971.

Kubler, George. *Mexican Architecture in the Sixteenth Century.* 2 vols. New Haven: Yale Univ. Press, 1948.

Lanning, John Tate. *Pedro de la Torre: Doctor to Conquerors.* Baton Rouge: Louisiana State Univ. Press, 1974.

Las Casas, Bartolomé de. *Devastation of the Indies.* Translated by Herma Briffault. New York: Seabury Press, Continuum Books, 1974.

———. *History of the Indies.* Translated and edited by Andrée M. Collard. New York: Harper Torchbooks, 1971. (Abridged.)

———. *In Defense of the Indians.* Edited and translated by Stafford Poole. Dekalb: Northern Illinois Univ. Press, 1974.

Leonard, Irving. *Books of the Brave.* New York: Gordion Press, 1964.

León-Portilla, Miguel. *Aztec Thought and Culture.* Norman: Univ. of Oklahoma Press, 1963.

——— and Garibay K., Angel María eds., *The Broken Spears: The Aztec Account of the Conquest of Mexico.* Translated by Lysander Kemp, Boston: Beacon Press, 1962.

López de Gómara, Francisco. *Cortés: The Life of the Conqueror by His Secretary.* Translated and edited by Lesley B. Simpson. Berkeley and Los Angeles: Univ. of California Press, 1966.

Lynch, John. *Spain under the Habsburgs.* Vol. 1. New York: Oxford Univ. Press, 1964.

MacLeod, Murdo J. *Spanish Central America.* Berkeley and Los Angeles: Univ. of California Press, 1973.

Mariejol, Jean Hippolyte. *The Spain of Ferdinand and Isabella.* Translated by Benjamin Keen. New Brunswick, N.J.: Rutgers Univ. Press, 1961.

McAndrew, John. *The Open-Air Churches of Sixteenth-Century Mexico.* Cambridge, Mass.: Harvard Univ. Press, 1965.

Morrall, John B. *Political Thought in Medieval Times.* New York: Harper Torchbook, 1958.

Motolinía. *History of the Indians.* Edited by Francis B. Steck. Washington: Academy of American Franciscan History, 1951.

Selective Bibliography

Padden, R. C. *The Hummingbird and the Hawk*. Columbus: Ohio State Univ. Press, 1967.

Parry, John H. *The Spanish Seaborne Empire*. New York: Knopf, 1966.

Payne, Stanley G. *A History of Spain and Portugal*. Vol. 1. Madison: Univ. of Wisconsin Press, 1973.

Paz, Octavio. *The Labyrinth of Solitude*. Translated by Lysander Kemp. New York: Grove Press, 1961.

Phelan, John L. *The Millennial Kingdom of the Franciscans in the New World*. 2d, rev. ed. Berkeley and Los Angeles: Univ. of California Press, 1970.

Post, Gaines. *Studies in Medieval Legal Thought*. Princeton: Princeton Univ. Press, 1964.

Prescott, William H. *Conquest of Mexico*. Numerous editions.

Ricard, Robert. *The Spiritual Conquest of Mexico*. Translated by L. B. Simpson. Berkeley and Los Angeles: Univ. of California Press, 1966.

Riley, C. Micheal. *Fernando Cortés and the Marquesado in Morelos, 1522-1547*. Albuquerque: Univ. of New Mexico, 1973.

Robertson, Donald. *Mexican Manuscript Painting of the Early Colonial Period: The Metropolitan Schools*. New Haven: Yale Univ. Press, 1959.

Sahagún, Bernardino de. *General History of the Things of New Spain: Florentine Codex*. Translated and edited by Arthur J. O. Anderson and Charles E. Dibble. 13 parts. Santa Fe, N. Mex.: School of American Research, 1950-69. (Book 12 is on the conquest.)

Sauer, Carl O. *The Early Spanish Main*. Berkeley and Los Angeles: Univ. of California Press, 1966.

Scholes, Walter V. *The Diego Ramírez Visita*. Columbia: Univ. of Missouri Press, 1946.

Scott, James Brown. *The Spanish Origin of International Law*. New York: Oxford Univ. Press, 1924. (Vitoria and translations of his treatises.)

Scott, Samuel P., tr. *Las Siete Partidas*. Chicago, 1931.

Shiels, W. Eugene, S.J. *King and Church: The Rise and Fall of the Patronato Real*. Chicago: Loyola Univ. Press, 1961.

Smith, Anthony D. *Theories of Nationalism*. New York: Harper Torchbooks, 1971.

Stein, Stanley, and Stein, Barbara H. *The Colonial Heritage of Latin America*. New York: Oxford Univ. Press, 1970.

Taylor, William B. *Landlord and Peasant in Colonial Oaxaca*. Palo Alto: Stanford Univ. Press, 1972.

Toussaint, Manuel. *Colonial Art in Mexico*. Translated and edited by Elizabeth Wilder Weismann. Austin: Univ. of Texas Press, 1967.

Ullmann, Walter. *A History of Political Thought: The Middle Ages*. Baltimore: Penguin, 1965.

Vicens Vives, Jaime. *Approaches to the History of Spain*. Translated by Joan C. Ullman. Berkeley and Los Angeles: Univ. of California Press, 1970.

————. *An Economic History of Spain.* Translated by Frances M. López-Morillas. Princeton: Princeton Univ. Press, 1969.

Warren, Fintan B., [J. Benedict]. *Vasco de Quiroga and his Pueblo-Hospitals of Santa Fe.* Washington, D.C.: Academy of American Franciscan History, 1963.

Wolf, Eric. *Sons of the Shaking Earth.* Chicago: Univ. of Chicago Press, 1959.

Zorita, Alonso de. *Life and Labor in Ancient Mexico.* Translated by Benjamin Keen. New Brunswick, N.J.: Rutgers Univ. Press, 1963.

Index

Index

Aristotle, 7, 9, 38–40, 85, 115, 128, 182
artisans: Indian, 71, 123, 127; morisco, 79, 101; Spanish, 109, 114, 123, 198; black, 137
Asensio, Eugenio, "La lengua compañera del imperio," 163 n.31
Augustine, 7, 9, 44, 72, 80
Augustinians, 44, 70, 91, 92, 106, 115, 182, 185
autos, 75–76, 123
Aztecs, 19, 22, 40, 76, 95, 96, 111, 113, 122, 147, 156, 174

Bacon, Francis, 62; *Works,* 175 n.51
Badajoz, bishop of, 32, 117
Badiano, Juan, 128; *The Badianus Manuscript . . .*, 195 n.30
Bailyn, Bernard, *The Ideological Origins of the American Revolution,* 202 n.3
Bakewell, P. J., *Silver Mining and Society in Colonial Mexico: Zacatecas, 1546–1700,* 191 n.57
Balboa, Vasco Nuñez de, 29
Banberniguen, Juan, 100
Bancroft, Hubert Howe, *History of Mexico,* 172 n.12
Barcelona, junta of 1519, 35, 37
Barlow, R. H., *The Extent of the Empire of the Culhua Mexica,* 165 n.14
Barrett, Ward, *The Sugar Hacienda of the Marqueses del Valle,* 186 n.6
Barth, Pius Joseph, O.F.M., *Franciscan Education and the Social Order in Spanish North America, 1502–1821,* 177 n.3
Basalenque, Diego, O.S.A., *Historia de la Provincia de San Nicolás de Tolentino de Michoacán del Orden de N.P.S. Agustín,* 182 n.55
Bassac, Arnaude de, 185
Bataillon, Marcel, *Erasmo y España,* 171 n.66; "L'Iñguiste et la Beata. Premier voyage de Calisto a México," 185 n.85; "Vasco de Quiroga et Bartolomé de Las Casas," 182 n.54
Bayle, Constantino, "España y el clero indígena de América," 185 n.86
beatas. See Franciscans
Beltrán, Diego, 138

Beltrán, Leonor, 62
Beltrán de Heredia, Vicente, O.P., *Historia de la reforma de la provincia de España (1450–1550),* 163 n.28; *Francisco de Vitoria,* 169 n.30
Beneyto Pérez, Juan, *Los orígenes de la ciencia política en España,* 161 n.16; "The Science of Law in the Spain of the Catholic Kings," 162 n.17
Berger, Peter, xiv; *The Sacred Canopy,* 159 n.2; and Thomas Luckmann, *The Social Construction of Reality,* 159 n.2
Berthe, J. P., "Las minas de oro del Marqués del Valle en Tehuantepec, 1540–1547," 187 n.12
Betanzos, Domingo de, 86, 89, 165, 180
Bible, 8, 16, 21, 73, 80, 85, 91, 92, 100, 128, 180; Complutensian Polyglot, 15, 73
Bisson, Thomas, "Military Origins of Medieval Representation," 187 n.14
black legend of Spanish cruelty, 170
black slaves, 45, 61, 62, 65, 79, 102, 132, 136–43, 148, 168
blacks, 44, 65, 136, 139–42, 152, 154
Bolton, Herbert, 159
Borah, Woodrow, *Early Trade and Navigation between Mexico and Peru,* 186 n.6; *Silk Raising in Colonial Mexico,* 175 n.40; "Los tributos y su recaudación en la audiencia de Nueva Galicia durante el siglo XVI," 177 n.73; and Sherburne F. Cook, *The Population of Central Mexico in 1548,* 195 n.2; and Cook, *Price Trends of Some Basic Commodities in Central Mexico, 1531–1570,* 193 n.64
Bowser, Frederick P., "The African in Colonial Spanish America," 201 n.53; essay in David W. Cohen and Jack P. Greene, eds., *Neither Slave nor Free,* 200 n.40
Boyd-Bowman, Peter, "Early Spanish Trade with Mexico; A Sixteenth-Century Bill of Lading," 193 n.85; "Negro Slaves in Early Colonial Mexico," 198 n.22; *Patterns of Spanish Emigration to the New World,* 187 n.15
Brading, David A., "Government and Elite in Late Colonial Mexico," 203 n.13; *Los orígenes del nacionalismo,* 203 n.13; and Harry E. Cross, "Colonial Silver Mining

212

Index

Index

King, P. D., *Law and Society in the Visigothic Kingdom*, 161 n.14

Knowles, David, *The Evolution of Medieval Thought*, 161 n.16

Koenigsberger, Hans G., *The Habsburgs and Europe, 1516–1600*, 167 n.5

Konetzke, Richard, ed., *Colección de documentos para la historia de la formación social de hispanoamérica*, 203 n.12

Kristeller, Paul Oskar, *Renaissance Thought*, 163 n.30

Lafaye, Jacques, *Quetzalcoatl et Guadalupe: La formation de la conscience nationale au Mexique*, 203 n.12

Landa, Diego de, O.F.M., 181; *Relación de las cosas de Yucatán*, 184 n.81

Landa, Rubén, *Vasco de Quiroga*, 198 n.20

landholding, 59, 65–67, 102–3, 107–10, 114, 124, 125, 144, 147, 150, 156, 176, 189, 192; *see also* Indian, property

Lanning, John T., "Cortés and His First Official Remission of Treasure to Charles V," 165 n.21

Las Casas, Bartolomé de, 20, 36–43, 70, 74–75, 79, 85–86, 92, 94, 108, 111, 112, 116, 137, 168, 178, 182, 190; *Apologética historia sumaria*, 169 n.29; *Historia de las Indias*, 164 n.4; *Tratados*, 163 n.26

latifundia, 103, 110

Latin, 15, 20, 57, 71, 73, 75, 90, 91, 112, 113, 128, 184–86, 193

Laws of Burgos, 18, 35, 43, 171

Laws of Toro, 5, 6, 9, 60, 162, 164

Lea, Henry Charles, *Chapters from the Religious History of Spain Connected with the Inquisition*, 170 n.50

Lejarza, Fidel de, "Franciscanismo de Cortés y Cortésianismo de los Franciscanos," 178 n.4

León, 5, 31

León-Portilla, Miguel, *Aztec Thought and Culture*, 194 n.1; *The Broken Spears*, 184 n.81; "Ramírez de Fuenleal y las antigüedades mexicanas," 173 n.26; and Angel M. Garibay, eds., *Fuentes indígenas de la cultura náhuatl: Informantes de Sahagún*, 184 n.81

Leonard, Irving, *Books of the Brave*, 164 n.7

letrados, 5, 163

limpieza de sangre, 13, 14, 100, 142; *see also* Old Christians

Liss, Peggy K. [Korn], "Jesuit Contributions to the Ideology of Spanish Empire in Mexico," 183 n.71; "The Problem of the Roots of Revolution: Social Crisis and Intellectual Ferment in Mexico on the Eve of Independence," 203 n.13; Topics in Eighteenth-Century Mexican Historiography: the Bourbon Reforms, the Enlightenment, and the Background of Revolution," 203 n.13

Livermore, Harold, *A History of Spain*, 166 n.29

Livy, 16

Lizana, Bernardo de, *Historia de Yucatán*, 177 n.3

Llaguno, José A., S.J., *Personalidad jurídica del indio y el III Concilio Provincial Mexicano*, 173 n.21

Loaisa, García de, 168, 170

Lockhart, James, *The Men of Cajamarca*, 202 n.3; *Spanish Peru*, 202 n.3

López, Jerónimo, 103, 123, 139, 191

López de Gómara, Francisco, 112, 116; *Cortés: the Life of the Conqueror by His Secretary*, 164 n.5

López de Zarate, José, 87, 88

López Sarrelangue, Delfina, "Mestizaje y catolicismo en la Nueva España," 184 n.79; *La nobleza indígena de Pátzcuaro en la época virreinal*, 194 n.7

Losada, Angel, "Hernán Cortés en la obra del cronista Sepúlveda," 170 n.45

Lourie, Elena, "A Society Organized for War: Medieval Spain," 162 n.23

Lowlands, 32, 38, 133

Loyola, Ignatius, 178, 187

Lunenfeld, Marvin, *The Council of the Santa Hermandad*, 160 n.8

Luther, 14, 185; Lutheranism, 80, 81, 100, 101, 180, 181, 187

maceguales, 55, 63, 97, 125–7, 136

Machiavelli, Niccoló, 3, 35; *The Prince*, 160 n.6

MacLeod, Murdo J., *Spanish Central*

Index

Index

character, xv, 159–60; nationalisms, 1, 154, 156; nationality, xii, xiv, 155–56; particularism, xi, 111, 131, 152, 154, 156; regional attachment, 63, 65, 67, 111, 115–17, 154, 156; Revolution of 1910, xii, 154
Mexico: term explained, xvi; church province of, 8; city of, 22, 65, 66, 71, 77, 78, 96, 97, 104, 109, 119, 121–27, 135, 144, 154; University of, 44, 60, 63, 64, 78, 85, 89, 109, 112, 115–16, 136, 193
Mexico, audiencia of: first, 51–52, 78, 104, 105, 137, 172; second, 52–57, 60, 65–67, 70, 77, 78, 86, 88, 90, 105–8, 110, 116, 120 122, 124, 127, 130, 134, 138, 178; and Mendoza, 43, 66, 174; and Velasco, 65, 66
Mexico, ayuntamiento of, 48, 65, 89, 104–17, 138, 139, 141, 152, 190, 194
Michoacán, 83, 85, 89, 115, 125, 173, 186, 194
military orders, 14, 16, 17, 20
Millares Carlo, Agustín, *Apuntes para un estudio bibliográfico del humanista Francisco Cervantes de Salazar*, 192 n.77
mining, 45, 54, 55, 64, 66, 75, 97, 99, 102–3, 108–10, 119, 125, 126, 132, 133, 135, 137, 138, 142, 168, 175, 187, 200; *see also* gold; silver
Miranda, José, *El erasmista mexicano, Fray Alonso Cabello*, 181 n.47; *España y Nueva España en la época de Felipe II*, 202 n.8; "La fraternidad cristiana y la labor social de la primitiva iglesia mexicana," 184 n.78; *La función económica del encomendero en los orígenes del régimen colonial*, 174 n.40; *Las ideas y las instituciones políticas mexicanas*, 201 n.2; "Notas sobre la introducción de la mesta de Nueva España," 189 n.33; *El tributo indígena en la Nueva España*, 172 n.7; *Vitoria y los intereses de la Conquista de América*, 169 n.30
Mixcoatl, 122–23
Mixtón Wars, 58, 62, 107, 125, 195, 198
Molina, Alonso de, O.F.M., *Doctrina breve*, 185 n.87
Montejo, Catalina, 187
Montejo, Francisco de, 139, 165, 172
Montesquieu, 155
Montezuma. *See* Motecuhzoma II

Montezuma, Isabel, 130, 136
Montúfar, Alonso de, 65, 87, 100, 153, 176, 201; *Información que el Arzobispo de México, D. Fray Alonso de Montúfar, mandó practicar . . . acerca de la devoción y culto de Nuestra Sra. de Guadalupe*, 203 n.12
Morales, Bartolomé de, 184 n.80
Morales, Diego de, 101
Morales, Gonzalo de, 101
More, Thomas, *Utopia*, 55, 83, 84
Morelos, José María, 156
Moreno, Juan José, *Fragmentos de la vida del venerable don Vasco de Quiroga . . .*, 173 n.28
moriscos, 79, 101, 140, 181, 198, 200
Mörner, Magnus, *La corona española y los foráneos en los pueblos de Indios de América*, 191 n.60
Morón, Francisca, 109
Moslems, 13–15, 26, 57, 73, 100–102, 152; *see also* Islam
Motecuhzoma II, 1, 22, 27, 49, 54, 76, 95, 113, 118, 120–22, 130, 147, 165, 195
Motolinía (Toribio de Benavente), 77, 87, 90–92, 94, 110–12, 119, 123, 128, 130, 138, 141, 142, 153, 180, 183; *History of the Indians*, ed. Francis B. Steck, 179 n.26; *History of the Indians of New Spain*, ed. Elizabeth Andros Foster, 178 n.5; *Memoriales*, ed. Luis García Pimentel, 173 n.23; *Memoriales o Libro de las cosas de la Nueva España*, ed. Edmundo O'Gorman, 178 n.5
mulatos, 61, 65, 140–42, 199, 201
Mun, Thomas, *England's Treasure by Forraign Trade*, 196 n.3
Muro Orejón, Antonio, comp., *Las leyes nuevas (1542–43)*, 170 n.43

Nahuatl, 71, 91, 128, 178, 184, 186
Narváez, Panfilo de, 1, 13, 101, 103, 137
nation, xi–xii, 2, 6, 14, 16, 21, 38–40, 60, 61, 67, 75, 76, 129, 153–56
nationalism, xv; *see also* Mexican, nationalisms
natural law, 4, 7, 8, 38, 39, 40, 56, 113, 169
Navarre, 63
Nayarit, 177

222

Index

Nebrija, Antonio de, 15–16, 163, 164, 171, 182; *Gramática castellana*, 163 n.31

Netanyahu, B., *The Marranos of Spain from the Late Fourteenth to the Early Sixteenth Century*, 188 n.21

New Christians. *See conversos*

New Laws of 1542, 37, 40, 44, 59, 62, 63, 79, 86, 88, 93, 108, 116, 130, 168, 170, 171, 191

New Mexico, 130

New Spain, kingdom of, boundaries, xvi, 172

Nezahualcoyotl, 82

Nezahualpilli, 82, 121

Nueva Galicia, 57, 58, 108, 186; audiencia of, 65, 66, 177

Nueva Vizcaya, 66

Nuñez, Hernán, 57

nuns, 70, 177, 184, 187

Oaxaca, 54, 89, 122, 126, 135, 174, 186, 189, 195

Oaxtepec, 181

O'Callaghan, Joseph F., "The Beginnings of the Cortes of León-Castile," 162 n.24

Ocelotl, 122–23

Ocuituco, 81

O'Gorman, Edmundo, comp., "Enseñanza del Castellano como factor político colonial: mediados del siglo XVI y finales del XVIII," 171 n.51; ed., "Una instrucción secreta a Don Antonio de Mendoza," 174 n.34; "Lewis Hanke on the Spanish Struggle for Justice in the Conquest of America," 170 n.50

Old Christians, 13, 100; *see also limpieza de sangre*

Olmedo, Andrés de, 23

Olmos, Andrés de, 91, 128, 174, 185

Oñate, Juan de, 130

Oran, 15

Ordás, Diego de, 191

"Ordenanzas de gremios de la Nueva España," 190 n.39

Ortega Martínez, Aña María, *Mujeres españolas en la conquista de México*, 187 n.15

Ortíz, Tomás, 86

Othón de Mendizábal, Miguel, *Historia económica de México*, 175 n.40

Otomís, 1, 125, 139, 184

Ots Capdequí, José María, *España en América: el régimen de tierras en la época colonial*, 189 n.30; *Historia del derecho español en América y de derecho indiano*, 171 n.52

Otte, Enrique, "Cartas privadas de Puebla del siglo XVI," 193 n.83; "La Nueva España en 1529," 173 n.15; "Nueve cartas de Diego de Ordás," 191 n.59

Otumba, 139

Pablos, Juan, 99, 174

Pacheco, María, 57

Pachuca, 109

Pacific coast, xvi, 99, 172

Padden, R. C., "The *Ordenanza del Patronazgo*, 1574: An Interpretative Essay," 183 n.71

Palacios, Beatriz de, 140

Palacios Rubios, Juan López de, *De las islas del mar océano*, 164 n.39

Pamplona, 78, 91

Pánuco, 51, 57, 91, 96, 105, 108, 172, 175, 195

papacy, 5, 10, 17, 18, 34, 35, 37–39, 41, 42, 53, 69, 70, 92, 166, 170; Adrian VI, 69, 137; Alexander VI, 41

Pareja, Francisco de, O.Merc., *Crónica de la Provincia de . . . la Merced*, 184 n.81

Paris, University of, 38, 92, 169, 178, 182

Parry, J. H., *The Audiencia of New Galicia in the Sixteenth Century*, 169 n.30; "Spaniards in the New World," in *Cambridge Modern History*, 202 n.4; *The Spanish Theory of Empire in the Sixteenth Century*, 169 n.30

Paso y Troncoso, Francisco, *Epistolario de Nueva España, 1505–1818*, 165 n.20

patria, 6, 13, 16, 153–56, 169

patronato real, 14, 18, 33–34, 69, 164, 172

Pátzcuaro, 83, 84

Payne, Stanley G., *A History of Spain and Portugal*, 160 n.5

Paz, Fray Matías de, *Del dominio de los reyes de España sobre los Indios*, 164 n.39

Paz, Octavio, *The Labyrinth of Solitude*, 196 n.1

Index